ANCIENT HAWAIIAN MUSIC

Helen H. Roberts

ANCIENT HAWAIIAN MUSIC

Helen H. Roberts

DOVER PUBLICATIONS, INC.
NEW YORK

Published in Canada by General Publishing Company, Ltd., 30 Lesmill Road, Don Mills, Toronto, Ontario.
Published in the United Kingdom by Constable and Company, Ltd., 10 Orange Street, London WC 2.

This Dover edition, first published in 1967, is an unabridged and unaltered republication of the work originally published in 1926 by the Bernice P. Bishop Museum, Honolulu, Hawaii, as Museum Bulletin 29.

Library of Congress Catalog Card Number: 67-18240

Manufactured in the United States of America
Dover Publications, Inc.
180 Varick Street
New York, N. Y. 10014

CONTENTS

I

ILLUSTRATIONS

PREFACE

A recent act of the Hawaiian Legislature provided for a long-felt want, voiced by many Hawaiian scholars as well as by students of Polynesian ethnology: the collecting, recording and preservation of ancient Hawaiian music and meles, or poetical compositions intended to be chanted. Aside from the interest which such a collection would have for the casual reader, its value for various lines of study cannot be questioned.

In order to insure the proper supervision for the undertaking, the Governor of the Territory of Hawaii appointed the Hawaiian Legend and Folklore Commission, whose duty it was to find someone qualified for the work and to accept responsibility for its accomplishment and for the publication of a report.

Although the appropriation made by the Legislature was hardly sufficient to cover the expenses of a thorough survey, provide for the publication of a study of the music, and for the sorting, translation and publication of the texts of hundreds of chants obtained without music, it was large enough to permit of the gathering of a mass of material and the preparation of this report. It is hoped that the chants obtained without music may also eventually be studied, translated, and published.

Most of the texts that accompany the tunes do not represent the highest literary achievements, the best versions, or the longest chants; for, as might be expected, what the people who are still living recall and can chant, reveal more of the breaking down process which is at work in all of the phases of the original Hawaiian culture than do such famous compositions as were too long or too sacred to be known to the masses and which were committed only to certain individuals, many of whom, as soon as they had learned to write, even imperfectly, recorded them in old account books and the like. A very large part of the meles for which no music was obtained was drawn from such books loaned by Hawaiians in various sections of the islands. Those interested in the subject of Hawaiian meles as poetry must realize, therefore, that as a representative collection, this volume is very inadequate. As a study of the ancient Hawaiian music, I believe that it gives a fair and comprehensive picture.

The work embodied in this report was not undertaken without a full realization of the size and difficulty of the problem and of the lack, on my part, of many qualifications, the possession of which would have materially added to whatever success may have attended the investigation. It was not without real hesitation that I assumed a piece of Polynesian research in complete ignorance of the language of the people among whom I was to work. Had there been anyone familiar with the Hawaiian language who had the requisite musical training and experience to identify, collect, and reduce to notation the tunes of the old type, and to analyze them with due regard for the requirements of ethnology, it would have been sheer impudence to have attempted the task.

There was, however, no such person available; the need of the investigation was urgent because few old people still live who are capable of furnishing reliable information. An ear capable of noting tones with discrimination should be able to catch the sounds of speech sufficiently to write down texts, while interpreters, if not as satisfactory as the ability to converse, could accomplish the rest.

With the many difficulties arising from these circumstances, the work would have been a failure without the hearty cooperation of countless individuals who have given cheerfully of their time, their knowledge, their conveyances, the hospitality of their homes, and their influence with those old people who were naturally reluctant to part with their treasured lore to a stranger whose motive they could not grasp.

Were each of these contributors to be mentioned by name there would be a volume alone devoted to the roll. It must suffice for me to say that this represents the work of the Hawaiian people as a whole and of many others who now look upon the islands as their home.

Particular thanks are due to Bernice P. Bishop Museum which offered all the facilities in its power to aid the work and which has undertaken for the Hawaiian Legend and Folklore Commission the difficult task of publishing the report; to Mrs. E. Lahilahi Webb, whose long and always patient labor corrected the spelling of the texts obtained in the field; to Mr. Thomas G. Thrum, who has given the texts a second revision and called attention to many obscure articles referring in one way or another to the problem, without a knowledge of which I would have missed much of value; to Mr. Kenneth P. Emory, who has read and discussed with me much of the manuscript; to Mr. T. F. McIlwraith, who has rendered invaluable aid in covering the literature on the Pacific; and to Mr. Thomas K. Maunupau, my interpreter, who procured on a loan and copied in his limited leisure, one of the most valuable collections of chants, and who posed for the photographs showing the positions in which the instruments were held.

Thanks are due not only to those Hawaiians who chanted, but to those others who, realizing the value to science, literature, and their own posterity of these records of their race, have loaned their collections of meles, copies of which will be preserved in the Bishop Museum until such time as they may be taken up for study and translation. The generosity of these patriotic Hawaiians will be acknowledged in each individual case, at present only through the press, but later, it is hoped, with their contributions as they are published. Some errors have been made in the music by the copyist. Unfortunately, very troublesome eyesight made impossible the checking of the music before the cuts were made.

A SURVEY OF ANCIENT HAWAIIAN MUSIC WAS
CONDUCTED, 1923-24, BY MISS HELEN H. ROBERTS
UNDER THE AUSPICES OF THE HAWAIIAN FOLK-LORE
COMMISSION REPRESENTED BY JOHN R. GALT, CHAIR-
MAN; EDNA J. HILL, SECRETARY; MRS. EMMA AHU-
ENA TAYLOR, HAWAIIAN MEMBER.

Ancient Hawaiian Music

INTRODUCTION

MODERN MUSIC AND INSTRUMENTS

Before discussing the ancient Hawaiian music and meles, something should be said briefly regarding the modern music and instruments, which the time allowed for the pursuance of this study prevents taking up in full, perhaps to the disappointment of those whose knowledge of Hawaiian music is confined to this period of its history and to whom it has made its irresistible appeal.

The subject of the development of the Hawaiian music since the coming of the missionaries, if a collection of tunes were given, would take a volume in itself. It is as different from the ancient music as it is possible for periods of the same art to be, especially when that art is practised by the same race of people. There is no mistaking the one for the other. It has been stated that formerly there was no word in the Hawaiian language for singing as we know it. The modern term is *himeni,* an adaptation of the word hymn. The natives first obtained an idea of real melody from the hymn singing of the missionaries. The terms *oli, hula mele,* and *leo* partly express the idea of singing but primarily refer to other concepts. However, a rather obscure book by Campbell (29), who was cast a wounded sailor, on the bounty of Kamehameha I for more than a year, about 1808, contains an extensive vocabulary including the word *hiva* for song or music, which is identical with the Tongan term, the corresponding Samoan word being *siva.*

In the days of whaling vessels, when the Hawaiians first became acquainted to any extent with the white race, a number of songs, composed

7

by the natives about the sights novel to them, and a few old chanties picked
up from the sailors, were current and provide examples of the music of
the intermediate period. The early Hawaiian compositions are either of
the old style, musically, with a few interspersed English words (as was
fashionable for a time), or, if there was an attempt at melody, the tunes
might be described as flat. They were not catching melodically, and not
easy to sing. They were rather formless melodic wanderings without
balance or point.

In somewhat later times there ensued a period of extensive composing
on the part of those Hawaiians who had superior educational advantages
and were gifted, like the members of the royal family, King Kalakaua, and
his sister, Queen Liliuokalani. Some of these compositions have been
published and have become very popular at home and abroad. A number
of songs written for or by her late majesty, Queen Liliuokalani, and others
in the collection of King Kalakaua, have fortunately come into the possession of the Bishop Museum. These songs represent a period in which the
foreign art, stamped with a fresh viewpoint, was being adopted by the
Hawaiians, and made to assume distinctive features at their hands with
perhaps all the more enthusiasm because of untold centuries of comparative
melodic silence.

If there are many other songs of this period not in these collections,
there are still enough people living from whom they may be obtained after
the study of the old music is completed. Although beautiful and worthy
of preservation, many of the later compositions have less value than the
ancient material which means so much to ethnologists, linguists, and historians, and to the musician presents a picture of the dawn of vocal music
of a peculiar type, for the old culture is vanishing, and the ancient material
if not taken now, would have been irrevocably lost in the rapid march
of race intercourse and civilization.

Rendered in Hawaiian fashion, these later melodies have an appealing
charm. Unusual harmonies, together with peculiarities of attack and voice
production, a few rather well-defined rhythmic styles and accompaniments,
a tendency to complete the cadences on unaccented portions of beats or
measures rather than on primary accents, and the use of the ukulele and
of the steel guitar, with its beautiful gliding tones, have given musicians
in other parts of the world novel sensations and aroused their interest.
That Hawaiians invariably sing with great expression, revealing a nice
feeling for the nuances of melody, often disguises the fact that the tunes
they sing are banal more often than not. There is, as yet, not a great

amount of character or variety to the compositions. Some possess individuality and create a demand for more, but the vast majority live but for a short time and the hearer is soon sated with their monotony. It is much too soon to pass judgment on the music of the new era, for it is still in its infancy.

A bald analysis of many of the songs shows them to be based on well-known hymn tunes or to carry a touch of old European folk songs, owing to the inspiration of one of the first teachers of music in Honolulu, the first band leader, Captain Henry Berger. With as great a natural love of music as the Hawaiians have, and as many moving melodies as are already credited to them in the brief period since they have, musically speaking, come out of bondage, they should make greater and greater strides, if their own styles are not absorbed in the international music which is sweeping the world.

THE UKULELE

The ukulele deserves special notice here, for it has been associated with the Hawaiians and carried far from the islands by tourists under the impression that it is an instrument of native invention, or if not that, an instrument invented there.

Up to the time of its introduction by the Portuguese, the only stringed instrument which the Hawaiians had known as a people was the primitive musical bow, the *ukeke* (*u-ké-ké*).

The truth of the statement that the Portuguese brought the instrument later known in these islands as the ukulele has been doubted by some, who are under the impression that although it was first made by the Portuguese, its form was not invented until after their arrival, and was the result of a desire for a more convenient size of instrument, which would also be cheaper to make and would on that account sell more readily.

This doubt led to further investigation and to the seeking out of an old Portuguese gentleman, Mr. J. A. Gonsalves, known to have come to Honolulu from Madeira among the first Portuguese immigrants. He was twenty years old at the time of his arrival (1879). On the same sailing vessel with him were three men, Augusto Diaz, Z. Santos, and Manuel Nunes, partners in the old home in the business of making musical instruments. They were the first guitar makers in the islands. That all three instruments were made and played in Portugal is proved by the fact that the largest, the guitar, was there called *viola*. It had six strings, like the present Hawaiian guitar. The taro patch fiddle, called *rajao* in its original home, had five strings, as it has in Hawaii, while the ukulele, with four strings, had its Portuguese representative in the *braga,* one of which Mr. Gonsalves brought with him when he emigrated. These statements have been corroborated by Mr. George Nunes, son of Manuel Nunes, who is now dead, as are also Mr. Santos and Mr. Dias.

STEEL GUITAR

During the years 1893 to 1895, Joseph Kekuku, a young Hawaiian man from Laie, Koolauloa, Oahu, was attending the Kamehameha School for Boys, in Honolulu. The guitar was a popular instrument among the students who were constantly strumming it. Like school boys all over the world, probably, they were not unfamiliar with the possibilities of the comb as a musical instrument, and one day as he was playing the guitar the idea occurred to young Kekuku to try the effect of a comb placed on the strings. It is not known just what suggested the thought to him. He was delighted with the result and played with his new toy for a time before it occurred to him to try the back of his pocket knife. This second inspiration was even more satisfactory and thereafter the knife was always used when he played the guitar. However, he wanted a more convenient piece of metal, so he appealed to John Padigan, in the school shop, to fashion for him a piece of steel suited to his needs.

By this time his singular and beautiful playing had become the talk of the boys, who were all emulating him, and one of them, Tilton, who went to his home on Maui during a vacation, performed on his guitar with the aid of his knife for the benefit of his family. His sister-in-law, now Mrs. Clement Parker of Honolulu, from whom this account was obtained through the kindness of Mrs. Webb, asked him where he learned to play in such a curious manner and he told her that Joseph Kekuku at school had been the first to think of it and had taught the others how to do it. She later met Joseph Kekuku, who verified the statement.

According to Mrs. Webb, the fashion spread very rapidly after a concert which she attended and at which, if her memory serves her correctly, Kekuku himself played. The audience was delighted and, as she expressed it, "it took the house," as it has since taken the musical world. This invention of the Hawaiian schoolboy is the most significant contribution by Hawaii to music, the introduction of an entirely new technique for the playing of stringed instruments, at least as far as the western world is concerned, although the Japanese employ a similar technique with one of their stringed instruments, and some African tribes north and south of the Congo do the same with the musical bow, using a shell or knife blade.

SOURCES OF ANCIENT HAWAIIAN MATERIAL

Since it was necessary to exercise a choice of the islands to be visited, I felt that by covering Kauai on the west, Oahu in the center, and Hawaii to the east, such differences in styles of composition or rendition as might exist between islands would be clearly evident, and that in case of a general uniformity, a representative collection would in this manner be obtained. There are no doubt many local specimens from unvisited islands which have been missed by this plan, but while the failure to obtain them is regrettable, their loss is not vital to the survey as a whole.

Practically all that can be gathered in a musical way from the country people on the three islands mentioned has now been taken, and the constantly increasing number of variants of meles already obtained, as the work progressed, argues for the assumption that the bottom was being reached in that well of information. This collection of poetry, comprising something near seven hundred chants, including variants, together with several large private collections which have been turned over to the Museum provides an enormous mass of literature from which to draw in the future.

Whatever could be learned of the mechanics of poetical composition and recitation as recognized and practised by the Hawaiians, together with quotations of various articles on the subject, and data on the musical instruments, will be incorporated in this paper.

It was not feasible to secure the vocal music for all of the chants, nor for the longest ones. In all, about two hundred tunes were taken, enough to provide a basis for a critical study, and as many of these will be presented as possible, not only to prove the points to be made, but to give the reader a clear idea of them. Sixty phonograph records, made for the purpose of casting into permanent form audible and exact representations of the old methods of chanting, have been set aside for preservation.

In making these collections, I have gone into the most secluded valleys, into the most outlying districts, away from the general path of travel, to homes, which, if seldom of grass, as in former times, at least show evidences of little but the old way of living. Many of my informants did not know their ages, and never had been outside of their districts; they could neither read nor speak English.

The younger members of the household, who, having had some contact with the outside world and are very apt to consider the old meles as foolishness and to frown upon old customs as antiquated and queer, have been surprised at the meles the old folk could recite and at their pleasure in doing so, once their confidence was gained and they were made to feel that they had a sympathetic listener. There were some, however, who, to the last, refused to tell what they were generally believed by their own old friends to know.

There is a tendency on the part of many writers who have discussed the old customs of Hawaii, to a belief that at least twenty years ago practically all traces of the ancient life had disappeared and that what was to be found was not likely to be genuine. As early as 1836, only sixteen years after the missionaries had arrived, Adolphe Barrot (16), who visited the islands in a French sloop of war, remarked that the instrumental music of the islanders was still found at a distance from the ports and some vestiges were to be observed on Hawaii—as though all traces would soon be obliterated.

It is easy to overestimate, as it is to underestimate, the extent of a foreign influence in a primitive community. Because articles of trade penetrate rather widely in a short time and a veneer of foreign material culture is soon apparent, it is often assumed that the change is complete. However, history and repeated observation have shown that at heart a people are slow to change and that, although to a casual observer there is little visible of the native life, to one who takes the trouble to win the confidence of those who carefully hide their intimate feelings from those they feel might misunderstand, much is revealed to show that old habits are strong.

There is no doubt but that year by year the survivals are a little more corrupted and broken down, and that it is not safe to trust overmuch information given by any of the younger generation, but those over seventy-five years of age, of families that continued to cherish old ways despite missionary efforts—and there were many—can still be depended upon to furnish reliable examples of chanting and playing of instruments, as well as trustworthy information concerning much of the old Hawaiian life.

No attempt has been made to translate the texts of the meles that are used. This, and that much larger work, the translation and preparation for publication of the great collection of meles for the present held in reserve, will require long and patient labor.

NOTATION EMPLOYED IN PRESENTING MUSICAL EXAMPLES

The theory is often expressed that the European system of notation, since it does not meet all demands made upon it by exotic music, should be discarded in favor of one which does. The advocates of this idea have devised systems in presenting their material which are in many cases not readily grasped and which at best convey to European musicians no ready and obvious musical impression, requiring long practise for facile reading. The existence of several such schemes tends to defeat the very object of comparative study, since the mastery of any demands more study than the average scientist or musician can give, and to present material so diversely noted would necessitate the adoption of a common system, thus heaping confusion on confusion.

In the final analysis some reference to the European system must be made in order to render an account intelligible to the majority of the reading public, already well grounded in it. For reasons of expediency, then, the European system of notation is employed in these studies, with only such modifications as are required. Tones which do not fall at such half-step intervals as are represented by European chromatic signs have their deviation from them indicated by oblique lines drawn through the heads of the notes, the direction of the lines when reading from left to right showing whether the modified or intermediate tone lies above or below that indicated on the staff. Single oblique lines represent deviations of about a quarter step from the staff degree, smaller deviations are indicated by double lines. No distinction in notation is made between quarter step deviations and those of a third of a step, nor between sixths and eighths of tones in the smaller deviations. Not only would such distinctions require for their detection delicate mechanical apparatus which was not available for this study, but their consistent use in vocal music presupposes not only the nicest discrimination on the part of the singers, and a highly developed music having the steadying and standardizing influence of complicated instruments of fixed pitch, but perfect voice control with a reduction to the minimum of all extraneous influences which are constantly at work in the case of fluctuation as against mechanical accuracy, such as emotional excitement, various physical conditions, like illness or old age, or phonetics of the accompanying words which some-times affect pitch.

A people with a highly philosophical bent, like the early Greeks, the Hindus and the Chinese, may evolve with the aid of theory and instruments ideal scales which their musicians seek to reproduce in singing, but that their attempts are accurately successful, especially in unaccompanied vocal music, is a statement needing no refutation. However, an excellent check on the consistent employment of fine tonal distinctions is the extent of variation, especially of the larger intervals, shown by individuals in giving more than one rendition of the same tune, and likewise the range of variation occurring in the renditions of the same song by different singers. Even if under these circumstances the range of variation is comparatively large, it does not follow that the effect of nuances of tone may not be observed, enjoyed, and emulated; but a lack of consistency in repetitions, even in a general way, but with larger intervals, proves beyond doubt the comparative unimportance of microtones in the musical scheme, although as whimsical embellishments they may amount to a stylistic feature.

Very great care has been exercised in reducing the Hawaiian instru-mental and vocal music to notation to indicate tonal deflections from the European chromatic scale as accurately as practical considerations demand, in order that tendencies to consistent usage might be disclosed; and, if necessary, more accurate methods might be adopted of measuring the microtones, than that of listening with a keen ear to repeated playing of every passage. More accurate methods have been deemed unnecessary, but, if they should later prove to be desirable, the records set aside for casting will furnish the material for further research, for while not identical, they are practically duplicates of the records transcribed.

Some students, in graphically representing exotic music, prefer to omit measure bars, indicating the accents by superior marks. If it be true that Hindu music substitutes the conception of contrast in length of notes, that is, long against short, and a subdivision of larger into smaller elements, which European music also has, for accent, then possibly the bar is superfluous under these circumstances, but the very difficulty involved in avoiding all accent, of word or tone, throws doubt on this statement. Accent need not be sharp to be accent, and length lends emphasis. The omission of measure bars in music constructed in irregular meter, although it obviates the necessity of inserting constantly changing time signatures and the indication of fractional beats, seems to remove those metric props in reading to which musicians of the European school, at least, are accustomed, thus giving to the very readers who would be interested a number of tunes apparently formless as to rhythm and meter, which are by no means lacking in these particulars and differ from those we are accustomed to write with bars only in that the measures are not of uniform length. Accent marks in place of measure bars are for that very reason useless for representing stress of other kinds, since to employ the same sign for two purposes would create confusion. In this study measure bars are retained and fractional time signatures utilized if necessary, or if the fraction reached a degree that seemed to give the impression of unnecessary meticulosity in notation, the plus or minus sign has been substituted.

Key signatures have been replaced by the insertion of chromatic signs immediately before notes requiring them, on the first appearance in the measure. Thereafter, throughout the measure, their presence is presupposed unless a cancellation occurs. This rule regarding signs holding for the measure follows the European custom. It has not been adhered to, however, where notes require oblique lines, and to avoid confusion and the necessity for carrying these unfamiliar signs in mind, as well as to avoid inventing cancellation signs which would not encumber the music, the lines have been inserted afresh, each time they are needed. The omission of key signatures, aside from obviating the use of some chromatics which might never once occur in the course of a song, disposes of committing the melody to any key, any tonality, or any tonic as an imaginary foundation by which the reader might be prejudiced.

The employment of the modified European system used in this paper must be understood to serve but a single purpose, that of conveying in a practically readable and sufficiently accurate manner the music of a people who have no system of their own. Where the greatest mechanical accuracy is necessary, as in a study of complicated instruments and the comparison of tones which, by consistent usage, hint at fixed ideal or real scales, theoretically the systems of the users of such scales must be mastered, but in actual detection and notation only that system devised by the physicists will serve.

In presenting problems of musical trend alone, without reference to rhythm, or vice versa, combinational notation is always hard for the average reader to follow, and prevents quick grasping of salient features. Curves or plots serve admirably for the one; dashes or numerals for the other.

That element which so largely influences musical impression—tone quality—has never been reduced to any kind of notation, and descriptions are at best in this respect unsatisfactory substitutes for auditory sensation. It may be that in time the photographed voice, as it is now being produced on screens in a series of complex waves by Dr. Carl Seashore of the University of Iowa, will be read for its quality as well as its volume, pitch, and rhythm, but it will be long before such reading will become general, and to accomplish it at all, the complex waves must be reduced to their elements.

INSTRUMENTAL MUSIC

This study is divided into two main sections, one dealing with instrumental music; the other, with vocal. The instrumental music will be discussed first, since an understanding of the instruments is desirable prior to taking up the hula chants.

Emerson (43) has listed and described in some detail most of the instruments which appear to have been used, but several which were quite common during his early life have now vanished and all are rare except the calabash drum and the coconut or gourd rattle. However, more definite information regarding some of these instruments has been obtained, together with pieces and typical rhythms, which it is desirable to give, because Emerson, hampered by his lack of musical knowledge and his dependence on occasional assistance, has so few represented in notation. His classification and treatment of the instruments is a little confusing, for he does not draw the line sharply enough between different methods of tone production, and he has been led astray in some particulars, yet were it not for his painstaking work, we would today have very little knowledge of the instruments or know how to look for vestiges that remain.

Other writers have mentioned some instruments that were particularly prominent in hula performances which they saw, but none, so far as I am aware, except Emerson (43) and Marques (103, 104) has attempted to give more than a superficial description. Marques' articles are the only discussions by a musician and are admirable summaries of the whole situation. He reviews the literature which has dealt, however inadequately, with the subject up to his time, but does not give musical examples nor does he describe the instruments in detail.

He divides the instruments into the customary classes, string, wind, and percussion, and remarks (104, p. 52) that the Hawaiians were not so entirely destitute of instruments as Cook made them out to be, giving as his list one furnished by Princess Liliuokalani, later the queen. Her description is somewhat cursory and was not intended to meet the requirements of scientific study, and some details, given by no one else, appear to be open to question, as for instance, the statement that the *ukeke* had tuning pegs. *Ukeke* with tuning pegs have not been seen in any museum collection, nor were any specimens discovered in the field. It would therefore seem that such an instrument, if there was one, may have been made specially for the queen and is of recent development. Dr. Marques, in personal conversation, states that he did not examine the specimens possessed by the princess.

In number and complexity the old Hawaiian instruments were limited

17

indeed, but they represent each of the three great families of instruments. Although the individual specimens belonging to these families are very primitive, they are, in some instances, so peculiar in their construction and use, that, were they found to exist in other parts of the world, there would be very good grounds for suspecting a more or less immediate contact between their users in ancient times.

THE STRINGS

There is but one Hawaiian representative of stringed instruments, a variety of musical bow, which, according to Linton (personal conversation) had its highest development in the Hawaiian islands, where it appeared with three strings, but which is also present in the Marquesas.

THE UKEKE

Emerson's description of this bow, or *ukeke* as the Hawaiians call it, is here quoted, for there are some points which he brings up which it is necessary to discuss. He says: (43, p. 147)

The ukeké, the one Hawaiian instrument of its class, is a mere strip of wood bent into the shape of a bow that its elastic force may keep tense the strings that are stretched upon it. These strings, three in number, were originally of sinnet, later, after the arrival of the white man, of horsehair. At the present time it is the fashion to use the ordinary gut designed for the violin or the taro-patch guitar. Every ukeké seen followed closely a conventional pattern, which argues for the instrument a historic age sufficient to have gathered about itself some degree of traditional reverence. One end of the stick is notched, or provided with holes to hold the strings, while the other end is wrought into a conventional figure resembling the tail of a fish and serves as an attachment about which to wind the free ends of the strings.

No ukeké seen by the author was furnished with pins, pegs or any similar device to facilitate tuning. Nevertheless the musician does tune his ukeké, as the writer can testify from his own observation. . . . When asked to give a sample of his playing on the ukeké, he first gave heed to his instrument as if testing whether it was in tune. He was evidently dissatisfied and pulled at one string as if to loosen it, then, pressing one end of the bow against his lips, he talked to it in a singing tone, at the same time plucking the strings with a delicate rib of grass. The effect was most pleasing. The open cavity of the mouth, acting as a resonator, reinforced the sounds and gave them a volume and dignity that was a revelation. The lifeless strings allied themselves to a human voice and became animated by a living soul.

With the assistance of a musical friend it was found that the old Hawaiian tuned his strings with approximate correctness to the tonic, the third and the fifth. We may surmise that this self-trained musician had instinctively followed the principle or rule proposed by Aristoxenus, who directed a singer to sing his most convenient note, and then, taking this as the starting point, to tune the remainder of his strings, the Greek kithara, no doubt,—in the usual manner from this one.

While the ukeké was used to accompany the mele and the oli, its chief employment was in serenading and serving the young folk in breathing their extemporized love songs and uttering their love talk-*hoipoipo*. By using a peculiar lingo or secret talk of their own invention, two lovers could hold private conversation in public and pour their loves and longings into each other's ears without fear of detection—a thing most reprehensible in savages. This display of ingenuity has been the occasion for outpouring many vials of wrath upon the sinful ukeké [by the missionaries].

The following description of the *ukeke* is based on an examination of a dozen or more in the collection in the Bishop Museum, on some described in the catalog of musical instruments in the Metropolitan Museum of Art, New York City, and on several specimens found on Hawaii in the hands of old players.

As to shape, all the old *ukeke,* with one exception, were only slightly bowed; in fact, so close did the strings lie to the wood, that in several specimens little bridges were inserted beneath them at either end of the instrument to allow them free play when struck. Thus the term musical bow, generally used for this type of instrument, particularly with Emerson's description, is somewhat misleading, although there is little doubt but that the derivation of the *ukeke* is from the primitive bow. Emerson offers no illustration of it, so that his description cannot be completely checked, but with one exception (fig. 1, *d*) all the old specimens collected by his brother J. S. Emerson (44), and the accounts or specimens offered by other authorities conform to the descriptions and illustrations given here. (See Pl. I, *B, C*.) The name, Hawaiian jew's harp, applied by so many writers, is technically not correct. The jew's harp is structurally a different instrument with a vibrating tongue fastened at one end to the body of the instrument and free at the other.

A great variation appears in the length of the *ukeke* studied—from fifteen inches to more than two feet—but all were about an inch and a half wide, except three which measured an inch in width and were smaller in every way. All were slightly narrowed toward the ends and smoothed into two distinct surfaces, an upper or flat face (over which the strings were intended to lie), and a slightly convex back or under surface. The depth of the cross section increased toward the center to about half an inch, on the average, and lessened toward the edges and either end. All specimens were provided at one end with a flange about an eighth of an inch thick formed by cuttting away the back of the *ukeke* to a depth of a quarter of an inch. Into this flange except in two cases, either two or three very narrow slits or notches were cut. The two exceptions substituted three small holes. Through these apertures were drawn the strings, which were prevented from pulling completely through by knots at their ends. Such a provision as a flange is not at all necessary to the efficacy of the instrument, for holding the knots in place, or for protecting them, as the wear on them would be very slight. It is merely a bit of nice workmanship which might be expected of a good carpenter, characteristic of Hawaiian wood work. In reality, the cutting away of the wood to form a flange weakens it as a brace against the tension of the strings. The fact that the flange is present in every specimen, considering that it is unessential, is one argument for the great age of this type of instrument which has become a stereotyped form.

FIGURE 1.—Sketch of types of *ukeke* stems.

All the specimens had the "fish tail" at the opposite end, as described by Emerson, and none had any pegs whatsoever to facilitate tuning. Most of the "fish tails" were of the shape shown in Fig. 1*a,* but one maker produced two, in the J. S. Emerson collection, illustrated by figure 1*b;* others were like *c,* while a more modern specimen, like *d,* is of a shape difficult to obtain with stone tools; *e* represents a Maui specimen.

Quite a variety of woods were used for the manufacture of the *ukeke,* some of which were deemed by the old Hawaiians superior for the purpose. On Kauai and Oahu no instruments were found, although informants had possessed and played them. One man on Kauai agreed to manufacture one of kauila wood (*Alphitonia excelsa*), which he considered the proper material, but failing to obtain some without making a long trip to the mountains, abandoned the attempt. On Hawaii the first expert player encountered, in North Kona, expressed the same preference. In the Joseph S. Emerson collection, largely from the island of Hawaii and now in the Bishop Museum, two *ukeke* have been tentatively identified by Forest B. H. Brown as of kauila.

A discussion among different natives in South Kona, Hawaii, as to the proper wood, came about in an unexpected manner. After trying in vain to locate an instrument with three strings which, according to Emerson, was the usual type, an *ukeke* was finally made in Kona by a middle-aged carpenter according to models which he could recall having seen.

It was therefore somewhat disappointing to find that wherever the modern instrument was produced, after a brief trial it provoked considerable mirth and even contempt. Several men declared that koa (*Acacia koa*), of which the instrument was made, was not suitable, for when strung up tightly it was too stiff to give as it should in order to keep the strings tense. Because it had been made of dead wood rather than from a green cut, seasoned, was another reason advanced for its reduced pliability, as were also its thickness and the extreme convexity of its under side. All of these points were thought to affect not only the spring but the resonance, when the wood was placed before the open mouth. Many held that the longer the instrument, the better the tone produced. Thus a defective specimen provided an illuminating discussion as to the knowledge the Hawaiians possessed of the properties of wood and the value of seasoning, as well as the ideas they hold on the causes of resonance.

Kauila wood was almost universally agreed to be the best, if obtainable; but the root of the puhala (*Pandanus tectorius*), the wood of the hau tree (*Hibiscus tiliaceus*), the iliahi (*Santalum sp.*), the ulei (*Osteomeles anthyllidifolia*), the aaka, aala, and the uhiuhi (specimens unidentified anatomically), were also declared suitable. Museum specimens represent, according to tentative determination or catalog data, kauila, ulei, puhala, iliahi, and possibly aaka, as well as the koaia (*Acacia koaia*). The second choice with the natives was the ulei, which although a scrubby tree, provides an excellent material for bows, since it is both tough and pliable, with a very fine grain. It seems to have been confused with sandalwood by someone, for two specimens in the Museum identified as such were said by natives to be ulei. Ulei, however, is not fragrant, and aside from the fact that the Hawaiians know both trees and their properties, J. S. Emerson's experience with ulei places beyond doubt that of the two, ulei is more suitable.

In old times strings were made of fiber. Some in the Museum are two-ply strings of twisted coconut threads. A few old people stated that formerly goat gut was employed, but that later horsehair was introduced. The much bowed, crude, modern *ukeke* in the Museum with the crescent-shaped "fish tail" (fig. 1, *d*), claimed by its maker in the late eighties to be the latest style *ukeke,* is strung with horsehair. One old three-stringed *ukeke* has a single remaining cord of fine gut, finer than any present-day ukulele string, the modern substitute, which may have been obtained as a gift from some foreigner in rather early times.

Mention has already been made of the original difficulty of procuring any *ukeke* in the field, and of the fact that after continual disappointment on Kauai and Oahu, the first reward for the search occurred in North Kona, Hawaii. Here a number of specimens were seen but they were all designed for only two strings, with but two notches in the flange end. Despite inquiry no three-stringed model could be found. It was necessary to procure one of each type to carry about. A two-stringed *ulei ukeke* was presented for this purpose and gut ukulele strings were purchased for it. Subsequently the *ukeke* of dead koa wood designed for three strings, with holes in the flange instead of notches, was obtained. With the exception of one old specimen in the Museum, this was the only example observed with holes. When some old people were asked to string it, the holes were not approved, so they were lengthened into slits. From this circumstance and the fact that only one other observed specimen has holes, it appears that slits were generally better liked, whatever may have been the original form.

For the *ukeke* with two strings, the method of stringing was as follows: after the cord had been knotted and drawn through the first slit, it was carried straight along the flat surface of the wood to the end, at the side of the "fish tail," then completely about it, starting from beneath, until several wrappings had been made, when the free end was drawn under the taut string and pulled up as far as possible and so fastened. A second string was adjusted in a similar manner to the other side of the *ukeke*. For three-stringed instruments, a third string was passed through a middle notch, along the *ukeke* and through the crotch of the "tail," thence about the whole tail several times. This was the method for separate cords and has been followed in such Museum specimens as still have strings upon them.

For my three-stringed *ukeke* I had one very long ukulele string, which, oddly enough, no one suggested cutting so as to have separate strings, although various informants used it from time to time. Cutting would have been an easier procedure, but invariably a knot was made in one end of the string which was then drawn through the first slit, carried along one edge of the instrument, back of the "fish tail" once or else wrapped around it several times after it had been pulled tight enough, then down over the surface on the other edge and through the third slit, with an attempt to pull it sufficiently taut, then back through the second slit, looking from beneath like a string around a tooth, and up the center of the *ukeke* to the crotch in the "tail" where, after sufficient tension produced the desired pitch, it was wound for the last few times about the two-forked stem and fastened as usual.

In tuning the instrument some persons placed the flange end on the knee and held the *ukeke* vertically, so that the "fish tail" came near the ear. In this way the tone, which was very faint, could be heard as the string was being tested with the thumb of the left hand, while the fingers of the right hand held it taut preparatory to winding it about the stem. But I witnessed what appeared to be perhaps a more primitive method of tuning by a woman of Kau, who refused to let me photograph her in the act. She sat on the ground, her feet out in front of her, her limbs somewhat flexed and the flanged end of the *ukeke* braced on the earth between her heels. Then, as she held the upper end with her hands, she placed both great toes on either side of the strip of wood and forced it into a slight bow, drew the strings taut and fastened them tentatively about the "fish tail" until she could pick up the instrument and bring it near enough to her ear to test the tone. If it was not right, she bowed the wood again with her toes and drew the string imperceptibly tighter. Once when the pitch was a little high, she ran her finger beneath the string, back and forth over its entire length as if to loosen it.

In all my interviews with old people who strung up and played the *ukeke,* little bridges or nuts, improvised from small twigs or matches, were inserted beneath the strings after tuning, at either end of the instrument, to lift them and to increase the tension. At the time I supposed that the idea had grown, as such ideas will very rapidly on occasion, from the bridge used in the ukulele and all of our stringed instruments. On later examination of *ukeke* in the Museum, however, two quite old specimens were found to be equipped with bridges made of small pieces of the rind of a gourd. Not being permanently fastened they could easily have been lost when the strings decayed or were loosened or broken, so that it is impossible to say with certainty if the stringless specimens also once had them. The *ukeke* in the Metropolitan Museum of Art is complete with bridges.

Data from the catalog of Joseph S. Emerson (44) show that his collection was secured from Hawaii, mostly from the Kona district, between 1885 and 1887. Since the introduction of the ukulele dates from 1879, it hardly seems likely that it would have been widespread in Kona at that time. The probability that the bridge was a native invention, very old, and inspired by necessity, is increased by the fact that a bridge is present in an Austral Islands musical bow and in the bow of the Marquesans (88, p. 408).

Most of the *ukeke* as illustrated by the Joseph S. Emerson collection in the Bishop Museum, all the specimens produced by old Hawaiians for me on the island of Hawaii, and the single old *ukeke* in the Metropolitan Museum, have only two strings. As most of these date back of the time when the Unwritten Literature of Hawaii was written, it appears that the two-stringed form always has been at least as important as the three. *Ukeke* described by Marques confirm this conclusion. This coincides with the theory that the derivation of the instrument is from the bow, and simpler forms precede the more complex.

Inquiry among the old people elicited the response from a number of informants that, as far as they knew, there had always been both forms, and all thought that the three-stringed was at least as old as the two, showing that it is not a recent improvement. One woman said that some *ukeke* had four and even five strings, but she had never played one and could not produce any. The method of stringing would make her statement very doubtfully true, for with only three places for the strings to lie at the conventional "fish tail" end, any larger number would necessitate a differently fashioned instrument, or else create an overlapping of the strings at that end. No one else has, to my knowledge, seen a Hawaiian *ukeke* with more than three strings.

John F. G. Stokes told me that he noticed in the Austral Islands a one-stringed musical bow more than two feet long, called *titapu,* which was plucked like the Hawaiian *ukeke* with one end held in the mouth which served as a resonator. A small piece of wood had been inserted beneath the string at one end only, to lift it from the stick. The instrument had been crudely made by a young boy who had traveled considerably, but not outside the Austral Islands. This specimen is apparently nearer to an ancestor of the Hawaiian *ukeke* than one known as the *utete,* brought to the Museum from the Marquesas by Linton. The Marquesan specimen is more truly a bow, with a curved stick about a yard long, which has, it is true, two surfaces, a flat and a convex, but whose position in regard to the strings as well as the curvature, however slight that may be in the Hawaiian form, is the reverse of that of the *ukeke.* No bridges are applied in this Marquesan specimen, and they would be difficult to keep in place on an instrument so curved even were they needed. Linton describes bridges of wood or stone on modern Marquesan instruments (88, p. 408). The knotted end of the string on the Marquesan specimen is inserted in a notch at the end of the wood, the other end is merely wound about the opposite extremity of the bow, which lacks the conventional flange and tail forms of the Hawaiian instruments.

Emerson (43) has remarked that the *ukeke* was primarily an instrument of lovers, who by use of a lingo of their own, talking while using the mouth as a resonator, could carry on conversations in public. It seems that it was not a matter of a different language but of a technique which rendered understanding to a foreigner difficult. The words, I found, were plain enough to all Hawaiians familiar with the mele who were within earshot.

Both Emerson and Marques were under the impression that the player talked to his instrument in singing tones, and it is possible that Hawaiians who have not learned how to use the *ukeke* or even those who do, might make the same assertion, because they are not inclined to strict observation. My experience with a number of old players who have certainly not changed their methods at this late date in their lives, has led to an entirely different conclusion. None of those whom I observed made any sound whatsoever with their vocal chords. They grasped the instrument in the left hand, with the palm next to the convex side, and the thumb pressing the lower edge. (See Pl. I, *D*.) The end containing the slits was held between the lips and the entire instrument extended horizontally to the left. The mouth cavity acted as a resonance chamber. With a small fiber, or more usually with a bit of cloth twisted into a point, the strings were picked with almost incredible rapidity. Twisting a cloth for a plectrum has become fairly widespread in the last century. Possibly tapa was formerly used. As the strings were picked, the shape of the mouth and lips changed, and the tongue was used exactly as it would be in speech, with the result that the sound issuing from the mouth almost resembled speech. At first I could hear nothing except tones on two pitches which were created by the plucked strings. They assumed the sound of an echo in a well when a pebble is dropped into the water. After numerous attempts, with a Hawaiian text before me, I was able to distinguish some words and have no doubt but that with a little experience, I could have understood the mele.

The *ukeke* was used for amusement as well as for love making and by husbands and wives as well as by those who had illicit love affairs. The tones, though faint, were sufficiently strong to be heard either side of a wall of a grass house. The *ukeke* was even used to accompany hula dances of the *olapa* variety on occasion, which were then sometimes loosely called *hula ukeke*.

There was some stopping of the strings with the fingers, but very little, according to one informant who had witnessed the *hula ukeke*. Those who played for me did not modify the tone of the vibrating string by stopping, but occasionally the thumb, which in holding the instrument nearly touched the lower string, pressed it when it was not being played.

Usually the player struck but one string at a time, alternating between the two or repeating, thus producing a little tune, but in a few examples all the strings were struck in one stroke. (See Nos. 6, 7, 8, 9, pp. 30, 31.) Again, although only one was struck, the other string would vibrate in sympathy, so that without the closest attention to the movements of the player's hand it was most difficult to tell whether it, too, was being struck. Whenever I heard two tones I indicated them, although I doubt that two strings were struck at once, except in the case of the two tunes on the three-stringed instrument. As the tone was too faint to record in the phonograph, the melodies were written down directly from the playing—a rather exhausting process for the players who could not be interrupted without becoming hopelessly confused and being obliged to start again. This continual repetition was an excellent way, however, in which to check what had been written. Fortunately one woman, with the promise of reward, patiently and good naturedly played her tunes again and again until they were correctly noted. Her renditions, even when irregular in meter, were very constant.

From six or seven performers were obtained eleven complete tunes and six fragments. Two of these were rendered on the unsatisfactory koa wood instrument, the other on two-stringed *ukeke*. In addition, a man, half Hawaiian, half Mexican Indian, who had been reared with his mother's Hawaiian people on Kauai, but who had moved to Hawaii after he was grown, offered to sing an *ukeke* tune which he could recall, although he could not play the instrument. He was about sixty years of age and had heard it long ago. Another man of seventy also sang an *ukeke* song. Both must have been played on the two-stringed instrument. (See tunes Nos. 14, 15, pp. 34, 35.) To show how difficult it is still for some conservative Hawaiians to sing, particularly instrumental music, the woman who played the *ukeke* so patiently was asked to sing the song that the words might be heard clearly and given their proper place beneath the notes, but she said she had never heard of such a thing being done and did not know how to go about it.

Each time but one that the two-stringed *ukeke* was tuned, the strings were brought to the interval of a perfect fourth, but with varying actual pitches. The exception was an augmented fourth produced by the Kau woman, who tuned the *ukeke* with the aid of her toes. (See p. 22.)

The two songs also contained but two tones each, standing in the relation of a perfect fourth to one another, and were rather faithful representatives of *ukeke* melodies as a comparison of them with the tunes actually played on the instruments will show. (See Nos. 14, 15.) One man played the *ukeke* on two different occasions, first tuning it to *d* and *g*, again to *c*♯ and *f*♯. (See Nos. 3, 4, 5.)

Another informant secured the interval of a major third, with which he was not at all satisfied, and finally abandoned his efforts, handing the instrument to a woman near, who tuned it to the interval of a perfect fourth and played a selection. (See No. 2.) The man made no comments on her playing. It was he who sang *ukeke* song No. 14.

Evidently then, this interval was customary for the two-stringed type. Its importance in very ancient times as the basis of the earliest Greek and Hindu music that we know, as well as its prominence in the music of other early nations, only supports the assumption that the *ukeke* is an archaic instrument or that its tuning goes back to some ancient musical concept. Although the fourth bears a simple relation to the fundamental, if it is not one of its near partials, and although it is readily determined, yet the great range of possibilities open owing to the free structure of the instrument makes its selection appear due to long custom, while the number of cases of its choice as against one exception prove that it was not due to chance.

The three-stringed instrument was tuned and played only once, by the Kau woman. (See Nos. 6, 7, pp. 30, 31.) The two outer strings were *gb* and *cb'* between an augmented and a perfect fourth, the middle string was *ab*, forming with the lower a major second and with the upper a neutral third. (See Nos. 8, 9.) This does not agree with the statement made by an old man in Kona, who, however had always lived around white people and had had many superior advantages. He remarked, in discussing the faulty koa model, that the three-stringed variety was tuned to *pa, ko, li*— the first three tones of the major diatonic scale as taught to the Hawaiians by the missionaries when they first learned to really sing. In our tonic sol-fa system these tones would be do, re, mi. The other tuning seems to my mind more likely to be correct, although the old man who discussed the tuning knew much about suitable woods and fashioned for me the only nose flute procured in the field. However, he was not at all particular as to the placing of the holes, showing that he did not realize its significance in producing certain tones.

In regard to the tunes themselves, Nos. 1 to 5 inclusive and 10 to 13 bear a marked resemblance to one another not only in actual pitch, but in their melodic and rhythmic structure, closer even than the limitations of the instrument would impose, although an analysis reveals considerable variety in the changes on the theme of two eighth notes combined with a dotted eighth and a sixteenth to form a measure. It may be said that these dotted eighths and sixteenths are characteristic of *ukeke* tunes and in this respect they differ from hula melodies quite noticeably. There is considerable regularity in the recurrence of accents defining the measures and few extra beats or fractions have crept in. This regularity is also somewhat of a contrast to hula tunes which, when not sung to the accompaniment of instruments, lapse into irregular meter, accommodating themselves more to the demands of the poetry and the breath capacity of the individual singer, as commonly happens when the stiffening influence of dance movement and rigid drum accompaniment is withdrawn.

No. 10, however, contains a number of rhythmic irregularities which were absolutely constant throughout many repetitions, so that these must be assumed to belong to the piece. No doubt the music followed the syllables in rhythmic values and required the extra beats, but that even the same song may be rendered differently by different singers is revealed by this song, "Aia i Honolulu," which was very popular and encountered again and again. In each rendition it differed as to text and this was reflected in the tunes to which it was fitted.   One version is represented by No. 11, another by No. 14, which was sung, not played, by one of the men.   The same mele has been adapted for hulas.

"Aloha Kilauea" is both an *ukeke* song and a *hula puili*.   It was played on the three-stringed model, first as given in No. 9, but a request for a repetition resulted in No. 8.   The difference between them proves that by this performer, the Kau woman, unique for so many peculiarities already mentioned, the rhythm was not regarded as important, if indeed the change was observed by her.   In rhythmic character, all her pieces differed from the others in lacking the dotted notes.

Comparison of these tunes with *ukeke* tunes recorded by Miss Elsner for Emerson (43, p. 149), reveals marked differences.   The tunes by Miss Elsner are all on one pitch, while the collection given here embodies at least two tones for every piece, as might be expected from the instrument. If a three-stringed *ukeke* was general in Emerson's time, as he has said (p. 18), then it would be but reasonable to assume that the tunes played on them would, as a rule, employ three tones, or if fingering was used, which is doubtful at best, more should be expected.   Therefore the tunes secured by Miss Elsner, although they represent one man's endeavors, indicate in but a limited way what the *ukeke* could produce with proficient players.

Ukeke Tunes

No. 1.—Played by Peter Kaawa, North Kona, Hawaii.

No. 2.—Played by Mrs. Kaimu Kihe, Puuanahulu, North Kona, Hawaii.

No. 3.—Played by Kaleihoohie, Waiohinu, Kau, Hawaii.

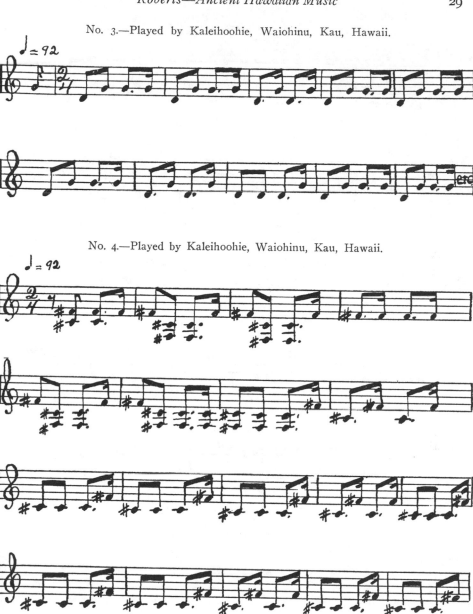

No. 4.—Played by Kaleihoohie, Waiohinu, Kau, Hawaii.

No. 5.—Fragments of tunes played by Kaleihoohie, Waiohinu, Kau, Hawaii.

No. 6.—Played by Mrs. Monika Keawe, Waiohinu, Kau, Hawaii.

repeated indefinitely

No. 7.—Kilauea, played by Mrs. Monika Keawe, Waiohinu, Kau, Hawaii.

No. 8—Kilauea, played by Mrs. Monika Keawe, Waiohinu, Kau, Hawaii.

No. 9.—Kilauea, played by Mrs. Monika Keawe, Waiohinu, Kau, Hawaii (supposed be identical with No. 8).

No. 10.—O keku iho oe, played by Mrs. Kawaimakaonalii Hao, Kalaoa, North Kona, Hawaii. (The single notes written in parenthesis were sometimes dropped by the player in favor of rests of the same value.)

No. 11.—Ai' i Honolulu, played by Mrs. Kawaimakaonalii Hao, Kalaoa, North Kona, Hawaii. (The only words recognized are those given.)

No. 12.—I aloha ia no Kilauea, played by Mrs. Kawaimakaonalii Hao, Kalaoa, North Kona, Hawaii.

Note: No. 12 is substantially the same as Nos. 7, 8, and 9. As sometimes rendered, the second section alternated with the first in repetitions.

No. 13.—Played by Mrs. Kawaimakaonalii Hao, Kalaoa, North Kona, Hawaii.

Note: At places marked 1, one of the groups of notes in parenthesis, usually the first, was omitted in repetitions.

No. 14.—Sung by David Alapai, Puuanahulu, North Kona, Hawaii.

E a i Ho-no-lu-lu Kou po ha tu'u ho(a?)
A-lo-hi la-ni i i ho ho' i i i i i au
Ka le-o o ta man(u) a' u le—hu-a i Mo
I-ka—u—le-le(?) ho-lo e ta we-la ma
Mo-etu pu-a ni-e etc.

Note: In No. 14 the various verses were adjusted to the time as indicated.

No. 15.—Sung by Samuela Akoni Mika, Hilo, Hawaii.

U ha'u he-a o-e e Ma-nu-o-te-tu]i(a) E-a-la ma-i o - e e

moe lo-a ne'i E - i -a ho'i a- u ma wa-ho a-ku nei O ta ua li-i-li-i i

ta ua mo-e -mo(e) Ho a'-e ta-u-a i ta'i-hu o ta li(o) I ta'u-lu ku-hu-i o

Wa-li-ka-ma-hel(e) U ha'u he-a o-e e tu'u Ho-a lu-(hi) Mei

tu-hu ma i o-e A-he po-no ke-i-i(a) E-i-a ti'u ti no i ta

u— la-i (a) I ka u-lu a - o'-a e Ma-ma-la-a A ho a-e ta-u-ai ta

i-hwi o ta li(o)i to u-lu tu-tu-i o Wa-li la-ha-hel(e).

THE WINDS

NOSE FLUTE

The most conspicuous musical wind instrument is the nose flute, variously known as the *ohe,* the *hano,* or *ohe hano ihu* (*ohe* meaning bamboo; *hano,* an instrument; *ihu,* nose). (See Pl. II, *C, E.*) The mouth flute was not known in Hawaii, according to Linton (88, p. 409), nor therefore the whole group of pan pipes. Alexander (1, fly leaf) does not mention the *ohe* at all, and classes the little gourd whistle as a mouth instrument.

At the present time probably not more than four or five persons are living who can play the *ohe.* The flutes in the Bishop Museum are all of bamboo, of varying lengths and diameters, with one end cut off short at the node, which closes the tube naturally, and with the other end open. A single nose hole is bored in the side of each instrument as close to the closed end of the tube as possible, and differs in size with different specimens. Some flutes have one, some two, some three finger holes, and these vary widely in their relative spacing as well as in diameter. Thus it may be seen that the fundamental and other tones would vary considerably with different flutes and that a flute played by one individual might not easily be played by another if a very much larger column of air than he was accustomed to must be set in vibration.

This was the case with a flute manufactured for me by the old man in Kona, who found after completing it that it required "too much wind." He had taken some pains to place the nose hole, and to shave away the wood at the node end, where the instrument was to be placed next to his upper lip, in order to bring the aperture nearer to his nostril. In determining the situation of the two finger holes he placed the instrument in position, holding it with such of his fingers as would not be needed to stop the holes, and then indicated the location of the first or nearest hole at a distance comfortably reached by the middle finger of his left hand, while the thumb and second finger were occupied in holding the flute in position. The second hole he rather carelessly marked at a distance down the tube.

The measurements of this flute were eighteen inches long with an inch and a half bore. The nose hole was half an inch from the end, held directly under the nostril, and was ⅜ inch in diameter. The first finger hole, a little smaller, lay 1¾ inches below, on a line with the nose hole, and the second 8 inches below that. The sounds produced on it subsequently by a younger man were the notes given in fig. 2.

FIGURE 2.—Diagrams showing tones produced by a nose flute: *a,* both finger holes open; *b,* upper hole open, the lower closed; *c,* lower hole open, the upper closed; *d,* both holes closed; *e,* both holes open and as result of embouchure.

In another part of the island of Hawaii a man about fifty years old had learned to make and play the flute from watching the old people. He is the only comparatively young man found who had retained an interest in the nose flute, and fortunately his breath capacity was unimpaired, so that he was able to play it well. He was very skillful with his own instrument, which he preferred to mine, although he played tunes on both. His flute was lower in pitch and did not record on the phonograph as readily as the shriller tone of the Kona specimen. I did not secure the tones which he could produce by various positions of the fingers, because he was very busy the day I visited him, and unwilling to take time, although he consented to play into the phonograph. Several of these tunes have been reduced to notation as well as some he played on the Kona flute.

The measurements of his own flute were as follows: length 18 inches, diameter of the bore 1⅜ inches, with the center of the nose hole ¾ inch from the outside node end of the tube and its diameter ⅜ inch. There were two finger holes, the first 4¾ inches from the node end with the same diameter as the nose hole. The second finger hole was 12½ inches from the end, and ¼ inch in diameter. The man said that he had not exercised any particular care in placing his holes but had put them where it was convenient for his fingers to reach them.

The Kona flute (p. 35) was first played by a man in Puna who produced the tones already given for the different stops in figure 2. (See p. 39, No. 16 for a tune produced on this flute.) He played another tune into the phonograph but with considerable effort, so a duplicate of it was not made and the first record has been reserved for casting and at present cannot be transcribed. When his wife sang a hula, Kenoi accompanied her in unison with the little tune No. 17, p. 39.

Considering the tonal possibilities of these flutes as demonstrated by Kenoi when he blew the various notes which I have given in figure 2, the tunes rendered by him, as well as by Kalepa Manu, the Hilo flutist, are extremely limited. (See Nos. 16, 17, 18, 19.) It must be remembered, however, that neither of these players was accustomed to this particular flute and had but a few moments in which to try it before playing, and that Kenoi had not handled an instrument in years.

Syncopation, which appears in these tunes to a limited extent, as it does also in the *ukeke* tunes, is worthy of note. Dotted notes contrasted with those of very small time value mark all of the flute music as in the case of the *ukeke* tunes.

Three pieces, Nos. 20, 21, 22, were played by Kalepa on his own flute and are rather ingenious variations of very simple melodic themes. In tonal content all of the flute tunes secured are very much simpler than that of Miss Elsner's specimens reproduced by Emerson (43, p. 146), with the exception of her first melody. Her player was undoubtedly a master of his instrument, as none of my informants pretended to be.

Concerning the nature of the tunes produced on the nose flute in 1836, when it was still fairly common, the following quotation has been taken from Barrot's article (16, pp. 33-35).

But what was admirable in this song [a hula] which, however, had a compass of only two or three notes, was the perfect accordance with which the five singers spoke and gesticulated. . . . Their song, like that of the first singers, was nothing more than an animated conversation. No other song, in fact, is known in the Sandwich Islands.

The instrumental music of the islanders which is still found at a distance from the ports, and some vestiges of which we observed on Hawaii, consists of tamtams and a sort of flute with two holes. Instead of the lips, the nose is used in blowing this instrument,—a graceful way, forsooth. The notes given forth by this instrument are not more varied than those of their vocal music.

The old man in Kona said that the tune he would have played had he been able to do so, was adapted to the words

Ku'-ulu-lu' a' ku' he o' a ku' he o' a

repeated over and over. He recited them in the rhythm indicated in No. 23.

The nose flute appears to have been chiefly an instrument for lovers. Its clear, soft, and sweet tone could nevertheless carry considerable distance with the right atmospheric conditions. A legend which deals with the circumstances surrounding its first manufacture and use, describes a prince on the mountain top above Wailua, Kauai, playing to call a princess living below him in the valley on the bank of the river, who awakened to the sound and followed it, accompanied by protesting members of her court, until she located the player who had been taught how to make the *ohe* and to use it by a god who wished him to win the princess for his bride.

Like the *ukeke,* it is said that the *ohe* could be made to sound as if words were being spoken through it, but not by the same method. Probably the sounds were modified in some manner by the embouchure and were played strictly in the rhythm of the spoken words. I have been told by Mrs. Webb that she once heard her grandfather playing the *ohe* and she thought as he played it that it sounded as if he were talking, and she could almost make out the words. She asked him in astonishment if he were talking and he replied that he was, and presently a neighbor woman came over who had heard and correctly interpreted his message. Drums in Africa could be made to speak in the same manner and carried messages for miles to those who could interpret the words. The natives of New Zealand also "talked" with flutes.

NOSE FLUTE TUNES

No. 16.—Played by D. H. Kenoi, Kapoho, Puna, Hawaii.

Note: As played by Mr. Kenoi, No. 16 had a variable, uneven rhythm with no apparent rule of variation; the melodic theme appeared over and over.

No. 17.—Played by D. H. Kenoi, Kapoho, Puna, Hawaii, accompanying a hula sung by Mrs. Kenoi.

No. 18.—Played by Kalepa Manu, Kalaoa, Hilo, Hawaii.

No. 19.—Played by Kalepa Manu, Kalaoa, Hilo, Hawaii

No. 20.—Same tune as No. 19, played by Kalepa Manu, on his own flute.

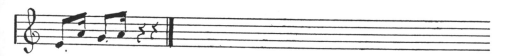

No. 21.—Played by Kalepa Manu, Kalaoa, Hilo, Hawaii.

No. 22.—Played by Kalepa Manu, Kalaoa, Hilo, Hawaii.

No. 23.—The rhythm only of a nose flute melody as it would have been played by
Kahikina Kaoo, of Hookena, South Kona, Hawaii, who sang the syllables to
indicate the rhythms.

Kuwu lu lwa kuheoa kuhe o a

THE GOURD WHISTLE

The *ipu hokiokio*, as the gourd whistle was named, is a small gourd
about the size of an ordinary pear, but according to Rev. Stephen Desha, of
Hilo, the shell of the Hawaii nut, *kamani (Calophyllum inophyllum)*, was
sometimes utilized instead. Four or five gourd whistles are in the Bishop
Museum collections, all pierced at the top by a hole slightly in excess of
half an inch in diameter for receiving air from the nostril, like the nose
flute. Midway down the side of the gourd, rather close together, are bored
two or three small finger holes. (See Pl. III, *B*.)

The name *"pu-a'"* for this whistle, mentioned by Emerson (43, p. 146),
was not heard, nor were any specimens of the instrument found, but in
conversation in various localities the whistle was called *hokiokio,* which
may be a more modern term. J. S. Emerson, who collected several specimens, noted (44) that they were also known as *ipu hoehoe,* although this
name is likewise applied to tubular bamboos, perhaps erroneously. The
simple nature of the instrument would preclude the possibility of its producing any but a rather monotonous tune and the whistle I heard gave
tones only half a step apart when the holes were stopped alternately. The
Andrews-Parker Hawaiian Dictionary defines the term *hoehoena* "to be made
quiet or charmed by the notes of the *hoehoe.*" If this definition refers to
the gourd, it would indicate that its tones were pleasing.

THE TI LEAF WHISTLE

The *pulai* (*pu-la'i'* : *pu,* trumpet, *la'i,* ti leaf), was a simple little whistle used
more as a plaything than as a musical instrument. (See Pl. III, *C*.) Emerson (43, p. 147), describes one kind which he saw as follows:

It is nothing more than a ribbon torn from the green leaf of the *ti* plant,
say three-quarters of an inch to an inch in width by five or six inches long, and
rolled up somewhat after the manner of a lamplighter, so as to form a squat cylinder an inch or more in length. This was compressed to flatten it. Placed between
the lips and blown into with proper force, it emits a tone of pure reedlike quality,
that varies in pitch, according to the size of the whistle, from G in the middle register
to a shrill piping note more than an octave above.

Those which I have seen were made in a somewhat different fashion.
The ribbon of ti leaf was folded by one person at an angle near the center

of a strip about eight or nine inches long. One half of the strip was then rolled about this fold; at first, for the first two or three turns, straight about it, and then with a gradually increasing spiral wrapping, which served to lengthen the tube. After the tube had attained a length of two or three inches with a diameter of between ¼ and ⅜ inch, the remainder of the ribbon was torn off, and the tube tied with a bit of leaf rib to hold it from coming unwound. The piece of the ribbon projecting from the point of beginning was also snipped off and this end of the tube was used for the mouthpiece, after being pressed flat for about an inch from the orifice, so that the inner spiral might partly fill the opening and the edge of the ribbon act as a reed or cord.

A whistle made by a second informant had no initial fold. This man was careful to see that one end of the ribbon was cut off square, with no ragged edge, and then began rolling it, as did the first. He was more successful than the first informant.

The tone emitted depended not so much upon the size of the whistle as upon the size of the opening and the way in which the compressed part occupied the space, and was controlled very largely by the way in which the whistle was blown. Much depends upon practise in blowing. It was possible to obtain tones covering a wide range of pitch, and varying from very soft to ear piercing sounds which could carry a long distance. It was the custom of the Hawaiians to cover the whistle with the hands, and by opening and closing the cavity made by the palms, to further modify the pitch.

There is some reason for thinking that the *pulai* emitted more than one tone at a time, according to the way it was rolled, so that a chord was produced which was said to be a "pretty tone," but this cannot be proved since no whistle of this type was found. In the Hawaiian Romance of Laieikawai (20, pp. 148-152), this little instrument is mentioned as having influenced the stubborn determination of a princess, who was so delighted with its sound that she forgot her intentions.

THE CONCH

The conch, one of the most frequently mentioned of all musical instruments of the ancient world, was also known in Hawaii. Although as elsewhere, it was more of a ceremonial trumpet than a purely musical instrument, it should be noted here. It could emit a tone of great volume, the secret of the production lying not in the breath capacity, but in the manner of blowing. The sound has been known to carry more than two miles. In Hawaii the conch was called the *pu* (blow), and was either the Cassis

or the Triton, with the apex cut away to leave a hole for blowing. (See
Pl. III, *D*.) I have not observed any with a blow hole in the side nor
heard of any. No artificial mouthpiece was fastened into the hole with
breadfruit gum as Linton describes for the Marquesan conch (88, p. 405),
so far as known specimens have revealed. Three Triton trumpets and
three Cassis are all that are known to me. Only one of the Museum specimens, a Triton, which was collected on Molokai, has two holes bored in
the side of the shell, not for modifying the tone, but for admitting a cord
by which the shell might be carried. This lashing has long since disappeared
but the edges of the holes on the sides next one another are worn shiny
and the tiny crevices of the shell texture at these points are full of dirt.

THE BULL ROARER

The Hawaiian name of this little instrument has not yet been obtained.
There is only one specimen in the Bishop Museum. (See Pl. III, *A*.)
It was used by children in play and not seriously as an instrument, so far
as I have been able to learn. It consists of the shell of a small coconut
which has been scraped thin. A hole about an inch in diameter appears at
the top, and on opposite sides of this opening are bored two very small
holes which were no doubt intended for cords of fiber. It is said that this
shell was held by means of a cord and whirled rapidly about the head so
that it gave forth a sound somewhat resembling that made by the wind
when it blows over the top of a bottle. Nothing further has been learned
of this instrument.

PROBLEMATICAL WINDS

HAWAIIAN JEW'S HARP

Of somewhat uncertain character are two instruments which are included
with the wind instruments, because they seem more nearly allied to them.

The jew's harp is not at all like the *ukeke*, which is frequently given
this name because of the manner of its use. It is a true jew's harp, the
Hawaiian name of which was *niaukani,* sounding coconut-leaf-stem. The
Andrews-Parker Dictionary confuses the two.

To quote Emerson first (43, pp. 147 and 132) :

The *niau-kani,* singing splinter, was a reed instrument of a rude sort, made by
holding a reed of thin bamboo against a slit cut out in a larger piece of bamboo.
This was applied to the mouth, and the voice being projected against it produced an
effect similar to that of the jew's harp. . . .

This was a simple, almost extemporaneous, contrivance, constructed, like the
jew's harp, on the principle of a reed instrument. It was made of two parts, a

broad piece of bamboo with a longitudinal slit at one end and a thin narrow piece of the same material, the reed, which was held firmly against the fenestra on the concave side of part number one. The convexity of the instrument was pressed against the lips and the sound was produced by projecting the breath through the slit in a speaking or singing tone in such a way as to cause vibrations in the reed. The manner of constructing and operating this reed instrument is suggestive of the jew's harp. It is asserted by those who should know that the niau-kani was an instrument of purely Hawaiian invention.

The performer did not depend simply upon the musical tone, but rather upon the modification of it produced in the utterances that were strained through it. It would certainly require a quick ear, much practice, and a thorough acquaintance with the peculiarities of Hawaiian mele to enable one to distinguish the words of a song after being transformed by passage through the niau-kani.

Although I did not discover any specimen of the *niaukani* in the field, and was therefore unable to observe its operation, there are passages in Emerson's description, clear as it appears to be, which make the exact province of this instrument doubtful.

In the Bishop Museum is one ancient specimen called the *niaukani* (Pl. I, *A*), which is quite different from the one described by Emerson. It is a thin strip of wood, about four inches long and an inch wide, cut square at one end and rounded at the other, resembling an elongated letter U. Upon it lies a coconut leaf stem, just as the name would suggest from a literal translation, *niau* being the stem of the coconut leaf, *kani,* to sound. Emerson's translation, singing splinter, is fanciful.

The extremity of this six-inch leaf stem is lashed to the square end of the strip of wood by a cord made of twisted coconut fiber, which is carried again and again about the stem and knotted; then it is directed once through a single very small hole placed in the center of the wood directly beneath the stem, and knotted again. Midway the length of the little board are two other very small holes, just the size of that through which the cord passed at the end, one on either side of the stem. They could not have been used to blow or sing through for they are so small that no appreciable amount of air could pass through them. There is no vestige of cord in them to indicate whether the stem was once lashed to the board at this point, but if that portion of it which projects two inches or more beyond the board were pulled back so that it would twang, after the principle of a jew's harp, unless it were so tied, there would be nothing to prevent the stem from hanging loosely by its single fastening and it would be necessary to hold it in place with the fingers, which would be very awkward since at the same time the instrument must be held to the mouth and the end of the stem must be flipped.

From Emerson's description and his rather far-fetched translation of the name, it would seem that the instrument he described was very different and borrowed its name from the coconut stem type. Linton (88, p. 408), describes also a bamboo jew's harp which corresponds almost exactly with Emerson's description, in that the bamboo reed seems not to have been fastened to the underlying strip and in both specimens air was propelled through a slit in the strip directly upon the reed which was assisted in vibrating by being struck at its projecting end. None of the three is like some metal jew's harps in having the vibrating reed cut in one piece with the background, free to vibrate at one end, and with the slit necessarily produced by its manufacture, lying beneath the reed.

As to the method of sound production, it is impossible to state definitely what may have occurred in playing the specimen now in the Museum. The stem was flipped, but how the voice was used is not known. It seems doubtful that the vocal cords were actually employed in conjunction with the sound produced by the reed as it vibrated, for the two small holes were evidently not intended for transmitting sound or air. The voice would also obscure the sound of the stem considerably. Mrs. Webb, who has heard it, says that the noise was not like speaking or singing, but rather a tick-tack, although the impression of words was conveyed, as we have remarked was the case with the *ukeke*. It does not seem too much to assume that the *niaukani* in the Museum was placed before the open mouth, which, acting as a resonator, changed shape in accordance with the words of the mele and thus appeared to emit words. Its other name *niau-ukeke* would strengthen this assumption.

BAMBOO TUBES

In the Bishop Museum collection are a number of bamboo tubes of varying lengths and diameters cut from between two adjoining nodes, with either end open and with no holes bored in the side. They could therefore not have been flutes nor the variety of drum called *kaekeeke* (p. 53), which properly had one end closed by a node. These open bamboos are not mentioned in Emerson's list nor by any writer on Hawaiian musical instruments that I have been able to discover, but in the Museum they are labeled as instruments with which to beat time. There was no sign and no mention of them in the recent field survey.

A statement was made by one informant who had seen old people performing on various bamboos but who had never examined them particularly or specially differentiated them, that a hollow bamboo, with both ends open, was held vertically before the player's mouth and blown across the end as one might blow across the mouth of a bottle. She said that there were little notches cut on the edge, on opposite sides, and one of these was placed against the lip. Such notches are not to be seen on the Museum specimens.

On the other hand, it is definitely known that sections of hollow bamboo were used in ceremonial procedure in connection with the prayer known as *kuni*. The prayer described was qualified as a clean *kuni* (not the praying-to-death prayer, *kuni anaana,* in which the kahuna secured bits of the person concerning whom he was to pray, such as nails, hair and the like, which he ate after burning). Over a dead body the clean *kuni* was uttered into the orifice of a tube of bamboo. While the kahuna was uttering the prayer he endeavored not to take a breath and sometimes his eyes positively bulged with the effort. If breathing became absolutely necessary, he quickly stopped the opening of the tube by slipping his palm over it as he withdrew his lips. When the prayer was concluded a plug of tapa was slipped into the opening of the bamboo to prevent the prayer from escaping, and the pipe was laid next to the body, beneath the garments. The informant, although then but seven years old, saw this done over the body of her mother, and only learned its true significance in after years from her grandfather.

INSTRUMENTS OF PERCUSSION

Instruments of percussion are divided by some writers into vibrating membranes and sonorous substances, which is the classification followed here.

VIBRATING MEMBRANES

There were two types of instruments with vibrating membranes, the *pahu* and the *puniu*. The *pahu* was a comparatively late importation by La'a from Tahiti, but the *puniu* seems to have been always known to the Hawaiians.

THE WOODEN KETTLE DRUM

The wooden kettle drum, *pahu,* was of varying sizes, from about a foot high with a diameter of seven or eight inches, to three feet in height with a kettle section the size of a bushel basket. (See Pl. IV, *D.*) The frame of the drum was cut from a section of a log, usually of breadfruit or coconut, according to Emerson (43, p. 140). The log was hollowed from either end with stone tools, but, so far as I could learn, without the assistance of burning, leaving a central partition in place.

The drum was designed to stand on end, and the walls of what was intended to be the lower section were cut into openwork patterns. Emerson describes the design as being "after the fashion of a two-storied arcade, the haunch of the superimposed arch resting directly on the crown of that below," but the drums in the Bishop Museum and other collections display almost as many patterns as there are specimens, including diamonds, zigzag and plain strips, and oval openings. At the extreme lower edge most of them have a solid ring of wood which reinforces a base otherwise liable to breakage.

The upper half of the log formed the resonance chamber, and the orifice was covered with tightly stretched fish skin, preferably that of the shark, according to several writers. The drum is said to have been beaten with the fist or open hand, not with a stick, and in this particular, as well as in its carved base, it recalls those of Africa and India. Ralph Linton tells me that the drum is also found in the Society Islands, the Marquesas, and parts of the Tuamotus. It is lacking in the rest of Polynesia. (See 88, p. 409.) Its history is given by Emerson (43, p. 141). No specimen was found in the recent survey and apparently the place of the *pahu* as a hula instrument has been entirely obscured by the original Hawaiian big drum, the *ipu* or calabash. Two *hula pahu* melodies were obtained (Nos. 104, 105, pp. 236, 237), in which the beats of the drum are indicated. Nowadays the *hula pahu* seems not to be distinguished from the *hula ipu* in a musical way.

THE COCONUT DRUM

The coconut drum, or *puniu*, the second type of vibrating membrane, was the snare drum of the Hawaiians. There are many specimens in various museums and the instrument has been described by Emerson (43, p. 141). (See Pl. IV, *B*.) The *puniu* is made of a coconut shell, the top portion of which has been cut off. Across the opening is stretched a fish skin, that of the kala (*Acanthurus unicornis*) being preferred because its scales are so small. This little drum was fastened to the right thigh of the player and beaten with a braided fiber. It has also become obsolete among the country people. One woman, at Kekaha, Kauai, who sang into the phonograph, brought a tin plate to lay on her knee, which she beat at the same time in quicker rhythm to simulate the *puniu*, for she did not possess one of the genuine instruments, its lighter tone contrasting pleasantly with the deeper notes of the *ipu*, for which she had substituted a tin dish pan in order that those notes could be recorded. The rhythms produced on these instruments are given with the hulas (pp. 215 ff).

The skin heads of both kinds of drums were lashed on with cords braided from fiber. Stitches placed near the circumference of the skin in an arrangement resembling consecutive V's, provided at their intersection a hold for the cords which passed beneath them and down over the face of the wood to a point in the openwork carving or to a ring at the base. The methods of lashing were different in nearly every specimen examined.

As these drums were not heard, it is impossible to say what may have been their original tones before their skin heads had lost their tension. Emerson mentions the tones of several he examined but it is doubtful if the drums were ever carefully tuned, although I have noticed that in calabash drum accompaniments, when a gourd possesses naturally a deep musical tone, the chanter gradually attunes his voice to it, if he sings several chants in succession, although the first one or two may sound quite at variance with it.

SONOROUS SUBSTANCES WITH AIR CAVITIES

The first two examples of instruments belonging to the class of sonorous substances lie midway between the vibrating membranes and solid substances which emit a sound when they are struck and caused to vibrate in their entirety. These two in being struck cause a column of air within their hollow centers to vibrate and thus augment the tone, as well as change its pitch.

THE CALABASH DRUM

The first is the *ipu* (calabash), or, as it is often called, the *paipu* or the *ipu wai* (or *hue wai*), water calabash. It is also known as the *ipu hula*. It consists of two gourds, the larger of which is placed at the bottom. An opening several inches in diameter at the top of this gourd and another in the bottom of the smaller gourd, placed together, connect the two air chambers. In a few instruments the two gourds are joined with one another by an intermediate section or collar cut from a third gourd, or they may be joined directly, all seams being glued with a pitchy substance which appears to be breadfruit gum. All specimens seen in the museums, or during field trips, had a mouth several inches in diameter cut in the top of the upper gourd, while the *ipu* varied in size from about eighteen inches for the height of the combined gourds, to nearly three feet. (See Pl. IV, *C*.)

For the purpose of transporting more easily these somewhat ungainly instruments, many are provided with cords or strips of cloth tied about the stricture, with a loop for the fingers. Emerson mentions tapa being used. It is very seldom that attempts at graphic art are to be observed on articles of Hawaiian manufacture, except on tapa. Three *ipu* in the Bishop Museum collection, however, show attempt at decoration. On one is scratched the upper half of the figure of a man, outlined by little dots. The second has a row of triangles about the collar. The third, which lacks an upper gourd and is very different in appearance from all others noted, is entirely covered by vertical stripes running from the top to the base in regularly alternating colors, red and brown. The edges of the stripes dovetail because they are serrated like the teeth of a saw. One gourd whistle has an out-lined figure of a man like those seen in petroglyphs.

The *ipu* was the popular large instrument employed in accompanying the hula. Its deeper tones marked the regularly recurring accent of the measure beat. Many writers have described the manner in which it was played. According to Emerson (43, p. 142), the tone was produced and modified at the same time, by striking it against the padded earth floor of the Hawaiian house. On occasions when I could observe its use, the player sat tailor-fashion on the ground with a small cushion or pad of folded cloth in front of him on which he placed the *ipu*. Two methods of manipulating it were observed. In the first it was quickly raised and dropped on the pad at the first beat, but the succeeding beats were marked by striking the side of the lower gourd sharply with the flat of three or four fingers in exceedingly rapid succession at the beginning of each beat, while the calabash was held in the air. The tone produced by the spatting of the fingers on the gourd is lighter and quite different in quality from that produced by dropping it on the pad and affords a pleasing contrast. The second method was to place the *ipu* on the pad, and to lift it at the first beat to the right on a level with the shoulders, striking it with the hand as it reached the end of the swing. It was then brought down and struck just as it reached the lowest point of the arc immediately above the pad. The third beat occurred when the highest point to the left was reached, and the fourth as it returned to the lowest point of the arc. Some examples of the rhythm of the *ipu* are given in musical notation under the hulas of that name (pp. 215 ff).

The calabashes used for the *ipu*, as well as for other purposes, were specially grown. It is not certain that either of two varieties for which I obtained the names were specially used for the *ipu hula*. They were known as the *manalo*, sweet, and the *awaawa*, sour or bitter. The sour gourds were preferred for general purposes because of the harder shell and the fact that the acid in the rind discouraged worms. They were, therefore, much longer lived. The Hawaiians were very careful not to disturb the tender vines at the season of blooming or before, for they knew that even a shadow on the flowers in the hot sun would cause them to wither, but waited until the fruit was well formed and approached the plants before dawn or after dark to "set" the gourds so that they would not lie on pebbles or become misshapen in any way. The high polish and the reddish brown color of the *ipu hula* and other calabashes comes only from long use. No coloring matter seems to have been applied, although the gourds may have been polished a little with stone.

BAMBOO PIPES

The second instrument which secured additional tonal effect by a vibrating column of air in its interior is the bamboo pipe known as the *ohe keeke* or the *kaekeeke*. Many specimens are preserved in the Bishop Museum but none were found in use in the country districts, although it is possible that on festive occasions which are still held now and then by the old people, some might appear from their hiding places.

The *keeke* was of different sizes, from a tube not much over a foot long and an inch in diameter, to one three or four feet long with a bore three inches across. Many writers have said that one end of the *keeke* was closed naturally by a septum of the bamboo and that this end was struck on the ground. Ralph Linton tells of the same instruments in Samoa and Tonga which were of varying length. Emerson (43, p. 143) says that their tones were pure and very pleasing and that with different sizes in use at one time in a hula, a number of tonal effects could have been obtained, when each player, holding a pair, raised and dropped them on the earth. The Bishop Museum collection, however, contains as many bamboos labeled *keeke* which are open throughout their length as those with one end closed. Two of the largest, several feet long, are open. (Pl. II, *B,* shows small *keeke.*)

SONOROUS SUBSTANCES, SOLID

STICKS

The most common of the instruments which vibrated solidly were the *kalaau,* or sticks which were used for the dance of that name.

The dancer held in his left hand a club of kauila wood, very heavy, about three feet long, grasped near its center, with one section lying along his forearm, close to his side, the other section projecting in front of him. (See Pl. II, *A,* upper.) The stick was too long to be photographed except at one end; it tapers toward both ends.

In the right hand the dancer held another stick, roughly shuttle-shaped, with one end more pointed than the other, and about nine or ten inches long (Pl. II, *A,* lower.) With this he tapped the club which proved to be quite resonant. The rhythms produced by this player may be found in the three hulas by Akoni Mika (pp. 264-268).

Footboards

The only person who demonstrated the dance with footboards was a Kauai man living on Hawaii, although a tune for the dance was sung by a Kauai woman at Kekaha. The man made no mention of any instruments operated by the feet, but it was observed that he stamped softly with one foot. This was taken to be a dance step at the time. It has since been learned that there are in the Bishop Museum collection two pieces of wood very much alike, from Kauai, which are said to have been used in the *hula kalaau*. (See Pl. V, *B*.) They are about a foot long and seven or eight inches across the center, narrowed at either end to about five inches, an inch thick at the edges and an inch and a half in the center throughout their length. One face is slightly convex with a curve more than two inches high in one specimen which is also slightly concave on the other face. The second specimen is flat on the under side and the convexity of the opposite surface is not more than an inch at the most.

Hulas have been described in which the dancer stamps with his feet on a stone leaned upon another stone, but the wooden slabs must have been much more effectual in creating a hollow sound. The name of these footboards has not been learned.

Two sticks used in the *hula manai,* not described by Emerson, perhaps because of its similarity to several other hulas, were rude little noise-making instruments. They were about two feet long and only thick enough to support without bending the streamers of the maile vine which hung from their ends. The dancer crossed these sticks and tapped one upon the other with the simple little rhythm given on page 272, until he decided which of the women sitting in a ring about him he preferred. He then designated her by touching her with the maile streamer.

Pebbles or Castanets

The *hula iliili* (*i′li-i′-li*) or pebble dance, required two small stones in either hand of the dancer. The *iliili* were employed very much as castanets are by the Spaniards. The idea was known in ancient Egypt, it seems, according to Stanford-Forsyth (143, p. 16) who mention tiny finger-tip pairs of cymbals which in later ages were carried by the Moors to Spain, where they were made of chestnut (*castaña*). Similar devices are found eastward along the Indian ocean to beyond the East Indies.

Rattles

Gourds

An instrument which survives in the hulas of today and is second in importance only to the *ipu* is the *uliuli* (*uli″-uli′*.) (See Pl. IV, *A*.) Early travelers visiting the Sandwich Islands mention in connection with the dances which they saw, these rattles made of a hollowed calabash or coconut adorned at the tip of the handle with feathers. Barrot (16, p. 32) says: " . . . . they waved with violence the feather fans which they held in the left hand, and the base of which, formed of a small calabash filled with shells and struck by the right at regular intervals, performed the office of castanets."

From this account it would seem that the custom of decorating the *uliuli* handles with feathers was ancient, and not, as Emerson suggests (43, p. 144) a modern fancy. At that time there probably were, however, as there are now, *uliuli* which were unadorned. The coconut shell or gourd was hollowed out by means of four small holes drilled at one end, and received a high polish, especially the coconuts, which were rubbed down until the light veins showed in contrast to the purplish color of the shell. According to Emerson and an informant whom I interviewed, the seeds of the little wild yellow canna (*ali'i poe*) were placed within it. Strips of ie (*Freycinetia arborea*) were drawn through the holes at right angles while they were green and pliable, and the ends, gathered together and wound about with more ie formed the handle. To increase the pliability of the ie for such purposes, bundles of it were thoroughly wetted and steamed in the imu before they were used.

The museum specimens are about equally divided between gourds and coconuts. One gourd has a small design picked out in dots. Only one lacks the feather decoration, the rest all have a disc surmounting the handle covered with tapa, skin or cloth, and thickly fringed about its circumference with feathers. A ruffle of tapa or cloth gathered close up under the disc about the handle hides it from view.

The *uliuli* rhythms are given on pages 237-260.

Gourds Strung on Sticks

An instrument concerning the antiquity of which there is some doubt is the *ulili*,[°] two specimens of which were purchased by J. S. Emerson on the islands of Hawaii about 1885, and which seem, from remarks in his catalog (44), to have been known to the people for a long time. A stout stick, perhaps fifteen inches long and an inch or more in diameter, is strung with three small gourds, the center one smaller, round and loose, the two at the ends pear-shaped, pointing outward toward the protruding two or three inches of stick at either extremity. These were held more firmly in place. There were no shot or small substances in them which could rattle. Through a hole in the side of the center gourd issued a cord, the end of

---

° Not the same instrument as the *uliuli*.

which, for convenience in grasping, was tied to a little stick or peg. The inner end of the cord was fastened to the center rod. (See Pl. V, *C*.)

The description of the manner of operation is taken from the catalog. The middle gourd was held in the left hand and the string, which was wound up around the rod by turning the center gourd, was suddenly pulled out with a quick motion by seizing the little peg suspended on the side of the gourd. If the motion were sufficiently quick, the string, as soon as it was unwound, wound itself up in the opposite direction, and a succession of quick pulls kept this top-rattle in operation indefinitely. There would not be much noise from such an instrument unless the gourds contained shot. The string was too old and frail to make a test of the powers of the *ulili* advisable.

Fringed Bamboo Tubes

The *puili* is a soft-sounding rattle made from a tube of bamboo about eighteen inches long. Three to five inches, including a node, are left to form a handle but the remainder of the tube is finely split into fringe. (See Pl. II, *D*.) Of four pairs of *puili* in the Museum only one has alternate slivers removed as Emerson describes (43, p. 144). The rest are intact. The *hula puili* is very graceful and pleasant to witness. In the hulas that I witnessed, each player held but one instrument, and sat tailor-fashion on the ground facing a partner. To every beat of the measure there was a movement of the *puili* with its accompanying "murmurous breezy rustle." The player tapped his partner lightly on either shoulder or wrist, the movement always corresponding for each, effecting a pretty cross-action. In some *hula puili* the place on the ground between the partners was also tapped at points relatively identical for the position of the two players. At certain intervals the rattles were exchanged in mid air.

Anklets

In times long past anklets made from hundreds of dog teeth which, strung on a foundation of olona netting in much the same manner as feathers were woven into the fabric of a fiber mesh to make the famous feather capes, were worn in the hula to accentuate the rhythms of the feet in dancing. They were called *kupee niho ilio,* dog tooth bracelets. (See Pl. V, *A*.)

POETRY

Before taking up the question of the vocal music it is necessary to devote a little attention to the meles, or poetical compositions which form the basis of the chants. Although the time allotted and the scope of this paper permit cnly a casual investigation here of the literary side of these poems (which must properly come when the general collection of meles is translated and published), something must be said concerning their salient features as giving rise to types of chants and particularly on the mechanics of their structure which, under most considerations might be suspected of having a possible influence on that of the accompanying musical compositions.

To the Hawaiian mind, the chief charm of the singing or chanting lay in the words, for their obvious meaning in many cases consisted of exquisite imagery, of word painting succeeding word painting, describing the beauties of natural scenery, used in a profusion bewildering to one accustomed to the restraints of most of our modern poetry. Those who look in Hawaiian poetry only for the secondary meaning referring to human passion, which is to be found in most meles, and declare that the Hawaiians appreciated only that aspect of their literature, entirely lose sight of the fact that a people could not use such imagery, such clean-cut and marvelous pictures of the natural beauty about them, without having seen and appreciated these beauties for what they are, in a manner analogous to the trained eye of the Japanese, who sees in the world about him all the tender grace and beauty of outline and color, but who, instead of putting what he sees into poetry, paints it with the same kind of bold, sure strokes on his scroll of silk.

That the Hawaiian, by means of such figurative language and beautiful similes can describe as well that one human emotion which has taken the untiring attention of the poets of all ages, is to his credit; although, child of nature that he is, he chooses to express what we would leave unsaid. To give the translation of these secondary or foundation ideas, as some would claim, in all their baldness, would offend not only modern taste but Hawaiian taste as well, for the old people expect that one should know the underlying meaning without being told, once the theme is understood. They would scorn a translation of this character, as well they might. Why use the beautiful similes at all?

On the other hand, there is no doubt but that the cleverness of well-composed meles which might be interpreted in at least two ways delighted them for this very reason.

Some of the most beautiful poetry contained in the chants about Pele and Hiiaka or other divine personages is said to have been inspired, is of unknown antiquity and authorship, and lacks the ambiguity of much of the poetry dealing with human beings. Those most finished meles ascribed to human agency which do carry at least two meanings achieve the second by pun, allegory, play upon words, and similar devices, as well as by the fact that many Hawaiian proper names are descriptive and nearly all are compounded and hence capable of at least one secondary translation, especially if purposely contracted or otherwise manipulated with this idea in mind.

The cleverness of the composers was aided materially by the structure of the language, for with its paucity of sounds the same phonetic combinations perforce carry many meanings not necessarily allied in sense. The custom of omitting in poetry all but the most essential words, left much to be supplied by the imagination, and the inferences thus drawn depended considerably on the predisposition of the auditor. Again, the key to an entire passage might lie in a single secret word, without the proper translation of which the entire meaning traduced might be very different from that intended.

There were those learned in the art of reading these secret or double meanings, but there were also composers so cunning in their manipulation of words and sense that none but those familiar with the circumstances inspiring the composition might discern the real intent, although other interpretations might serve the general listener. Under such circumstances a few very small errors or changes might cause all sense to be lost and this is particularly true of very ancient meles which contain words now obsolete.

The statements of a number of writers to the effect that these compositions were handed down from generation to generation with faultless accuracy is misleading and even untrue. The natural result of transmitting by word of mouth would be the gradual growth of many versions of a single mele; even those that deal with genealogies are known to have different versions, although the intent was to preserve them accurately. It is extraordinary that compositions some hundreds of lines long have been kept as accurately as they have, even with the memories of the race trained for this purpose. The chants to the gods, notably to Pele and Hiiaka, are remarkably constant, a fact which can be partially accounted for by the directness of their language, but even these chants have versions, while the topical chants show a wider range, as might be expected.

These remarks, together with a few quotations from articles dealing with the subject will afford an understanding of the nature of the poetry. A good general review of the subject has been written by George W. Stewart (145). A history of Hawaii, by S. M. Kamakau (82, chap. 52), contains the following passage on the composing of poetry:

The composing of meles was a special education in those old days and certain people became very famous for their achievements along this line. The recital of some of these meles, such as the *ko'ihonua* or genealogical history, was somewhat different from other recitals, in that the tone was almost of one note, in order that the words could be distinctly heard and understood; the voice was held in the throat so that it would not be so harsh. A *ko'ihonua* mele is one which relates to the forefathers of the Hawaiian people and to the history of the kings and their accomplishments together with the deeds of their ancestors. In the *ko'ihonua mele* of Kuali'i, the Kumuali'i and the Kumulipo were preserved, and in the mele of Peleiholani, the genealogical tree of Ololo and Haloa was given, and in the mele of Kamahanao, the history of Palikú and Punaimua were made known.

In these compositions great care was taken in order to have the details accurate and the names correct, and this is the reason for the great value of these genealogical histories of the ancestors of the Hawaiians today. These genealogical trees go further back than the time of Wakea who is commonly known as the forefather of the Hawaiian people.

There were many kinds of meles and several important items of historical value have been found in them which relate to the people of old. Meles have been composed about the heavens, the sky, the ocean, the earth, the sun, the moon, the stars, and many other natural objects and they contained many words of wisdom. Others were composed in honor of the ancestors, the land they lived in, about chiefs, for the glorification of kings, for thankfulness, for love, to heap reproach on enemies, to offer prayer, to lament, for persons when sleeping or when they arose, to supplicate, to announce a withholding, to call for certain persons, to accompany gifts and to announce them, to announce an elevation in rank, to prophesy or tell the future, to mock, or for various other purposes, and in some of them may be learned many things of value, and again in some one can find only chaff.

In the *olioli* or hymnal meles there is the underlying purpose of worship. The tone of the voice is different from that used for the other *meles*, being lighter, although held very low in the throat. The sound issues gurgling, the breath is held for a very long time and as the words come out as though falling from the tip of the tongue the mouth is opened only slightly and no heavy veins are to be seen along the neck. When one can do this in the manner described he is considered an expert.

The composing of the *ko'ihonua, ha'ikupuna* [relating one's ancestors] and *kamakua* [telling of one's parents] meles was conducted under very strict tabu and only by those who were well versed in the history of the time. The tabu placed on the spots where these meles were composed was no less than that employed at the composing of a genealogical history. Meles foretelling the future and those for worship were generally composed when the spirit moved the prophet. Meles in honor of persons, for the glorification of a king, for thankfulness or for expressing lamentation and various other kinds, were often made by a single individual and were completed in a short time, but on the other hand, if a mele was to be composed to reveal that a given individual was stingy, good, bad, brave, and so on, then two or more persons together composed the mele. In large compositions the composer generally had several persons with him and to each a line was assigned, and sometimes two, and as each line was completed the composer designated one person who took that line and studied it, committing it to memory. In this manner several lines were composed at one sitting and and when completed they were recited by the different ones. Then the others took them and in a short time the whole mele was learned by heart. Should the mele be short, one or two could sit and compose it. These meles were beautifully made, fitting in as wanted by the composer.

Most of the honorific meles were made for kings or for children loved by their parents and held as favorites. Meles often times were very vulgar and unfit to be heard. The tone of the voice might be all that was required, but the words were very disgusting. Then, again, they were couched in language that very few could understand, but the tone and the voice was all that some people cared about.

There is some difference of opinion concerning whether the word *koʻihonua* refers to a genealogical chant or to the method of chanting. A note, presumably written by Dr. N. B. Emerson (100, p. 184), gives the following:

Haku mele, literally to weave a song. A mele for the glorification of a king, born or still unborn, was called a *mele inoa*. This was a eulogy or panegyric of the ancestral and personal virtues, real or fictitious, of a king or princeling . . . Ko-i-honua was not, as mistakenly supposed, a particular kind of mele. It related to the tone or manner of utterance of the *mele inoa;* it meant that the *inoa* was to be recited in an ordinary conversational tone, and not after the manner called *oli,* that is applied to a singing tone. The *ko-i-honua* manner of reciting a *mele inoa* made it more intelligible and therefore more acceptable to the king. . . . In making out the origin of the phrase *ko-i-honua,* the *ko* seems to be the causative . . . *i,* to utter . . . *honua,* the earth, earthly, as distinguished from an inflated or stilted manner of speech used in the singing of the *oli.*

Among modern Hawaiians *koʻihonua* is interpreted by some as Kamakau has it, by others as a kind of mele. Senator John Wise is of the opinion that Emerson has gone far astray on the derivation of the meaning of *koʻihonua* which he thinks is compounded of two words—*koʻi,* axe, *honua,* earth—the derived meaning being that of clearing the ground or stripping a tree of all but its trunk, from which the Hawaiian lovers of figure of speech applied a secondary interpretation, that is, the bare recital of the essential details of a family genealogy stripped of all doubtful details and encumbrances and standing forth in bald outline.

This same kind of conversational chanting is also known as *kepakepa,* which, as illustrated to me by a man who once held the position of reviser of meles in the reign of King Kalakaua, was merely a rather rapid and expressionless reciting of the syllables, in what might be written as sixteenth notes, without regard to accent and with no variation in length.

As Kamakau has it, the meles recited in olioli fashion were primarily religious chants. At the present time, whatever may have obtained in the past, although prayers and any kind of religious chants are recited in olioli fashion, others are also given in this manner.

Andrews (5, pp. 26, 27, 30, 31) gives some light on the question of the types of meles.

The word MELE signifies a *song*, or words so arranged that they may be cantillated or sung. To arrange or put words in such order is termed HAKU. The specific and perhaps original idea of *haku* was to sort out feathers of different qualities and colors, and arrange them in the ancient war cloaks, *kahilis*, or wreaths for the chiefs. It was a work requiring art and skill. A secondary idea was to regulate, to reduce to order; to compose, to put words in order, and is used like the Greek *poieo*, whence *poiete* and the English *poet*, i. e., an artificial composer of words. . . .

Among Hawaiians the *oihana haku mele*, the skill of the poet has been honored from time immemorial. Among them were several grades of poets, as hakumele *maikai* or *akamai loa*, exceedingly skillful; this was the highest class. Haku mele *olioli* or makers of common songs, and haku mele *paeaea*, the makers of low vulgar meles. Hawaiians had different classes of meles themselves such as mele *kaua*, war-songs; that is, celebrating the exploits of warriors. Mele *koihonua*, that is detailing, celebrating the genealogies of chiefs. Mele *ku'o*, that is singing meles, pronounced with protracted musical sounds. Mele *olioli*, that is, songs on joyful subjects, comprising a great variety. Mele *kanikau*, that is *elegiac*, expressing sorrow for the death of friends. Mele *paeaea*, a class of low meles. Ipo's, or love songs, and *inoas* or songs composed at the birth of the chief and recited at his funeral.

Again, meles may be divided into three classes as to their *excellence* in the judgment of the Hawaiians themselves. Mele *maikai*; this is the highest and best class, exhibiting more skill in its structure and containing good sentiments. Secondly, mele *olioli* or mele *lealea* embracing a large class of various kinds, but of a middling quality as to skill and composition. Thirdly, mele *paeaea*, wanting in many respects the high qualities of poetry. This class embraces much that is low, vulgar and indecent in sentiment, and ranges from high to low in composition, and resembles the low songs of grog shops or the forecastle of ships. It has different names applied to it, as mele *kamalii*, mele *pupule*, etc., as the English say, prose run mad. Most of the modern meles that appear in the newspapers belong to the class *olioli* in sentiment, but *paeaea* in quality.

. . . . Keeping in mind Greek and English poetry, the Hawaiian has

1. No measure of feet, as dactyl, spondee, trochee, etc.

2. It does not consist in any particular number of syllables or words necessary to constitute a measure, line or verse.

3. Hawaiian poetry has nothing like rhyme or the correspondence in sound of the termination of one line with another as in English. Hawaiians do not seem to see much beauty [in] or set much value upon rhyme, even when introduced into their hymns.

4. As their Meles were anciently unwritten, they had nothing like Acrostics as may be seen in some of the Hebrew poems and sometimes in English.

Though Hawaiian poetry lacks all these, nevertheless, it has certain qualities which render it at once distinguishable from prose. It has laws and rules of its own, among these are

1. Measure of proportion, that is, in number and proportion of things and their accompaniments, that is, there must be *subjects* and *predicates* with their adjuncts . . .

2. Although there are no measured feet, yet even a stranger listening to the pronunciation of poetic ideas at once recognizes a different movement of voice from that of pronouncing prose. This movement may be termed, as in common language, the *poetic jingle.* In reading or reciting the voice seems to float along easily, throwing off letters or syllables or adding on, as best suits the flowing of thought. . . .

Hawaiian poetry for the most part consists of short, terse carefully adjusted sentences; all matter that can be is thrown out that the principal idea may make the stronger impression . . .

4. Abruptness or suddenness of introduction is a quality of Hawaiian poetry. The poet seldom prepares or warns his hearers of what is coming. He instinctively follows the advice of the Roman poet and rushes *in medias res* into the midst of his subject. . . .

5. The Hawaiian has what may be called a Poetical Dialect. As was remarked before, every person [foreigner] though tolerably well versed in Hawaiian prose, when he takes up a mele, feels himself in difficulty. . . . It may be the result in part from the following:

1. In unusual or ancient words which he has not seen before, or which are very seldom or never found in prose.

2. In some peculiar construction of sentences.

3. In short, concise, bold elliptical expressions, connected with but few qualifying terms, but the whole arranged in entirely different order from prose.

4. Many ellipses appear—particles which he considers unnecessary are dropped.

5. In constant allusions to unknown circumstances of persons, times, and places.

6. In different and new forms of words, such as reduplications and sometimes triplications of syllables in verbs; letters and syllables added to the ends of words and especially to the ends of lines.

7. In abrupt changes of tense and person, with many other anomalous peculiarities.

6. As what in other languages would be called lines or verses have no definite length, that is, no definite number of syllables, they are mostly complete in themselves as to sense. Every line seems to convey one complete idea, simple or complex. To this, however, there are many exceptions, especially in historical details. The Hawaiian poets were fully aware of the effect of a "refrain" repeated at regular intervals and had distinct parts for solo and chorus.

7. . . . [Hawaiian poetry] makes the harmony of the verse arise from *tones, accents* and musical undulations, such as in English is called *cantillation,* something like an English *chant,* admitting, however, slight modulations, but without any *cadence.*

8. Though the haku meles do not confine their verses to any set number of syllables, words or terms, they do, however, observe rigidly a relation when things answer to things and words to words, and also the proportion of one verse to another, and this relation appears both in the idea and in the number of words, hence they observe a rhythm of proportion and a harmony of sentences. Their meles are all adapted to music, that is, to cantillation.

Again in the third article of the series, p. 35, Mr. Andrews says:

A few words respecting the different methods of composing meles. Some of the Haku meles, male or female, would retire by themselves and think out the ideas and words of their meles and afterwards repeat or cantillate them in public. Such meles, however, were never very long from the difficulty of retaining them in their memory. Another method was the opposite extreme. A chief would select his most able warriors, and his principal men, and propose the subject of the mele and appoint each one to furnish what we would call a line or verse and the others to act as critics or correctors, and so on till the whole was furnished. Another method was for the poet to collect a few only of his poetical friends and after explaining to them his subject, would commence by reciting the first line or thought and then ask the opinion of all the others as to its merits. They would approve, reject or amend till it was approved by all; then he would suggest another line or thought which must undergo the same process of revision, but at the same time adjusting the words and sense to what went before and so from time to time they composed until the mele was finished. What was singular, the corrected lines were *paa naau*, fixed in the memories of each, and thus each had what we should call a copy. . . .

Many of the points mentioned by Andrews have been confirmed by the present study, but others need correction or revision and addition. Not all may be mentioned now, but will come out as the subject progresses. It should be noted particularly that he uses olioli in several different senses, perhaps correctly, but that he does not differentiate clearly between the kinds of meles dealing with certain subjects, and the manner of their rendition. While he gives some of the important classes of meles, he omits others.

Although Andrews says there are no measures of feet in Hawaiian poetry, as in Greek poetry, old people, some of whom did not know their ages and certainly could not have learned to recite English poetry, recited to me meles which were regularly scanned, with the same number of accents to each line, if not the same arrangement of syllables within each foot. None of these meles is ancient, but, on the other hand, none of the composers was especially familiar with foreign poetry; to have acquired the style would have necessitated such a familiarity unless it was a Hawaiian idea as well. Mrs. Lahilahi Webb, who knows one composer personally, is quite sure that his composition was not inspired in any way by foreign poetry. Except for the mele composed for King Kalakaua, whose retainers may have adopted their style from poetry heard at court or learned at the royal school, it seems likely that the scanning of the different poems given here was a Hawaiian idea.

Again, nearly all meles composed for hulas have lines of uniform length, as regards feet, if not the actual number of syllables, and are frequently scanned. Some olis in which the lines are of nearly uniform length may be scanned, as for instance, that given here as an *inoa*, or name chant, for King Kalakaua, but there was not the same uniformity of lines in most olis. The *inoa*, by the way, was composed not only for kings, but for every child that could lay claim to being anyone of any consequence, even a commoner. Parents were considered lacking in their duty who failed to have an *inoa* chant for each child. This was chanted by friends on any occasion of greeting and not reserved merely for the funeral.

Only a portion of the mele for Kauikeaouli is marked for scanning, for I could not keep up with the chanter in some places. The division of the lines into three feet is rather exceptional. Most of the meles capable of being scanned have four-foot lines.

The feet created by the accents were not uniform in the arrangement of long and short syllables, which seems to have been a matter of indifference. The correct accents of words were in some instances displaced by the measuring of feet, and the same lines have been divided differently by different chanters. For example, the third line of the mele beginning *"Hanohano Kapulani"* was said by one informant to be improperly accented and should read *"O ka pá kolonáhe á ke keháu"* instead of *"Ó ka pa kólonahe á ke keháu."*

A study of the music of the chants will reveal differences of accenting there for identical passages, which differences if occurring in the chanting might also appear in the reading out, or scanning. It was noted that in the chanting the scanning was apt to be broken down, for the musical accent did not necessarily coincide with that in the scanning, and that neither need coincide with the accent of the word as spoken. The mele to Kauikeaouli, with the three-accented lines, however, followed the same accenting for scanning and music.

MELE FOR KING KAUIKEAOULI
Singer: Kaahaaina Naihe, Honolulu, Oahu

This is a *mele olioli inoa* from Molokai. The singer, who is ninety years old, says that it was known by her father and mother.

Hé inoa é Kalani é
É Kauikéaouli é
Hóʻomoe á he inóa
Í lua nó ke kanáka
Pá iho ía Kináʻu
ʻWái olu wále ka manáo
Mé he ua liʻíliʻi lá
Mé he ua nóenoe lá
Ó ka pa a ké kona é
Ó ka makáni nui éa
Hé lawe ná ka hau é
Háu mālíelie é
Ólelo ná ka Hawáiʻi

Kú kapiháʻa i kái
Káu iki káha olua éa
Máluna ó ka moáʻe
É hele ána o Kaláni
Í ka lai í Onoulí
Káhea áʻe o Kaláni
Héaha lá nei makáni
Óua pú kona páha
Hó aʻe káwaʻa iwáho
Í poho ólu *aa* na péʻa
Hé lawe ná ka hau é
Háu malíelie lá
Nínau é ke kialúa
Páki wai óle keáma
Etc.

---

a The italicized letters represent sounds inserted for euphony in scanning.

CHANT FOR KALAKAUA

Singer: Moha, Kekaha, Kauai.

This is a *mele inoa*, a welcoming song, composed by Kalakaua's musicians. It is part of the mele honoring his world tour.

Anoái ke alóha e naló ia Éhu
Kahitúonaláni imi pómaitái
I niáu iho néi ma ka Pénekía
Nené au tái oiá tai lóa
Ekólu oukóu ha í ka mikíni
I álo i ka makáni i ka éhuehu kái
Ale ó ka moána o ka Pákipíka
Iho mái e ka nóe halí'i e ka óhu
Anú o Kalepóni he aína malihíni
Tu'upáu ia mái na hó'ohiluhílu
Hoíke na móku me ná papú
E nakólo na pú kowélo na há'e
Ole hála na péle hone ána na píla
A máki na kóa ka'uléle na páhu
Ulu wéhiwehi lúa na méa a páu
Kahíto a óki a pá ihííhi
Lawé a linoháu a mítihilína
Kenéla kopíla hano ná ho'okípa
E niníu na hóa na wíli akáu
Ho'i héma me ke hóa i te húleilúa
He ahá la ía na méa i o tíki
Ho'onúa ia mái na áno a páu
Aóhe mea ími a ka máka i tóe
Ua unúa ha ia mái a ákoatóa
Na hó'ohiehíe aía kapitála
A'e áku o kaláni ma ná kaáhi
He makána i lohía a náni lua óle
Na ka huíla e láwe o keáhi kona péa
Naná e ahá'i i náni ai hó'i
Hiki má ka hikína oni ná mea hána
Nóme i ke alaháo
O Maúna Poháku he wáo kanaka óle

He nahéle anoáno kai ó Mekíko
Hiki áku oukóu i Wákinekóna
Halelú me kaláni pule wále na hóa
Kipá aku i ka hále keía kapuláni
Huli hó'i o kaláni ma ó Niakála
Noe mái e ke ánu hone ána i ka póli
Tupúni pa'a mái na kápa hulukiá
I mehána i keáhi lala ó ke kanáka
Huli hó'i o kaláni i ke óne oíwi
Ua íke na láni á me ka moána
Ua íke e ka lá a mé ka mahína
Ua íke e ke ka'upu au ó ka moána
Ua íke na kólu o Púoína
I ka wélo ha'ahéo a ka háe kalaúnu
I ka íli o ke kái o Háaluéa
Ho'óle ke káuna ike óle na kílo
Tuhitúhipu'uóne olélo hewahéwa
Malihíni kamahá'o ma ke kómohana
  mái
Aóle ikéa penéi mamúa
O ke kúhiná ia máoli iliháu
He wái pahe'e wále na olína léo
Ku'u í ka nanáhe me ká wawali pú
Ma Núhawená na léo huró
He mamá e kelá he pahé'e keia
Ma Bókekóna papa Ámeliká
Kelá kauá o Komó'oaluálu
Keiá kumu héa awaáwa ahúna
Ho'i mái o ka láni me ke óla maiká'i
Ma ke áwa o Kóu pulehéte na póki
O koú inoa iá-é-o-é————

MELE INOA [1]

Composed by Miss Lucy Peabody.

Hánohano Kápulani í ka ulu hála
Ika hale ánini pé'a launíu
Ó ka pa kólonahe á ke keháu
Kóana ké ala á o ka hináno
É mapu ké ala í ku'u póli
É moani í ka wai kú'i a kekéla
Ía wai káulana káu i ka lá'i
A'e ona í'a ne'i é ka malihíni
Í ke ani péahi á ka launíu
Ike aka láwe malíe a ke éka

Ká makani kólonahe pá ahiáhi
Hóne ana í ke kai málino a Éhu
Áia í ka maka lá o ka opúa
Ó ka lihilíhi wai ánuenúe
Ké nihi á'ela i Há-li'ilú'a
Nóenoe í ka uka ó Alanapó
Óla ï ké kini ká uka o Kóna
Í ka ua lóku i ka láu laáu
Háina i'a mai ána ka puána
Ó Kalani kí'eki'e kú'u lei ía

---

[1] Scanned by W. H. Kahikina Kaoo, Hookena, Hawaii.

With the remarks on measure of proportion by Andrews (p. 63) properly belongs a statement to the effect that Hawaiian meles intended for hulas, and occasionally other kinds, are always composed in couplets. In some olis so composed the couplets are chanted with an interval of trilling at the end of each.

Contrary to Andrews' statement, there is one prominent method of rhyming which is so characteristic of Hawaiian poetry that it may be said to be one of the signs of genuine old compositions by master composers. This is what Prof. E. H. Sturtevant has suggested to me may be called linked assonance, which consists in beginning a new line with a word or words sounding the same or very like the last words of the preceding line or some words in it which are of outstanding importance. This assonance may not be carried consistently throughout, although it forms a feature of the poety. Some meles show a marked use of it but apparently followed no rule. Evidently the more skillful composers could introduce it oftener than others. It appears to have served the purpose of a mnemonic device, which might well be needed in chants hundreds of lines long. It may be imagined that a composer might have to go to some lengths to secure words suitable for this linked assonance which at the same time might be made to convey two meanings, all in keeping with the context. It requires considerable exercise of the translator's imagination, at times, to derive any sense in some of the more ancient specimens where old meanings of words have been lost. On the other hand, no doubt a successful combination in some of the difficult passages would evoke storms of applause which might win a composer deserved fame.

The following poem, recited by a centenarian woman of Kona, Hawaii, is a fair example of linked assonance. Here the couplets are linked:

Ku'i aku e ka lono puni ke kaona	Eia ka iini i ka pu'uwai
Ka hikina a ka la ma Kumukahi	Waiwai ke aloha hi'ipo'i nei
Akahi a lana ko'u mana'o	A na'u a nau no kekahi
E hui olelo me keonaona	Ho'okahi ho'i au ho'okahi oe
Onaona na maka o Leialoha	A i kolu i ke aheahe makani
Ua pulu i ka wai lohi o Maleka	Ke aheahe kehau na ke ahe laua'e
Ma ka leka ku'u i ke lihi ana iho	A i lawe mai ka eleele waha ole
Ho'opulu i ka welelau lihilihi	A ku'u aloha e ha'i mai ana i ka
A he lihi kuleana ko'u ilaila	nuhou, etc.

Where actual repetition of sounds is not feasible, there is occasionally a transposition, as a line ending in *"loke"* followed by one beginning *"ko lei,"* or one ending with *"nuhou"* followed by another ending with *"honua."*

Any number of such examples of linking lines may be observed in the meles presented in this book by those who care to pursue the subject further, many of them going beyond the mere repetition of the same syllables and utilizing words which have the same general sound but which are different in spelling. Some of the best examples are among the meles reserved for future publication.

A general idea of how meles were composed, learned and given out to the people, and some particulars as to their form have now been obtained from the writers quoted. In some respects they contradict one another, in some cases they have not told the whole truth. Keeping in mind their remarks, the chants offered here and the observations on them will supply some additional information.

It has not been mentioned by any of the authors quoted that in composing meles, especially name chants, the utmost care was taken that none of the lines could be given by the most evil-minded enemy any sinister secondary interpretation which could later be turned to the disadvantage of the one for whom the mele was composed, for ill fortune would attend not only the subject of the mele but the composers as well if such lines were discovered.

Any person not an expert, wishing to compose a sarcastic mele (calculated to arouse derision for the unlucky object and end in his complete discomfiture), consulted with old relatives who could be counted upon not to divulge the secret and who would assist in inventing the most scurrilous attacks possible. Persons have thus been taken entirely by surprise in some public gathering by suddenly hearing a mele chanted abusing them in the most uncanny fashion, leaving no room for doubt concerning their identity. There was no recourse except to improvise on the spot an answer, or to retire, as some women at least have done, in tears, to await a suitable opportunity for inventing a reply and delivering it at the psychological moment. If the unlucky object of spite could contrive an extemporaneous answer clever enough to silence his tormentor, great was his reward, for the delight of the audience would know no bounds.

Helen Cadwell (28, p. 72) quotes Alexander, but does not name the publication, as classifying meles into four divisions: (1) religious chants, prayers and prophesies; (2) *inoa,* or name songs, composed at the birth of a chief in his honor, recounting the heroic deeds of his ancestors; (3) *kanikau,* the dirges or lamentations for the dead; (4) *ipo,* or love songs. Roughly this classification covers the field, but under the last group would fall all the topical meles of a more secular character, which in number seem to have outstripped the others as time went on and to have survived in better condition on the lips of the country folk. As a corollary of this statement it should be remarked that they are, generally speaking, poorer in composition and quality, although many love songs are very subtle and beautiful, and some sarcastic meles are extremely clever. A better term for the fourth group would be topical, secular and love meles, including such war songs as would not fall under the other headings.

Under these four divisions might be made many sub-groupings according to the subject treated. Thus there were many kinds of prayer chants used in all sorts of ceremonies, the different names for which are given by Fornander (56, vol. VI, 1, pp. 2-52).

Under the class of *inoa* are genealogical chants; *lei* or complimentary meles; those dealing with sports, such as the *nalu;* those dealing with significant garments, such as malo and *pa-u*; others for parts of the body, notably *mai,* for which not only chants were composed, but which with different individuals were given special names; and so on. The dirges, or *kanikau,* are qualified by terms like: *manewanewa,* extreme sorrow; *uwe helu,* reciting or proclaiming in wailing the virtues of the deceased; *mele paha,* to call upon gods, men or the dead in figurative language; or *mele uhane,* in which the method of burial was recited in detail. The *mele kau,* used in connection with oli chanting, was the explanatory section which was recited *kepakepa* fashion between different *oki,* or verses. There is some doubt about the *mele paha* being a kind of *kanikau,* but some informants thought it was.

The topical meles have many descriptive titles, such as: *hooipoipo,* to cause to love; *hoonaikola,* sarcastic; *haku kole,* literally, to make inflamed, in which everything that can be thought of as detrimental to a person is listed; *mele mahalo,* giving voice to admiration; *mele hana'loha,* composed by a person having supernatural powers, to act as a love charm; *mele hoalohaloha,* for the purpose of showing affection; *paipunahele,* a mele composed by parents or elderly relatives for a favorite child; *mele hei,* composed to be recited when making the different passes of the string figures; *mele kimo,* juggling meles to be sung when making passes in juggling; and so on without end.

So far as I have been able to learn, all these sub-titles refer only to subject matter or the purpose of the mele, and not to different kinds of poetic composition having rules for number of lines, way of ending, methods of rhyming, verses, and the like. Typical hula chants of more modern type provide at the end for a restatement of the theme of the mele in the line *Haina ia mai ana ka puana* preceding the last, which may be translated, "let the echo of our song be," followed by the name of the person in whose honor it was composed, or failing that, by a restatement of the prominent idea in the mele. But that these lines were not considered indispensable is shown in that they were not always given with the rest of the text.

The *mele inoa* as a class always ended with a call of *"E o mai"* or similar hail, and the name of the person for whom the *inoa* was composed. It was the custom for this person, on hearing the hail, to respond with *"E o e."* Aside from these points and the fact that hula chants are generally composed in couplets, there appears to be no difference in the approved styles of composition for the different kinds of meles. Their classification as given was determined by their subject matter. There were certain styles of poetic composition, such as verses and refrains, which were adopted by individual composers, or which were the fashion generally for a time, but they were not essential features for any given type.

VOCAL MUSIC

In the vocal music a peculiar situation arose, evidently at a very early time. According to the general descriptions of travelers who had the advantage of visiting the islands while they were practically untouched by outside influences, there was no singing as we understand the term. Instead of more or less free, spontaneous melody which could be appreciated for its own sake even though associated in the minds of the singers inseparably with the words, and which could express beauty apart from the manner of its rendition, there was merely an intoning or chanting on two or three pitches as principal tones, so that the resulting melody was at best rudimentary and monotonous. Even under these circumstances which have apparently remained practically unchanged down to modern times for meles composed in the ancient style, the humming of a hula tune occasionally evoked a remark from an informant that that was an old hula, that it was the composition of a certain individual, or that it was also used for a hula other than the one under discussion, so a recognition of melody existed.

The expression of emotion as set forth in the text was supported by the melody only inadequately, by the general character of the movement of the piece, although not necessarily, or by the swelling or diminishing volume of the voice and its quality, but not invariably, and was regularly achieved only by the facial expression and gestures of the singer. Even these were more or less prescribed and set in their form and were used over and over again.

Quite aside from Marques' remarks on Hawaiian music (103, 104), which came to my attention long after I had finished collecting and to the general conclusions of which I had also arrived, a subsequent critical analysis of such music as was recorded established the fact that the meles as chanted fall into two distinct classes. The first is rather loosely termed by the people "olioli" or "oli," and covers a variety of chants, not only as regards their content, but also as regards several methods of chanting. The second is called "hula," and covers that great number of chants which may be used as dance accompaniments, although this is not a necessary condition.

THE UNACCOMPANIED RECITATIVE OR OLI MELE

The oli method of chanting is fairly well described by the English word recitative, which Webster's International Dictionary defines:

A species of music recitation in which the words are delivered in a manner resembling declamation; also a piece of music intended for such recitation;—opposed to melisima or melody. Recitative is thus characterized by freedom from strict form in its tonal and metrical structure, by being rhetorical rather than melodic in its phrasing.

It might be added that while the oli is free from strict form it is very circumscribed as to tonal content, by comparison with which the hula is much more spontaneous in melodic expression.

Before turning to the presentation of the music of the chants and a discussion of the results of their analysis, it is important to give what the Hawaiians themselves have said about their olis, in addition to what has already been mentioned in the section on poetry. In any study which borders upon ethnology it is worth while to investigate the ideas the people hold of their art and other phases of their culture and to see if in actual accomplishment they do or do not approach their ideals, when their achievements are critically analyzed.

There were well-defined standards of excellence in the performance of both kinds of chanting. In the oli the chief requisite was a deep and powerful chest tone, with an ability to hold the breath almost indefinitely. According to many old informants one who desired to become a master at the art of chanting olis should begin his training in childhood and devote himself to the sports which develop lung power and endurance. It was considered of little use for an adult to try to learn. Children would vie with one another in running given distances without taking breath, in diving and remaining beneath the water, or in simply holding the breath as long as possible whenever it occurred to them to do so.

There is a popular mele from Kona, Hawaii (p. 98), which mentions this training for chanting. I collected it with music several times and also the story concerning it. The mele and a less detailed story were obtained by Emerson and are given by him (43, p. 118). It refers to a little pool of shallow water in the rocks by the sea at Kailua, Hawaii, where the sun was reflected late every afternoon for a considerable interval. This and similar pools were called *poho na'u*, *poho* meaning both a depression in the surface and to blow gently. These pools were great swimming centers in the olden times. When the sun was setting and some part of it had disappeared below the horizon, the children would go to the *poho na'u* and lie down with the breast on the pahoehoe lava, and gaze into the pool facing the sun. In each *poho na'u* only two children could *na'u* at one time. A third, between them, acted as judge, and gave the signal to commence. Inhaling a deep breath, each child whispered to himself slowly, "*Na'u-u-u-u-u,*" and the one who endured longest was pronounced the winner. When this group had finished, another took its place and so the game continued until it was very dark. This place at Kailua was not the only one where the children could *na'u,* but they played at any spot where there was smooth pahoehoe and pools of water. Some called *"Na'u-u-u-u, Na'u-u-u-u ke kukuna o ka la,"* meaning "For me-me-me, for me the rays of the sun." The prolonging of the *u* sound in calling, as all singers know, was admirably adapted to the development of full, musical tones.

As described by Kamakau in the passage quoted on pages 59, 60, the breath control was from the chest and there must be no strain visible. It has been said, however, by the old folk, that a chanter's eyes sometimes bulged with the effort on a long chant.

An increase and diminution of tone was greatly admired. The Hawaiians described it as "the voice going high and low," which remark I at first thought referred to pitch and was mystified since the pitch variation is so limited. It applies to volume, however, and students took as their teachers for this difficult phase of chanting, the incoming waves of the sea or the roar of the waterfall. A devotee of the oli would practise for hours on the sands, imitating the sounds of the breakers as they gathered power, broke, and dissipated.

Considering the strain to which a chanter was subjected in reciting long stanzas, and the idea which developed that ill luck would attend the breaking of the flow of sound by the taking of a breath except at proper points, it is not surprising that a peculiar mouthing of the syllables crept into vogue which rendered them all but unintelligible to the uninitiated. This is the condition that may have made desirable the *kepakepa* or *ko'ihonua* style of chanting already mentioned. The slurring of syllables varied greatly in extent with different individuals whom I heard, and there were some localities where the usage was more prevalent than in others. Thus on Kauai and Oahu, particularly, *k*'s were apt to take a sound intermediate between *th* and *z,* which I have represented in the text beneath the music by substituting *z*'s for *k*'s. Individuals were not absolutely consistent in this change of a stop for a spirant, but in the localities mentioned its use was general and with each individual likely to be the preference throughout the chant. I have made the substitution only where it was heard; therefore inconsistencies in the texts will be understood. No rules appear to govern the change. The most that may be said concerning it is that in chanting it was a feature on the islands mentioned.

It has become a matter of common knowledge that on Kauai and

Niihau formerly *t* was a regular substitution for *k* in the spoken language. It is still to be noted in the speech of the older inhabitants and where the softer sound (*th* or *z*) did not occur, was prevalent in the chanting. If a question was raised about a word or a clearer pronunciation was sought, the old people rather impatiently repeated the word using *k* instead. This lapsing into *t* sounds is evident to a keen ear in the *kepakepa* recitations of old people anywhere, and was even found occasionally on Hawaii in common speech, and generally in chanting.

Thus it would seem that the observation made by a number of writers and heard again and again in general conversation, to the effect that the people of Kauai and Niihau differed from those of other islands not only in the use of many words and expressions but in the regular substitution of *t* for *k*, must be modified—at least as to present-day conditions—to permit of the statement that in chanting a *t* or its softer substitute is generally employed on Oahu and Hawaii as well. If there is anything in the theory that songs and rituals tend to preserve archaic forms of language, and the meles do contain many obsolete words and expressions, this use of a *t* sound in chanting, or its modification, would indicate that the sound was once common to the people of all the islands, possibly in an earlier home. The softer spirant may be an affectation of comparatively late date, but it is exactly the sort of an enunciation which would tend to develop with the manner of oli chanting.[2]

A tendency to certain vowel changes was observed which was general enough to appear as a feature of chanting although it was not sufficiently fixed to reveal any rules. Wherever these changes were observed they are represented by underlined letters in the text beneath the music, while the sounds theoretically correct for the Hawaiian of today have been retained in the texts printed separately after each musical example. By comparison of the two sets of text these changes may easily be observed. They may also be differentiated from the nonsense syllables or fillers, which are likewise underlined beneath the music, but not italicized in the separate texts except now and then at the ends of lines. Fillers appear more frequently in hula than in oli chants, except for the trill sections which are a feature of olis.

Examples of phonetic change which were sufficiently frequent and consistent to attract attention were: the substitution of *o* for *a* in the article *ka* before words having *o* in the first syllable, or in the preposition

---

[2] Edwin M. Loeb, recently returned from a field trip covering six months on Niue, or Savage Island, reports the use of the *t* there in former times, which among the old generation now living has become *ts*, and in the language of the younger generation *s*. This he ascribes to Samoan influence. The Hawaiian *th* or *z* may have no such derivation but it is worth noting that the sound is not foreign to the tongues of the older generation in Hawaii.

ma under similar conditions, although not so regularly; the combining of two adjoining vowels like *a* and *i* into *e*, or *o* and *u* into *u*, and the tendency of *a* before *e* to change to *e*. A peculiarity of enunciation in chanting is the interpolation of letters as fillers between the syllables of a word, like *e* between two syllables containing *a,* and this is not necessitated by the tune, which is of very loose construction, rhythmically. Some traces of alliteration are noted, exemplified by the selection of filler syllables which begin with the same consonant as that preceding or following in the beginning of a text word, but these filler syllables may take different vowels.

The lack of consistency between different individuals and even between the performances of the same individual indicates that there is either a breaking down of an old usage, that its adoption was never complete, or that it is recent. It will be difficult ever to settle the question, for the missionaries, although they recognized the subtle difference of sounds, in reducing the language to writing standardized it and so taught it. All the written chants of collections belonging to natives thus contain but very poor evidence of the sounds as spoken. Only rarely does one in laboriously writing out his meles slip into a *t* for a *k*. Almost no attention is paid to the very noticeable glottal stop that interrupts the smooth flow of sound in the language of all the old people, the presence of which is often vital to the sense to be derived from words otherwise identical in spelling. It was used by the missionaries only in a few cases, like the indirect pronouns, and is totally ignored in the newspapers. I have been at great pains to represent all of these stops in the text using the inverted apostrophe in distinction to the apostrophe, since the apostrophe, aside from the English usage, represents temporarily dropped letters in certain combinations, which in others are retained. I have also applied accent marks to those words which break the general rule of the emphasis on the penult. Reduplicated words ordinarily take two accents, one for each half.

It is hoped that this scrupulous attention to phonetics, although I admit that with such a brief time in which to learn the language there is ample room for mistakes and the omission of some diacritical marks, will be of service to linguists who may wish to pursue the subject. Above all, it should help in the proper translation of the texts collected and in revealing the correct pronunciation of the old Hawaiian to those who would like to see it preserved in its true form, for the pronunciation of the younger generation is very slovenly. To have diacritical marks in the dictionary is not enough, for without such marks in the texts there is often nothing to indicate how a word should be translated, especially when double meanings are so common a feature of meles. Properly written texts likewise furnish material for more detailed and exact comparison with chants elsewhere.

METHODS OF CHANTING

According to old informants on the three islands, there are several varieties of oli chanting. These include the plain oli, most frequently used, the hoaeae and the hoouweuwe. The *ko'ihonua* and the *kepakepa* are more like conversation than the oli or recitative, as has already been said, and have practically no musical qualities, although they are classed by the people as varieties of oli. The hoaeae and the houweuwe are considered by many to be the same; one informant thought the hoouweuwe was merely the crying of children without cause, but there is so much evidence of its being a style of chanting that his opinion cannot be accepted. Andrews (p. 61) mentions the *kuo* (*kuó*) as a chant with a singing tone but nothing concerning it was known by any of my informants, who had never even heard of the term. I was not able to learn of any other styles of oli than these and did not discover any chants not to be accounted for under these groups. The term *mele namu* has been mentioned as a rough-voiced chanting, opposed presumably to more finished performances, but it is a term not generally known, at least at the present time.

Oli

The oli fashion of chanting was prevalent for all kinds of meles not intended for dancing, and the plain oli, as it has been called, might be used for all occasions except mourning or when specially clear enunciation is required. Topical meles may also be olis, and many are known both as hulas and as olis. A study of the examples which I have selected will make clear the character of the oli. Individual style is discernible in each, but doubtless every one of the better known chants here given would show considerable rhythmic or even melodic differences if rendered by other performers. Within limits, olis are very flexible. The texts are likewise subject to variation. There is not a mele in the entire collection, I presume, which someone would not find incorrect according to his version. Some meles have been branded as senseless by one translator only to be cleared up by another.

No. 24 has been chosen as the first example, partly because of its length, for, as there is so little melodic variety to these recitatives, it has not been thought necessary to give many in their entirety. This chant reveals in its general aspect the idea of the oli as a whole, its monotonous pitch, its rhythmic features marked by notes of small time value and hence rapid movement, and its long periods. In examining these chants the reader must bear in mind that the singers were old people, and that the fine lung capacity of youth was past. All of them deprecatingly said that they could not now oli as they had formerly and most of them were reluctant to try. Therefore the positions of the rests are as often indicators of temporary incapacity as of customary pauses. A break was supposed to occur only at the end of a natural period in the poetry.

Some of my informants took advantage of the ends of lines as breathing points and thus their chants are phrased somewhat as the music of our songs would be, with due regard for musical pauses or occasionally cadences falling with the poetic phrase endings. The typical oli is extremely difficult to divide musically into sections and phrases, as we know them, not only because of the lack of rests but because of the lack of melodic or rhythmic variety which would make clearer the definitions of parts by the creation of melodic groups or possibly patterns. In the olis there are no melodic groups which, as such, can be repeated as thematic material with or without elaboration.

The only melodic change of consequence in this oli occurs at the breathing spaces where the voice drops in pitch, either before or after the rests or at both points. In the beginning there appears to be a rather constant relationship between the musical sections of two measures each covering six beats and single lines of the poetry. After the fourth line this system breaks down; even counting one of the quarter rests as part of the fourth section leaves too many beats and more than two measures for the fifth section. The sixth requires four and a half beats, the seventh five, the eighth four, and so on. Later the relationship between music section and line of poetry is regained temporarily, but it is soon lost.

No. 24.—Sung by Becky Kawaa, Honolulu, Oahu.

Note: In copying, a final sixteenth note has been omitted in the first measure of staff six.

Note: In staff three, fourth measure, a dot should follow sixth note.

i ke ka-i U-a ku o-no-o-no ka u-a o ku-nai-mo-a-na U-a a-i e

i-a'e la e Ka-la-na-ma-i-hi-ki U-a le-lu po-no i-a ka ma-la-ma

o I-ku-a' la U-a pa-a na a ma-na a u me Na-u-e ke ka-i O na u-ke-lo ana u

a me Ha-u-a-i-li-ki Me a kuu ho-a le-le i ke a-ne o lu-hi He

lu-hi-he-wa ke-i-i a o-e e ke a-loha ke ka-ka-li a-nai ka mo e

o ka hi-hi ma — ai He me-a no'-i ke-a-u a Nau-e

i-hi ma-i e ———

Note: Read *helu* for *lelu* (second line); *hele* for *lele* (fourth line); *nau-e* for *Naue* (sixth line).

Ha‘aheo i luna ke ahi a Kamaíle
Ka lele anoano a ke ahi i Makuáiki
Kunihi kokolo a ka auhau i na pali
Ke lawea mai la e Nu‘alolo i ka
  papala
Ke aka lele a ke ahi o Kamaíle
Ke oni a‘e la e like me A‘ahoaka
E akahele mai oe e Makana ia kaua
E a‘u lehua i luna o Makamaka ole
Ua lohe ia kaua e Ainaike
Ua haina‘e la e Kauka‘opua
E eia la ua kapu ka luna o Koaikini
Ua malu pono ka pua hau i Maluaka
Ua ana puni i‘a ke one o Mahamoku
Ua kau kanawai a Limaloa
Ua pa‘a i ka puke helu ana ka li‘ulá
Oki pau ka hana i Kekaha pua ohai
Hikiki‘i lua i ka luna o Ainaike
Le‘a kaena a ke kini o Maná
Ke hiu nei ke hele i Waialoha
Ka ho‘onalonalo a ka moe i ona
Ke pe‘e ela e nalo i Kahihikolo
Kokolo mai ana ka uahi a ka moe iou
  nei
Loku ana i ka pe‘a kua o ke kanaka

Ka wale walania i ka maka me he
  uahi ala
Ooe o au ana kekahi ilaila
Ooe ia e kekahi lau pali o Makana
E ke oho lau lena o ka awapuhi
Heaha la ka hana a Manu‘akepa e
  hana nei
Keena wale ala no ena i ka luna o
  Kawaikini
E au oe o ikea mai e Kauko‘opua
Ina no ilaila ke kini o makou
Ou kini aloha i Māmalahoa
E huli mai ka pono me Papiohuli
Aoe hemo ka pili a Maka‘li‘i
Ua kakia kui nao ake akamai
O Kaula aku ia he moku lewa i ke
  kai
Ua ku onoono ka lua o Kuhaimoana
Ua ai ia”ela e Kalanamaihiki
Ua helu pono ia ka malama o Ikuá
Ua pa‘a na mana au me Naueikekai
O na olelo ana ia me Ha‘uailiki
Me a ku‘u hoa hele i ke one o Luhi
He luhi hewa keia ia oe e ke aloha
Ke kakali ana i ka moe o ka hiki mai
He mea no ho‘i kau a naue iki mai—e

This chant reveals a not uncommon psychological situation—a general shifting of the pitch of the chant as a whole. With some chanters such a shifting occurs gradually, so imperceptibly that it is not observed by the listener until the end of the song when testing with a pitch pipe proves that the entire level has been raised or lowered. Again the change is made abruptly, between sections. The fact that this phenomenon is observed universally among singers, not only among people whose knowledge of music is confined to spontaneous outbursts but among trained European singers as well, tends to discount its value here as evidence of intention, or as a feature of oli chanting, especially as plenty of chanters do not have this peculiarity.

The tonal content in the first third of the chant is the note c with a or ab below forming with it the interval of a minor or a major third. After a break the singer drops to b as a principal tone, maintaining the major third interval by substituting g for ab. Whether she felt that she was flatting, or her sudden rise in pitch was due to some nervous reflex, $c\sharp$ presently becomes the tone level and a or $a\sharp$ produces the interval of a major or a minor third. C as a principal tone is restored near the close. The variation between the major and minor third and an apparent indifference to these changes in intervals marked much of the Hawaiian chanting heard by me.

The rhythmic character of all olis is determined by the large number
of sixteenth notes, and the absence of striking contrast in note values
except where there is a play on a vowel by trilling as at the end of a
period. A study of the changing meter of this song reveals no design or
even an approximation to one. Two part meters predominate but a
larger number of measures with three beats appear than is generally to
be observed in the olis. The impression received by me from hearing
very many of these chants is that the single beat is uppermost in consciousness, in hula tunes generally as well as in olis, and that the recurrence of accent in the olis particularly is more a matter of seeking relief
from continual evenness of inflection, or is controlled by some outstanding
accent of the word than a recognition of its value in forming rhythmic
or metric patterns. The number of syllables in a line and their customary
emphasis in speech very largely control the situation in the mele oli, and
most of the measures containing fractional beats may be accounted for
in this manner. The scanning that was mentioned in the section on
poetry, if it obtains in the oli as a framework, is so distorted by fillers,
trilling, holds, and the like that it is entirely lost sight of, in nearly
every case.

The second oli, No. 25, shows slightly more melodic variation than
the first and suggests a melodic division which I have indicated by means
of the brackets above the notes. These are not sections, strictly speaking, for the Hawaiians are quite unconscious of them as elements of form,
while their occurrence here is as likely as not only temporary, and perhaps
the divisions might change with the next repetition of the chant. The
demands of the poetry create sections of constantly varying length
throughout the oli. The rests which now and then cause appreciable
pauses are seen at some points to come in the middle of poetic phrases—
a circumstance which theoretically runs counter to European standards
as well as to Hawaiian. On the other hand, musical divisions, if they
might be considered as sufficiently delimited to be identified as such, are
now and then split by the breaking off of one line and the beginning of
another. It is a question of how far practice followed theory even in
the old times, in recitatives like these.

This oli illustrates very well the wavering effect of tone which was
much sought, although not generally in so obvious a fashion as is
attained here by the comparatively large half-step intervals. Other
examples will be noted where trills of less magnitude are employed. The
trilling at the end is found in many olis but is not a fixed feature for
plain oli chanting.

No. 25.—Mele inoa chanted by Kalani Ku Kama, Waiakea Homesteads, Hilo, Hawaii.

I-a Ka-o-u-li Kōo-te-a e Ta-la-ni Hea e-lū-i he a pu—

to-a tu u Hea pa-pa-u-na-o-a i a Lo-no He a-hu— e ku no e

te ta-i no ho-ho-nu e ta-la-ni-nu-i — i-a(m)ma-o— ma— o e te-a-e Te—

a-o-e hi-a-po e ta-pu no e i-a O te hu tu-lu o te-a hi-nu

o ta .ho-u o e te Ka-pu la a i-a ae te Tu li-ae ma-i Ta

la-ni Ho— a hu—a i-a ma-i kōo-te-ae ta mo-e-tu Pa-o-pa-u i-a Ko-ho-la-

lo(a) Ke a-li' Na-ha ma-i ka lua u-le— o la-ha o-le Ka a-la'

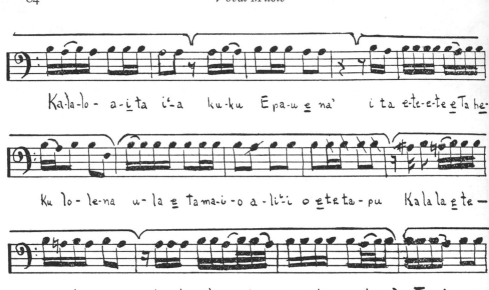

Ka-la-lo - a-i ta i-a ku-ku Epa-u e na' i ta e-te-e-te e Ta he-

Ku lo-le-na u-la e Ta ma-i-o a-li-i o e te ta-pu Kala la e te-

i e ta o ma-no te a-hi a-le e ta ni-u-hi mo-e-la-u' O Te a-la-ni

o-pu-u hou ho-uo ta mu-tu O ta ho'-e-lo e o we-la o-le i-a

o ta a ma-e-ta O ta u-lu na-na-i ha-ha-o e ta e-na-e-na o ta

we-lo lo-lo-a I na-nge i ho-a-li-ali a a-a' no e Ta-la-ni Ta-u-

(li) - hi-wa e Ta-a-ma o ta A-ta-la-pa no e ta la-u-a e

Ia Kaouli-Koʻokea-Kalani
Heʻliʻi he pukoʻa ku
He papaunaoa ia Lono
He ahua ku no ke kai hohonu
No ke kai hohonu o Kalaninuiiamamao
O ka Keawe hiapo kapu no ia
O ke kulu o ka hinu o ka hou o ke kapu la iaia
Ku lia mai e Kalani kohohonu
Hoa hua ia mai koʻokea ka moku
Pa paʻu ia Koholaloa i ke ʻliʻi
Nahá mai i ka lua uleo laha ole
Ka alaihi kalaloa ka iʻa kukú
E pau ai nālima i ka ekeeke

Ka haku lolena ula ka māio aliʻi o ke kapu
Ka la la la kea, ka mano, ke ehi ale, ka niuhi moalawa
O Kalaniopuʻu hou o ka moku
O ka hoʻelo wela ole ia o ka maka
O ka ulu nana i hahao ka enaena o ka welo loloa
Nana e hoaliali a aá no Kalani
Kaulihiwa a Kama
Alalapa no ka laua keiki
O ka Pūlikolikoikalani
Ka mano, ka hailawa, ka hāhalua, ka iʻa nui hihimanu
Ke koaʻe lele uka a o ke aku lele kai
E o mai a ka Kaoulionalani i kou inoa.

Nos. 26 and 27 are different renditions of a *mele inoa* or name chant by a very old woman of Kailua, Hawaii, who said that it had belonged in her family for a long time. The poetry is considered to have no merit by those who have passed on the texts so it is omitted here, except under the notes, but the music is given to illustrate the kinds of variation that obtain when the same singer gives the same chant twice in succession at the same interview. This is a typical case.

The brackets above the music show the nearest approach to musical divisions that can be made with due regard for the lines of the poetry. It is a question as to how far one is justified in making them at all except that they are valuable in tracing the existence or absence of design elements. The trills and holds, although necessary features of olis, are so variable from chant to chant that they are to be regarded more as whimsical embellishments than as fixed elements of structure.

In the second rendition there is more fluctuation in pitch, but nothing to indicate that the deflected pitches are intentional even though any number of them occur. The differences in this respect between the two renditions, and a closer similarity of rhythms than is generally to be observed under these conditions would indicate that with this informant, pitch was harder to control than rhythm.

Although Nos. 26 and 27 together with No. 25 might be expected to reveal similar musical features if it were customary to chant the *inoa* in any particular way, study and analysis have indicated no peculiarity by which they may be differentiated from other olis except that at the end of the chant it was customary, before announcing the name of the one for whom the chant was composed, for the chanter to call upon him with a musical call of "*E o*" and for the other to respond with a similar hail. There is no metric or rhythmic arrangement, no style of beginning, of trilling or of holding notes, no pattern of repetition of parts, no tonal content that distinguishes them from other olis.

The next examples offered are sufficiently ancient in text to satisfy the most critical, and probably were true to tradition in being chanted. Chants to the goddess Laka and the goddess Kapo, like those to Pele and Hiiaka, are of unknown antiquity. Laka was the patron goddess of the hula and although the hula included a great variety of dances, and, after graduation the dancers might use for the amusement of their audiences almost any kind of meles they chose, the proper performances were always preceded by a ritualistic ceremony when the goddesses were invoked by means of prayers, *pule,* chanted in oli fashion. During the strict novitiate which those who desired to become proficient in dancing

No. 26.—Mele inoa chanted for her family by Mrs. Koleka Naia, Kailua, North Kona, Hawaii.

No. 27.—Another rendition of No. 26.

Ku mai au i ka mo-ku Ni-nau-a-na na-wai la o-e Na Ku-mu-o-ka-la-w

a-u i ha-na-u Na ka la i-ki-i ki ha-na ka la ha-na ai a po-a-hin(a)

Na Ma'-i ke-u-e na' Ke-o-pu la'- i Na ke a-la ul-a na ka-hu-na

ai o Ku Na Ka-ma i ka hu'- Na-na ka-hu-ko po'-ou o

Ka-la-ni Na 'la-ni e-wa-lu Na Ta-u-h. Ta-e-o-lo -o-o-

a I-lai-la'u a ho'-i mai e No-u ho'-ke-i' an'nei e e

a-ki he-wai ka u-ku O Ka la-ni-ho'-o-ka-ha Ko ku-pu-

u-na Ke-ku-pun̄o na 'li'-i.

the hulas were required to undergo, the rituals and tapus must be meticulously followed (Emerson, 43, p. 15). The effect of this long period of training and religious observance was to instill in the pupils a life-long allegiance to the goddess, and such a feeling exists to the present day quite generally among the country folk. One well-known hula teacher of a district in Kona severely criticized a famous leader of tourist performances in Honolulu for not knowing the invocations and not observing the customary rituals. He was not condemned as having fallen from grace so much as for his supposed ignorance of convention. His performances were considered incorrect. So much for the persistence of ancient belief and custom!

One of the best known and very ancient invocational chants to Laka, which has already been given in text by Emerson (43, pp. 20, 42), was encountered again and again in various districts with remarkably slight variation in words. It was always chanted in oli fashion as the first mele a hula chanter wished to sing into the phonograph. The chant was given complete by a hula dancer of Hilo, Hawaii.

The metric regularity of this chant is almost perfect, thus differing from most, but there is no outstanding rhythmic pattern. It is merely a recitative, like the others, with a trilled section at the end such as is often to be found with the plain oli, but here the "trill" is not achieved by any perceptible fluctuation in pitch but by a bouncing or throbbing of the voice on a single pitch. I have indicated by the brackets a possible division into musical sections which, controlled by the lengths of the lines of the poetry, are of the following dimensions according to the number of measures or primary accents included: 3, 2, 3, 2, 2, 3, 2, 3, 1, 2, 3, 3, 5, which is the nearest to a metric pattern repeated that any of the olis reveal. It seems probable, however, that these sequences of metric groups are not the result of conscious musical design.

No. 28.—A prayer to the goddess Laka, chanted by Mrs. L. P. Kahema, Hilo, Hawaii.

Note: Staff five, last measure, first note should be followed by a dot.

Eia au e Laka
Ka wahine i noho i ke ala i nu'u
E Laka mai iuka
E Laka mai kai
O ka ho'oulu a Lono
Ka ilio o nana i hae ka aha
O ka ieie ku i maka a wao

O ka maile hihi o ka nahele
O ka lau 'i lei a ke akua
O na ku'i o Hauoli
O Hina-i-ka-malama
O Hina wahine a Kina'u
O Laka i ke kuahu nei la e
E ho'i e.

Another rendition of this same chant in a slightly different version was obtained near Hilo, but the notation covers only a part of it since the record proved too faint to transcribe. (See also Emerson, 43, pp. 19, 143, for texts.)

No. 29.—A chant to the goddess Laka, given by Kalani Ku Kama, Waiakea Homesteads, Hilo, Hawaii.

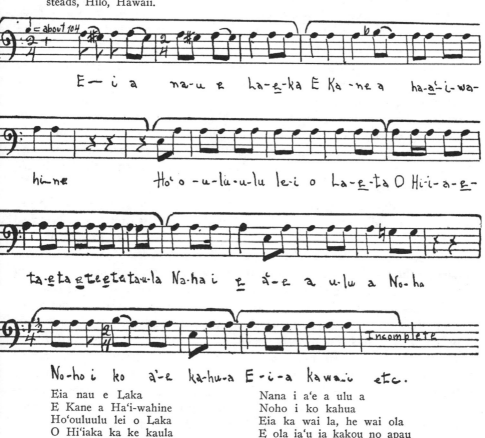

Eia nau e Laka
E Kane a Ha'i-wahine
Ho'ouluulu lei o Laka
O Hi'iaka ka ke kaula

Nana i a'e a ulu a
Noho i ko kahua
Eia ka wai la, he wai ola
E ola ia'u ia kakou no apau

The differences in the chanting of this and the preceding example are very striking, and the notation makes plain as no audible impression would, the part played by the individual singer in chanting. For instance, both renditions are on the same pitch level; in both two-part meter predominates and the general relative time values of the notes are the same, only one chant moves somewhat faster than the other. In both the voice occasionally drops to the neighborhood of a fourth below. But with all these similarities the reader may pick out many differences.

A second rendition by the same singer differed greatly from the first, especially rhythmically, but was unfortunately too faint to bear transcription after being played a few times.

W. M. Kalaiwaa, of Kamuela or Waimea, Hawaii, known all over the island for his chanting, gave a famous old mele oli for that place, text versions of which are given both by Fornander (56, vol. 6, no. 1, p. 203) and Emerson (43, p. 68). I also obtained it on Kauai, and on Oahu as a hula. Kalaiwaa made two records of it which were transcribed and are here presented for comparison.

The first, No. 30, is not absolutely reliable as regards actual note values for the record was not perfect. A record of an oli, if it is not absolutely clear, is very difficult to transcribe because most of the chant is on one pitch and the syllables are apt to be blurred in enunciation through the softening of the *k*'s to *th* or *z*. With a dim record or one that might be termed "ragged," it is almost impossible to tell where one note ends and another begins. Were there more changes in pitch, even with the blurred enunciation transcribing would be comparatively easy.

Even with its defects, the transcription is sufficiently correct to furnish a fair idea and to make evident the fact that only two pitches, a principal one of *g* and another a fourth below, which takes a rather prominent part, make up the melodic material, for the slightly flatted *d* is not a significant part of the tonal content. The musical divisions are, as usual, of different length, to accommodate the poetry. A peculiarity revealed in the chanting of Kalaiwaa but not in that of anyone else, consists in partly stating a line of poetry, every so often, then taking a breath and stating the line completely, after which the mele is resumed. In this chant every fourth line is so treated. A musical analysis at first seemed to indicate that the partial statements, covering what might be taken for a musical section, might have been used by the chanter to increase the apparent number of lines and thus to create a kind of balance in pairs which was impossible in the nine lines as they stood. There was nothing in the poetry or the music to show that a division into three parts was intended unless this partial statement of every fourth line could be taken to mean this. As many points about the olis made me wish that I could have secured more information from the

No. 30.—Chant for the village of Waimea (Kamuela), South Kohala, Hawaii, chanted by W. M. Kalaiwaa of that village. (Record indistinct.)

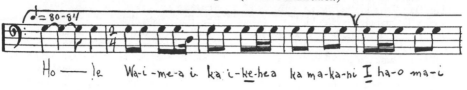

Ho — le Wa-i-me-a i. ka i-ke-hea ka ma-ka-ni I ha-o ma-i

nā le e ke ki-pu-u-pu-u Hela-a-u Ka-la-i-hū'a na ke a-nu O-ó ei ka na-

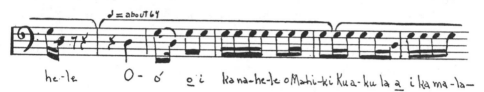

he-le O - ó o i ka na-he-le o Mahi-ki Kua-ku la a i ka ma-la-

na a ke ki-pū-u-pū'u Holu o ka ma-ka o ko o-hā- wa-i o u -li Ni

= ai-a-u e-Aa a ta pu-a Ni-ni - a-u e -ha tapu-a o Koa-i'-a E-ha i

ke a-nu Ka na -he-le o Wa-i-ka A-lo-ha Wai-ka-i-ā-u mei-po o-o-o-o-o-o

o-o-o-o-o - o-o - la

Hole Waimea i ka ihe a ka makani
Hao mai na ale a ke ki-puʻupuʻu
He laau kala-ihi ia na ke anu
O-ó i ka nahele o Mahiki
Ku aku la i ka malana a ke Ki-pu-
    ʻupuʻu
Holu ka maka o ko oháwaï o Uli
Niniau, eha ka pua o Koaiʻa
Eha i ke anu ka nahele o Waiká
Aloha Waiká iaʻu me he ipo la

Hoe Puna i ka waʻa palolo a ka ino
Hauleule i ka la i hala o Koʻokoʻolau
Eha e! eha la!
Eha i na makani kuʻi a kaulumanu
Halaʻʻe ka makapehu ihe a ke Aʻe
Ku iho i ka pahu ku a ka awaawa
Hana neʻe ke kikala o ko Hilo kini
Hoʻi luʻuluʻu i ke one o Hanakahi
I ka palolo ua mea wahine o ka lua
Eia e hoʻi a

chanters, I decided to put a number of questions to Kalaiwaa by letter, after having given in my own mind the answers to most of them. Whether his style was or was not proper according to the canons of oli chanting, it is such departures by famous individuals as he which frequently lead to the adoption of new styles by the community as a whole. I put to him these nine questions:

1. I have noticed that in chanting an oli you have chanted now and then to the middle of a line, and then have gone over this line again from the beginning. What is the reason for this?

2. In the mele Hole Waimea and in Kona Kai Opua there are only nine lines each. How are these meles divided, into parts with three lines each, or do the lines go, perhaps, correctly in pairs?

3. Is Kona Kai Opua a mele hoaeae the way you chanted it?

4. What is the difference between the hoaeae and the oli?

5. What is the difference between the hoaeae and the hoouweuwe?

6. What kind of voice would you call that you used for the *mele kimo?* A hula, perhaps? If a hula, what is the name of that kind of a hula?

7. How many kinds of voice are there in chanting?

8. What is a *mele kuo?* For what kinds of chants is it used?

9. In your chanting of the dirge mele for Kahahana what was the kind of chanting you did, oli, or hoaeae, perhaps, or possibly the hoouweuwe?

Many of the general questions I had put again and again to other informants and was merely seeking confirmation from Kalaiwaa. His answers will be given, as they are pertinent. Concerning the nine-line poems, in making inquiries among his acquaintances in order to have correct answers for the questions, he learned that for "Hole Waimea" there were additional lines. He replied concerning his own version:

1. He repeated the lines every now and then because his breath had failed. He would go over the imperfect line again, and then would chant on until his breath failed again, and he rested whether the line was finished or not. He did this also that he might be sure of the next line, for when

No. 31.—Repetition of No. 30.

Note: In copying, one too many sixteenth notes has been included in the final measure of the second staff.

he was at a loss to know what came next this repetition filled in and at the same time helped his memory.

2. As to the two nine-line poems, the composers had never been exact in the matter of lines. The meles were according to what the person had done. When the account was finished, then the mele was complete regardless of the length. No one ever paid attention to see if meles were alike in number of lines.

3. Kona Kai Opua was a mele oli as he had given it.

Therefore it is apparent that form as we know it had no part in the consciousness of the chanter, but it is interesting psychologically to observe the regularity with which Kalaiwaa made his pauses and to note that he used practically identical sequences of notes for setting forth both of his partial phrases in chanting "Hole Waimea."

The second version of this chant, No. 31, leaving aside the general pitch, is considerably different from the first. Only one line, the eighth, is partially stated before it is given entire. The two versions were made in immediate succession and the singer was asked to give it again only that I might have two copies in case one was damaged.

The second nine-line piece of poetry (No. 32) beginning *Kona kai opua* is treated by Kalaiwaa in a different fashion. (See also Emerson, 43, p. 117 for a version of the text.)

A comparison of this with the preceding chant will show that the chanter is verging on habit in form. For instance, in both he has taken two musical sections to cover the first line of the chant, and about one for each of the two succeeding lines. Instead of partially reciting the fourth line and then pausing for breath, he has varied the procedure in this chant by using the fillers *o e* prolonged over a section, but it is evident that he has established the habit of doing something different after the end of the third line, for, had he wished, there was nothing to prevent his taking a breath at this point instead of a little later.

After the second pause there is a reversion to the general scheme set forth in the first part of the chant, that is, the sixth line of the poetry, or the first of this part, covers two musical sections, the seventh and eighth each one, after which there is an extended section corresponding to that in the first part, but now the fillers *e* and *i* are used. There is little doubt but that here is a beginning of a design in chanting, of which, perhaps, Kalaiwaa was hardly conscious.

A prayer for Lohiau, figuring in the Pele and Hiiaka myths (Emerson, 42, p. 210), presents more of the aspect of a hula than an oli. The rapid

No. 32.—Oli chanted by W. M. Kalaiwaa, Kamuela, South Kohala, Hawaii. (Transcription is doubtfully correct; the record is worn.)

I o   Ko-na e ta-i   o-pu a e ta '- i O pu-a hi-na-

no u-a a ma-li-e Hi-o - lo na wa-i na'o a ke-ha-u O e e

e e e   O ku-ia la ko-i-li i te ta-i i Ta-na-r-a

al'ta-ma-li'- i Te to-hi la   Ke- e to-a-hi-i-la i ka

ku-ku-na o ka la Pu m hama wa-le i-a a-i- na A-lo-ha wa-le ke ki

ni (O) Ho'o-lu-lu e e   e e e e e i A- oh' ka he lu'

i-a o-e ke a-lo-o-ha   ?

O Kona kai opua i ka la'i
O pua hinano ua malie
Hiolo na wai na'o a ke kehau
O ku'u la koili i ke kai
Ke na-ú ala kamali'i

Ke k'ohi' la i ka kukuna o ka la
Pumehana wale ia aina
Aloha wale ke kini o Ho'olulu e
Aohe kahe lua ia oe e ke aloha

sixteenth notes are replaced by those of greater time value and more prominence is given to other tones than that of the general level, bb. Because of the slight increase of melody over monotone a melodic design becomes more easily discernible. Although not necessarily existing under such conditions and certainly not characteristic of olis as a class, such design is to be found in this example.

In chanting, the singer has altered the first three lines into two, whether accidentally or by design it is now unfortunately too late to determine. Probably, however, it was an error, but as they stand the lines make perfect sense and sound well. Even though a repetition of this chant might prove disappointing in being quite different, such examples as this show that the threshold of melodic design has been reached.

I have lettered the phrases, each containing two melodic sections, so that their structure may be compared. The same letters refer to the same melodic ideas. The characteristic partial statement of a line of poetry appears at B″, just before the pause.

No. 33.—A prayer for Lohiau, by W. M. Kalaiwaa, Kamuela, South Kohala, Hawaii.

We- la ka la-ni we-la Ma ka—li-i Ka-e-lo i-a e ka

ka-u-lu a' Ka-i-a-hu o ka mo-ku pa-pa-pa-ka a-i-ni ka-a (words missing in text)

—ke kai o ka ma-u-na Ha ka mo-an'a-le po-po-i

Ki-la-u-e-a Ku mai Pu-nu ki-e-ki-e i ka la-ni Ha-ha-a ka

ul' o ka o-pu-a pu- e- hu mai la ka u-la E—

hu mai la ka u-ka i Ke-a-hi-a- la-ka Ke-a- hi ka ua-hi

le-hu-a Pa-ku-i Kau- a-hi ka-na-ka E-a ho'-o-ma-hao-le i ke

po-i a ke a-hi I-a-hi i Wa-i-mo-a-ka e u-we ma

Defect at end

- - - - - - - - - -a-i

Wela ka lani wela ka hoku' ka ma-
 lama iluna
Wela Makali'i Kaelo ia Kaulua
Kai ehu ka moku papapa ka aina
Kaiko'o ka mauna ha ka moana ale
 popo'i i Kilauea
Ku mai Puna ki'eki'e i ka lani
Ha'aha'a ka ulu o ka opua

Pua ehu mai la ka uka i Ke-ahi-a-
 Laka
Pūmehana i ka Wai-welawela
Ikiiki i ka uahi lehua
Paku'i i ka uahi kanaka
Ea hanu ho'omaha ole i ke po'i a
 ke ahi
I ahi i wai maka e Hi'iaka e
E uwé mai

A second prayer for Lohiau, No. 34, as chanted by Kalaiwaa, being short, required no considerable pause and contains no restatement of lines. Like the first, it resembles a hula more than an oli both in rhythm and in giving more relative prominence to notes other than that of the general level. Both of these prayers have the long-drawn ending of the final phrase that characterizes many olis.

No. 34.—A prayer for Lohiau, chanted by W. M. Kalaiwaa, Kamuela, South Kohala, Hawaii.

No. 35, a modern mele, seems to defy analysis from any but the standpoint of the comparative lengths of lines as they were recited. The first two phrases shown by the brackets are capable of subdivision into two musical sections each, but the third does not lend itself to subdivision. It also contains a mistake committed by the chanter, the extent of which cannot be exactly determined because although the entire phrase is immediately repeated as if to correct the error, it is not begun as before and may be different from what he would chant at another time. There is very little evidence of design and the phrases of the music are of very uneven length. The chant is not complete but enough is given to show its character. Two-beat measures predominate, with occasional variations. The measures, listed by the number of beats, show a rough grouping with irregular passages

No. 35.—Oli inoa, chanted by W. M. Kalaiwaa for his grandchild. (Incomplete.)

ma-i-ke ka-mau' o-hu-o-hu-i na pua le-hu-à le-i o Pi-ko-i-le—

i È ka-hi koa-na i k'e-hu kai O ka la pu-ka i a Ha'-e (hà'e)

Ke e ha-i a'e la li ka-ma Ma-ka-no-ni Ka no-ho na-ni ma-i Ha-na—

Ka-u-lu-a i Ka ma-li-e E le-i a—na o-pu-a o pi-o-pi-o i ke a-o ka'

i La-ma-u-la   E   e he ka t a—ku'i na pu'k u-wa-u

i nawa-i ma-u-u ka maka-i a ke ku-pu-a' Ki-la-hi a-na—— etc.

Ki'eki'e Kuki'i hanohano i ka malie
Auau i ka wai o Waiwelawela
E lei ana i na pua lehua kau iluna
    o Kalehuawehe
I pulu i ka huna ua o Kauapaka
E nana ana i luna o Koa'ekea
Oili Kumukahi au i ke kai
E nana ana i na ale hulilua i ka
    moana

E lawe ana ke au lawe i ka miloholo
    i Waiakaea
Ea mai i ke kama ua ohuohu i na
    pua hala lei o Píkoilei
E kahiko ana i ke kapa ehukai
A ka la puka i Ha'eha'e
Ke hahai a'e la e pili me Makānoni
O ka noho nani mai a Hanakaulua
    i ka malie

E lei ana i na opua o Piopio i ke ao
    kau i Lamaula
Ike aku i na puʻe uwai mauka makai o
    ke ala a ke kupuna
E kilohi ana i ka ulu hoʻonoho i ka
    papa pili o Huaʻilua
Huaʻi ka nalu o ka iwi huaʻi iluna
Pae na kini heʻenalu holo ana i ka
    lala hoʻi ana i ka muku
Pae aku i ka iliili nehe o ka aina
Auau aku i ka wai kapipí i ka wele-
    lau o ka lima
Komo aku i ka uluwehiwehi o Ma-
    nuʻuhale
Inu i ka wai o ka punawai kau i ka
    lewa
Wai a ka ua i hiʻiai iluna
Wai a ka ua i pulama ai iluna
Wai a ka ua i malama ai iluna

Wai a ka huna o ka ua a me ka
    makani i lawe mai ai
Kahake ka upu kaha i ka ili o ke kai
Hoʻi ka uaʻu kau iluna o Malama
Malama ka iiwi ai lehua o ka nahele
    i lei no ke kama
Malama ka apapani inu wai lehua i
    lei no ke kama
Malama ka o-o kanikua mauna o ka
    nahele i lei no ke kama
Malama ka aʻo kani kohakohá i ka
    nahele i lei no ke kama
E hoʻolohe ana i ka leo o ka nihi-
    nihi kanikua mauna
E nana ana i kānaka loloa o ka
    mauna
E o e Alowena lei a Ane i kou
    inoa a.

between. Thus there are thirteen of two-four meter, one slightly less than two beats long, then ten measures of two-four and three which are irregular, fourteen of two-four and four irregular, again ten measures of two-four and one of three-four, after which there is a general breaking down.

A final chant by Kalaiwaa is a juggling mele, or *mele kimo* which, in its poetic structure, is adapted to the turns of the juggling and affords an excellent basis for musical design. Nine lines are recited during which a pass in juggling is performed and the chanter sings *"puni"* meaning "termination of the period," or "successfully completed." Then there is a refrain section of three lines to the effect that the first pass is completed without mishap and the second being successful, the third will be a tie. There follows the second part, six lines long, after which *"puni"* is again sung, followed by the three lines of refrain. The third pass is only three lines long.

An analysis shows other points worth noting in the music. In the actual number of beats the measures are somewhat irregular, particularly at first. Although no order or pattern of metric groups is disclosed by listing the measures according to their beats, there is a tendency, after about fifteen measures, to insert one of four beats between periods of anywhere from seven to sixteen measures of three-four meter. This three-part meter largely predominates and in itself is unusual in Hawaiian chants.

I have divided the music as it would fall, regardless of the words, into divisions which are, strictly speaking, extended sections, which are also built on the principle of three, for there are three measures in each except those numbered XI, XII, XX, and XXI. Section XI and XIX cover the second and third lines of that part of the poetry which is repeated between passes of the juggling, and aside from balancing one another, in their altered form of four-measure phrases provide a musical passage of different character which calls attention to the finishing of a division. Sections XII and XX imitate this form in the opening of the new parts but XII covers

No. 36.—Mele kimo, or juggling mele, chanted by W. M. Kalaiwaa.

I

Eono moku ia Kalani
Kona, Kohala, Koʻolau,
O Kalihi o Paieie
A pua i Okiokiaho
Ke naʻi aku nei makou
E ku ka hale i Punaluʻu
I ka wai hu o Kauwila
I ka iliili o Koloa
I na mauʻu o Malaia
    Puni
Ahia aʻu puni akahi
Kahi e ka lua lua e
Ke kolu paʻi wale

II

A Ko-há-koʻ-há-i Kalani elima
O na lima ia lohelohe eono
O na ono aina ehiku
O kaua hikuhiku ewalu
O Kamalalawalu eiwa
O ka holo kuaiwa o ka holo kekeʻe
    Puni
Ahia aʻu puni akahi
Kahi e ka lua lua e
Ke kolu paʻi wale

III

Ke noho ala no o Paiʻea
Ilalo i Laupahoehoe
Ma uka aʻe o Ulekiʻi
    Puni

only one line of the poety while XX, by a mutilation of the design of repeating the final word of a line, which has been maintained up to new except for the second and third lines of the intermediate sections, embraces two lines of poetry. The breaking down is further shown in XXI where two words are introduced not in the text as given separately. They are fillers taken from the word *Ulekiʻi* in the last line which is now introduced and completed by means of a four-measure section. The whole is completed by a little coda consisting of one melodic motif for the word *"puni."* This is the most interesting and consistent musical composition of any among the olis. It is not, from the considerations just discussed, a typical oli, and in some respects resembles a hula, but the meter is different from the majority of hula meters. I asked Kalaiwaa whether it was a hula, and if so, what kind. He answered that it was merely a *mele kimo* and that the game of juggling was for children and grown people as well, and proceeded to show me two ways in which the juggling might be done, with two objects manipulated by one hand only, or ten in two hands.

Nos. 37 and 38, supposed to be the same, are two renditions of an oli for Liliana, by an old woman of ninety, Kaahaaina Naihe of Honolulu. In reciting the text she evidently omitted the second line, which could not be identified on the records. These examples are given merely to represent another individual's method of chanting. In general character they resemble the plain oli with one prominent tone, another slightly above it, and an occasional drop to tones a perfect fourth or a minor third below. The movement is not quite as rapid as the oli generally takes, but most of the notes are of uniform length.

No. 37.—Oli for Liliana, chanted by Mrs. Kaahaaina Naihe, Honolulu, Oahu.

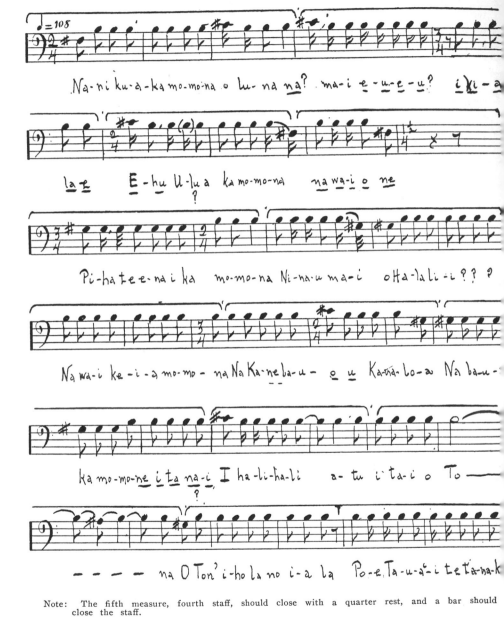

Note: The fifth measure, fourth staff, should close with a quarter rest, and a bar should close the staff.

ma-la-mai — — —i a Pi' i mi no' li mi a-wa-he (U) ho - ni - ho-

ni-ho-ni a-u a a A ke i-no a ho-ni-ho-ni o li-li-a na-ka

1

Nani kuaka momona o luna la
Ulu ia mai ka momona a koakoa
Piha ka ena i ka momona
Ninau mai o Halali'i
Na wai keia momona
Na Kane laua o Kanaloa
Na laua ko momona
I halihali aku i kai o Kona
O Kona iho la no ia la
Poe Kaua'i ke kanaka malama ia
Pi'i mai no alima i awaha
Honi la
U honihoni au la i ke inoa
Honihoni o Liliana

2

Ka momona i {Ka momona o Kiholo / paia Kona mai o Aanei
Ea Kohala ka aina i ke a'e loa
A la'i ha puluhi ke kai
Ke ho'olale maila ka wa'a e holohā
Ke keiki nanā makani
E ai Liliana i ko momona
Ma ke ehukai o neue i keawehala
Ke ho'ohalahala maila ka wai kapu
Ka wai leleopu i ke po'o o ka pali
I ka pali ka wai hui pu me ke kai a
Honi e
Honihoni ia au la
I ke inoa honihoni o Liliana

3

E ai Liliana i ka momona
A na wahine e kui nei
I ka hope ka ipu a ko momona
Na nele oe e ke kanaka makua
I ka momona ole ua lawe a nei au
Ke keiki i ka momona ua pau
Ua lohe Waipi'o mai ka uka a ke kai
I ke inoa momona o Liliana
E ai Liliana i ka momona ka'a poe
  o Ko'olou ia ala

Malama o ko laila kini
I na ilaila pau ewalu
Ewalu ho'i ka momona
Ewalu ho'i ka lihaliha ua
Piha iho nei o na pele
Ha kou hoa e ho'ohoa ia,
Honihoni, etc.

———

Ka momona o Wailoa[a] o Ko'olau
E ai Liliana i ka momona o na pu'u
E kupele ia e ka wahine
He manu ai na ke keiki
I ke kula o Āhinahina
I hina i ke a ku no aloha maoli
  honiele moe
E ai Liliana i ka momona wai o
  Wailoa
Moena haunu ole o Kekaha e
Mai Kekaha aku no a Wainana'li'i
O ke ali'i noe ko opú o ke kau ano
  ko hokua honi e
Honi e honihoni au a
A ke inoa honihoni o Liliana

———

Ne'ene'e kai a ka pipi
U pa ka'i a ka pipi
Hua ma ona no hamuana no
E hamuana i ka laupawale
I ka lau ama'uma'u
Aohe koe lau a ma'uma'u
I ke kahili a na pepeiao
A Kanekopa laua Kanaloa
Koele iho ka manea pahihi
A inoa na Liliana

———

He ai Liliana i ka momona
Moe wai Lehua i uka o ke aki
O kaia haawe pa'a kaiehu
Nana nana no ia ha'i mai
Honihoni o Liliana
I ke inoa momona o Liliana.

a Not Wailua.

No. 38.—A second rendition of No. 37, by the same performer.

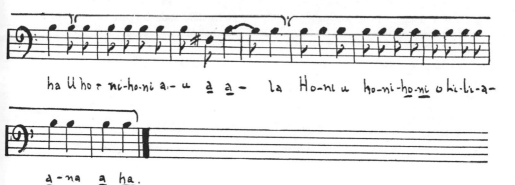

ha U ho r ni-ho-ni a.- u a̱ a̱- la Ho-ni u ho-ni-ho-ni o ki-li-a-

a̱-na a̱ ha̱.

A fragment of a *mele inoa* was also given twice by Kaahaaina. The text as sung with the music is different from that recited, and the two renditions vary considerably. The first, although slower moving, is more like the majority of olis in its melodic structure. The major third interval in the second is rather uncommon. Differences between major thirds and perfect fourths seemed not to be noticed by quite a number of informants.

No. 39.—Oli, chanted by W. M. Kalaiwaa.

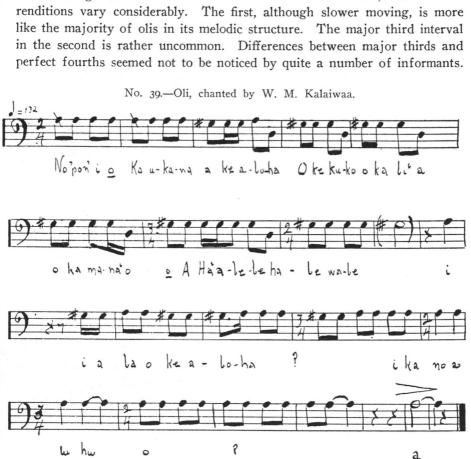

No'poni i o̱ Ka u-ka-na a ke a-lo-ha O ke ku-ko o ka li' a

o ka ma-na'o o̱ A Ha̱'a-le-le ha - le wa-le i

i a la o ke a - lo-ha ? i ka no a

lu hu o ? a

Noho pono i loko ka ukana a ke
  aloha
O ke kuko o ka li'a o ka mana'o

A ha'alele wale i Puna na hoa aloha
  e iala.

No. 40.—Another rendition of No. 39, by the same performer.

A *mele inoa* of considerable length by Kaahaaina is given here rather than with the group of *inoa* near the beginning of this section, because the singing of this informant appears to conform more closely to the hula than the oli style of chanting and as much of what she gave is imperfect or incorrect, for her advanced age made her subject to lapses, it is of doubtful importance in determining the characteristics of chants, although interesting to observe.

No. 41.—Name chant for Kamehameha III, Kauikeaouli, supposed to have originated on the island of Molokai, chanted by Mrs. Kaahaaina Naihe, Honolulu, Oahu.

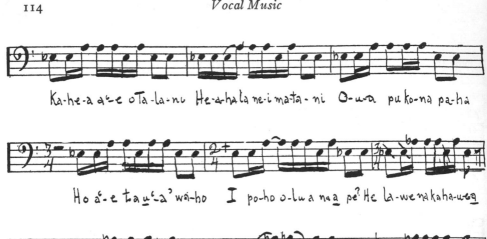

Ka-he-a a'-e o Ta-la-ni He-a-ha-la ne-i ma-ta-ni O-u-a pu-ko-na pa-ha

Ho a'-e ta u'-a' wá-ho I po-ho o-lu a naa pe? He la-we na-kaha-u-ea

Ha-u ma-ha-lire-le-e e-a. Ni-na-u e ke ki-a-lu-a Pa kimiwai-o-le-kea-ma

Le-le-kali-u o o ka wa'-a I ka lu mai-a ka ho-e Pa ka ma-ka-ni he pe-lu

U-a lo-no o a-ku la o ka-hi-ki I ke l-no-aa o Ka-la-ni He mai-'ha Ta-hi-ti e a

La-pa ma-i i-ke o kai O ka i-a la-u o ke a-ha Oka i-a la u o ka pu-hu

I la pu a-la ko i-ke Ina ha-a u-amohi-o-e Ke-i o-lo-lo Mo-ola w

The chant begins òn the lower of two tones forming the interval of a
perfect fourth, which in itself is not typical of olis. They usually start
and end on the general level. The gradual flatting is not to be considered
as significant.

The interplay between the low and the high tone is almost equal and
igves a swinging effect to the melody called by the Hawaiians *anuunuu*
(waving or vibrating). It is not at all characteristic of oli chanting. I
have marked the melodic sections for a distance to show that in substance
they are practically the same, of nearly .uniform length, and that each
covers two lines of poetry. All these features, so different from those of
the olis so far discussed, will by this very difference help the reader to
realize the nature of the true oli, very difficult to define because of numerous
little exceptions in any particular specimen, but fairly clear when a number
of examples are observed together.

This is one of the few meles which were scanned. (See p. 65.) It
was no doubt an oli which has been adapted to hulas because of its regular
structure, which may account for its having been chanted somewhat after
the hula style, but named an oli by the chanter. The regular movement
of the poetry has made impossible any but three-part meter, without strained
and unnatural treatment in delivery, but the measures reveal slight irregularities almost constantly throughout such as might creep into any sort
of a recitative. This "near regularity," together with the fact that the
meter is three-part rather than two, is another departure from the oli
style. That the chant comes from Molokai, one of the islands not investigated, adds interest.

No. 42 is a *mele uhane,* in which a human being holds conversation
with a spirit, or ghost god. The dialogue feature is rare in my collections.
The island of Oahu was peopled in Hawaiian mythology with ghost gods
who lay in wait for persons passing from Kauai to the windward islands,
captured and ate them. A legend relating to these gods is given by Fornander (56), but the story accompanying this mele is quite different:

There was an eight-headed god, known as the *Akua poowalu.* Each of his
phases displayed some terrible physical affliction. Thus there was the *Akua
kuapuu,* hunch-backed god; *Akua muumuu,* maimed god; *Akua pupule,* crazy god;
Akua makapaa, one-eyed god; *Akua makapo,* blind god; *Akua kuli,* deaf god;
Akua lolo, paralyzed god; and the *Akua oopa,* lame god.

A girl lived in Kau and the home of her parents was the only house in that
district. She was an only daughter and was bewitched by Halalii, king of evil
ones who was living in the valley of Waipio. Once the daughter confided to her
mother about her dreams of the delightful spot down in Waipio, the flowing
water, the beautiful pali towering above, the people and their fine homes. The
mother realized what lay back of the dreams and warned her daughter that she
was under the influence of Halalii and that she must forget such dreams. But

No. 42.—Mele uhane, or ghost mele, chanted in oli fashion by Mrs. Kaoulionalani of Waiakea, Hilo, Hawaii.

"Pahupahu e owai mawaho?"
"O wau no keia ke akua kuapu'u
I ki'i mai nei wau ia oe
E hele a'e kaua i ka po le'a o Halā-
    li'i."

"O ho'i a ha'i aku aole au e hiki aku
No ka mea he mau malihini ka'u
    ka hale e nonoho nei."

the daughter would not and gradually pined away, and died. The bundle of her bones was kept in the house and when her parents were there alone she came out in her spirit and talked with them and cooked for them. Some strangers came to the neighborhood and fled in terror from the house but meeting the parents were persuaded to return, assured that the ghost was only their daughter. They returned and went to the place where the bones lay and begged forgiveness of the girl, and proved that they were kahunas who could save her and bring her to life.

In the night a knocking was heard outside, and it proved to be one of the eight gods come to take her, as usual, to Halalii. But the girl had been given strength to resist by the kahunas and refused to go. The mele translated reads:

"Who knocks, oh, who knocks with-
    out?"
"'Tis I, the hunchbacked god, you
    see,
Come to fetch and carry you

To a rendezvous with Halalii."
"Return, say I may not comply
For two that are unknown to me
Within my house are sitting nigh."

All night long the gods knocked one after the other and the girl was nearly dead with terror as were the kahunas and the parents, but they held out and in the morning the spell was broken and the girl was restored to her usual form, after which she went with the kahunas into Kohala.

As the mele is chanted here, it is an oli of the type which remains almost entirely on a single tone without dropping, especially at the ends of the word phrases, to tones about a third or fourth below. The musical divisions marked by the brackets correspond with the word phrases and are uneven in length. Some might be subdivided, but the melody, if it may be so called, is such that longer sections might as well be considered to be lengthened by extensions as to be composed of two smaller sections. The second rendition by the same woman differed greatly from this but was too faint to be transcribed.

No. 43 was chanted by J. P. Hale, of Hilo, who once had the position of reviser of meles to King Kalakaua. This mele he said was not a true oli because it lacked the *"i-i"* or quaver in the voice.

In general aspect it is similar to some olis already discussed, which were slow moving. The sentiment is suitable for regular oli. Beginning with the second measure *o* is prolonged considerably and at other points throughout the chant there is playing with the vowels, which takes the place of the trill. Near the end there is a little trilling. This is very like the style of chanting hoaeae as it is done by some informants.

No. 43.—Chanted by J. P. Hale, Hilo, Hawaii, who states that it is not a true oli.

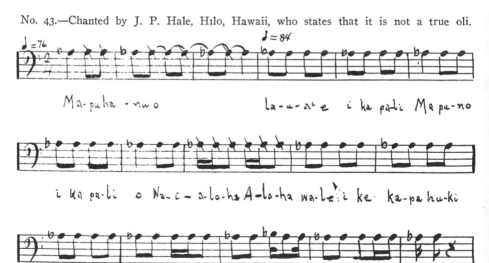

Note: The last note, third staff, should be followed by a dot.

No. 44.—A repetition of No. 43.

Ma-pu ha-nu o ka a-la-u-a-e i ka pa-li Mapu no i ka pa-li

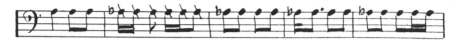

o Wa-i - a-lo-ha A-lo-ha wa-le i ke ka-pa hu-ki pa-la-i Pa-la

i ka hw-ki le-o le-a Kū ka o A-la-ka-i I no-e-no-e A

wa-le i   ma-i no e ka le-hu-a ma ka-no-e wi-wo i ke-a-nu

Mapu ka hanu o ka laua'e i ka pali	Anu aku la i ke alanui kuilima kana-
Mapu no i ka pali o Waialoha	ka o Maunahina e
Aloha wale i ke kapa huki palai	E hina ho'okahi ia la ho'i owau
Palai ka huli leo le'a i ka uka o	wale no
Alaka'i	E hihina pu a'eno kaua i ka ahanui
Noenoe wale mai no ka lehua maka-	Ua ike a.
noe wiwo i ke anu	

The second rendition, which after a few lines was too faint to transcribe, lacks the hoaeae characteristics and is different in other small particulars from the first, but the identity in pitch of the first three measures of No. 43 and the first two in No. 44, and again in the measures in which the word "aloha" appears, is very unusual and shows that at least with this singer the smaller intervals could be reproduced exactly from time to time.

The Hoaeae and Hoouweuwe

The hoaeae and hoouweuwe are the best examples of Hawaiian chants which directly express emotion by the quality and manipulation of the voice, although nothing in their tunes makes an appeal to the foreign ear.

Several informants state that the hoaeae is a form of chanting to be used only for love meles. The hoouweuwe is a wailing chant. The word hoaeae means to cause to *aeae,* this being the onomatopoetic term for the sound of the voice as it lingers over the vowels occurring in the final syllable of the couplet and prolongs them with a passage similar to a trill. Thus the hoaeae chanting is distinguished from the plain oli in being interrupted at more or less regular intervals by periods of prolonged vowel sounds, for if such a passage occurs at all in the plain oli, it is properly at the end, and it has been demonstrated this is by no means an invariable condition.

Many Hawaiians confuse the hoaeae and the hoouweuwe or say that they are the same. Others state that the hoouweuwe goes further than the hoaeae and in addition to using the protracted vowels converts them from the rather lilting sound of the hoaeae into the most doleful wailing, the effect of which on the auditors causes them to weep in sympathy.

It will be recalled that two of my questions to Kalaiwaa were concerning the difference between the two kinds of chants, and the oli. These were his answers:

4. The difference between the oli and the hoaeae is that the hoaeae hangs on to the last of the line but in the oli the going is smooth and soft.

5. The difference between the hoaeae and the hoouweuwe is that the hoaeae is light and the hoouweuwe is heavy. Sometimes the one who does the hoaeae has a heavier voice and it sounds very much like the hoouweuwe and the listeners cry.

It may readily be seen that these distinctions of voice quality are very subtle and not easily to be conveyed except with the demonstration of actual hearing. I was not fortunate enough to obtain many specimens of the hoouweuwe for there is a natural feeling of reluctance to chant in this manner without cause. One or two persons were prevailed upon to give wailing chants and my impression as I heard them was that not only at the places where the vowels were prolonged, but even more in the enunciation of the words, there was the very real effect of weeping. The *mele kanikau* and others of that description are chanted in hoouweuwe fashion. In order to observe better the features of these chants and to clearly distinguish between them, if that may be accomplished, examples of them will be discussed separately.

The hoaeae.—The late Mr. S. Kekoowai, an old Hawaiian resident of Honolulu, who chanted regularly at the meetings of the Daughters of Hawaii Society, endeavored to explain the principle of the hoaeae method of chanting and gave the following illustration:

No. 45.—Type of oli called hoaeae, chanted by Sam Kekoowai, Honolulu, Oahu. (Incomplete.)

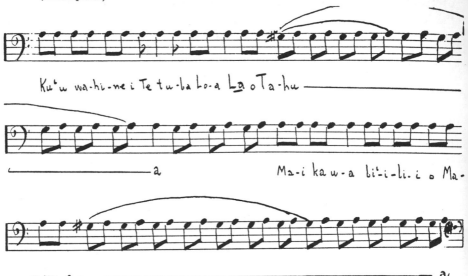

Ku'u wahine i ke kula loa o Kahu'a
Mai ka ua li'ili'i' o Manoa
Ke lihau mai la i ke oho o ke kukui
I kuhi no au he ehu kai no Mamala
He aina i kaihu o na moku
A moku mai ka pawa o ke au a la
     e o e

E ala a'e kaua ua ao e a
Ua puka ka la puka ke kanawai
A puka mai no he mea hilahila
I kaulana ai na lehua i Nu'uanu
A he wahi aloha no moe i ke anu
     ke ahi ke kapa
            (Unfinished)

The two lines as chanted were supposed each to represent the ending of a couplet. The properly constructed mele hoaeae should be capable of being divided into couplets, the lines of which should be of about equal length. The final vowel of the final word in the couplet whether it is *a, e, i, o,* or *u,* should be trilled, but it was permissible to substitute *a* or *e* for the other vowels thus producing the sounds which gave the style of chanting its name.

Two renditions of a hoaeae by Kekoowai are given in Nos. 46 and 47 and reveal the usual range of variation which seems to attend the performances of single individuals.

It is worthy of note that the lower tones occurring twice in the first line of the music differ by a whole step in the two renditions; that is, in the first case the interval created is a minor third and in the other it is a perfect fourth. An analysis of the tonal content of both renditions shows that in the first and third parts of the chant in the first rendition the minor third is used, while in the middle part the perfect fourth is substituted.

No. 46.—Oli for Queen Kaahumanu, chanted by Sam Kekoowai, Honolulu, Oahu.

Note: In fourth staff for *f* read *f♯*.

No. 47.—Another rendition of No. 46, by the same singer..

Ka manu kóa'e hulu ma'ema'e keawe	Ka'a ālapalapa i ke one o Luhi
O Keawe ke ka'upu lele kauahua	E luhi oe aua nei i ka moe
Ka iu uli, ka pueo hoanoano	Ina ke aloha la he ai liliha
Nana e popo'i keaewa o ka lani	Ua ike a—
Me kalani nei no a nei ka nui o ke	Lihaliha i ke ho'olua ke kini o Puna
aloha	Pāku'iku'i i ka momona a ke kiu
Pela no ka mana'o ke hiki mai	Ina kohi kelekele a ka pu'ukolu
Ua ike a—	A ka málualua makani mai lalo
————	Nana e ka'a ka laulá o Kapa'a
Ike i ka wai ula iliahi o Waimea	Ka nani o ke kalukalu o Kewá e
He wai ula na ke kiu waiahulu	Awawá ia no he hale kanaka
Ke oko ala i ka poli o ka pohaku	Nawai ewawá ka hale kanaka ole
Me he hina ma'i ala i ka houpo o ke	Ua ike a.
kai	

In the first part of the second rendition the perfect fourth obtains in all but one case; in the middle section both intervals are employed and in the third part likewise. The principle of the hoaeae is very nicely demonstrated and there is an undoubted introduction of intervals finer than a half step in the trills. These are quite common in the first rendition but appear only in the final trill of the second. There is no consistent order revealed in their use by a comparison of one trill passage with another, or of the second rendition with the first.

No further examples of hoaeae chanting were obtained on Oahu but on Hawaii the specimens collected seemed to have purely individual peculiarities which roughly conform to the general description given.

The first man interviewed could recall but one couplet of a hoaeae and demurred at giving so little of the chant, but was finally induced to sing what he did know over and over again, in the same way and without interruption, that I might hear how the hoaeae was done. He gave the first couplet three times in the phonograph and it is produced here not only to show his method, but also because this is one of the few cases where three renditions of a very short section of music were secured from the same individual in rapid succession. Being short, they should have a closer identity than they do, were minor differences in chanting considered of any importance. A somewhat fuller text of this chant was supplied by a very old woman of Kailua, Hawaii.

No. 48.—Three renditions of the first couplet of a hoaeae, given by Peter Kaawa, Kalaoa, North Kona, Hawaii.

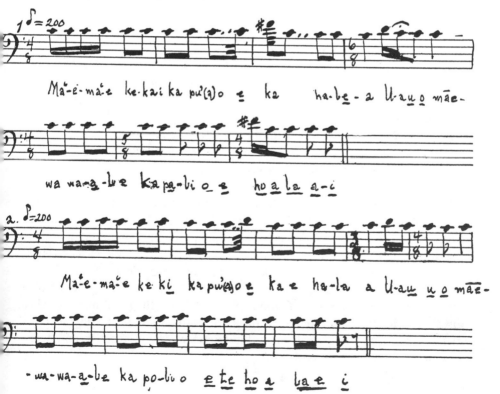

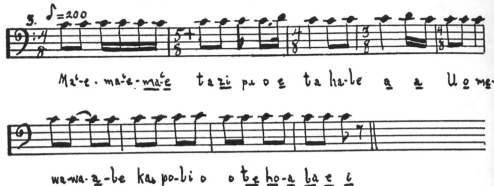

Note: In the second measure of the first staff, the third note should be dotted.

Ma'ema'e i ke kai ka pua o ka hala
Ua maewa wale i ka poli o Kahiwa
He hiwahiwa lipolipo o Papalauahi
Ka nani hemolele a ku'u mea aloha
     i ona

Hele oe aohe hala a ke kīopua
O ka nawe malie wale no a hiki i
     Haihala
Heaha ka'u hala nui ia oe e ke aloha
     (Incomplete)

I think that this little example proves perhaps better than all the rest, how flexible the chants are, not only in the music but in the poetry which governs it. As one old Hawaiian put it, "The beauty of the mele is that you must know the theme," and evidently knowing the theme, or the thought, it did not make very much difference if words or lines were changed now and then, or the voice varied so long as the general effect was obtained. As to text, a chanter would be apt to adhere closely to that version which had been taught him, but I have many examples of variants from different localities in which there are changes in vocabulary and not a few which have wide differences in ideas, although many very old chants are surprisingly uniform, even from island to island. One mele given by two Hawaiian scholars living near one another was identical for the two versions except for a single word. The second scholar, Reverend Stephen Desha, reviewing the contribution of the first, Judge Simon Haaheo, discovered it, and remarked that the two words were practically identical in sense but that the one given by his friend was now obsolete and therefore probably more correct.

A hoaeae chant by Kalaiwaa has very little of the trilling prescribed by Kekoowai. Nevertheless, its features conform to the hoaeae design. The place of the trilling is taken by prolonged vowels sounded in most cases with one rising and falling of tone. These are found, not regularly at the end of couplets, but more often at the end of each line.

No. 49.—Hoaeae, Nalu of Kalakaua, chanted by W. M. Kalaiwaa, Kamuela, South Kohala, Hawaii. (Incomplete.)

Note: The second measure, fourth staff, should close with an eighth rest.

Ku'u aloha la, ku'u aloha
Ku'u aloha i ka pua o ka ōhāwai
Oia pua luhe wale mai no i ka nahele
He nahele aloha na'u ke ala me ke
onaona
Onaona ia pua ke pili mai owau ke
hoa
Hai amu ka manu i ka pua o ka
mamane
Akahi au a ike i ka ino o Hilo
Ke huea mai la na piha á moe wai
o uka
Ke heluheluia mai la e ka ua na
manowai

Ne'e papa ke helu a ka la i Punahoa
He hoa no oe no'u i ka pua o ke
aali'i
He 'li'i no oe he hiwahiwa na ka
punohu ula
He milimili ho'i au na Panaewa
He nui oko'a no na ka ua kanilehua
Makemake wale au e ike ia Waiakaea
I ka mimiki a ke au ko i Halaea
Mimiki no ka ua lawe no ka makani
Homai ho'i ka uahi ua anu au
(Incomplete)

This chant is more like a hula in tonal content, for aside from the general prominence of the note *a* which establishes the level and is like a tonic, the fifth and third of this fundamental in inverted position are also stressed, while the second above it as a changing note adds to the melodic fullness. A careful perusal of the music will reveal its features in the light of discussions which have already been made. The musical divisions differ in length, each corresponding to a line of poetry. Most of them end in a similar manner.

Two chants to Ļaka and Kapo, already mentioned as patron deities of the hula, which were obtained on Hawaii, are puzzling as to classification because their form is roughly that of the hoaeae although the protracted vowels occur for the first time only after the fifth line in both cases. The one for Kapo was simply called an oli, and the other, of which there are two versions, was termed a hula although it does not resemble such tunes. In this case the informant may not have been clear in her distinction between an oli to Ļaka for the hula and the method of chanting itself, which I may have noted mistakenly. Chants made to deities were always given oli fashion.

No. 50.—Oli for the goddess Ļaka, chanted by J. S. Kiaha, Kohanaiki, North Kona, Hawaii.

Noho ana Kapo i ka ulu wehiwehi
Iluna o Moalae
Ohi 'a-ku ku ia i Maunaloa
Aloha mai kaulana-ula

Eia mai ka ula la, he ula leo
He kanaenae ia oe e Laka
Ho'oulu ia eia no ka uku o ka leo.

No. 51.—Called by the performer a mele hula to the goddess Laka, but certainly an oli. Chanted by Mrs. Kawaimakaonalii Hao, Kalaoa, North Kona, Hawaii.

Note: The fourth note, first measure, last staff, should be dotted.

(A)-lo-' ma-i Tau-la-na-u-la-'i-a ma' i-a ma-i ta u-la la
he u-la le' i e e e i e i a He u-la i ta-
na-e-na-e a-lo-ha na'-u i-a o-e E La-e-ta-e E
ma-li-u ma e-a-e-i a-e a' e i a e a ? E ma-li-u mai
o-e a a-e mai o-e po-no'' i au a e a e a e

Noho ana Laka i ka ulu wehiwehi　　He kanaenae aloha na'u ia oe
Ku ana iluna o Mo'ohelaia　　　　　E Laka e
Ka Ohi'a-ku iluna o Maunaloa　　　E maliu mai oe a a'e mai oe
Aloha mai a'u kaulana-ula　　　　　A pono ho'i au a.
Eia mai ka ula la he ula leo

No. 52.—A repetition of No. 51.

An examination of the two chants has influenced me to classify them with the hoaeae meles. They will readily be seen to possess roughly the features of this kind of chanting if they are compared with the positively identified specimens. The music divisions of No. 50, if attempted without consulting the texts, might be differently marked, but as their boundaries prior to the appearance of the first rest are principally a matter of arbitrary selection, it is necessary to fall back on the texts for a decision. The breath taking at the end of each phrase causes a measure of three-part meter in nearly every instance, following a comparatively long succession of two-part meter.

In poetic content, No. 50 is almost identical with Nos. 51 and 52. The one is addressed to Kapo, the others to Laka, but it is quite evident that in either No. 50 or Nos. 51 and 52 the poetic idea was borrowed. These meles should be compared with Emerson's versions (43, pp. 44, 33). Nos. 51 and 52 also resemble the hoaeae but the method of trilling is different. Rhythmically as well as melodically there are the usual variations between the two renditions of the Laka chant. The second rendition was interrupted at the end of the record but enough is given to illustrate this point. Its reduced tonal content as compared with the first might be taken to indicate that the steadier tone was the singer's ideal. Often nervousness is the cause of a poor first rendition, and as the singer gains confidence the quality of his work improves.

The hoaeae chants from Kauai each reveal individual features but all have the lines of recitative interrupted by passages of prolonged vowels.

No. 53.—Famous old oli belonging to the old chiefs, chanted hoaeae fashion by Mrs. Lucy Kapohaialii Kaili, Honolulu, Oahu.

Ike ia Kaukini he lawai'a manu
He upena ku'u i ka noe ko Pokahi
Ua ho'opuni a'e la i ka ohu ka
    kikepa
Ke na'i la i luna o Kaauwana

Ka uahi noe ke kapeku e hei ai ka
    ia manu Pu'oali'i
O ke 'li'i wale no, ka'u makemake
O ka luhi o maua me ia nei
O ka makou le'ale'a no ia
Ua ike a.

This chant is different in having a long trill passage almost at the beginning, after which several lines are recited before there is another. At the end of three more lines there is a third trill, and almost immediately following, a fourth. The first three show some very interesting and consistent uses of microtones. This consistency is scarcely matched by any other chanter. For the sake of comparison, I have inserted here the same chant sung by one of her fellow-townsmen, as he said, oli fashion, but the evidences of hoaeae are plainly visible in the series of tied notes. This man's accents were too faint to make the insertion of measure bars anything but guesswork except in one or two cases. A comparison of the two examples shows that Mrs. Kaili was an adept at her art beside which the second example is but a vague outline. Many people who chanted for me, including this second singer, offered as excuses for not singing the fact

No. 54.—Same oli as No. 53, chanted by Aiamanu Pauole, Hanalei, Kauai.

that they had but picked up the knowledge of chanting. Aiamanu Pauole was not a chanter with training but he knew some meles which he consented to sing into the phonograph after much urging. Although his rendition was not a finished piece of work it is valuable as a contrast with one which is.

Another hoaeae by Mrs. Kaili, No. 55, instead of prolonging the final vowel sound of the line, carries it over a brief interval only, and then substitutes the regular refrain, *"uoki e."* This comes at the end of every line rather than at the end of each couplet and is accompanied by one of three melodic motifs. The music may be divided into sections, two to each line of poetry except for the last pair. It should be noticed how the breathing period atones for the short phrase at the end of the second line of the music. Such a mele, I was told, might be called *Uoki* from the number of times this phrase is used.

No. 55.—Hoaeae for Nahienaena, chanted by Mrs. Lucy Kapohaialii Kaili, Honolulu, Oahu.

Ho‘i au e pili me Ka‘uiki, uoki—e—
He nanahe upalu no ko laila kini,
　　　uoki—e—
E aka hele mai oe makana ia kaua,
　　　uoki—e—
　　　A uoki—e—

Heaha ka hana a kauka‘opua, uoki e—
Pahe‘e, pakika kaua i ka welowelo,
　　　uoki—e—
Ilaila ho‘ohihi ka mana‘o, uoki—e—
Hoeu na Honoaopi‘ilani, uoki—e—
　　　A uoki—e—

The hoouweuwe.—Two renditions of a famous chant which originally came from Hawaii were obtained on Kauai from two different singers living in rather widely separated localities.

No. 56.—Hoaeae from the island of Hawaii, chanted by Waiwaiole Kala, Kapaa, Kauai.

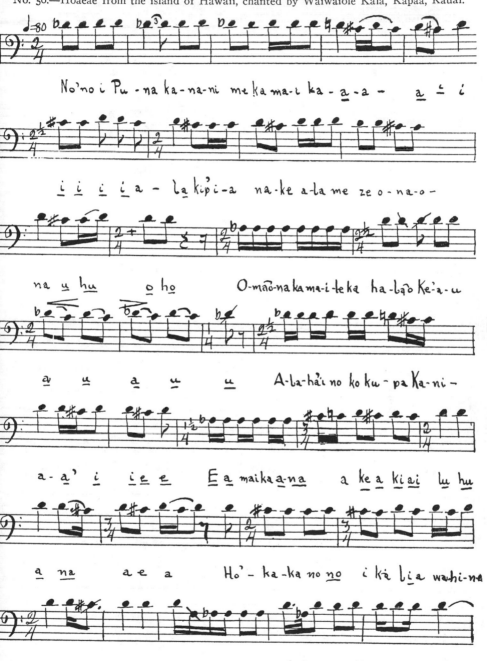

No'no i Pu-na ka-na-ni me ka ma-i ka-a-a-   a ¯ i

i i i i a - la kipi-a na-ke a-la me ze o-na-o-

na u hu   o ho   O-mao-na ka ma-i te ka ha-lao Ke'a-u

a   u   a   u   u   A-la-hai no ko ku - pa Ka-ni -

a-a' i   i e e   E a maika a-na   a ke a ki ai lu hu

a na   ae a   Ho'- ka-ka no no i ka lia wahi-na

za-a-a   a-pu Pu-a-pu-a'i mai no belo wa-hi-a a za ma-ka

Note: In third staff, last measure, read d♭. In fifth staff, the first measure should have the time signature 2/4, the second measure should have the time signature 2½/4 and close with a quarter rest.

No. 57.—Hoouweuwe from **Puna**, Hawaii, chanted by Mrs. Koiahi, Hanalei, Kauai. (Incomplete.)

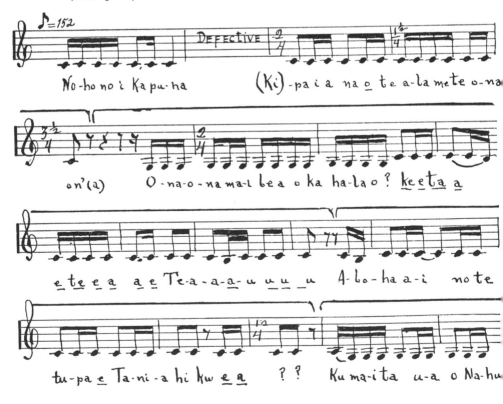

Note: The last two notes in the third measure, staff three; and the first two in the fifth measure, staff four, should be sixteenth notes.

Noho no i Puna ka nani me ka
maika'i
He hale kipa ia na ke ala me ke
onaona
Onaona ka maile ka hala o Kea'au
Aloha ai no ke kupa Kaniahiku
Ku [ea] mai la ka ua o Nahunahu
ki'eki'e i luna
Ho'okakano lua i ka la'i o Wahine-
kapu
Puapua'i mai la na { leo awahia
{ olelo

a ka { manu
{ makani
Na kauna olelo a ka pu'ulena i ka
uka
Kaka'o ka waha o ka ua nahua i ka
nahele
I ka i mai no ua lilo o Omaolala ia
Panaewa
Heaha no ka hewa ke ai ia ka'u
hakina
He po'o maunu ia na'u i ai a kau i
ka **laau**

Ua pau mai la i ka makapehu o ka
uka
Ia kini noho nahele noho pololi Ola'a
Mana'o a'e ke ola i ka hakina pua ai
a ka manu
He koena ia na ka naulu i ai a
ha'alele
Ke pane mai la e howawa, ke koena
waianuhea
Peulaka u ka hauanu a ka Waiapo
O ka'u hana akamai loa ia o ke
konane

He helu ekahi au i ka pulapu i lono
oe
O oe no ka ole he mauka uka e'e
pakeke
He sela oe no mua he huki kaula kau
hana
He pulumi oneki oe no ka papahele
Owau mai no ka haku ka ona e ko'u
waiwai
A he wahi aloha, no puia
I ke onaona ka paia o Puna

The first, No. 56, has the prolonged vowel period at the end of each line of the poetry, accompanied by a rather slow rising and falling of the pitch, like a trill but not fast enough. This chant was called a hoaeae.

The second, No. 57, really moves a little slower than the first and was given as a mele hoouweuwe. It is unfortunate that the first part of this record was defective, but the latter part of the chant has the same underlying principle as the hoaeae. The vowel periods are at the end of each line of poetry as in the first rendition. A slight preponderance of *o* and *u* sounds over *a* and *e* or *i* changes the style and it must be admitted that these two sounds give a much more mournful impression. The two renditions have about the same kind and degree of differences that mark successive performances of an individual. The presence of some trills which are inverted in position as compared to others in this and in those chants already given, is very exceptional.

A mele from Hawaii designated by Mr. Kalaiwaa as a *kanikau* has the features of a hoaeae in modified form and was said by him to be either a hoaeae or a hoouweuwe. It resembles No. 54 in substituting tied notes for trills.

No. 58.—Kanikau for Kahahana, chanted by W. M. Kalaiwaa, Kamuela, South Kohala, Hawaii. (Incomplete.)

Pili-lua oe o hele lua i Ewa [3]
O ka hele oe a Kaʻulani
O ka awili kolo o lua ia lua mea
O mea wale ia iho i ke kula e
O ka ōneanea i ka wai lele
Nolaila ka o Kahápuʻukolo
O ka pahu i loko o Kekeleiaiku

He malama no o Hikileiakaakaleʻa

Ohionaloli o ka maka o Kemilia
O hiki naʻuele o naʻuele kona lua e
Elua ka laua i ka moana
Oia kai ke awalau i Puʻuloa
I luna o Waakai o Lohiolani
E i lau hoe ia ai Kalani
Oia ka iluna i ka pola waʻa e
Kupu maikaʻi Leahi i ka malie
I aea ke kai a moku o koa

[3] This mele was published in Na Mele Aimoku, the collection of King Kalakaua, pp. 233-241, Honolulu, 1886.

SUMMARY

I have attempted by this series of examples to show, as clearly as may be considering the great range of variability, the difference between the plain oli, the hoaeae, and the hoouweuwe. Not a single example of the *mele kuo* was found. The opinion has been given that Andrews was mistaken in including *kuo* as a separate class and that they were the same as hoaeae and hoouweuwe. The dictionary defines *kuo* as weeping for joy, or crying with a loud voice.

Mr. Kalaiwaa in answer to my question (p. 94) as to what was a *mele kuo* and for what would such chanting be used, replied: "It is probably done when they are chanting the wailing mele. At the end they say *'kuo.'*" Taking it for granted that he was right in his assumption he continued that there were three kinds of *mele kuo* used on different occasions: (1) When any of the family had gone away and returned after a long time they all chanted and cried at the same time. That was when the family cried loudly and chanted the mele for the person that had just returned; (2) if anyone died in the family, man, woman, child, grandparent, grandchild, then there was reciting and crying; (3) when a couple had lived together and one passed away and the other was left, then even after a long time, when love arose within one like a flood, then the one who was left would begin to wail and chant as if the loved one were present, even though he had long been gone.

A tabulation of the tonal content of thirty-nine olis, given in figure 3, brings out one or two striking points.

FIGURE 3.—Tonal content of hulas. The numbers of the examples correspond with the numbers of the songs given in more complete form on pages 77-147, examples not numbered are from songs not otherwise reproduced. The slurs indicate that the examples connected are different versions of the same song. The names of the informants indicated by number are as follows: (1) Peter and Mrs. Kaawa, Kalaoa, North Kona, Hawaii; (5) Mrs. Kawaimakaonalii Hao, Kalaoa, North Kona, Hawaii; (11) Mrs. Becky Kawaa, Honolulu, Oahu; (12) Kalani Ku Kama, Waiakea Homesteads, Hilo, Hawaii; (13) Mrs. Koleka Naia, Kailua, North Kona, Hawaii; (14) Mrs. L. P. Kahema, Hilo, Hawaii; (15) W. M. Kalaiwaa, Kamuela, South Kohala, Hawaii; (16) Mrs. Kaahaaina Naihe, Honolulu, Oahu; (17) Mrs. Kaoulionalani, Waiakea, Hilo, Hawaii; (18) J. P. Hale, Hilo, Hawaii; (19) Sam Kekoowai, Honolulu, Oahu; (20) J. S. Kiaha, Kohanaiki, North Kona, Hawaii; (21) Mrs. Lucy Kapohaialii Kaili, Honolulu, Oahu; (22) Aiamanu Pauole, Hanalei, Kauai; (23) Waiwaiole Kala, Kapaa, Kauai; (24) Mrs. Koiahi, Hanalei Valley, Kauai; (26) Kainoa Kawelu, Waiohinu, Kau, Hawaii; (28) Solomono Huihui, Honolulu, Oahu; (43) Mrs. Kaluaikapahukapu, Kailua, North Kona, Hawaii.

All the chants, regardless of whether they are plain oli, hoaeae or hoouweuwe have one principal tone, which in frequency and emphasis is at least five or six times as prominent as the most frequently used of the remaining tones. I have roughly represented these values by different notes. The whole notes are the most prominent in the chant and constitute the general level.

In a few chants (like Nos. 24, 41, 37, 46, 47) a gradual shifting of pitch occurred while practically the same interval structure was maintained. The tonal content of these chants has been represented by a series of measures with dotted instead of full measure bars and the notes in any one of the measures represent the tonal content for a part of the song. The tonal variation is apt to be so great between two renditions of the same chant by the same singer (as for instance, between No. 26 and No. 27, or between No. 51 and No. 52), that one is hardly justified in attempting to say which of the tones actually struck in a chant, except the general level and notes of large denomination, are intentional and which are accidental deflections. Other chants which are the same but sung by different singers, together with these just mentioned, are represented in the figure by being connected by slurs.

Disregarding the tonal shifts which seem to be due entirely to a tendency to flat, which is not confined to Hawaiians but is generally common, all but nine chants have, in addition to the outstanding tone, another ranging in different cases from a minor third to a fifth below it, which, on account of its prominence, deserves to be considered as having a definite melodic connection with the principal tone and to be a structural rather than an embellishing note in the melody. This feature of a principal and a secondary tone is common to both plain oli and hoaeae so that the presence of the lower tone may not be taken as characteristic of either type. Its employment depends apparently on the individual preference of the chanters. The variation of the lower tone in its relation to the upper, which is evident in a single chant or from chant to chant, is also either a matter of whim, or of indifference, showing that an interval of a perfect fourth or major or minor third was not clearly established or differentiated in the minds of the people. The same tendency to variation appears in different renditions of the same chant by the same singer. The stressing in chanting of two tones which lie a third or fourth apart may have had some ancient connection with the prevalent tuning of the two-stringed *ukeke,* for the lower of the two notes in by far the greater number of the olis also stands in the relation of a perfect fourth to the upper, which assumes the character of a tonic, but others ranging around the lower note to a distance of a whole step either way, or even further removed, are occasionally found. It is important to note that the "tonic" lies uppermost, thus giving the definite impression of a scale built downward, not upward, from a fundamental.

There are, in addition, some notes which cluster around the "tonic" like satellites attracted to it. Many of them are less than half-step deflections, particularly those used in trills, others lie a whole or half step from it and come into play usually as changing or grace notes and are constantly varied by the singer. Two, however, which are more frequently encountered, not only in the different renditions of a single chant but in various ones, are the whole step above the general level and the half step below, or in

European musical terminology, the major second or super-tonic and the seventh or leading tone.

Roughly speaking then, there are two groups of tones in the chants, which in some overlap. One group lies around the general level and one around the fourth below it. Between the groups there is some play, by selecting tones from either; but the most play occurs between the tones within the upper group, with an occasional selection of one of the tones of the lower group by way of complement or contrast. There is not much play between the individual tones of the lower group.

These are loose descriptions and there are exceptions to all of these statements, but they fit the general situation and are the best that can be given in view of the great fluctuation in performance and the poverty of melodic design which renders the distinction between structural and embellishing features exceedingly difficult and even arbitrary at times.

That intervals smaller than those employed in European music, namely microtones, were used in these chants and appreciated for their effect has been shown from examples where something like a consistent appearance of them may be discerned, but that they are part of an established scale about which there was even the vaguest philosophy, or that their use was ever a matter of exact determination, mechanically, I was assured of the contrary. Other evidence shows that the Hawaiians were only on the threshold of fixed melody aside from the fundamental and its lower dominant. This matter will be taken up again in the final conclusions of the report where its importance for various considerations will be discussed.

An examination of the tabulations in figure 3 in connection with the examples from which they were drawn will give a far better conception of the problem than pages of description. The tabulations have been grouped according to performers, that it might be possible to observe any personal preference in the choice of tones, or any local styles, since they had previously been studied for differences for the three types of chanting. I think, however, that there is nothing to be determined in this direction.

The choice of pitch level of the chants is rather limited in view of the wide range of lower tones possible for men's voices or higher tones for women's.

The greatest range selected for any one chant is in two chants by Kalaiwaa, Nos. 31 and 49, and in one by Kalani Ku, No. 25. The predominating range of any chant, if it may be called such when it covers only the principal tones, is not more than a fifth and generally less.

Twenty-one olis begin and end on the general level, twelve begin but do not end on it, and three end but do not start there. Three start a perfect fourth below, or on the lower dominant, and one a major third below.

The single beat appears to be uppermost in consciousness. In many passages the fixing of the measure bar was extremely difficult and in some cases impossible, so even was the flow of sound in single beats. The impression was gained that two- or four-part meter, the most conspicuous, has come about in the manner similar to that which gave rise to the expression *"tick tock"*—the outgrowth of the demand for variation in monotony— while variations beyond this regular alternation are largely due to the natural accent of words rather than to an appreciation of meter for its own sake. However, one or two meles with considerable three-part meter show that this time was not unfamiliar, although probably it had hardly reached the point where it was recognized for what it is.

In the matter of direct attack in the beginning of an oli, the word accents undoubtedly have some influence, but many words begin with light syllables. It is therefore worth noting that of thirty-four examples only five begin on unaccented portions of beats or on weak beats. In one such case the second rendition of the chant begins with an accented beat.

The complicated rhythms of olis, about which so much has been said, as it has in the case of much American Indian music, are really, I believe, in one sense not complicated at all. They have not been appreciated or studied by their users apart from the text and there is little evidence of more than the simplest play with them. They are merely the transferred rhythms of speech more or less whimsically treated. To prove that any language may be based on a certain set of general laws of rhythm would, naturally, require a much firmer grasp of its principles, with sufficient time to examine quantities of texts, than it would be possible to accomplish in this study of Hawaiian music. The music in itself appears to reveal only the roughest general patterns in the olis, and the simplest rhythmic structures in the hulas, for the Hawaiians were, evidently, only at the beginning of the abstract study of rhythms, not on the heights.

MODERN OLIS

A few olis which are confessedly modern are not distinguishable from more ancient types, as far as chanting is concerned, nor in their poetry, except for the use of modern terms. They are given here without comment merely for purposes of comparison, and are but further proof of the fidelity of a people to the customs of their ancestors, even in the face of more than a century of friendly invasion bringing with it much that they have cared to adopt.

No. 59.—Chant for Kalakaua, recited by Kapeliela Malani, Kawaihaeuka, South Kohala, Hawaii.

No. 60.—Same as No. 59, and by the same chanter.

He ha-le o Mau-i o e   Ta-ma'E ta-hu-a Lai-na He tu mu no e tha-le O

ha-le tu mu-i-ta-la-ni Ta pu-ka o na ha-le Ta-ho-no'na mae tu E ho-a-e-ta no

i ta ha-le   Ho- a-ta   o e ta e po-u-ha-na Ha-wa-i'i ma e ta hi-

ki-na He ta-ba-tu-a o Hi-lo a-me Wa-i-a-e-te-a   E au-h'u-ar-ne va

Mo-e-ta-u-le l'(e) He-le ma-i tha la me ta la-hu-a E ki-ite a-li-i me

ta-ma-ma-ne Ho-a-hu ta na-he-le o Pa-i-e- i- e E a-to   i ta mi-lo ho-lu

Wai-a-e-ta-e-a l Ia la-u e te-e té té te-we-me Ko a-u te ta u-e ta e

Note: In staff two, third measure, also in staff six, third measure, read f#. The last two notes in second measure, staff three, should appear as sixteenth notes.

Eo i ko'i-no-a e Ta-le-ta-ua e o e — — e eo — o

No. 61.—Same as No. 59, and by the same performer.

(Note: The first part is a doubtful transcription as the record was faulty, but from the metronome mark at 108, the transcription is definitely correct.)

He ha-le o Mau-i o e Ta-ma'Eta hu-a Lā-i-na Hetu-mu noe ta ha- le O

ha-le tu-mu-i- ta-la-ni Ta pu-ka o na ha-le Ta ho-o na mo e (tu) E'o-

a-e-ta no i ta-ha-le A'o a a a a a-e-ta-e pou-ha-na Hawai-i ma etahi -

ki-na He ta-la-e-tu-a o Hil'(o)' me Wai-a-e-t-a Ea-u-hu a-

na i-a Mo-e-ta-u- le-le He-le ma-i ka ka ha-la me ka-le-hu E

ti'te a-a-li-i me ta ma-ma-ne Ho a-e'ka-na-he-le o Pa-i e-i - e

E a -to i ta mi- lo ho- lu Wai-a -te-e -a I-a la-u-e a .e e

E o i to'i -no-a -e Ta-la-e-tau e — — —

He hale o Maui o Kama	He kalakua o Hilo ame Waiakea
He kahua o Lahaina	E auhau ana ia Mokaulele
He kumu no ka hale	Hele mai ka hala me ka lehua
O hale kumukalani	E ki'i ke aali'i me ka mamane
Ka puka o ka hale	Ho ahu ka nahele o Paieie
Ka hono o na moku	E ako i ka milo holu Waiakea
E hoaka no i ka hale	Ia laua keké ke kuene
A aho aka e pouhana Hawai'i ma ka hikina	E o mai oe i kou inoa, e Kalakaua

No. 62.—Oli chanted by Mrs. Kawaimakaonalii Hao, Kalaoa, North Kona, Hawaii.

Ma-i Pu-na a-u i he le me-i i ne-i O ta u-a pa-ka-ka-hi

o ta u-a pa-ta-lu-a O tu-lu o Ma-he-a-la-ni ho-a le-le

ho-i o teta-i li-to Po-ki-i o teta-i ma lin(o) Ho-mai

ho-mai u a a e i a-e-i i i a i na e-tu-a

e a e a e e E-i Ho-no-lu-l(u) ku-u po-ha-e-

ku Ke-a- lo-hi-la-ni-ku-u ha-ku i-a (Pun) -i-a

ho-i a leo e ta ma-nu a-e a e ta le-o a

e a ta mo-a-nu—

Mai Puna au i hele mai nei
O ka ua paka-kahi o ka ua paka-lua
O kulu o Mahealani o hoa hele ho'i
 o ke kai liko

Poki'i o ke kai malino
Homai homai i ai na akua

No. 63.—Repetition of No. 62, by the same performer.

Ma-i Pu-na a a i a a i he-le ma-i nei O ka u-a paka-kahi

o ka u-a paka-a-lu-a O ku-lu o Ma-he-a la-ni

ho-a he-le ho-i o ke ka-i Li-ko Po-ki-i o ke ka-i m line

Ho-mai ho-ma-i lu-na a-i a e a a e a a e a a

i a-i na-a- ku-a a e a a

No. 64.—A chant sung by Kainoa Kawelu, Waiohinu, Kau, Hawaii, for his sister.

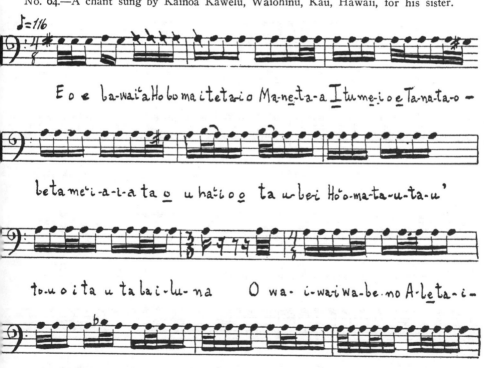

E o e la-wai'a Ho bo ma i te ta i o Ma-ne-ta-a I tu-me-i o e Ta-na-ta-o –

be ta me'i-a-i-a ta o u ha'i o o ta u-bei Hö'o-ma-ta-u-ta-u'

to-u o i ta u ta lai-lu-na   O wa- i-wai wa-be no A-le-ta-i-

hu-i te tu-pa a-i O e te ti'ö o Hai-li-la-ni te-i te tu-a-i-a-to O wai-uo Lu-mahe-i

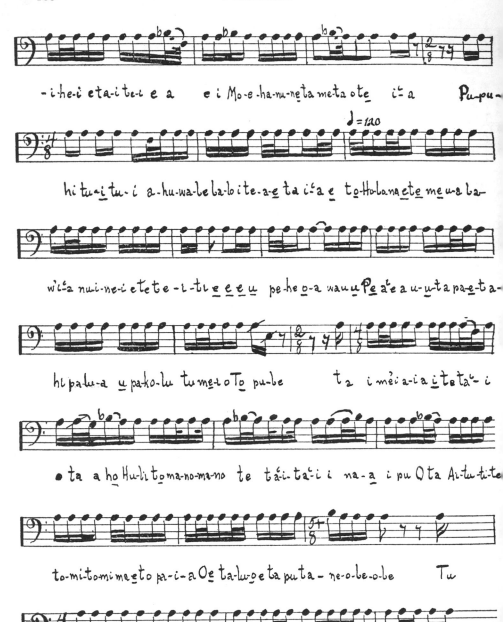

-i-he-i eta-i-tu-i e a   e i Mo-e-ha-nu-nе̣ta meta ote   i⁼a   Pu-pu-

𝄽=120

hi tu-i tu- i a-hu-wa-le la-lo i te-a e ta i⁼a e to Holana ete me wa la-

w⁼i⁼a nui-ne-i ete te -i-tu e e u pe he o-a wa u u Pe a̷ e a u-u ta pae ta-

hi pa-lu-a u pa-ko-lu tu me-ı o To pu-le   ta i me̲i a-i a i to ta⁼ i

o ta a ho Hu-li to ma-no-ma-no te ta⁼i-ta⁼i i na-a i pu O ta A-tu ti te-

to-mi to-mi me̲ to pa-i-a O e ta-lu o e ta pu ta- ne-o-le-o-le   Tu

me̲-i ta hi-ti-wa-we te a-we-ha no lo he a-tu la e ta-u ta Ma-u-ho-ku-a

Note: At the end of staff one, read two thirty-second notes for two sixteenths. At the end of staff five there should be a measure bar.

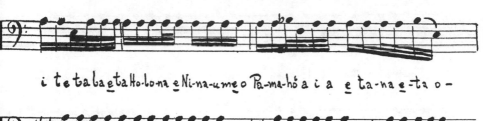

i te ta ba e ta Ho-lo-na e Ni-na-u-me o Pa-ma-hó a i a e ta-na e ta o-

be u-a he-i i a au-ta ue tei-a ha-a e he'e e U-a hei o

ma-e to'e i te' a h'a ta-hi la-u me na e ta-a-u te-u e-lu-e Tu ma-io Ta-ha

li-tu-a ta ma-no-ma-no Ta hi-hi-pe'a e ta i po-no'na ta-i-tu-a-a-na A-o-

he no he ma-mo e la wa i he ma-mo ma-hi-a-i-i kahi i ta e ta u ba me ta-z-u-a

Ku-hi-he wau-a ba-wa-i-a nu-i ne-i i o-o e ta ba-e i mi-no to po po-luna

Te hol'a li te-a o ma-e-to-po-u-bi O tu'u ai-ne te te-i o ta wa-iu-hu

Note: In the fourth staff, last measure, the third, fourth, sixth, and seventh notes should be thirty-second notes.

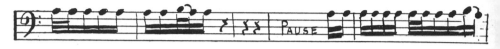

Note: The final note should be *bβ*.

E o e ka lawai'a holona i ke kai o Manaka'a	O Waiu o Lumaheihei kai kaa i o moehanuna ka maka o ka i'a
Ku mai o Kanakaole ka mea iaia o ka uha'i o ka ulei	Pupuhi kukui ahuwale lalo i kea ka i'a a ka holona
E ho'omakaukau kakou oi kau ka la iluna	Kahea mai ua lawai'a nui nei e ke keiki a pehea wau
O waiwai ole o Alakaihu i ke kupa ai	Pa-e a'e a uka pakahi, palua, pakolu, ku mai o Kapule ka mea iaia ke ka'i o ka aha
O ke kipi o Haililani kai ke kua-iako (?)	

O huli o ka manomano ke ka'ika'i i
  na ipu
O ka Aiuki ke komikomi ma ka
  paia
O kalua ka pu kane oleole
Ku mai ka hikiwawe Keawehano (?)
Lohe aku la ka uka Maulukua i ka
  i'a a ka holona
Ninau mai o Pamaho'a ia Kanakaole
  ua hei ia oukou e ka i'a
A—e ua he'i makou e ka i'a ho'o
  kahi lau me na kaau keu elua
Ku mai o Kahalikua ka manomano
Ka hihipe'a ka imi pono o na kai-
  kuaana
Aohe no he mamo lawai'a he mamo
  mahiai i
Mahi i ka la me ka ua
Kuhihewa ua lawai'a nui nei i o'o
  ka lae i mino ka papalina

Ke holo ala i ke—á makapouli o ku'u
  aina
I ke kai o ka waiuhu
Uhu mai na keiki lawai'a nui a ka-
  hai moku ninau pehea la ka i'a
  o Manaka'a
Ho'ole ua lawai'a nui nei aohe i'a he
  i'a na ka holona
Aohe no he lawai'a nui i ole ka ai i
  ka pipipi i ka hulalilali
Piha ka waha ou-a lawai'a nui nei o
  na inoa papakolu keia o na
  makua o'u i hea aku ai i ku'u
  keiki
O ka lawai'a holona kona
O ka inoa ko ia nei a o mama he
  makua
E—o—a.

No. 64 was composed more than fifty years ago for a child by its grand-parents. I feel that it is true to the old style except in the matter of more breath interruptions. It is peculiar as a piece of poetry in having the longest lines of any of the chants in the entire collection, with or without music. The pause in the music is not significant, for the chanter was out of breath and forgot the lines in his confusion.

THE TRUE SONG, OR MELE HULA

The hula, as Emerson has said (43, introduction), was the opera of the Hawaiians. Under the designation mele hula fall all those chants which might be described as adapted to dancing purposes, and, generally speaking, less formal in character.

I have already mentioned the outstanding difference between oli and hula music, that in the hulas there is somewhat freer movement of melody, more equalization in the use of such tones as are employed, rather than a predominance of one which binds all others to it, giving them, if a simile be permitted, the aspect of sparks flashing from a piece of metal resounding as it is struck. The hula chants more nearly approach true song. The olis, moreover, were not accompanied by musical instruments or dances, while many hula tunes had some such support. The oli was a solo performance. Only rarely did two chant together, or relieve one another. The hula was usually ensemble.

The general term hula embraces two classes of songs, those intended as accompaniments for dancing and those merely to be sung after the same style. A second classification might be attempted from the fact that some hulas have instrumental accompaniment and some do not, but these two classifications do not coincide.

The songs not intended for dance accompaniments invariably have been termed plain hulas by my informants. One said that formerly none but trained performers chanted hulas, but that in modern times others have picked up the art of chanting, if not of dancing, and it is these outsiders who introduced plain hulas. It is probable, nevertheless, that in early times non-professionals might have occasionally produced topical meles for their own amusement.

The plain hulas are not so important for the study of musical form, perhaps, as those adapted to certain kinds of dancing, where music with well-defined structural features, such as regular metric and rhythmic patterns, repeated sections of melody, might be expected. Therefore the dance tunes will be considered first. In order to discuss them with suitable clarity it is necessary to touch upon the dancing and drama that accompanied them.

DANCING AND DRAMA OF THE HULA

The instrumental and vocal music of the Hawaiians was, like that of most other peoples in a similar stage of culture, intimately, almost inextricably, associated with the intoning of poetry, and in the hula, with dancing and drama as well. It is not my purpose to deal in detail with dancing and drama. Early true drama, that is, dialogue and action as distinguished from a chorus uniformly portraying by gesture the words of a mele as it was sung, if ever developed, has disappeared leaving no trace. The only reference to drama I have found is by Barrot (16). In the rare examples of dialogue chants it is doubtful that the parts were taken by more than one individual. Very little is known about antiphonal chanting which some say existed.

Chamisso (31, p. 15) describes the dancing as he witnessed it between 1815 and 1818.

Poetry, music and dancing, which, in the South Sea islands appear hand in hand in their original union to adorn human life, deserve to be particularly attended to. The spectacle of the hura, the festive dances of the Owhyeeans, filled us with admiration.

The words mostly celebrate, like the Pindaric Odes, the fame of some prince. Our knowledge of the language was not sufficient to judge of their poetry. The song in itself is monotonous; with the accompanying beats of the drum it measures the turns of the dance, bearing, as it were, upon its waves a superior harmony. In the varying dance the human form develops itself to this measure in the most admirable manner, representing itself in a constant flow of easy, unrestrained motion, in every natural and graceful position. We fancy that we see the antique starting into life; the feet only bear the dancer. He moves with composure. His body, his arms, all his muscles are expressive, his countenance is animated . . . The drummers sit in the background, the dancers stand before them in one or more rows; all join their voices in the chorus. The song is at first slow and piano, and is gradually and regularly quickened and strengthened as the dancers advance and their action becomes animated. All execute the same motions. It is as if the dancer stood several times repeated before us. . . . Their usual songs are danced in the same spirit, standing or sitting. They are of very different characters, but always accompanied by graceful motions of the body and arms.

Barrot (16, pp. 33, 34) gives a picture of the hula at a somewhat later date, 1836.

But what was admirable in this song, . . . was the perfect accordance with which the five singers spoke and gesticulated. They must have been rehearsed many times to attain to this degree of perfection. Each one of the five pronounced, at the same time, the same note, the same word, made the same gesture, and moved his calabash in the most perfect time, either to the right or to the left, or striking it against the ground, he caused it to give forth sounds somewhat similar to those of a bass drum. It might be said that they were all moved by the same impulse of thought and will. Sometimes the gestures varied and became inconceivably rapid, yet I was never able to discover a mistake. The voice, the hands, the fingers, the calabashes, the bodies of the five singers were always extended, moved, regulated, by a spontaneous movement.

Again, in the same article, referring to a dance:

The dancing was at length announced. But the time is past when the swarms of male and female dancers assembled on the green grass, and there, in their graceful dances, accompanied by songs, recounted the glorious achievements of warriors. . . . Only one thing was remarkable in this dance, and that was, that the dancer regulated the measure and from time to time gave the musician the subject of his song. The musician endeavored to make his time accord with the movements of her feet, and he succeeded with remarkable precision. Yet, at the end of half an hour the dance began to seem long. . . . The dancing, so mean and monotonous, was far from realizing the idea we had formed of it. Only the singing and the singers appeared to have preserved all the originality of ancient times. . . . Formerly the women were passionately fond of these sports and public dances. Many females, even of the royal family, had the reputation of being finished actresses, for this people once had plays, and the members only of distinguished families appeared upon the stage.

The native talent for drama, especially a talent for pantomime, is clearly shown even at the present time in the facial expression and gesture which accompanies not only the hula of today, but the most ordinary conversation or acts of daily life. A mere lifting of the eyebrow, a turn of the eye, or even a change in its light, conveys a meaning which could not be expressed in many words, while the traffic policeman by subtle and delicate movements of his hands, which a European or American could not hope to imitate without long practice, transmits his thoughts without possibility of misinterpretation, to the utmost nicety even when his back is turned.

The difference is very marked between the dancing and gestures of those trained in the old school, even if they are no longer young, and of those who have attempted to pick up a knowledge of the hula, or have learned it, in loose modern fashion. Whatever may be claimed to lie back of even the ancient hulas, it is impossible not to feel from the traces of the classical types that survive, that a very wide gap separates them from the coarse hula of today, and that in them we have but a hint of the "tender grace of a day that is dead."

Emerson (43) has given full description of the long training necessary to the mastering of the intricacies of the hula, the rigid discipline imposed upon the students, the devotion paid to the patron goddess, the rituals performed and the graduation ceremony of the novitiates. He has also practically exhausted the list of various kinds of hulas, giving in many cases the explanation of their origin and purpose, so far as it was obtainable, and presented typical meles for each. But he has done this more in a descriptive style, with sympathy and great grace of expression, rather than analytically. He does not classify the dances in any way which would assist in grasping differences and similarities readily and testing them out with the tunes. He does not enter into a discussion of the dance figures to any extent, for at the time of his writing it probably was already too late, as it certainly is now, to make a critical study of them. It could never have been satisfactorily accomplished without the aid of moving pictures and diagrams worked out by a professional dancer.

From what Emerson has said and from what I have gathered here and there, the standards of excellence in hula performance lay, apparently, not so much in the voice production, although no doubt attention was paid to training the chorus,[4] as in the possession of a repertory, a feeling for rhythms and meters and in the ability, above all, to execute the motions with finish and precision, following the sentiment of the meles.

In the absence of more detailed information concerning the dances, it is necessary to resort to a classification of them from one standpoint or another, while by analyses of the tunes under certain groups it may be possible to discover rhythmical, metric or other features which distinguish the different types. Thus the identification of the tunes of certain kinds of hulas may be achieved by an analysis of the structural features rather than by association, which was the Hawaiian method.

---

[4] See the line in the oli chant to Laka, Nos. 51, 52, where *he leo ula*, a ringing voice, is mentioned. The word *ula*, commonly translated as red, has another deeper meaning referring to the psychological effect or the stimulating sensation aroused by the sight of rich red—the flaming or striking quality of it. *Ula* is applied in the same way to describe a penetrating, powerful or delectable perfume, and here to that voice quality which fills the hearer with delight—a full and joyous richness of tone.

Aside from the two classifications of hula tunes which have already been suggested—a division of them into those which were or were not intended for dancing (which divisions will be followed in presenting the music), and a grouping into those having instrumental accompaniment and those which do not—there are other possible classifications which must be considered.

The names which have been bestowed upon various hulas are of little assistance toward making a satisfactory grouping, for they are drawn from many sources and relate to totally different aspects. Some hulas take their names from animals, and apparently the meles chanted for them mention the animals, while the gestures of the dance attempt to depict their characteristic actions. A large number of hulas take their names from the form of instrumental accompaniment employed. A small group are named for the kind of gestures used, as the *paiumauma,* or chest-beating hula, and the *kilelei,* or *kielei,* in which the dance is performed with feet widespread. Others receive titles from the subject of the mele like those hulas enacting incidents in the story of Pele, and still others from the fact that they are games, like the *manai* and *kilu* in which the players try for love forfeits. Finally one hula, which Emerson has mentioned, although it is a question as to whether it does not represent a class of hula rather than a specific dance, is the *hoonana,* to cause to be quieted or amused, a name derived from the purpose of the dance.

Some difference of opinion existed among my informants regarding general terms applied to the hulas, which, because of the amount of action involved, required the division of performers into two groups, the musicians and the dancers. Emerson (43, p. 28) has given the term *hoopaa,* steadfast ones, as that designating the musicians while *olapa* was the name for those moving about. The *olapa* seems to be also a particular kind of hula in which this division of performers always obtains and the question has been raised as to whether the terms should be extended to divisions of performers in other hulas of a similar nature. In many of the hulas performed sitting, as well as in one or two performed standing, the instruments were played and the chanting done by the same individuals. In some hulas performed standing, the term *olapa* was not, so far as I know, given to those who danced.

There were evidently no class terms to designate all those hulas named for instruments, for animals, for games, or for gestures. While the distinction was recognized, it does not seem to have been sufficiently clear or important in the minds of the people to require a special terminology. The only general names that I have discovered differentiated the standing from the sitting hulas, that is, the *hula ku iluna* and the *hula noho ilalo*.

These two terms cut directly across all other classifications except that which differentiates between regular and plain hulas, but they also distinguish dancing, as the word is strictly understood, from gesture and from motions made only from the hips. On account of this distinction, which the Hawaiians themselves have made, and because it is as satisfactory as any grouping which might be found, for there seem to be exceptions in all other directions, this classification will be followed as far as may be in presenting the different hulas and their music. Only those hulas for which tunes were secured in the recent survey and concerning which something was personally learned from watching the motions will be discussed in this report. They do not include some mentioned by Emerson, but additional light was obtained regarding a few and one was found which he has not given.

It is evident that other distinctions in types of hulas, if ever made by the Hawaiians, have been blurred with the passing of time. Among those taking their names from instrumental accompaniment are a few which appear to be interchangeable; that is, the mele and tune are capable of being adapted to several kinds of instruments and the name of the hula changes accordingly. They are all performed sitting, however.

Others, which are performed standing, although with instrumental accompaniment in some cases, may derive their names from the motions made, while others, like the *kalaau,* also a "standing up" hula, again look to the instrument for a title.

In bestowing terms the Hawaiians seem to have taken the most appealing characteristic; and the fact that many of the meles intended to be used in hulas with instrumental accompaniment may be adapted to several kinds of instruments would indicate that the differences in accompaniments except in tone quality, could not have been very noticeable or fundamental.

DANCE TUNES

The Noho Ilalo, or Sitting Hulas

The *hula noho ilalo,* performed sitting, will be presented first. This class includes the greatest number of hulas, both with and without instrumental accompaniment. Among those without accompaniment is that strange group, the animal hulas.

The Animal Hulas

On Emerson's list (43, pp. 219-233) are four animal hulas, the *hula kolea,* plover dance; the *hula mano,* shark dance; *hula ilio,* dog dance, and *hula puaa,* pig dance, in which "the composer of the mele developed some characteristic of the animal in a fanciful way, while the actors themselves aimed to portray the animal's movements in a mimetic fashion." Emerson says that the accompanying movements were performed without instrumental accompaniment. The first two hulas were enacted sitting or kneeling; the *ilio,* Emerson says, shifted between sitting and standing. It was performed sitting when I saw it. There is nothing in the description of the *puaa* given by Emerson to indicate what was the position, and as my informant could not perform the motions, its place among the *noho ilalo* is only doubtful.

It is beyond the scope of this report to attempt to discover the origin of these peculiar dances, so different from all other hulas, even were it possible to do so at this late date, but they do suggest a totemic significance which must have been lost very long ago. There are indications, however, that animals, as guardian spirits, are even to the present day regarded with veneration by the Hawaiians and that not long since there was a reluctance to partaking of their flesh. See also the Fornander collections of legends (56) for references to such spirits who were called in some cases *aumakua* and again *unihi pili.* Rougier (131, p. 470) reports a dance of animals in Fiji called *méké ni manumanu,* not totemic but highly amusing and performed with the intention of creating laughter. The meaning which Emerson derives from the animal hulas hardly accounts for their being named for animals and danced in a fashion mimicking them.

Hula mano and hula kolea.—Emerson states (43, p. 231) that the last and only mention of a performance of the *hula mano* in modern times was in 1847 on the island of Oahu, in the "lonely and romantic valley of Waimea" during a tour made by Kamehameha III. No trace of it was found in the recent survey.

The *hula kolea* had evidently all but passed from memory at the time he wrote, for he gained his information about it from an informant and not from having observed it.

Hula ilio.—The *hula ilio* had long been "out of commission" as Emerson has it, at the time his book was written, and it was therefore very surprising to discover, at Haena, Kauai, an old fisherman living almost as a hermit who recalled what purported to be a *hula ilio* which he performed for me. It was enacted in a sitting posture and the words were emitted with rather explosive breath, somewhat after the manner of a dog's bark, while the ribs were thumped with the elbows and that part of the upper arm which could be brought sharply against the sides as the bent arms were lifted and dropped. Only one example of this hula was obtained with music. Wherever I read it to old Hawaiians in the hope of stimulating their memories it created some amusement but no one else had heard of one. Very recently another has been reported from Hilo but it is claimed that the words are modern and the music has not been obtained.

The Kauai example is somewhat playful and childish, according to ideas nowadays, and the text does not seem to be particularly archaic, yet Paikulu, the old fisherman who recited it to me, thought that it must be "pretty ancient," at least two hundred years old.

No. 65.—Hula ilio, chanted by Paikulu, Haena, Kauai.

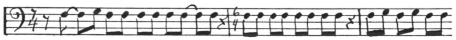

Note: In the fourth staff, second measure, a quarter note *f* should precede the rest. In the second staff a measure bar should appear before the time signature 1/4.

Me he ilio mai ana oe	Mohalu aku a nei loko
Ka papani ma'u ilaila	He taiko'o ko kai
Kohi ana i ka pu'u	Te mau linalina nei
Ho'i aku au lalau	Ho'oku o ka waiwai
Kao'o ana lalo	Hoite he ole mai

The tune to which it was chanted has all the marks of antiquity. It is very circumscribed, melodically, for the tonal content consists of but two notes, a whole step removed from one another, the lower of which occurs the more frequently, by far. The rhythms are very simple and almost unvarying and what is most striking, the meter, which is fairly regular, centers around six-part groupings which might be written as a slow three-four time with each quarter note subdivided into eighths, but which cannot be written as six-eight, divided into two groups of three beats each, for the movement is 1 2, 3 4, 5 6, not 1 2 3, 4 5 6. The slow time of the chant which six-four expresses better, and the almost equal weight of the six beats, except the first which receives the primary accent, was responsible for the choice of time signature.

There is, on the other hand, enough metric irregularity to show that the meter is influenced by the poetry, one line of which is chanted to each measure, with a breath taken at the end. There is an even number of lines permitting of an arrangement into couplets but the tune is so monotonous that the couplet idea as expressed by a melodic question and answer which is found in many hulas is not apparent here. The chant begins on the accented beat.

Hula Puaa.—The same old man also knew a *hula puaa* which Emerson says (43, p. 228), was apparently native to Kauai, and of the performance of which on any other island within historic times he had not been able to learn. Paikulu could not make the motions but he recalled the mele.

The tune, in addition to the two tones, a step apart, as in the case of the *hula ilio* (although the higher is rather infrequent), has another note a minor third below the general level which takes an important part. The note values are small, but the beats not very rapid, and the predominating

No. 66.—Hula puaa, chanted by Paikulu, Haena, Kauai.

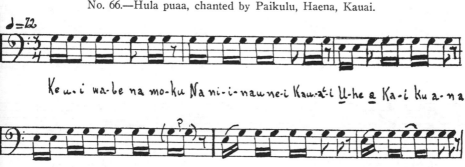

pu-a ki-i ta   ha-u Ae mai ăheu bẽ bo-a ạ ne be ta-i o

Ma-pu Pu-a mu-i ta u-a ba-i o ki-lo Ha-na-u kău to wa-i a-i

hi-u O pe pe i' au   ke-a O ka ni-ho a-i o po   Ha wa-i-i-ii:

Nạ i wa-be o   o ma-hi-ti i ta pu-a o ta ạ be-hu-a Pạ'u   o ba-u wa

hi-ne Ka-hi-to a ma-i-tạ-i O ka nu-ku hu-mu-hu-mu Ho-bo ku u-a   u-a O ka

ne wa-hi-ne i na mo-bu (O) Ka-i tu-a-a na ko in-oa) A o te a-u o ta ma-i

ta-ni O-le-bo i-te o be O ta pọ'e u mạ i tạu Ta mẹa lẹ-ạ au ma-i E

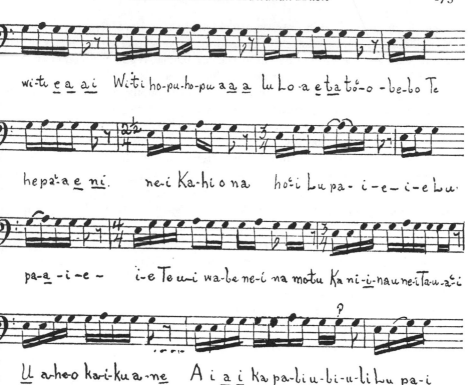

Ke ui wale nei na moku	Kahito a maitai
Ke ninau nei Kaua'i	O ka nuku humuhumu
Ahea kai ku ana	Holo ku ua ua
A i ka pali uliuli	O ka ne wahine i na moku
Lu paieie he ino	O Kaituaana ko inoa
Kanaka pua ki'i pua ki'i ta hau	O ke au o ka makani
A'e mai ia he u leo loa	Olelo ite ole
O ka tai o Mapu	O ka po'e o ma tau
Pua nui ta ua lai o kilo	Ka ma'a lau maia
Hana { u ko / kau } to wai a hi'u	E witi e witi
	I hopuhopu a lulu
O ka pe pe ia au kea	E loa ko'olelo
O ka niho aio po Hawai'i	Ke he pa'a ku nei
I wale o mahiti	Kahi o na ho'i
I ta pua o ka lehua	Lu paieie lu paieie
Pa'u' o lau wahine	

meter is three-four, with only occasional lapses. I have repeatedly noticed that like other tunes, dance tunes tend to become uneven in meter when given without the stiffening influence of some regular accompaniment, especially by untrained performers. This is not only true of Hawaiians but any music teacher can cite experiences with pupils, and I have noticed it among many other persons of different races. Possibly with a group of dancers to sing for and a more urgent need of regular meter this and similar chants would be given with stricter attention to time on the part of the singer. It is unfortunate that after chanting the mele correctly on the first record, which has been reserved for casting, Paikulu forgot his lines near the end of the second rendition, before the texts had been written down, and could not recall them, despite many trials. The lines given here are incomplete.

The first lines are each covered by a measure of music and are broken by rests. The metric irregularities at the appearance of the long line are noticeable in both renditions which the singer made. This line also destroys the correspondence between the music and word divisions. The chant begins on the first beat of the measure.

Two renditions of another *hula puaa* chant were obtained from a man at Kapaa, thirty miles from Haena.

No. 67.—Hula puaa, chanted by Waiwaiole Kala, Kapaa, Kauai.

U - be pa-hu ka mot(u) U no a te-le al'(a) Ae pa hue ta mot(u)

U ho'-o hi-o-bo ka a'(ha) E tu wa-le na ki'-i E ta-u ma-i na hail'(o)

E ma-na'-o ho-bo ta mot(u) U li-li i ta ha-ol(e) E tu ta hoe ul'(i)

I ko-hi ta pa-le-ka-i I howa ke-be a-la Ae pa-a-hue ta mot(u)

E po-a-i i te bo'(a) I he u-ku ko a-i wa-i I he me-a he me-a o'(e)

Ule pahu ka moku	E tu i ka hoe uli
U no a tele ala	I kohi i ka palekai
A e pa ahu e ta moku	A e pahu i ka moku
U ho'o hiolo ka aha	I nou a kele ala
E tu wale na ki'i	E poai i ke ko'a
E kau mai na hailo	I he uku ko ai wai
E mana'o holo ka moku	I he mea he mea oe
U lili i ka haole	I he mea he mea oe

The first, No. 67, is seen to have a slightly different tonal content from No. 66 by Paikulu, for in place of the minor third below the general level the perfect fourth appears. Even were the two tones considered interchangeable, a matter which has already been mentioned in the section on the olis (p. 151), a quite different tune from No. 66 is produced. What is particularly noteworthy is that the meter of this example is six-four and that rhythmically it is almost identical with No. 66. Taking into consideration the fact that in value the notes of No. 67 are double those of No. 66, but that the chant moves almost twice as fast, it is perceived that No. 67 might be regarded as moving in three-four meter with the quarter note unit set at Mm. 60, or that No. 66 might be written as a six-four movement with the quarter note at Mm. 144.

No. 68.—Another rendition of No. 67, same chanter.

The second rendition of this chant by the same singer gives again a quite different melody with an added note one-half step below the general level and the minor third below instead of the perfect fourth. But the metric conception of six parts, or three, subdivided into two, and the rhythmic pattern, are practically the same as in the other two chants. Here occurs one of the very rare examples of metric uniformity and rhythmic pattern carried out in three tunes for the same kind of a hula rendered by two different people. The metric and rhythmic character of the *hula puaa* seems to be then a movement in three-part meter, each part subdivided into two with a rhythmic pattern as shown in figure 4, with variations.

FIGURE 4.—Sketch showing meter and rhythm of the *hula puaa*.

The movement of No. 68 progresses at about the same rate as the others, for a quarter note taken as the metric unit would be set at half 152, or 76. Both of the renditions of the *puaa* chant by Waiwaiole begin on the accent.

GESTURE HULAS

For want of a better term I have given the name gesture hulas to those which were performed in a sitting posture, without instrumental accompaniment, the names bestowed by the Hawaiians referring to the type of movement accompanying the chanting. I obtained meles for only one such hula, the *paiumauma,* or chest-beating. There are others which should come under this head, such as the *ohelo,* described by Emerson, which, however, was performed in a reclining posture; the *pahua,* the accompaniment being pebbles used like castanets (but not the same dance, evidently, as the *hula iliili*) ; the Pele, the *muumuu* and the *kolani* (all without instruments) ; as well as the *kilu,* or one of the game hulas.

Hula paiumauma.—Of the first of the eight *paiumauma* tunes that were secured, No. 69 was given by a very old informant in Honolulu. The *mele,* she said, came from Maui. (See Emerson, 43, p. 204.) With a different tune, also said to be a *hula paiumauma,* the same words were chanted by Mrs. Webb who first heard the melody sung by a Maui man, while an old woman on Kauai, who identified the tune she gave to the same chant as a *hula paipu* or *ipu wai* ascribed to it the same origin. (See p. 228.)

No. 69.—Hula paiumauma, chanted by Kaahaaina Naihe, Honolulu, Oahu.

Manono e Manono e	Moe aku kaua i ka wai welawela
Manono a'e ai	I ka papa lohi la
Kau ka opeope i ka ulu hala ae ae	O Maukele la e ae
Hali'i pulana[5] no huli mai	A kele a kele ko aloha ea
Huli mai oe la moe kaua	A he oi e

The chanter of this hula gave two phrases and part of another at which point she made a mistake in the words and began again. I have given the chant as she first sang it to show the difference in her tunes. The rhythms are the same as far as the first tune indicates them. Although the meter is not uniform throughout the second rendition, two-four time predominates and the tune is built on the plan of four measures to each musical division which covers one line of the poetry. If necessary, fillers are added to the text to make this possible.

The mele, like all hula meles, is composed in couplets and the condition is met in the music by a somewhat different melodic scheme for the second division of each pair from that in the first. There is not much variety, as the letters designating each melodic phrase indicate, but there is enough between those forming pairs to reveal something of a complementary nature in the second. According to one informant the mele is not finished. She had heard it a number of times but never completely. The last line stands alone, as would its musical accompaniment but for the presence of a coda put on in the form of a call, which acts as a short complementary phrase for it.

The rhythmic pattern, with more or less variation, is composed of three measures in eighth notes and a fourth containing an eighth and a dotted quarter, throwing the weight of the movement on this last measure of the phrase, which is syncopated, so that the weight does not fall until after the primary accent is past, which accentuates the effect. The tune begins on the accent.

As to the tonal content, especially if the coda is considered, many pitches are involved, but the most prominent, occurring in the body of the chant, as might be expected in the more archaic olis and hulas, are the general level, the major second above it or the super-tonic, the half step below it or the leading tone and a group of tones lying between the minor third and the augmented fourth below, including those pitches.

The tune begins not on the general level but below it; in the first rendition a fifth below, in the second a major third. The long series of notes, practically on one pitch, so characteristic of the olis, are here broken up. There is more equal employment of the general level, with its surrounding group of tones, and the notes in the lower group.

---

[5] Observe the substitution of *l* for *n* in *pulana*. The confusion of *i* and *n* seems to have occurred in several Hawaiian words in more recent times.

No. 70, in metric and rhythmic features, is very similar to No. 69. The meter is mostly two-four, but there are some constant irregularities like a three-four meter in nearly every case for the final measure of every second phrase and a tendency to a slightly lengthened measure at the beginning of each pair. Aside from four measures to each phrase, the

No. 70.—Hula paiumauma, chanted by Solomono Huihui, Honolulu, Oahu.

ao boto o ba e Oka pi-pi u-a-hi o Ta-le-po-ni i ba e

Kama-no u-la o Te-a-mo-k-wa a ba e Ke ba-we ca-laci —

Lu-na-li-lo o la e a e E ka e-he-o a o no a manu u-a e

A-lo-ha a o ta u i o to k-wa e ba e a i I ta-e

he-u a o ta-ma-ta-ni i ba e Ha-e-na u ma-i a-na ta a pu a-na

a ba e a Ha-a-he-o i ta ma-ta o ta-o-pu-a o ba e

At first, the singer gave the first four measures thus, later changing to the form given above.

U he a wa le o e e ta u u ba e

beats tend to break up into eighth notes and the rhythmic pattern is very similar to that of No. 69 with three measures of eighth notes followed by a fourth in which the presence of a quarter note, and in every second phrase an added beat as well, lends the weight to the last part of the phrase.

At first the singer started the mele with the line which is given below the example, but later he omitted it. It appears to belong, however, as a comparison of this version with two others given by him will show. (See Nos. 75 and 78.)

In tonal content the chant is not so extended as No. 69, for it lacks the coda, which in that song was a contributory factor. In addition to the general level there is only the minor third below which is now and then supplanted in the same setting by the perfect fourth or a tone a fraction of a step higher. This song begins below the general level, also, and on the accent.

Metrically and rythmically No. 71 resembles the first two *hula paiumauma,* although it has a quite different tune. The fact that the song begins on the last half of the first beat rather than on the accent gives it a somewhat different swing, but it is a question as to how important this is in this particular case. In Hawaiian singing, especially with dance tunes which move rapidly and in regular meter, there is seldom room for breath between syllables and it is therefore robbed, one might say, from the mele by half enunciating the syllable as the breath is being taken. Very often the final syllable of the word at the end of the line is so treated. When it is faintly sounded this syllable is written in parentheses beneath the rest. If it is not heard at all it is written in the same way, but after an apostrophe.

This habit of breathing has become so strong with hula singers that it is followed even when it is not necessary. In this chant the initial *"A"* is not heard, but it is meant to occupy the time of the eighth rest, and as several other first phrases of musical pairs begin on the accent, the beginning on the last half of the first beat in the initial phrase is not so significant.

The meter is absolutely regular, two beats to the measure. There are four measures to each musical phrase which covers a line of poetry and the lines are arranged in pairs. The couplet idea is very nicely brought out by the melodic character of the two complementary phrases, which are carried through the song with only slight variations. This is a good example of simple two-part form.

In tonal content the melody is more varied than any studied so far, assuming that frequent appearance of tones at important points or other

No. 71.—Hula puili, uliuli, or paiumauma, chanted by J. P. Hale, Hilo, Hawaii.

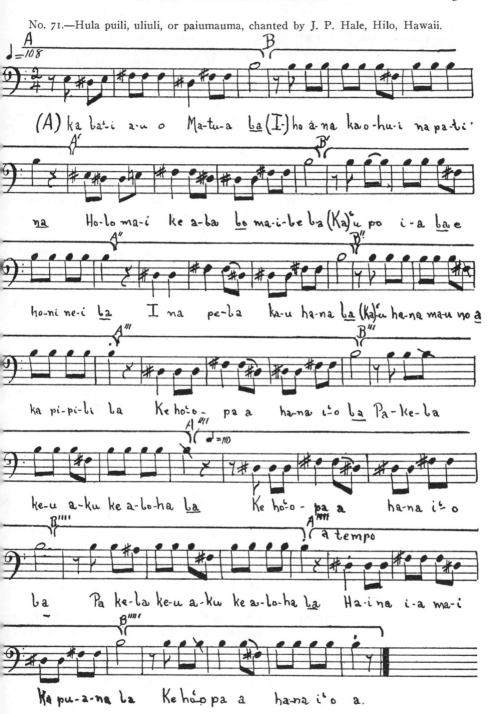

A ka laʻi au o Makua   Kaʻu hana mau no ka pipili
Iho ana ka ohu i na pali   Ke hoʻopa a hana iʻo
Holo mai ke ala o ka maile   Pakela keu aku ke aloha
Kaʻu no ia e honi nei   Haina ia mai ka puana
I na pela kau hana   Kaʻu no ia e honi nei

emphasis of them justify the assumption that they form part of the melody structure and are not merely embellishing features. The general level is supported not only by the frequent appearance of the fourth below, but by the augmented fourth, the fifth and the sixth, all apparently part of the melodic scheme. Thus it is evident that here the major triad in the first inversion, taking the general level as the fundamental, is a noticeable feature, combined with the subdominant. Like the other two *hula paiu-mauma,* No. 71 begins below the general level and works up to it.

Several new features appear with No. 72, which comes from Maui— apparently the home of more melody than is found elsewhere in the islands, as far as the old type of music is concerned. The attention of the reader is here called to the Maui tunes as they are encountered in this report. It is to be regretted that a survey of that island could not be made to ascertain if there really was a greater tendency to melodic development there.

In meter and the number of measures to the phrase, this tune is almost perfectly regular except for additional measures of rests, sometimes one, again two, at the end of the couplets, which were no doubt due to the short breath of the singer and not to any difference in the structure of the melody. They would probably be omitted if the chant were sung by a group of hula performers, to the accompaniment of the gestures.

In rhythm the weight of the emphasis is reversed from the final measure of the phrase to the first, while the last three measures tend to divide into eighth notes as did the first three in the previous examples. This shift gives quite a different swing to the piece but its underlying movement is the same as in the other specimens.

The complementary character of the two musical phrases forming pairs is indicated by the lettering and is carried out in the same fashion as in No. 71. Here too, aside from the general level, other structural melody tones appear, most prominently the fourth and the sixth below, forming with it an inverted major triad, but also the major second above the level and the leading tone, with a cluster of microtones, just below it. The song begins and ends on the level or fundamental, which, however, is not the highest tone achieved, so that the effect of beginning nearer the middle of the range of the song and working up higher is still maintained.

No. 72.—Hula paiumauma, for Kalakaua, chanted by Mrs. Lahilahi Webb.

a-na la Ka mo-a-na o Ma-a-hu- ko-na la Ka ma-ka- ni

a- pa-'a pa-'a la Le'- i ma-i o Ko-ha- la I ka

nu- ku na ka -na-ka la Ha-i -na ma-i ka pu-a na la

O Ka-la ni Ka-la-a-ka-u- a la

Note: All the divisions marked A should have been shown as starting after the rests.

A Kona hema o kalani	Hae ana e ka naulu
Na ná ia Kaawaloa	Ka makani hele uluulu
Ike i ka la'i a Ehu	Ku ka e'a i ka moana
Ehuehu oe e kalani	Ka moana o Mahukona
Ke hele'na o Hawai'i	Ka makani āpa'apa'a
Malamalama na moku	Le'i mai o Kohala
Ekuku' ana i ke kai	I ka nuku na huapala
I ke kai hāwanawana	Haina ia mai ka puana
Olelo o Kawaihae	Ka Lani Kalakaua.

The same words as given in No. 72 were chanted also as a *hula paiumauma* to a different tune by another informant on Kauai (No. 73). This evidently an old stock hula tune for it was encountered again and again in different guises. It begins peculiarly, but falls into the swing at the second measure. As I have written it, one musical phrase of four measures covers two lines of verse. Properly each note should be doubled in value and the tempo as well, and then, if the measures were divided in half a situation would be produced similar to those occurring in the other tunes. Although rhythmically the pattern is different, even speaking relatively, the faster movement comes at the beginning of the line and the slower at the end. The meter is almost uniform throughout, and if the music were altered so that the notes received twice their value and each measure were cut in half it would be seen that four measures constituted a melodic phrase in each case, and that these phrases were in melodic relation of a statement and answer, to cover each couplet of the mele, with a measure of rest at the end. Thus it might be said that this tune conforms in general pattern to the others.

With but two exceptions, each occurring once, the tonal content is confined to the general level, the fourth below and the major second above. The exceptions are the leading tone, half a step below the level, and a tone lying very slightly below the major second. The song begins and ends on the fundamental or level, but the same idea of working to a higher tone after starting is maintained, as in the other chants of this group. Beginning with the phrase covering the second line of the mele, here appearing as a section, this effect is more marked by using the fourth below as a starting tone.

The first part of No. 74, a fragment, which was sung by Kalaiwaa of Kamuela, Hawaii, whose chanting has already occasioned some attention, is very irregular. It appears as if the second measure should have been combined with the third in more rapid movement after the pattern of

No. 73.—Hula paiumauma for Kalakaua, chanted by Aiamanu Pauole, Hanalei, Kauai.

Ko-na-he-mo ka la-ni a Na-nai-a Ka-a-wa-lo-a I-kai-ka la-i-a

E-hu ae-a na E-hu-e-hu-o-e' ka-la-ni (ke)he-le-na a o Ha-wai-i

i i i ae-a-na Ma-lama-la-ma na mo-ku(E)-ku-ku a-na i-ke

Vocal Music

the second phrase. These irregular beginnings of songs may also, I believe, be taken less seriously than might seem to be justified, considering that this peculiarity too, is not confined to the untrained singers of Hawaii, but is to be found in school rooms and church choirs all over the world until training has eradicated it.

After the first few bars the chant falls into phrases containing four measures, usually with two beats each. The rhythmic pattern is new; in fact there are several quite well defined. In the first part of the chant covering the second, third and fourth pairs of phrases, the first measure of the first phrase of each pair, that is, phrases marked C, C′, and E, is subdivided into eighth notes and the emphasis or weight of the movement falls on the last three measures, each with an eighth note and a dotted quarter, creating syncopation. The second phrases of these pairs have the last two measures covered by one prolonged note, preceded in the phrase marked D by a measure containing a dotted quarter and an eighth note, but in D′ and F by a syncopated measure which in effect amounts to an eighth, a quarter and an eighth. With all this variation the idea is still maintained of throwing the weight on the last measures of the phrases.

At G the scheme is altered, for after the usual measure of eighth notes there are three measures of what is equivalent to a dotted quarter followed by an eighth. In F′, the complementary phrase to G, the rhythm of the D phrases of the first part of the chant is roughly followed. At A′ there is a melodic return to the idea set forth at the beginning of the chant, but the rhythm is reversed here, continuing that which predominated in G, with a quarter note coming first in the measure, while the phrase B′ roughly follows the D rhythms. At H again occurs a new pattern composed of only two measures, one containing the dotted quarter and eighth, the other two slurred eighths and an eighth rest and then the final eighth note. This pattern is doubled to cover the first phrase of the couplet and used again in the first half of the second phrase, where, however, it is combined with the final rhythm of the D phrases thus connecting this section with what has gone before, linking the design. In the rhythms as well as in the melody, EG and D″ reflect earlier themes, as do EG′ and F″, EG″, and D‴.

Rhythmically as well as melodically this is quite a complicated tune, for all its apparent simplicity, and the manner in which the patterns are carried out gives the impression that the composer was not entirely unconscious of them.

No. 74.—Paiumauma hula, chanted by W. M. Kalaiwaa, Kamuela, South Kohala, Hawaii.

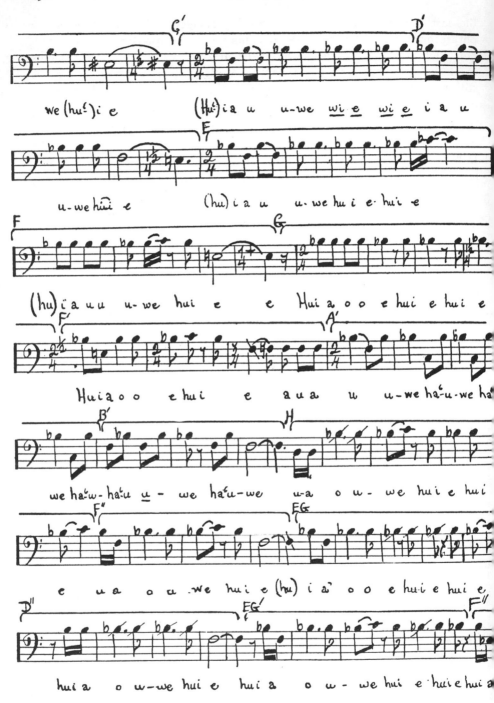

Ha'uha'u uwé ha'uwé
Ha'uha'u uwé ha'uwé
Hu'i a u uwé hu'i e

Hu'i a u uwé hu'i e
Hu'i a'o o e hu'i e
Hu'i a'o o e hu'i e

There is not the close resemblance between this melody and the others which have preceded it, but in rough outline it can be seen that it might serve for the same kind of a dance. The gestures however, unless they were very simple and occurred only on the beats, must have been quite different. The tune begins on the accent, like the others.

In tonal content the melody is peculiar in stressing so often the note standing in the relation of the major second or super-tonic to the fundamental or general level, both as one step above it and in the lower octave, where it forms with the level the minor seventh, that interval generally considered by the European school so difficult to sing. These two scale tones, if we may call them such temporarily, seem almost to vie with one another for prominence and with them the lower dominant, as usual, acts as the other "pole" defining the principal range of interplay. The shift of pitch in the song, beginning with C', should be disregarded as unimportant, and reduces the apparent number of tones comprising the tonal content. There are some deflections around the general level and some around the fourth below, one of these being the slightly lower pitch of the final tone, which, however, as it is prolonged, rises to the true dominant.

Nos. 75 and 76 are renditions by the same singer and are supposed to be the same chant as No. 70, with which they should be compared. Excepting No. 71, they are different from the other *paiumauma* in starting on an unaccented beat. They are also very irregular in time and in the number of measures to the phrase.

They have but two tones, the general level and the fourth below, and begin on the lower and ascend to the upper. The statement and answer idea in the pairs of melodic phrases is carried out consistently with little variation from pair to pair.

75.—Hula paiumauma, chanted by Solomono Huihui, Honolulu, Oahu.

Note: As chanted, the words of No. 75 are very different from those recited. The tunes are always repeated in more or less the same phrases. In the third line, first measure, the sixteenth notes should appear as eighth notes.

No. 76.—Hula paiumauma, chanted by Solomono Huihui, Honolulu, Oahu.

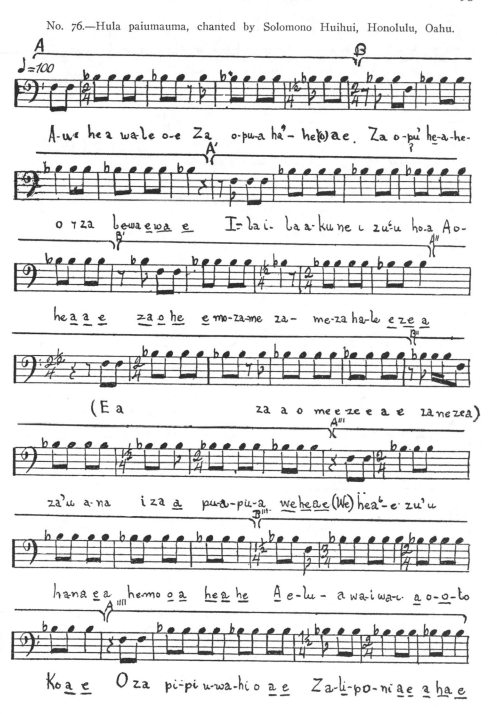

Note: The fourth staff should end with a bar.

Auhea wale oe e keau	Elua waiwai o loko
Ka opua haʻaheo i ka lewa	O ka pipi uwahi o Kaleponi
Ilaila aku nei kuʻu hoa	Kamano ula Keamolewa
Aohe makamaka o ka hale	Kelawe iala e lunalilo
Hoʻi mai kahi manu me kanele	E ka eheu o na manu
Aohe pua loke o ka nuku	Aloha a o ka uʻi o ka lewa
Hoʻokahi puolo mahope	I ka eheu o ka makani
E kau ana i ka puapua	Haina mai ana ka puana
Wehe aʻe kuʻu hana a hemo	Haʻaheo i ka maka o ka opua

The Instrumental Hulas

Hula Iliili.—One of the ancient sitting hulas was the *iliili* in which the performer held in each hand two pebbles which he caused to click together as he opened and closed his hands in time with his chanting. Aside from this nothing was learned of the gestures. Four tunes were obtained, two of which are different renditions of the same chant given by one singer, but they are not at all alike, melodically.

No. 77 was transcribed from a record; No. 78 was taken in notation directly from the chanter.

A moment's comparison will show that although the melodies differ, the rhythms of these two versions are almost identical, beginning with two sixteenths on the last half of a weak beat and following more or less closely the pattern of two eighths, two sixteenths, and an eighth. The meter is regular, with two beats to the measure. Divisions of three measures each are needed to cover the lines of the poetry and these are uniform in length throughout, so that the *hula iliili* as represented by these tunes, at least, differs from the *paiumauma* in having three-measure phrases instead of four. These phrases go in pairs, although for either melody there is very little difference between the first and second phrases in each case. The characteristic feature of the rhythm is also different from those of the *paiumauma* in having the weight of emphasis at the beginning of each measure and a turn resembling a mordent in the last half.

In No. 77 the tonal content consists of the general level which once is slightly flatted, and a series of tones downward, from the leading tone, half a step below, through the minor third, the major third, and a tone between, the fourth and the augmented fourth. The tune begins on the fourth below the level, or the lower dominant, and the second phrase of each pair ends, usually, on a lower tone than the general level, so it may be assumed that the chant closes possibly on the fourth, although it is not complete.

No. 78 is more circumscribed in range, for with one exception there are only the general level and the minor third below, the exception being the flat seventh, a whole tone below the level.

Almost the same tune as No. 79 was given again by the same chanter as another *hula iliili,* with a different mele. The same rhythm and meter

No. 77.—Hula iliili, chanted by Waiwaioli Kala, Kapaa, Kauai.

Note: In the second staff, fourth measure, read *c#*.

No. 78.—Another rendition of No. 77, by the same chanter.

I a - - li̓o-ha e-a Ti-i-le̲-u- e a li̲-o ka-ke-le o

ka mo-a-na Ho-lo ma-mu-a ho-lo ma - ho-pe Hu-li po-no ka i—

hu i ka ma-ka-ni Ha-ki nu̓-a ka u-a-hi i-te ta-o No-me

a̲-e ta hu - i-la ma-a̲-la-lo A waho ka-i a-w o Ka—

i- wi.

I aloha ia Kilauea	Haki nuʻa ka uahi i ke kai
Lio kakele o ka moana	Nome aʻe ka huila malalo
Holo mamua holo mahope	A waho kai au o Kaiwi
Huli pono ka ihu i ka makani	Huli lua ka ale i ka moana[6]

---

[6] This mele is incomplete, according to the informant. Another says that the last two lines
should be

Haina ia mai ka wahine
O Kaleionehu he inoa

No. 79.—Hula iliili, chanted by Waiwaioli Kala, Kapaa, Kauai.

A ka la'i au i Kuhiau
Alo ana o Heki ka moana
Ua hele a hilala na kia
Kiki'i kape'a i ka makani
Walawala ka pumi mahope
Hulei lua ka ili kai

Ka huliuli kapapa o luna
Ua lewa lalo oni pono ole
O ke kau a ka manu o Kaula
Hai ia ka ino ka moana
Haina ka puana lohe ia
Alo ana o Heki ka moana

are used as in Nos. 78 and 79. There is somewhat more tonal content to this chant, for in addition to the general level there are, in downward order, the leading tone, the submediant, the submediant flatted, which is a major third from the level, and the dominant. (See No. 80.)

No. 80.—Hula iliili, chanted by Samuela Waiki, Kawainui, Hilo, Hawaii.

Note: Another half note should appear under the last measure. The first measure bar after the eighth rest should be a dotted line.

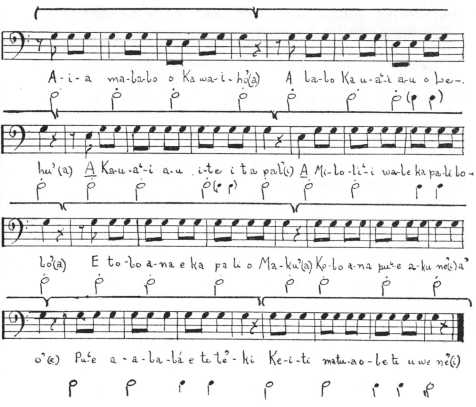

Hiki mai, hiki mai, e ka la e
Aloha wale ka la e kau nei
Aia malalo o Kawaihoa
A lalo Kaua'i au o Lehua
Kaua'i au, ike i ka pali

Miloli'i wale i ka pali loloa
E kolo ana e ka pali o Makua
Kolo ana pu'e aku nei ia oe
A pu'e aalalá e ke keiki
Keiki makua ole ke uwé nei

The fourth tune was given by Waiki, a chanter near Hilo, who illustrated the rhythm of the pebbles striking. It is possible that the three-measure phrases of the preceding three examples may have been peculiar to their chanter, for in the tune by Waiki four-measure phrases again occur, with the beginning of many of them on the last half of the first beat, making the shift to starting with the accent in the last three phrases all the more marked, especially as it is a recapitulation of the idea in the first phrase. There are two rhythmic patterns of prominence, that of the first phrase and that of the third. In the second phrase there was fluctuation from rendition to rendition. At times the phrase would start with the second half of the beat, and the bar would occur where the dotted line is, while the last note of the following measure would be omitted. Again the phrase would omit the initial rest, starting on the accent and shifting the bar half a beat further along, and the note at the end of the next measure would be sounded.

The melody of this tune is confined to the general level almost entirely, but the minor third below occurs often enough and with sufficient emphasis to show that it is structurally important. There is nothing about this tune which would distinguish it from the *paiumauma,* for even the weight of emphasis in the phrases is toward the end. On account of the few examples and the possibility of the tunes by Waiwaiole being peculiar to him in their metric and rhythmic structure, the distinguishing features of the *iliili* tunes as a class cannot be determined.

Hula puili.—This hula has already been described on page 56. It is occasionally performed at the present time. Nine tunes are here presented, Nos. 81 to 89 inclusive. With what has already been said in detail about the preceding hulas, not much may be added which the reader might not readily observe for himself in the light of the foregoing discussions. It will therefore perhaps be sufficient to touch on only a few points.

No. 81 is unusual in being sung by two individuals together. Two records were made, and in one, which was reserved for casting as being a single instance of part singing, the man chanted throughout a perfect fifth lower than his wife. The melodic phrases are in pairs and are practically the same, repeated again and again except that in the first phrase the augmented fourth below the level is used, but in subsequent passages

No. 81.—Hula puili, chanted by Mr. and Mrs. Keawe Nainoelua, Amaulu, Hilo, Hawaii.

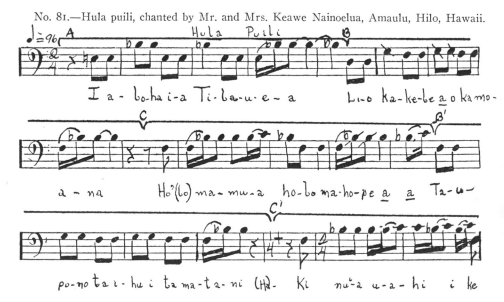

E oľ o Ka-la-ni Me-ha-me-ha O-la ne'i a pu-a

hi-pa Na hi-pa a ta Mu a'-i-pu'u pa-a la a(la)la-u i ta

la-u o a Li-wa Ha- i-na he-i-no-a Ke a -li-i na O Ka

La-ni Me-ha-me ha he i-na-a

Note: In the last staff, for *inaa* read *inoa*.

Ia aloha ia o Kilauea   Lu a'e la Palaau ho'okahi
Lio kakele o ka moana   Ho'okahi ka pahuna malalo
Holo mamua holo mahope   Kohu auna manu i ke one
Kaupono ka ihu i ka makani   Kaholoholo i ke alialia
Haki nu'a ka uahi i ke kai   E ole o Kalani Mehameha
Nome a'e ka huila malalo   Ola ne' ia puá hipa
Hala e ka lae o Kalaau   Na hipa a ka Ma'ipu'upa'a
Pili makou me Moloka'i   Lalau i ka lau o Liwa
Huli aku e ke alo Lahaina   Haina ia mai ka puana
He ukana ka Kilauea   O Kalani Mehameha he inoa

the perfect fourth takes its place. The swing of the movement is in two's, with four measures to the phrase, but a number of irregularities are observed. The phrases begin on the unaccented part of a measure, on either the second beat or its last half.

Although No. 82 has fewer tones and simpler rhythms it is the same in metric structure, with four two-beat measures to the phrases which are in pairs and begin on the second beat of the measure. A second rendition of this chant, No. 83, has the customary minor variations in melody, but metrically and rhythmically it is similar to the first except in one important particular, that of the phrases beginning on the accent rather than on the second beat of the measure. The result is quite a different swing. This is the only example of a *hula puili* in this group beginning its phrases on the accent, but one very irregular specimen which appeared to be so unreliable in many ways that it was not considered, had this feature, as well as one or two modern examples.

No. 84 is unusual in the presence of a triplet at the end of the majority of the measures, but after the first one, these eighth notes are given their full value so that the measures contain four and a half instead of four beats. Possibly the measures should be subdivided into two each, of two-four meter, for as it is, only two four-beat measures are required to cover a line of poetry. The point, however, is not important. I have marked the divisions to conform with the lengths of lines of the mele and not to the accepted rule of four measures to each, which would double their length.

Nos. 85 and 86 require no discussion. Their limited tonal content and the minor third downward as the important interval rather than the perfect fourth, should be noted.

No. 82.—Hula puili, chanted by Solomono Huihui, Honolulu, Oahu.

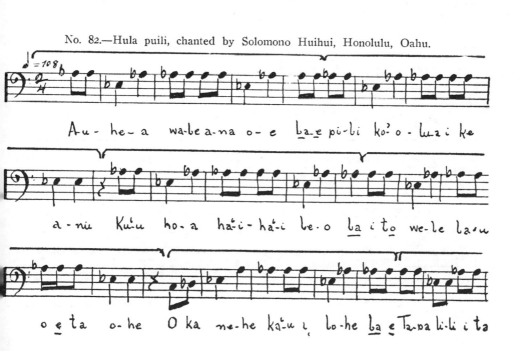

a-na ba e Tu-u ho-a h'a-i ha-i be (o)

No. 83.—Hula puili, chanted by Solomono Huihui, Honolulu, Oahu.

A-u he-a wa-le a — na   o – e ba o pi-li za-o- lu-a i ze an(u)

Zu-u-ho-o a ha-i- ha-i be-a-o ha i za we-be-la-u ez a a o-

(he) O za ne- he   za-u i bo-he za he Za-pa-bi-li i i za

a u i   I ba-we a i za i za ma i za -we-be-la-u ma-za-ni

ba-u-hu   A-bo-a-a ma-i ho-i a-u a i za ha-wa-na

a o Zon'(a) He i-ze na-bi-hi a-na i ho a.   No o zu-u-pa-a

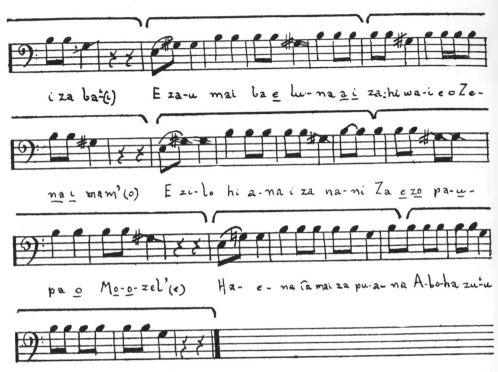

Auhea wale ana oe pili koʻolua i ke
    anu
Kuʻu hoa haʻihaʻi leo i ka welelau o
    ka ohe
O ka nehe kaʻu i lohe
Kapalili i ka welelau lima
I lawe a lima ia mai
E ka makani pahu pua
A loaʻa mai hoʻi au i ka hau anu o
    Puna
He ikena lihi ana iho i ka nu hou
    o Kona
He manaʻo paʻa no koʻu
No kuʻu pua i ka laʻi
E kau mai la i luna kahi wai o
    Kemamo

E kilohi iho ana i ka nani
I ka papa o Maukele
I pakele aku no oe i ka mea o ka
    hilahila
Mai noho a hana mai i ke koa
    Pelukia
Hoʻi a ua nei
O ka hana i ko piko
Aia oe me manuʻa
I ke alanui malihini
O ka nui pahu wale no
A he iki na mea hana
O ka iki ape iho ia
E pehu ai ko nuku
Haina mai ka puana
No pili aloha i ke anu

Nos. 87 and 88, two renditions of the same chant by one singer, are
alike in general outline, if different in actual melody. The complementary
relation of the pairs of phrases is very marked. These two are distinguished
from the preceding tunes in beginning on the last half of the first beat,

rather than somewhere in the second, but the effect is the same—of beginning after the accent. The tonal content is strongly marked by the first inversion of the major triad, which in the second specimen is supplemented by the leading tone. The turns so frequently appearing at the end of the measures make the rhythm of the second rendition practically identical with Nos. 77 and 78, which are *hula iliili.*

No. 89 also begins on the last half of the first beat, and while its tonal content includes the major second above the fundamental as well as the first inversion of its major triad, and even the major third above, which is not common in any chants, there is nothing in this tune strikingly different from the others of the group. The text was considered worthless, and so has been omitted. The melody has the most extended range of any of the *hula puili* except No. 81, which is said to have come from Molokai. No. 89 is from Maui.

It can hardly be said that there are any marked features of these *puili* tunes which plainly differentiate them from the *paiumauma* except that the rhythms instead of throwing the weight of time and emphasis at the end of the phrases distribute it more or less evenly from measure to measure and the tunes themselves begin on the unaccented beat, either on the second or its last half, in the majority of cases, or on the last half of the first.

No. 84.—Mele hula, chanted by Solomono Huihui, Honolulu, Oahu.

ti ma-nu-a-hi wa-le ma-i la e Po-no i ta ma-o-na le'-a-lé-a la e a I ta a

i ho'o-nu'u a o pi- ha la e Tu a - i no ka he-le-a-na la e a He bo-a'-

a i te we-le-la-u li- ma la e I ta a-pa-na na-mu ha-a-o-le la e Ha-e-

na mai a-na ka pu-a-na la e a-na A-u-he-a wa-le o-e e ka wa- i la e La-i

ma-li-a i Ha-u-o - la la e

Auhea wale oe e ka wa'i
Lana malie i Hauola
Ua ola a'e nei ke kuewa
Ike ka kahiaka inu kope
Ai i ka meaono a ke kuke
Me ke ki manuahi wale mai
Pono i ka maona le'ale'a

I ka ai ho'onu'u a piha
Ku ai no ka hele ana
He loa'a i ka welelau lima
I ka apana namu haole
Haina ia mai ana ka puana
Auhea wale oe e ka wa'i
Lana malie i Hauola

No. 85.—Hula puili, chanted by Solomono Huihui, Honolulu, Oahu.

No. 86.—Hula puili, chanted by Moha, Kekaha, Kauai.

A-u he'wa be a-na o-e E za pu ha-u o Ma bek(a) Ke a-u ni ka ma-

na-o o Pe-he - ao Ni-a-ka-ba Ke ba wai ta-ma-ha-o Wa-iha li'i ta mo-a-n(a) No

nei mai na mo-e-ku(Lo)'he a-kune'i bu-kin'(i) Ua' nai a-Ku-be-ke A-ob'i-ho-po La

kan(a)(O) kani u-o A-e-kia Hu-e-a e Kau na nu(i) Ka mo-a-na Ini-a-na E hu-hu

no' E-na-la-ni(Te)to-a Te-to-e-i-ti' A-li' o-e pa-la-u O o (Lines

missing in text)   Ha-i-ne ta pu a-na Ka-la-ka-u-a i-no(a)

(Note: At the end of this hula the words *"He inoa no Kalakaua"* were spoken.)

Auhea wale ana oe
E ka pua hau o Maleka
Ke au nei ka mana'o
Pehea o Niakala
Ke la wai tamaha'o
Wai halulu i ta moana
Nene mai na moku
Lohe a ku nei Lukini
Ua ana ia Kuleke aole i hopo Lakana

O ka nui o Akia
Huea e ke kai na nui
Haiti ka moana Iniana
Ehuehu no o E-na-lani
Te toa o Ketotia
Alia oe e palau
Haina mai ta puana
O Kalakaua he inoa.

No. 87.—Hula puili, chanted by Solomono Huihui, Honolulu, Oahu.

No. 88.—The same as No. 87, repeated by the same chanter.

He aloha ku'u lei pua oliwa
I pilia i ke anu pili ko'o lua
Elua maua e'e pakeke
Maluna o ka mokuahi Kaleponi
Ia lawa iho wau ma ka palekai
Ka pipi'i a ke kai pi'o mahope
Aia Hiloone ka pua o Kina
I lokua e ka ua kanilehua
Onaona Paliuli i ka ua noe
I ka holu a ka niu o Kalapana
I na paha oe e ike ana
I ka papa opiopi o Kaiwiki
Ike la paha oe i ka mea nani
Ka uahi pu'unohu mai i ka lua
He alele waha ole kai hiki mai
Na ka manu kiko pua lehua Ola'a

I ka ike a na iho hakuko'i loko
Lelele kaha uli pau ka palena
Pa ka makani nui naue ka moku
Hiu na pe'a heke o ka holo ia
I pae mai au i kahi manu
Nene holo hau o Maunakea
Aole kahi nui ia Kohala waho
Ua like laua me Kohala loko
Kau aku ka mana'o no Hi'ilawe
I ka papa lohilua o Maukele
I pakele ho'okahi mai nei Puna
I ke ahi pi'i o Kilauea
Me oe ka haili a ke aloha
Me au ka halia no kaua
Haina ia mai ana ka puana
Ku'u hoa o ke anu pili ko'olua [7]

There is so much variation in many particulars, however, for the individuals of any group, that these differences are less sharp than any attempt to state them would indicate. There are exceptions to nearly every statement that could be made. The meters of the *puili* tunes are predominantly two-part, with some irregularities like fractional beats and very occasional three-beat measures. Four measures constitute the phrases in all but one tune which has phrases of two four-beat measures, and in each tune the phrases tend to fall in pairs.

No. 89.—Hula puili, from Maui, chanted by Solomono Huihui, Honolulu, Oahu.

[7] The informant who sang the chant did not know all the words and began in the middle. Mr. Kekoowai supplied a fuller version.

Hula ipu and hula pahu.—Possibly at some distant time the *hula ipu* and the *hula pahu* were really distinct in particulars other than the type of their instrumental accompaniment, but at present the same tune may

No. 90.—Hula pa-ipu, chanted by Antone Kaoo, Honolulu, Oahu.

Ko ma'i keia lawea mai
Ho'ohene i ka puni hiu a wela
Hiu a'e ko mai lawea mai
Aole mea koe hiu a wela
Ua nani Kilohana lawea mai

Kuahiwi kapu ia la o Kaala
He ala e ke oho a o kapalai
Ka maile lauli'i a o Koiahi
Haina ko ma'i lawea mai
Ho'oheno i ka puni hiu a wela

La a e a a a e a a e a

serve for both and is called a *hula ipu, ipu wai,* or *pa ipu* when the calabash drum is used, and *hula pahu* if it is associated with the wooden drum with the skin head. No *pahu* was seen, for when the two *hula pahu* were secured the *ipu* or even a tin box was substituted, and was used exactly as the *ipu*—swung in an arc to the right and left of the player as described on page 52.

Thirteen tunes were obtained for the *hula ipu,* Nos. 90 to 102, inclusive, but not many with the *ipu* accompaniment. However, as all the *hula ipu* which I did see were played in very simple rhythms, the accompaniments presented here will give a good idea of them and presumably may be taken as typical.

In No. 90 the rhythm of the *ipu* is represented by the two lower lines of notes. The calabash was played by raising it quickly and dropping it on the pad with a thud for the first beat, and by slapping it on the side with the fingers of the right hand, as it was suspended in the air, for the succeeding beats. The lowest line of quarter notes and rests represents the dropping of the *ipu* on the pad, the upper the slapping of the fingers. Throughout, the heavy beat of the *ipu* comes at the first of the measure, so that the beginning of the voice part after the accent is perhaps not so significant for the movement of the piece as a whole as if the song were unaccompanied. The structural design of the music is very well marked and is carried out consistently. There is an introduction of four measures or one phrase by the drum, after which the voice begins. The lines of the poetry are arranged in couplets and to each line there are four measures of two-four meter. The meter is regular throughout. The two melodic phrases constituting a pair do not differ much from one another yet there is enough diversity in the second each time to make it complementary to the first. At the end of each phrase the beats change, the end of the first phrase having one ground thump for the initial beat and one tap for the second, while only ground thumps on the beats close the second phrase. Between the couplets are interludes of drumming covering three measures exactly and this design is carried throughout. Our ideas of sym-

No. 91.—Hula ipu-wai, also serves as a hula alaapapa, chanted by Moha, Kekaha, Kauai.

Ho'oputa i kai i ka la inu lau   Puta hele i tai tulili i taua
E lulumi ana na ale o kauná   Ka papa a Lohiau a pua
Hati kakala mai ana ka makani   E lohi mai ana e maukele
Puta ka hala ka lehua o Panaewa   Ta papa o Papakanené
                                                         E puta a ua nei ka makani[8]

metry would suggest interludes of four measures as more in keeping with
the form of the voice phrases, but this musician has chosen to contrast one
three-measure phrase with two four-measure phrases, which results in an
effective metric pattern.

The introduction of the chant, on the other hand, is four measures
long. As if to emphasize the contrast between the interludes and the open-

---

[8] The text is said by one informant to be incomplete; by others, to have no meaning.

ing and closing parts, after the last couplet the coda begins with a four-measure phrase chanted to filler syllables, and this is paired with a phrase partly sung but finished with a new rhythm of drumming. To balance the introduction the chant closes with a complete phrase of drumming in a still different rhythm. This is one of the best examples of structural design in any of the tunes collected. The chanter, who is a well-known hula master in Honolulu, said that the same mele and tune might be used for a *hula uliuli*. In response to a request for a demonstration he gave No. 105. I do not know whether the fact that this man is par₁ negro is any reason to advance for the superiority of his examples from a metric and rhythmic standpoint as well as from that of design, but the ability of the negro along these lines, which amounts to a racial trait, is too well-known to need discussion here. This was the only informant in whom negro blood appeared to dominate.

In tonal content the tune is extremely limited, covering only the general level and the minor third below.

In No. 91 the ground beat of the *ipu* was on the quarter notes until the dotted rhythms began, after which it occurred at every beat, the sixteenth notes being tapped with the fingers. This tune also has its introduction. There is nothing noteworthy in the melody; the meter is almost absolutely regular and the phrases are about four measures long. There are only two digressions from a monotone, the first of which, near the middle of the chant, is uncommon. The tonal content, besides the general level, includes the minor third below, and the major second and minor third above. This chant was also called a hula *alaapapa*, with *ipu* accompaniment, and will be referred to later under the hulas of that name. (See p. 268.)

Although No. 92 is also in straightforward rhythm, the meter is a little

No. 92.—Hula pa-ipu, chanted by Mrs. Kaahaaina Naihe, Honolulu, Oahu.

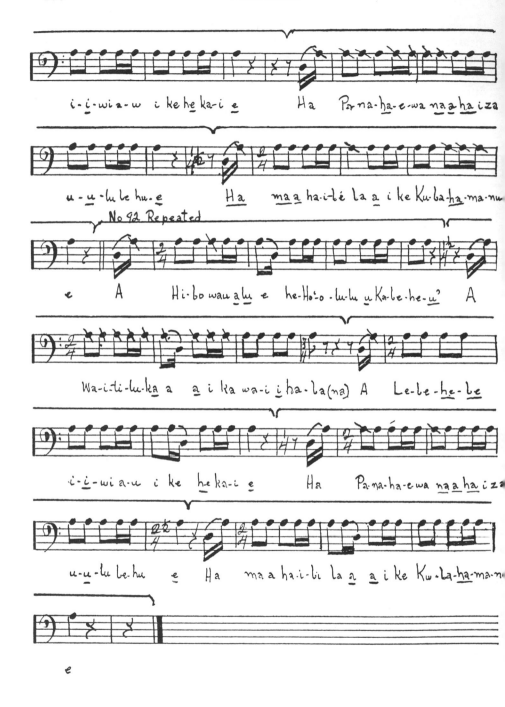

No. 93.—Hula pa-ipu from Hilo, chanted by Mrs. Kaahaaina Naihe, Honolulu, Oahu.

A Hi-lo ho wa-u e - he Ho-o-lu-lu hu ka le-he-ua A Wai-

hi-lu-ku wa a hai ka wa-i hi ha-ba-na A Le-e -he-le-e -

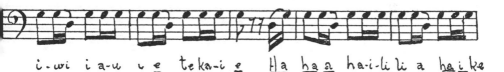

i - wi i a-u u e te ka-i e Ha ha a ha-i-li li a hai ke

Ku-la-ha-ma-nu e Ha Pa-na-hae-wa la a ha i ka u-lu hu be-hu-e

A Hilo no wau ehe
Hoʻolulu ka lehua
A Wailuku a i ka wai halana

A Leleiwi au i ke kai
Haili la e ke Kulamanu e
Panaewa i ka ulu lehua
(Incomplete)

irregular. The majority of the measures have two beats, but show a tendency
to shorten the intervals between phrases. Each phrase contains four
measures, but there is no particular evidence of their belonging in pairs.
Only five lines are given which are repeated with slight rhythmic and pitch
differences. All the phrases begin on the last half of the second beat.
The rhythmic pattern set forth in the first phrase is closely followed in all.
Even though this piece also has the beats subdivided, a very different swing
characterizes it from that observed in Nos. 90 or 91.

The tonal content is unusual. Not considering the flat *a*'s which are
probably not intentional, or the raised *a* at the end of the second phrase,
only two tones occur, the general level and the fifth below, a tone which
seldom occurs alone in connection with it. However, in still another

rendition of this chant by the same singer, the interval is changed to a fourth. (See No. 93.)

Nos. 94 and 95 are different versions of the same mele from Niihau. The words are not very ancient, but the mele is good.

No. 94.—Hula ipu-wai from Niihau, chanted by Kamehaitu Helela, a native of Niihau living on Kauai.

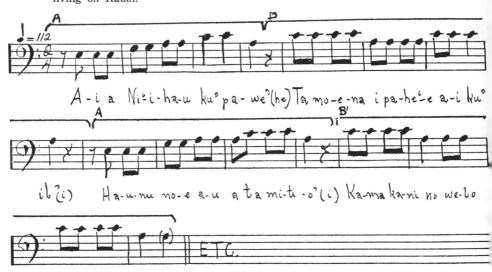

Aia i Ni‘ihau ku‘u pawehe
Ta moena i pahe‘e au ku‘u ili
Haunu noeau a ka mikioi
Ka makani nowelo piko o lehua
Elua maua me ke ala me ka ulu
    hua noho i ka‘apapa
Kau aku ka mana‘o e i ke maka
I ke ko eli lima o Halali‘i
Ailana o Kaula noho i ka mole
Home pohai a na manu
He aloha Nihoa i ka ehukai
A ka naulu e ho‘oipo nei
Ooe ku‘u hoa alo o ke anu
Na ale holu mai o Kaulakahi
Ho‘okahi a‘u lei e lei nei
O ke ahi kau mai o Anaki
A ke aku ka mana‘o e ike maka
I ke ahi kaulana o Kamaile
Ka nihi nowelo i Makuaiki
Ahe iki ko aloha eha ku‘u kino

Aloha Nu‘alolo i ka haka lewa
I ke ala kunihi a ka malihini
Kau aku ka mana‘o e inu wai
I ka wai kau mai o waialoha
Aloha ka makani ahe Ko‘olau
Ka makani noho o lae o Kikiopua
Ku‘u pua lehua i Haena
Kahela i ka wai o Limahuli
Ka huli ke ala o ka na‘ena‘e
Ku‘u ipo laua‘e noho i ka poli
Kaua i ke one o Maniniholo
Ku‘u ipo i ke kai holu o Makua
Ulu hala o Naue kau aloha
I ka nou hala ole a ka lupua
Onaona na lehua o Lulu‘upali
Noho ana i ka poli o kau maka
Kau aku ka mana‘o no Haohila
Hue pau ke kai o ke alahula
Kau aka mana‘o no ka ua loku
E ike i ka nani o ka aina

Only two couplets were given by the first informant, in which the melodic phrases are complementary. The couplets begin on the last half of the first beat and the phrases are four measures of two-four time. In tonal content this tune recalls some of the hulas from Maui, for aside from the upper note, which might be regarded as a tonic of a melody with major tonality, and the two tones of its inverted major triad, the minor third below it receives considerable prominence and is the final tone of each phrase. This fact makes it possible to regard the tune as having its

No. 95.—Hula ipu-wai from Niihau, chanted by Hanohano Makea, a native of Niihau living at Hanapepe, Kauai. (Incomplete, would be continued after the same manner.)

A-lo ma-i Ni-i-ho-a i ta e-hu-kai A ka na-a-u-lu a-e ho-o-u-po ne'(i)
O — o e tu-u ho-a a-lo o ke a-n:(u)
Na a-le ho-lu ma-u o ka u-lu ka'(hi)et

general level on the lower tone, and as being minor in tonality. The tune differs from the Maui hulas in beginning on the lowest of the four notes and working up through all of them to the highest.

The second version of this chant, No. 95, begins on the accented beat, thus differing from the *hula ipu* tunes so far examined. It is written in four-four time, and only two measures are required for a line of the poetry. Some of the phrases are sufficiently different, melodically, to form complementary pairs, but there is little variation and most of the time the same melodic idea occurs in both. Taking *g* as the general level, it is evident that the tonal content is the same as in the first version, except that the lowest tone is missing. The chant begins on the highest and works down. It ends, as did the first version, on the minor third below the level. There are some instances of syncopation in the second version but none in the first. The beats of the *ipu* were not obtained for this hula.

Beginning with No. 95, are several *hula ipu* which start on the primary accent. The long first line of the poetry in No. 96 is responsible for running the melodic phrase past the usual four measures of two-four time to the middle of the fifth, after which the remaining phrases start on the last part of the measure. The time of the second phrase is thrown out in the three-four measure. The third phrase is five measures long, with an extra beat in the first measure, as well. This sort of irregularity continues throughout the chant. The mele is given by Emerson (43, pp. 63, 155).

The melody is very unusual, the only one of all that were collected which shows a suggestion of modulation. The general level is easily determined as *c*, but the tune starts a major third below it. These two tones, with one appearance of the major second above, are all that are found until the *ab* changes to *a♮* at the beginning of the third phrase, thus shifting the tune from a tonality suggesting *ab* major to one of *a* minor. In this new melodic setting the fourth phrase, with the introduction of the fourth below the level, appears to modulate definitely to a tonality which we would be apt to designate as *f* major, for although the tonic is not heard, it is the more forceful because it is expected and does not appear.

No. 96.—Hula pa-ipu, chanted by Mrs. Kaimu Kihe, Puuanahulu, North Kona, Hawaii.

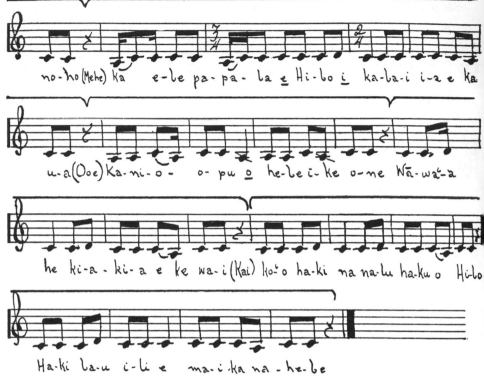

(Note: The chant has two verses.)

No luna e ka hale-kai noho ia e ka
  ma'alewa
Nana na maka ia Moana-nui ka
  lehua
Noi au i e kai o Mali'o
Ku a'e he lehua ilaila a o oe ia a ia

II

Pa ko Keaau o lulu Waiakea
Noho i ka la'i o Hanakahi
O Hilo i holo ke'a ia

Kau keikei o Leleiwi o Makahanaloa
Me ka ele papala he la i lalo e
  Kanoho
Me he kaele papala Hilo kalai ia e
  ka ua
Ooe Kani-o-opu hele i ke one
Wa'awa'a he kiakia e ke { wai
                          { anu
Kai ko'o haki na nalu haku o Hilo
Haki lau ili e mai ka nahele

However, the Hawaiians probably would not miss it, lacking as they
do the harmonic background, and the melodic mode, as they perceive it,
would be very differently colored on this account. The fifth phrase of the
chant acts as a coda. At the introduction of the second verse syncopation
appears. The perfect fourth below the general level is lost, and the tune
is henceforth confined to the minor third interval and the major second
above, as at first. No instrumental accompaniment was obtained.

Two versions by different chanters of another *hula ipu* are Nos. 97
and 98.

No. 97.—Hula pa-ipu, chanted by Aiamanu Pauole, Hanalei, Kauai.

He wahi maʻi *e he a*
No Iolani *e he a*
Aia ko maʻi *e he a*
I Hiʻi lawe *e he a*
E lewa ana *e he a*
Ko kikala *e he a*

I kalaau *e he a*
A ka pahi olo *e he a*
Ko ia nei lima *e he a*
E umoki ana *e he a*
Haina ka puana *e he a*
No Iolani *e he a*

No. 98.—Hula pa-ipu, chanted by Kaha, Moloaa, Kauai.

Both of these chants start on the accent, and with a major third leap upward from the first to the second beat, but the individual rhythms are quite different, and in the first example the major third interval is soon replaced by the minor. Except for this little shift both versions have but two tones. The first ends on the same note on which it began, but the second on the upper note. The tunes might be described as *anuunuu*, wavering, for the distribution between the two tones is so equal that a designation of the general level could only be arbitrary. This term as applied to melody was one of the rare technical terms encountered.

Tune No. 99 from Maui has already been referred to in connection with the *hula paiumauma,* No. 69. It is almost entirely regular with four-measure phrases in two-four times. The first phrase is composed of two identical sections, a rare occurrence, and the rhythms are somewhat similar to those of No. 97.

No. 99.—Hula ipu-wai, chanted by Mrs. Lahilahi Webb, Honolulu, Oahu, from words furnished by Mrs. Koiahi, Hanalei Valley, Kauai.

hu-li ma i i A hu-li ma-i noho o-e mo-e

ka-a- u-a Mo-e a-ku ka-u-a O ka wa-i

we-la we-la o ka pa-pa lo-hi a o Ma-u-ke-le

la e a O i e A i e (2nd Verse) A ke-le a ke-le ko-a-lo-ha

Incomplete

la e a

E Manono *la* ea e Manono *la* ea
Kau ka opeope i kaulua
Hali'i punana no huli mai
A huli mai no oe moe kaua

Moe aku kaua o ka wai welawela
O ka papa lohi a o Maukele
A kele a kele ko aloha.

Although *bb* is not particularly frequent, the situations in which it is used would indicate it as the general level, in addition to which there are the other two notes of its major triad in downward inversion and the major second and third above it. This introduction of the upper third is also very unusual, for in only one tune so far examined has it appeared as a melody note. The two slightly raised *bb*'s are probably unintentional deflections. This tune should be compared with No. 100 which has the same mele but an entirely different melody. The tonal content varies in No. 100 between a major and minor third. Both the upper and lower tones are prominent, so that the general level is problematical.

No. 100.—Hula ipu-wai, chanted by Mrs. Koiahi, Hanalei Valley, Kauai.

Note: In the third staff, first measure, *b* should be an eighth note.

The rather uncertain beginning and the metric and phrase irregularities may mean that No. 101 is not a particularly good specimen. The deflected pitches which are not consistently used in phrases alike in conception may be only unintentional wanderings or may be an attempt to vary the monotony. Leaving them out the tonal content is *ab*, general level, and two tones forming its major triad in the first inversion, together with the leading tone and the lower dominant.

No. 102 is one of the rare examples of three-part meter throughout, with two measures to each musical division covering a line of poetry. There is not much melodic variety from division to division and no evidence of their forming pairs. The tonal content is again the general level and the minor third below.

The last of the group, No. 103, was also given as a mele oli. (See No. 30.) As a *hula ipu wai* its time varies between two-four and three-four, with four or five measures to the phrase. From the phrase marked E there are five measures to the phrase, except at F, where occurs a short interlude with considerable change in melody, and at which point the singer began to forget his words, which may account for the irregularities.

No. 101.—Hula pa-ipu, chanted by W. M. Kalaiwaa, Kamuela, South Kohala, Hawaii.

e — A-o Pā:na-ha-e-wa la a ha i ka u-lu hu le-hu' e — A

Pā-na-ha-e-wa la a ha i ka u-lu hu le-hu' e e A Ha-a-il' la a i ke

ku-la hau ma-nu e — A Ha-a-il' la a i ke ku-la hau ma-nu e A

Wa-i e-lu-ku a a a i ka lu-a a ka na-ka A Wa-i e-lu-ku

a a a i ka lu-a a ka-na-ka

Note: In the fourth staff, third measure, read a♮. The first and second staves should be closed with measure bars.

A Hilo wau e hoʻolulu ka lehua   A Panaewa la i ka ulu lehua e
A Leleiwi la au i ke kai   A Wailuku la i ka lua kanaka
                                 A Haili la i ke kula manu e

No. 102.—Hula ipu-wai, chanted by Moha, Kekaha, Kauai.

Note: In the fourth staff, third measure, read *f#*.

A Waialeale a nui ta hele kua
I te a Pu'utapele halulu koai'a
Nehe mai ta uila hela a Maunahina
Pili no a ka manu i te he naele o
    Alaka'i
He wai opua ka makani

Halulu ihola ke wai
Awawa mai Hanakahi ka luna o
    Kawako'o
Ko'o ha me no oe hano o noe i ta
    piina
Papaume ka ua mo'a i te alapi'i

The general level is *g,* but the major second above it has almost as much prominence. The minor third below the level is the next important tone, while the leading tone occurs only once, and the lower dominant only at F.

From these examples it will be seen that there is no one feature on which all the tunes are agreed. Part of them begin on weak beats, part on the accent. Some have regular two-four meter with four measures to the phrase, some are irregular both in meter and phrases; one has three-four meter throughout. In some the melodic phrases form pairs, in others they are apparently independent. The rhythms are different for all of them. Only one feature appears to be characteristic of the majority of tunes and that is the prominence of the minor third interval downward from the general level. While some tunes have quite an extended range, this interval is stressed more than the others, and in a few of the tunes there are only the two notes, the level and the third below. Whether

No. 103.—Hula ipu-wai, chanted by Louis Nakeu, Honolulu, Oahu.

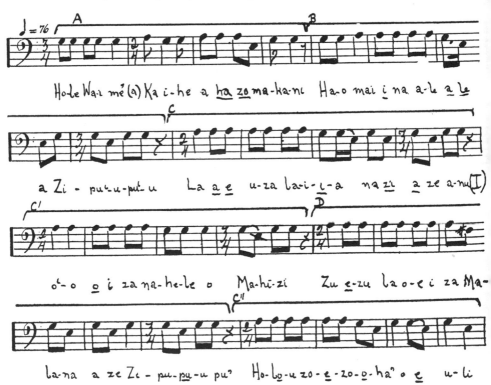

Hole Waimea ka ihe a ka makani
Hao mai na ale a ke Kipuʻupuʻu
Laau kalaihi ia na ke anu
I oʻo i ka nahele o Mahiki
Ku aku la oe i ka malana a ke
    Kipuʻupuʻu

Holu koʻohai ouli
Niniau eha ka pua o Koaia
Eha e ke anu o Waiká-é
Ka nahele o Wakai-e aloha
Kona aloha ka i hiki mai i oʻu nei
Mahea la i nalo iho nei
(Unfinished)

this should be taken as the distinguishing mark of the *hula ipu* melodies, however, is a question. Its prominence here may be merely a coincidence.

Two tunes for the *hula pahu* are subjoined to the *ipu* chants.

The meter of No. 104 is absolutely regular two-four. The first five phrases are four measures long, but in the D phrase the extra length of line requires an additional beat which is taken from the following phrase. F is also lengthened by a beat, but G, instead of being shorter, has one more measure than usual. The heavy beat of the *pahu* or *ipu*, as the case

No. 104.—Hula pahu, chanted by Peter Pakele, Waiakea, Hilo, Hawaii.

We-li-na mai nei i ke kini o lalo
Na hoa i ka uka nahele o Puna
A kahi kanoho ua e kauakahi
Noho a Kane ka papa lohia
A lau o Kalohelani o Pi'ilani

Alo nei ia poe ka maanu lei
Na ka manu i kai o Halulu
Ha no ka lani ka papanio ni'oni'o
Ni'oni'o oi ala e i a
Mimiki ke kai o ahu wale ka papa

may be, shifts from the second to the first beat of the measure without apparent design, and the lighter taps are now and then reduced to two eights or a quarter on the second beat only. No other varieties of rhythms were heard during many repetitions of the piece, but these were interchanged constantly.

In tonal content there is the general level, with one deflected tone at the end of the G phrase, and the lower dominant, a perfect fourth below, which is changed to the minor third at the beginning of the C phrase.

No. 105.—Hula pahu, chanted by Waiwaiole Kala, Kapaa, Kauai.

(Note: Beats of the pahu and the niu are indicated.)

No. 105 was a continuous repetition, without variation, of the musical section given here, so far as the tune continued. The tonal content is the general level and the minor third below.

Hula uliuli.—Probably the most popular of the hulas at the present time is the *hula uliuli* and tunes for it, as well as meles, are composed in greater number than for any other. I have selected fourteen out of nearly thirty, all very similar, to present for discussion, but they are so much alike in many particulars and the reader is so familiar by now with the methods of analysis adapted, that it will not be necessary to say much concerning them.

No. 106.—Hula uliuli taken from his grandfather's book and chanted by Antone Kaoo, Honolulu, Oahu.

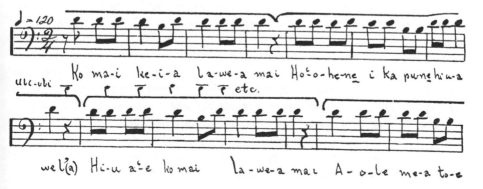

hi-u a wel'(a) U-a na-ni ki-lo-ha-na la-we-a mai Ku-a-he-we

ka-pu i-a la o Ta-al'(a) He a-la e ke o-ho a o Ta-pa-

lai Ta-ma-i-le-la-u-ki-i a o To-i-a'(hi) Ha-i-na za o

ma-i la-we-a mai Ho-o-he-no i ta pu-ne hi u aa we-la la

e a a a e a a e a

With one exception, and possibly a second which will be discussed when it is reached, all the tunes begin on the second half of a beat. The time is almost absolutely regular in the most examples and two-four meter predominates, but there are a number of tunes with four-four, and in most cases the phrases contain four or two measures as the case may be. In some of the chants the phrases form pairs with complementary melodic material, in others they are merely one theme repeated over and over with very little variation. No. 106 is one of this type.

Only two tones, a minor third apart, form this chant. The upper is the most frequent and probably should be taken as the level. The *uliuli* was shaken only on the beat, but in returning after a shake there was a slight rattle occasioned by the movement, which has not been represented in the notation. This piece should be compared with No. 90. It is one of two demonstrations made by a hula master of the method of adapting a tune and mele to two different types of hulas, in this case the *ipu* and the *uliuli*.

No. 107 is the only example I have observed in all the Hawaiian chants in which the extension as a device is regularly employed throughout the song to lengthen phrases of melody which in their usual number of four measures would be too short to accommodate the poetry. The first phrase, A, has an extension of two measures. B is really composed of extensions only, repeated, and forms a complement to A. It is eight and a half measures long. The A' phrase is two measures longer than A, with a second extension, while B' is shorter by two measures than the corresponding B, and so the tune proceeds.

The tonal content resembles that of some of the earlier hula tunes. The general level is *bb*. In addition, there are the two tones of its inverted major triad, as well as the major second above; and twice the leading tone comes in, a half step below the level. The song begins on the lowest tone and works up. No accompaniment was secured for this or the remaining tunes, but all the *uliuli* rhythms which I have heard are very simple, with a shake usually on the beat, and now and then on the half beat, with no syncopation.

No. 108, from Maui, has a rhythm very common to *uliuli* melodies. Its phrases are in pairs, with complementary melodic material. The measures

No. 107.—Hula uliuli for Lunalilo, chanted by Solomono Huihui, Honolulu, Oahu.

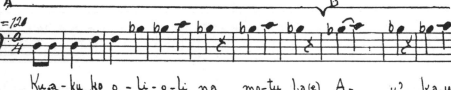

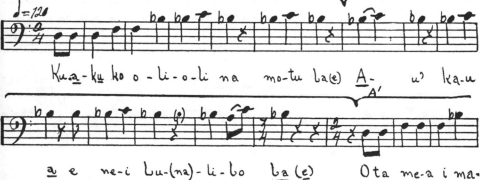

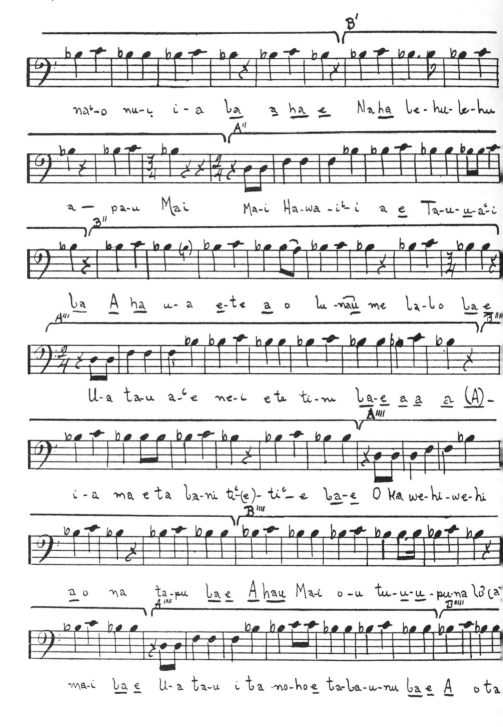

ba-ni Lu-na-li-lo he (i) -no-a ba e

Ku ka olioli i na moku
Ua kau a‘e nei Lunalilo
O ka mea i mana‘o nui ia
E na lehulehu a pau
Mai Hawai‘i a Kaua‘i
Ua ike o luna a me lalo

Ua kau a‘e nei e ke kini
Aia ma ka lani ki‘eki‘e
O ka wehiwehi o na kapu
Mai o‘u kupuna loa mai
Ua kau i ka noho kalaunu
O Kalani Lunalilo he inoa

No. 108.—Hula uliuli, for Kalakaua, chanted by Solomono Huihui, Honolulu, Oahu.

He me-le he i-no-a no ze u-na-on(a) No ka ha-i za-la-u-nu i Ha-le a-

li-’i He li-’i na ma-za la’ e za u-il-a E a-na-pu i i’li-’i

za pa-e o-pu-a Zu’u pu-a li-i-li a la lai Wa-i-

lu - ku Ua i -nu i za wa-i o I-i- a-o U-a’o za-u-a

e za i - nu (w)ai U-a pa zo ma-za-ni a he zi-lipo(he) (A) he po-e

me-i a-u no Ha-wa-i’-i He ma-za hu-a-po mu-a na-e Zo-mu-

a-i - e n'(a) Ha-i-na i-a ma-i a-na ka pu a-na He me-le hie-i-

no-a no li - -lo a

He mele he inoa no ke onaona	I'ane'i mai oe me mi nei
Ka hae kalaunu e Hale ali'i	He wai hau ia no ke kanaka
He 'li'i na maka o ka uila	Akaka wale no Haleakalá
E anapu mai la ka pae opua	Ka ue a ke kini o Ko'olau
Ku'u pua lilia la i Wailuku	Lalau i ka pua ke aali'i
Ua inu i ka wai o Iao	Laau kunihi alo i ke kona
Ua ao kaua e ka inu wai	He a'e ale au no ka moana
Ua pa ka makani he kilipohe	Alamihi o ka lae iliili
He poe mai au no Hawai'i	Ilihia i ka pa a ka puewai
He maka hiapo kapu na Kumukahi	Ka makani anu o ku'u aina
Ho'okahi lihau pua i Kaua'i	Haina ia mai ana ka puana
Hu'e lapa koni hu'e i'ane'i	E ola ku'u lani milimili

are somewhat irregular but the phrases are of nearly uniform length. In tonal content the tune is like many that are known to have come from Maui and very similar to the preceding, except that the major second above the level is lacking, and once the perfect fifth below is introduced. The tune begins on the lowest note and works up to the level. Practically the same melody is used for many meles, and may be called one of the stock hula tunes. Another rendition of it by the same chanter shows the type of variations that exist. (See No. 109.)

No. 110 is again very similar melodically to the preceding chants, but its time is definitely four-four, and four measures constitute each phrase. There is but one melodic idea repeated over and over for each, with scarcely any variation. It contains only four tones, the general level, the two forming its inverted major triad, and the fifth below. This tune also begins on the lowest note and works up.

The text of No. 111 was faulty, so it has been omitted. The tune is not very different from the others, with each phrase composed of practically the same melodic idea. The phrases are unusually long, the first four of seven measures, while all but one of the remaining have six measures, but two of them end in a measure of three-four rather than

No. 109.—Repetition of No. 108 by the same chanter.

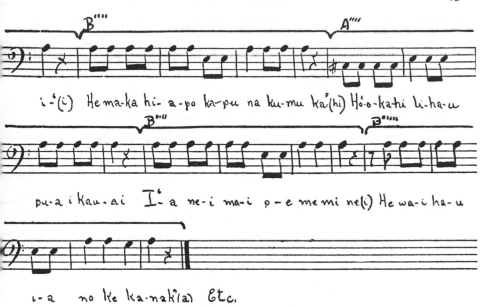

Note: In the last staff, first measure, the final two notes should be eighth notes and *g* should be *g#*.

No. 110.—Hula uliuli, chanted by Solomono Huihui, Honolulu.

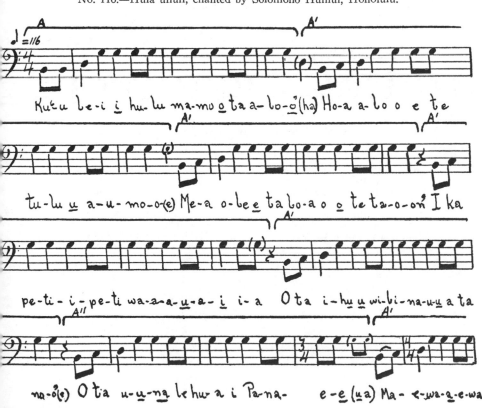

wa-u <u>u</u> e te ho-<u>o</u>(a) U-a tu'u a-a<u>'</u>e o-e e i ta nu-<u>u</u>(i) Na-u i-i-

i-mi ta-a-<u>a</u>-<u>u</u>-pe na ho <u>ho</u> A-no e h<u>e</u> <u>e</u> ta no-ho-na <u>a</u> u-a li-te <u>ko</u>-i

ma-i <u>i</u> ta <u>a</u> u-a <u>a</u> b<u>a</u> e pi-i (li) O i ta<u>a</u><u>a</u> ma-u a-<u>'</u>a-e te a-

bo-o-(ha) E pi- pi-i i ne-i i ta a pu-<u>u</u>-wa-<u>a</u>-(i) Ha-i-na <u>a</u><u>a</u> ma-i

a-na ta pu-<u>u</u>-a- an(a) Ho-a a-bo<u>o</u> <u>i</u> te tu-lu <u>u</u> a-u-mo-o'(e)

Ku'u lei hulu mamo ke aloha
Hoa alo o ke kulu aumoe
Mea ole ka loa o ke kaona
I ka pekipeki wawae ia
O ka iho wilinau a ka noe
O ka uka lehua i Panaewa
Maewaewa wau e ka hoa

Ua ku'u a'e oe i ka nui
Nau i imi kapena hou
Ano e ka nohona ua like
Koi mai ka oe e pili
Oi ka mau a'e ke aloha
E pipi'i nei i ka pu'uwai
Haina mai ana ka puana
Hoa alo au o ke kulu aumoe

No. 111.—Hula uliuli, chanted by Solomono Huihui, Honolulu, Oahu.

Note: Last two measures, staff two, also second and third measures, staff eight, should carry repeat marks.

two-four time. The tonal content consists in the general level, the two tones of its inverted major triad, the subdominant, and the leading tone.

Although each phrase of No. 112 is like every other and contains two measures of four-four time, the interlude of a single measure at the end of every second one shows that they are conceived of as complementary.

No. 112.—Hula uliuli called Kanaenae for Laka or Kona Hema, chanted by J. S. Kiaha, Kohanaiki, North Kona, Hawaii..

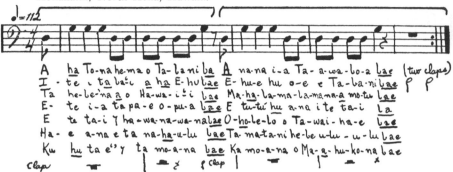

There was no *uliuli* but the chanter clapped in place of it. It is doubtful if he would use the instrument so sparingly, for it seems to be customary to shake it at least on every beat.

The tonal content has but two pitches, the general level and the perfect fourth below, which is the more frequent of the two, but the points at which the upper occurs indicate that it should be considered as the level.

The text of this chant has appeared before, in connection with Nos. 72 and 73, as a *hula paiumauma,* and is therefore omitted here.

No. 113 and a second rendition of it, No. 114 by the same singer, differ markedly from the other *uliuli* tunes only in their more rapid movement and the smaller time unit. There are four eighth-note beats to the measure, and two measures to each phrase. Two melodic ideas group the phrases in pairs which are repeated more or less exactly. The contrast between the perfect fourth in the first phrase of each pair and the minor third in the second, for the chief interval below the level, is an unusual play. In addition to the level, *db*, and the two tones of the inverted triad, are noted the major second above the level, the half-step or leading tone, the minor third below, and some deflected pitches which are apparently occasioned by the fact that the tune is pitched near the upper limit of the singer's range, for in the second rendition, which shifts to a pitch a whole step lower after completing the first couplet, they disappear except in the one case of an altered leading tone.

No. 113.—Hula uliuli, chanted by Nahaleuli Nahialua, Kekaha, Kauai.

(A) i-a i Ma—na' kou be-i na-ni Ko o—ha-i o   Pa-pi-o-

hu-li (I) pi-li-a Ko²lu a no ta-u- no²a   No-no-no u ba-i ta wai bi²u

la   I na— pa-hao-e   ei-te   a-na (I) ta ho lu a ta ni-u

o Kau-na-be-wa (He) a-be-be wa² o-le tai hi-ti   ma- i (Na) ka u-li a-i le hu (a)

o ka-na— he-be

Note: The third staff should be closed with a measure bar.

No. 114.—Repetition of No. 113, by same performer.

(A) i-a i   Ma-na' Kou be-i na-ni Ko o o- ha-i o   Pa- pi-o

hu- li (I) pi-li-a ko²o-lu a   no ta-u- no² a No-no-no u-bai ta wai li u

le-a I na a pa-hao-e ei-te a-na (I) ta ho-lu a ka ni-u

Ka-u-na-be-wa (He) a-le-be wa-ha-o-be tai hi-ti

Aia i Maná kou lei nani	I ta ite a na iho lana ka mana'o
Ko ohai o Papiohuli	I ta hea a ka leo o ko Waikini
I pilia ko'olua no ka tauno'a	Kau aku ka mana'o no Wailua
Nonono ula i ta wai li'ulá	No ka wai ho'oipo ka pua hau
Ina paha oe e ite ana	He ole ka heluna no Waimea
I ta holu a ka niu o Kaunalewa	Ua like laua mea Makaweli
He alele waha ole tai hiti mai	Haina ia mai ana ka puana
Na kaili ai lehua o ka nahele	Na niu holu mai o Kaunalewa

No. 115.—Hula uliuli, composed by Kalala and chanted by Wahineikeaouli Paa, Haena Wet Caves, Kauai.

Ha-no-ha-no ka-u-ka i Pu-ha-na-ka-ba-ni (I) Ka be-o o ko o-he ka-na-

i-ka-wi̅   Na-ne ho̤o i-po-i po ke a-bo-ha

A bo-a̤a o Ka-i-lu-ba-u-o-te-to̤(a)   Ke kui-ni

i ka ho-me a o na o ma-nu Ke a-ba a-nu-he-a pu-a mo-ki-han̤(a)

He e ko-na pu-li-a-hi no ko-wa-i ku-ni Hṳ-i ba i ka lu-na

Hanohano ka uka i Pihanakalani
I ka leo o ko ohe kanikawí
Nana ho'oipoipo ke aloha
A loa'a o Kaililauotetoa
Ke kuini i ka home o na manu
Ke ala anuhea pua mokihana
He kona piliahi no kowaikini
He uila i ka luna Waialeale

Aneane no au e laiwalé
E noho kapena no ka welowai
Pa ha, pa lima, ku'u lohe ana
Ua hui Huleia me Niumalu
Ua malu Kuhiau noho i ka iu
Ua pa'a i tapono a Lihue
Haina ia mai ana ka puana
O Hali'alaulani kou inoa

The chanter used No. 115 again and again with slight variations for any number of meles, and on some occasions embellishments in the form of passing and changing notes made it very melodious. Although the phrases are so much alike, it may be seen that they are intended to fall in pairs, with an interlude of three measures after each couplet, an arrangement which recalls the *hula ipu,* No. 90, and the *hula uliuli,* No. 112. The interludes are practically regular throughout the piece. The phrases have the customary four measures of two-four time.

Difficulty in determining the general level is encountered because of the almost equal use of *d* and *e.* Experience with many tunes, however, inclines me to consider it as *d,* and the *e* as the major second above, while *b* is the familiar minor third below, and the perfect fourth appears at the end of the first phrase of each couplet except in the first instance. To ears accustomed to major scales and harmony, the *d* sounds like the fifth in a scale of which the tonic, though absent, is continually suggested, but as intimated before, this predisposition to harmonize background must not be considered to color the Hawaiian viewpoint and should be ignored in an attempt to appreciate Hawaiian tunes as they are.

In No. 116 there is the same tonal content as in the preceding chant, with the lower addition of *f*♯, but the progression of the melody is reversed. The introduction of the *f*♯ gives the inverted major triad of the general level, while the major second above, and the minor third below also occur. In another *hula uliuli* this tune is used again with the addition of the leading tone, and is much elaborated rhythmically.

In structure No. 116 is practically identical with No. 115.

No. 116.—Hula uliuli, chanted by Wahineikeaouli Paa, Haena Wet Caves, Kauai.

Ki-li-o-e ta-u a-no-a-i a (Ho-) o-pu-lu i-a ne-i e ta e-hu ta-i

a e   A-ka-hi ho-i a-u a i-ke ma-ka a e Na ku-pa

ta-u-la-na o ka a-i-na a e   Ha-i-na i-a ma-i a-na ka pu-

a-na a e (O) ka li-hi-li-hi o ta po-li la-u-a-e a e

Ka poli laua'e ka'u aloha	I ka poli kapu o Lohiauipo
A Makana ho'i e hi'i mai nei	Ku'u ipo i ke kai o Keé
Hi'i poi ia e ka wai ama'u	Kai hāwanawana hone i ka poli
Ka makani kaulana o ka aina	Poli o Kilioe ka'u anoai
Ua like a like me Kanaloa	Ho'opulu ia nei e k'ehukai
Me ka wai aniani o Kapala'e	A kahi ho'i au a ike maka
Ma'ema'e ia pua o ka hinahina	Na kupa kaulana o ka aina
Ia lei makahehi a ka malihini	Haina ia mai ana ka puana
Iini ka mana'o e ike aku	O ka lihilihi o ka poli laua'e

Beginning with No. 117, the remaining tunes commence on the accent. The same rhythms prevail, however, except for this feature, and as if it were impossible to depart from the customary style, now and then in the course of the chants phrases will begin on the half-beat. There are no points about No. 117, except the manner of beginning, which have not been observed for the *uliuli* tunes in general.

Although No. 118 has a very different sounding melody because of its movement in curves from the lowest note up to the level and down again to the fourth or minor third below, it is practically the same as the others in tonal content, except that the major second above the level is missing.

The meter and the phrases are uneven, but the irregularities are rather consistent throughout the piece and make an unusual and interesting rhythm. There are only three measures of irregular meter to a phrase and the phrases are in pairs, although only the difference of a single note at the end of each couplet, except one, reveals this. It may be thought that there is some mistake in placing the *e*'s which begin the phrases; at times they appear on the last measure beat and again after the bar. These differences in accenting did exist, but they were not consistent with regard to the position in the first or last part of the couplet, as the notation shows. The mele has already been given in part on page 251.

No. 117.—Hula uliuli, chanted by Solomono Huihui, Honolulu.

ti - no   Hi-ki-ma-i te-a-bo-ha zu-pou - li   (A)-ne-a-ne no a-u

e-u-e a   i - ho I ka me-a ma-i-ta-i za he-a-bo-ha A-bo-ha

ta-hi wa-i a o te-i ho-e Ho-i o-e i-ba-i-ba pe-he-a wa-u

Pe he-a ho-i a-u   ko ho-a bo-e To-ho-a i-ta nu-i a-lu-a ta

be-o   Ne-e me-i e ta u-a pa-a na-u pa-li Pa-li o-e pa-li

a-u   pa-li ta—u-a   Ha-i-na   i-a ma-i a-na ta pu-a-na

Te pi-li ba-u ho-bo o a lu-a - nu-i

Auhea wale oe e Kauanoe
Ka ua koʻi aweawe i ke kula
Kuʻu hoa o ka ua lei koko ula
Ke pili lau holu o Luanui
Nui mai ko aloha eha koʻu kino
Hiki mai ke aloha kupóuli
Aneane no au e uwé iho
I ka mea maikaʻi he aloha

Aloha kahi wai o ke hoʻi
Hoʻi oe ilaila pehea wau
Pehea hoʻi au ko hoa luhi
Ko hoa i ka nui alu a ka leo
Neʻe mai e ka ua paʻa na pali
Pale oe, pale au, pale kaua
Haina mai ana ka puana
Ke pili lau holu o Luanui

In No. 119, as in Nos. 113 and 114, the movement is more rapid. Possibly the time might have been written as four-eight. Only two measures constitute the phrases which form pairs, and the meter is almost regular. The exception is the lengthening of the final measure of the second phrase in all but two instances, and with perfect consistency after the first time. The tune contains only two tones, the level and the minor third below.

With this group of tunes is concluded the survey of the *hula uliuli* and also of the sitting hula. Many features have appeared again and again in the melodies for this dance, and I have purposely stressed and repeated them that they might be impressed upon the memory, not only because some have appeared throughout all the hula tunes, but also because some are more typical of the *uliuli* chants even if practically never all present in the course of a single example. Therefore no one is representative; and since none is invariably characteristic it has been impossible to group the tunes according to any of them.

In the *uliuli* tunes the most distinguishing feature is the tendency to begin phrases on the half-beat, very frequently on the last half of the first in a two-beat measure. The phrases tend to be eight beats long, whether divided into four or two measures, and the meter is more regular, perhaps, for these tunes as a group, than for any other. The phrases fall very noticeably in pairs in many tunes, because there are two distinct melodic complementary ideas, one for each, and even where there is but one small theme, the difference of as little as one note at the end of the couplet, or the presence of an interlude, reveals the conception of two-part structure. The melodies in most instances are not nearly so circumscribed as in the other tunes, for although all along as many pitches have been encountered, they have seemed more ephemeral, outside of the level and its major second above and the minor third or fourth below, which built the main melody structure. In the *uliuli* tunes the inverted major triad of the level, the major second above the level, the minor third and the fifth below, and at times the half step below (a true leading tone) have greatly enriched the tonal content by becoming important in the melody. Where the previous hulas have generally begun on the level and worked down and back, most

No. 118.—Hula uliuli, chanted by Nahaleuli Nahialua, Kekaha, Kauai. (Incomplete.)

A-lo-ha Wai-me-a i ta wa-i te-a   Pa-i - hi ta wa-i u-la-i li

a'(hi)   U-a- hi u-tai   a a a a Ka Ti-u   I-te i ta a-u

wa-i a-ta me-ne-hun'(e) Ka tu-pu e-u o o Ki-ti-a-o. la

Na na i o-ni   pa-a po-li o Le-hu'(a) A - i-a i ka ba-i o

Ma-lu- a-ka Tu'u be-i o - ha-i a-boe-hu tai   I ho-a ka

a-na no a Li-ma-lo-a No ka o-ba- li o La-na-ma-i hit'(i) Hi-ti

mai ke a- lo-ha we-la Wa-i - ne-ki Ho-a pa-a-pa a-na Pa-a-pi-u

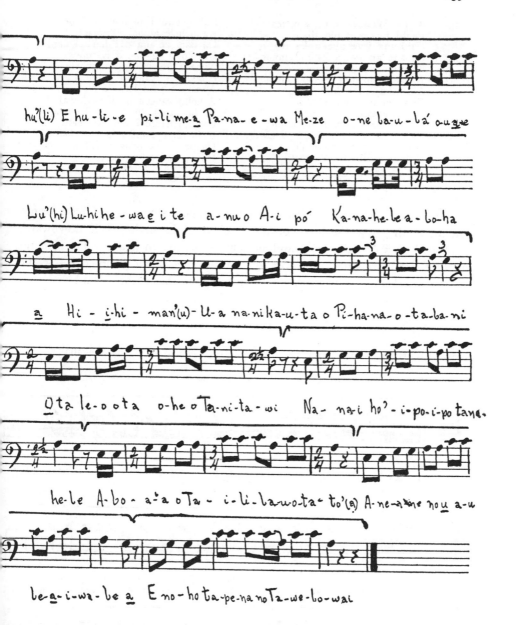

Aloha Waimea i ta wai tea   Luhi hewa i te anu o Aipó
Pa'ihi i ta wai ula iliahi   Ka nahele aloha Hihimanu
Uahi uta i te ahe a ka tiu   Ua nani ka uta o Pihanaokalani
Ite i ta au wai a ka menehune   Ka leo o ka ohe o Kanitawí
Ka tupu e'u o Kitiaola   Nana i ho'oipoipo ta nahele
Na na i oni pa'a poli o Lehua   A loa'a o Kaililauokatoa
Aia i ka la'i o Maluaka   Aneane no au leiwalé a
Tu'u lei ohai alo ehu tai   E noho kapena no Kawelowai
I hoa kaana no Limaloa   Pa lua, pa kolu, ku'u lohe ana
No ka olali o ka Lanamaihiti   Ua hui Huleia me Niumalu
Hiti mai ke aloha wela Waineki   Noho mai Tuhiau la i ta la'i
Hōapaapa ana Papiohuli   Ua pa'a i ta pono a Lihue
E huli e pili me Panaewa   Haina mai ta puana
Me ke one laulá ou e Luhi   Paihi i ta wai ula iliahi

of the *uliuli* tunes have taken directly the opposite course and have begun
on the sixth below the level, or the mediant of its major scale downward,
and worked up to the level and in some tunes down again. The general
feature is still retained, however, of the melodies being grouped below the
general level and rarely going above it except to the major second.

No. 119.—Hula uliuli, name chant for Kapiolani, chanted by Moha, Kekaha, Kauai.

(Note: At the end of the chant, the performer shouted, *"He inoa no Kapiolani."*)

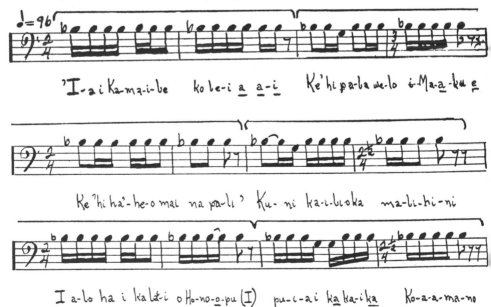

Aia i Kamaile ko lei nani
Ke ahi papala welo i Makua
Ke ahi haʻaheo mai na pali
E kukuni i ka ili o ka malihini
I aloha i ka laʻi o Honopu

I puia i ke kai Koaamano
Noho mai kilioe wahine i uka
Na kalo Aola kau i ka pali
Haina ka wahine nona ka lei
O Kapiʻolani i ka iu o ka moku.

THE HULA KU ILUNA, OR STANDING HULAS

Only five dances classed as standing hulas are represented here: the *hula kalaau,* the *olapa* or *alaapapa* (for they are said to be the same), and the *manai,* all with instrumental accompaniment; the *kilelei,* or *kielei,* and the *kui Molokai* without accompaniment. In the sitting hulas the motions were chiefly gestures, of well-defined types in the animal hulas and the *paiu-mauma,* although they in part portrayed the sentiment of the words of the meles; while in the instrumental hulas of this class the gestures illustrating the texts were combined with movements required or customary in the playing of the instruments. The standing hulas, on the other hand, were real dances.

Hula kalaau (stick hula).—Takes its name from its instrumental accompaniment. It was danced to the tapping of one stick (about nine inches long, and tapering at the ends like a cigar) on another several feet long, about two inches thick, tapering also, which was grasped by the left hand, palm upward, and held on the forearm close to the side, with a foot or more of its length projecting beyond the player's hand. Both sticks were of heavy dark wood, preferably kauila, which is resonant.

David Malo (100, p. 303), says that the *hula kalaau* was most frequently performed by chiefs. Emerson describes the dance (43, p. 116) and also quotes a description of a performance seen on Maui by Ellis who says that each musician beat time with the right foot on a stone placed on the ground beside him for that purpose. The two wooden instruments mentioned on page 54 were not seen in use but Sheriff Samuel Pua of Hilo, who is from Niihau, states (correspondence) that he has often observed them in the *hula kalaau* on Kauai, but does not know the name for them. He thinks that the concave side was covered either with shark or with *kala* skin.

The *kalaau* is a classical hula very seldom seen now, but those who have witnessed it say that the arms were flung about in a manner somewhat resembling wrestling. This must have necessitated two groups of performers, those who played on the sticks and those who danced. I did not see a regular performance, but obtained one tune from a woman of Kekaha, Kauai, without accompaniment, and others from a man on Hawaii who accompanied his hulas with the sticks and stamped with his feet. Sheriff

No. 120.—Hula ka-laau, chanted by Moha, Kekaha, Kauai.

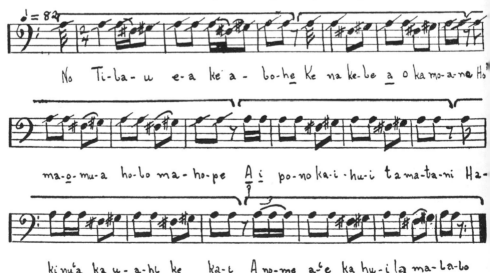

Pua states that both instruments, the sticks and the foot boards, were played in the same time, keeping up to the rhythm of the dance. The significance of the foot boards and sticks will be discussed on pages 364, 365.

The mele obtained from Moha, at Kekaha, Kauai, has been pressed into service for many kinds of hulas. (See Nos. 77, 78, 81.) It is also a favorite *ukeke* song. All the lines of the chant are begun on the last fraction of the final beat of the measure. The meter is absolutely regular two-four, and three measures constitute a melodic division. The general effect of the movement of the tune is quite like that of the animal hulas, Nos. 65 to 68. It would be allowable to combine three measures of two-four time into one of six-four.

The tune is confined to three principal tones, the general level, the leading tone, half a step lower, and the minor third below the level. In the first part of the song these tones are slightly sharper.

The other three examples obtained on Hawaii from a single informant all have the same melodic idea but are nevertheless distinct.

No. 121, instead of having three, has four measures to the phrase, so that it is fundamentally different from the one given by Moha. Two-four meter, however, is maintained. In addition to the last, which forms a coda, are six phrases, falling in complementary pairs. The coda has no other than a musical reason for its presence, for it would have been quite possible and even easy to have included the word *"ala"* at the end of the sixth phrase. As it is, the coda provides a very satisfactory ending to a little composition, which, if limited melodically, is nevertheless quite perfect from the standpoint of design.

After the first phrase, where their rhythm may have been made intentionally different so as to provide a contrast for the coda, the sticks are tapped in a rhythmic pattern carried consistently to the end of the chant.

The general level is *b,* and in addition to it there is the very uncommon whole step below, or, as we would call it, the flat seventh, and also the minor third below, with some deflected pitches or microtones between these two.

Although No. 122 sounds very much like No. 121, because of the tonal content and the play between the general level and the whole tone below, the differences are clearly marked. The tune is like No. 120 in beginning on the final quarter-beat of the measure, but like No. 121 in having four instead of three measures of two-four time to the phrases established as the structural plan during the first five phrases of the chant. With the sixth, which is the last half of a couplet, an extension of three measures is added, anticipating the end. The final odd line of poetry is prolonged

No. 121.—Hula ka-laau, chanted by Akoni Mika, Waiakea Homesteads, Hilo, Hawaii.

Note: Both rests in staff three should be followed by dots.

A ka lae i Koʻokoʻolau ka makani
Huli e mai la ka ino hele iwaho
Popoʻi i aku la i ka lae hala o
    Waʻawaʻa

Me he waʻa kaulua ala Puna i ka
    makani
Me he punua naiʻa ala i ke kai
Oa-oá me he hula ka-laau ala

No. 122.—Hula ka-laau, chanted by Akoni Mika, Waiakea Homesteads, Hilo, Hawaii.

Note: At the beginning of this chant the accompaniment was drowned by the voice, therefore it is uncertain whether all four eighth notes were beaten with the stick or only three as indicated. In the last part of the song there was clearly a rest on the first half of the second beat.

He moku Kaula, Nihoa ame Niʻihau
I ka ulu laʻi a ka Waihoa a Kane
O kaulana a ka la i Halaliʻi
Hala ka la kau ma ke kua o Lehua

Kau ka ma lehulehu o ke ahiahi
Moe e no Kauaʻi i luna ka la e
E o ana no o Lehua i ke kai.

by an extension occupying the time of a normal phrase, which musically provides a balance to offset the fact that balance is lacking in the poetry. The tapping of the sticks follows a single pattern throughout, practically, although in the first part of the chant the beats were so faint on the record that it could not be determined whether the first half of the second beat was tapped or was a rest. Rests occurred at the first half of the second beat in all the measures of the last part.

In tonal content the tune is more limited than No. 121, for there are only the general level and the whole step below, with microtones between them in the third phrase, and the half step or leading tone below the level, as well.

In No. 123 the four-measure phrases of two-four time start just after the accent. Only at the end of the chant is there an extension of four measures to balance the odd line of the mele. The structure of the melody is practically the same for each phrase during the first part of the tune, but the last part shows that the couplet plan underlies the structure.

The tonal content provides one new tone that has not been previously observed in any chant as a melody tone, and that is the minor second above the general level, which is brought out quite prominently near the end of the tune. There are also the minor third and the whole step below the level, with some deflections from each.

These are hardly enough tunes to furnish material as a basis for conclusions as to the outstanding features of the music of the *hula kalaau* in general, but the procuring of any at this time was fortunate, and such as there are will give the reader an idea of it and show that these melodies, with their limited range and prominence of the general level, their simple rhythms and lack of variety, belong to the archaic period along with the animal hulas and the *paiumauma*. The minor third seems to be the prominent interval in three of them. One by Akoni is limited to an even narrower range, but its melody is clearly related to his other two in which the minor third appears.

No. 123.—Hula ka-laau, chanted by Akoni Mika, Waiakea Homesteads, Hilo, Hawaii.

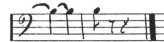

Pauli hiwa mai la Kalani o Hilo	Hapai'na a'e la e ka ua a kelakela
Kalani a ka ua i o-o a nakele	Kelakela moku lau i aá ka lehua
A nakele Hilo i ka ua a nahá	Lehua noho make anu iuka o Kali'u
Nahá mai kekahi maha o ka hala	I nani ka pili e aia me ke aloha
Ma pepe i holo ka maha o ka ohi'a	A hele a'e ke aloha a hemo ka pili

Hula olapa or *alaapapa.*—These were claimed to be the same by all informants questioned about them. Quite vigorous motion characterized dances and the duty of providing the instrumental accompaniment, such as the drumming on the *ipu,* was assigned to a group of musicians, the *hoopaa,* while the *olapa* performed the steps. Emerson (43, p. 57) states that this was one of the classic dances and in its best days belonged to the highest rank. Those of which I could learn, however, had degenerated considerably from this standard and become gross performances.

Only three tunes were obtained, two from Kauai and one from Hawaii. One of the Kauai tunes has already been given as a *hula ipu.* (See No. 91.) In melodic structure it is very similar to No. 124 by the same singer.

The *olapa* by Moha, No. 124, is not ancient in text (see page 236), or else the fragment as it appears here has been adapted to modern conditions, but the tune is as archaic as any in the entire collection.

The introduction, consisting of a three-beat measure chanted to filler syllables, begins on the accent, and the song proper starts at the bracket over the notes, with a meter which is predominantly two-four. Two measures constitute a melodic division which accommodates a single line of poetry. The divisions are practically identical, but though they do not fall in pairs as regards their melodic material, the lines of the mele are probably so conceived until the odd line is reached at the end. It is not certain that there is any intentional musical balance to this odd line in the final musical motif covering the word *"inoa,"* for, although it has a more melodious intonation than usual, it may be accidental. As soon as the chant was finished it was customary to call the name of the person for whom it was recited.

The tonal content is limited to the general level which eventually shifts to half a step lower. The deflected pitches near the end were probably due to the same causes that occasioned the general flatting, and are probably

No. 124.—Hula olapa accompanied by the ipu-wai, chanted by Moha, Kekaha, Kauai.

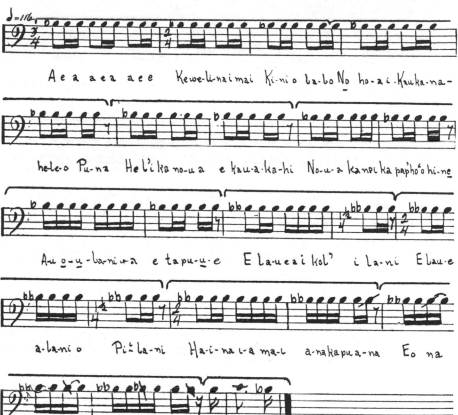

A e a a e a a e e Ke we-li-nai mai Ki-ni o la-lo No ho-a-i- Kau ka-na-

he le-o Pu-na He l'i ka no-u a e kau-a-ka-hi No-u- a ka nou ka papho'o hi-ne

Au o-u-la-ni ʋ-a e tapu-u-e E Lau e a i kol' i La-ni E lau-e

a-la-ni o Pi-i la-ni Ha-i-na u-a ma-u a-na kapu a-na E₀ na

la-ni ko- u i no-a i-a i no- a

Ke welina mai nei ke kini olalo
Na hoa i kau ka nahele o Puna
Hele i ka nou e kauakahi

Nou a ka nei ka papaho'ohina
Auahilani ta pue tauahoa
E lau e kolo he lani o Pi'ilani

not of the same nature as the inflections used in the olis. Compared with this tune, No. 91, by the same singer, is found to be very similar. There the *ipu* provides an introduction by itself, which is followed by the same kind of a voice introduction as in No. 124, probably a peculiarity with this chanter. In No. 124 the voice introduction is combined with the words of the first line to create a phrase of four measures. Subsequently in No. 91 two lines of poetry are required to match the introduction. As in other tunes these lines might be considered separately with the smaller musical sections. They would then be almost identical with the sections of No.

No. 125.—Hula alaapapa, chanted by J. P. Hale, Hilo, Hawaii.

Mahiki i luna la
Ha'ule i lalo la
Ku ka oe wahi o Kikala e
Ole o neio e mau mau la
Aohe ho'olale a koe aku e

Aohe ho'olale a koe aku a
Mahiki i luna la
Ha'ule i lalo la
Ku ka oe wahi o Kikala e
Ole o neio e mau mau la

124. The only difference worth noting is the use of the minor third and the major second above the general level in the middle of tune No. 124 and the appearance of the minor third below near the close.

No. 125 presents a very different type of tune, with the prominent use of the fourth below the level, the presence of the leading tone, and the low start of some of the phrases which work up to the level or even to the major second above it during the first phrase of the couplet, for this tune has the couplet structure, and on to the level again in the following phrase. The low start is reminiscent of some of the *uliuli* tunes and the *paiumauma*. The meter is similar to that of the animal hulas in being three-part. The divisions are in pairs, with two measures covering a line of text, comprising each division. The rhythm is the most complicated of any in the hula tunes, and very unusual in its dotted sixteenth notes.

In tonal content the tune is the same as many others encountered all through the groups. It has the general level, the leading tone, the fourth below the level, and the major second above, with some microtones between the leading tone and the level. The poetic design is unusual and good, and the melody sections conform to it.

These three examples are also too few and too varied to permit of any generalizations concerning the types of melodies, meters, or rhythms which might be considered to distinguish the *hula olapa* or *alaapapa,* if indeed there are such features.

Hula manai.—Only one *hula manai* was secured, and that by accident. Emerson does not mention this hula but it was well-known and was probably very similar to the *hula ulili* he describes. That dance, however, had nothing to do with the instrument of the same name, the combination of gourd tops discussed on pages 54, 55. If the *ulili* was used to accompany a hula no record has been made of it. It was not encountered in the recent survey.

The *hula manai* was also known as the *maile,* the name of the vine, or as the *makoi* or *mokoi,* also the word for fish-pole. It was danced by a man who stood in the center of a circle of women sitting on the ground. In each hand he held a short stick from the end of which depended a long streamer of the maile vine. The sticks thus looked very like two little fish-poles, hence the other name. The man tapped these sticks one on the other in the rhythm shown in No. 126.

The meter of the tune is three-four as is that of a number of the older hulas. It is also syncopated and four measures constitute each phrase, which begins on a weak beat. The tonal content is the general level and the minor third below. The tune begins and ends on the lower note.

No. 126.—Hula manai, chanted by Samuela Waiki, Kawainui, Hilo, Hawaii.

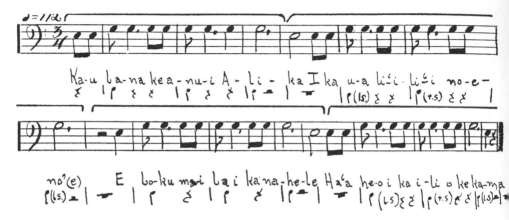

Kaulana ke anu i Alika	Hoike mai ana i ka nani
I ka ua liʻiliʻi noenoe	Nou a mau loaʻku
E loku mai la i ka nahele	Haina ia mai ka puana
Haʻaheo i ka ili o ke kama	E o kuʻu kama kuʻu lei
Ka wahine i ka {iu / liko} o ka lehua	

Hula kilelei.—Malo (100, p. 303) gives a short list of hulas among which is the *kielei,* a name which Emerson also uses but adds *kekelei* as alternative. Emerson describes the dance (43, p. 210) and places it in the classical group. It was performed without instrumental accompaniment. I found it remembered only on Kauai and both informants who chanted tunes for it called it the *kilelei.* One, a native of Niihau, illustrated it. She first placed the right foot forward in a rather emphatic manner, presently withdrawing it and advancing the other. There were some gestures with the arms and a little jumping with both feet planted squarely, but the action did not resemble that described by Emerson. No doubt the words of the mele controlled it somewhat, and if there had been a company of dancers there might have been more animation.

Two renditions of a tune for the *kilelei* were given by a man at Kapaa. The differences in accenting the first two or three measures of the two versions should be observed. The melodies diverge considerably as they proceed. Of the first Mr. Waiwaiole remarked, "This one has a rather crooked voice," as his daughter translated it. He employed the term *anu- unuu.* It was not clear whether he referred to the evenly divided beats which frequently occur, and, which as he sang it, seemed to pull against one another, or to the occasional dropping to the minor third below the level, but the opinion of other informants is that it refers to the change in pitch in the sixth measure, where the melody oscillates between the two tones.

There is no possible division of the tune until the end of the third measure, and the three are sufficient for two lines of text. Taking this as the plan, the next division comes at the end of the sixth measure, the next at the end of the ninth, and the next at the end of the twelfth. In the first three divisions two lines of poetry are accommodated, but the end of the third couplet, which is composed of filler syllables, is divided, and part is carried over to the phrase covering the fourth couplet. The tonal content is extremely limited, with only the general level and the minor third below.

In the second rendition the time was more definitely two-four than four-four. Five measures were therefore included in the first musical division and four in each of the two following. The two last are much extended and do not coincide with the beginnings and endings of the lines

No. 127.—Hula kilelei, chanted by Waiwaiole Kala, Kapaa, Kauai. (Incomplete.)

E-i-a   o ka pa ma-ka-ni Ka-la-a-lau Ota la-wa- la-wa tu-a   Nu-nu-i

to-bo-ti-ni   na-na-a Mau-na-hi-na He a-nu o A-ba-ta-i Pu-lu e-bo i ta

u-a   Tau-a-hi tau-na-na E-a la e-a   c-i e-i-a Wi-wi-li tama-ta-ni

wi-wi-li pu-a nu-i

No. 128.—Repetition of No. 127, by same chanter.

Eia o ka pa makani kalalau
O ka lawalawa kua
Nunui kolokini naná Maunahina
He anu o Alaka‘i
Pulu elo i ka ua

Kauikananá
Ea la e a, ea i-i eia
Wiwili ka makani, wiwili pua nui
Naue o Nu‘alolo ka haka a ka ma-
  kani e e

of poetry. Although this circumstance is common enough in olis, it is not often encountered in hulas. The tonal content is quite changed. The minor third below the level occurs only as a passing tone, while the leading tone, a half step, and the flat seventh, a whole step below the level, are fairly prominent. There is also the very rare diminished fourth below the level and the major second above, with a few deflected tones between the level and the leading tone.

No. 129.—Hula kilelei from Niihau, chanted by Moha, Kekaha, Kauai, a native of Niihau.

Akamai makou i ka pi‘i moku
Ke huki kaula ina peaihu
A ke o wa‘awa‘a kane e ke ahi
Ke kalia nei kapaia

O keaha atu ia
Ta uahi ho‘okele lapalapa
Huli ka moku Kaua‘i ti.

No. 129 differs from the two previous examples in beginning on the last part of a beat rather than on the accent, and there are only two measures of approximately two-four time to each division covering a line of poetry. It is like them in the combinations of eighth notes with sixteenths. The tonal content is not so extensive as in No. 127, for it consists in only the level, the flat seventh a whole step below it, the minor third below and the major second above.

The tune of another *kilelei* was sung by Waiwaiole, and was merely the simple theme shown in No. 130, repeated over and over. It is exactly the same melodic framework that is used in many different hulas, and may be classed as one of the ancient stock tunes. The general level, the fourth below and the major second above are the familiar pitches of its tonal content.

No. 130.—Tune of a hula kilelei, indicated by Waiwaiole Kala, Kapaa, Kauai.

Hula kui Molokai.—This hula is said by Emerson (43, p. 207) to belong probably to a period later than the classical and to have been performed on other islands than the one to which it owes its name and probably its inception. The dancers were lined up in pairs and the motions they made resembled boxing. There was no instrumental accompaniment.

The tune of No. 131 is similar to those of the other classical hulas in being extremely limited in tonal content, having only the general level and the major third below it. The meter is irregular but three-four time predominates and about four measures cover two lines of the mele during the first part of the chant, but later the lines are shorter and there is no obvious connection between their limits and the logical divisions of the music. Dividing the tune according to single lines of the poetry would result in irregular sections beginning at different points in the measure. This melody recalls some of the olis.

HULAS USED FOR VARIOUS PERFORMANCES

Several of the examples already given have been used for more than one kind of hula performance but a few others were collected which are capable of adaptation to three or four, as their contributors stated when giving them. Thus No. 132 and No. 71 as well were said to serve equally well as a *puili, uliuli* or *paiumauma.* The predominating two-four time with four measures to the phrase is characteristic of the *puili* and *uliuli.*

The manner of beginning the phrases on the last half of the first beat is like the *uliuli* hulas, and so is the tonal content, consisting of the general level and its inverted major triad, with the leading tone, the perfect fifth below the level and the other pitches, which are used as passing-tones and which may be seen in the general table on pages 313-316.

The informant stated that No. 133 was a mele which could be chanted olioli as indeed many of the hulas can be, or could serve as a *hula ipu, pahu, alaapapa, kalaau, kaekeeke*—evidently any of the drumming hulas. Its meter is quite regular two-four and most of the phrases have four measures, but

No. 131.—Hula kui Molokai for Halaki, chanted by Solomono Huihui, Honolulu.

e i ne he ɩi Mo-lo-ka-ɩ-ɩ

the tendency to extend the final measure by holding the final note for two rather than one measure, or interpolating rests, should be noticed. The tonal content is confined to the general level and the minor third below.

No. 132.—Hula (incomplete), adaptable for several dances, chanted by J. P. Hale, Hilo, Hawaii.

(Note: This hula was composed in 1875 at Kahuku Ranch, Kau, Hawaii.)

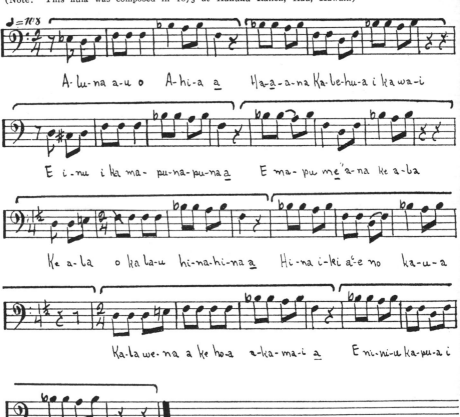

A luna au o Ahia
Haana ka lehua i ka wai
E inu i ka māpunapuna
E mapu mai ana ke ala
Ke ala o ka lau hinahina
Hina iki aʻe no kaua
Ka lawena a ke hoa akamai
E niniu ka pua i ka nahele
Hele a oluno palaai

O ka nelunelu o ka opuʻu
A he meli ka hoa e like ai
Waiu kahe o ka nahele
Hele no oe a manaʻo mai
Eia ia neʻi ko aloha
He aloha ke kumu i hui ai
Ike ia na pali Koʻolau
Haina ia mai ana ka puana
E niniu ka pua i ka nahele

No. 133.—Hula of the nose flute, chanted by Sam Kekoowai, Honolulu.

O ka wai halau i Wailua la
Wai awili pu me ke kai e
Ka'ika'i ana i ka mana'o
I ka ho'ohihi a hihimanu
Manuahi auhau
Huna a ka pu'ulena
Lu i ke ala waiho ia'u
Owau wale no i ka uka laau

I ke ano o Pihanaakalani
Ho'olale mai a ka naulu
Ulu no ka mana'o ka lia iloko
I ka wai pua hau o Maluaka
O ka ka ia'u ka anehe a ka ipo
Ku'u ipo i ke one o Luhi
I ke kalukalu moe ipo o Kewa-la-oie

No. 134 was declared equally good for the *ipu,* the *uliuli,* or others like the *puili.* It is so like No. 133 in its general plan that it hardly calls for comment. The rhythm occasioned by the presence of the dotted notes and the alternation of the major with the minor third below the level are the only points worth noting. The mele is a variant of that in Nos. 72, 73, and 112.

No. 134.—Hula ipu, uliuli, etc., for Kalakaua, chanted by Mrs. Kawaimakaonalii Hao, Kalaoa, North Kona, Hawaii.

No. 135.—Hula uliuli or puili, chanted by H. W. Kahikina Kaoo, Hookena, South Kona, Hawaii.

ma-i ka-i ma-nu meka ne-be nae a-ha Hoʻo-ka-hi puʻo-bo ma-ho-pe ba

ha (Pu) e-lu-a ma-ho-pe i ka nu-ku ba e a ha (I) We-he-a e ka

ha-na a he-mo ba e ba E-lu-a wa-i-wa-i ka oʻko ba i a-ha Pi-

pi-u wa-hi o ho Ka-be-po-ni a-ha Aʻ-e he O-i e he ka ma-no u-ba

o ke (A)-mo-le-wa ba e a-ha ka ma-no u-ba o ke i A-mo-le wa ba Aʻ-

e he O-i-e he ha-i-na ma-i a-na ka-pu-a-na ba e a ha o

Shouted

ma-e a o a ka u-a ba a ma-ni

Note: In next to the last staff, the following corrections should be made: First measure, the last two notes should be sixteenth notes; fourth measure, the *f*'s should be *e*'s; last measure *c* should be *c♯*.

A'e Oie akahi ho'i au a ike
E kahimanu ai pua oliwa
Nomenome i ka lau laiki
O ka iki nalo meli iho ia
Aia ka eha i ka huelo
Pa mai ia'u welenia
Hele i ke au a ka makemake
I ka huaka'i imi le'ale'a
Ilaila aku nei o Pahua
Aohe makamaka o ka hale

Ho'i mai kahi manu me ka nele
Ho'okahi pua loke i ka nuku
Ho'okahi pu'olo mahope
E kau ana i ka puapua
I wehea e ka hana a hemo
Elua waiwai oloko
Kamano ula o ke Amolewa
He pipi uwahi no Kaleponi
Haina mai ana ka puana
Kahikina na maua no

No. 135 was pronounced either a hula *uliuli* or *puili,* and therefore its time in three-eight is very singular. There are approximately four measures to the phrase. The tonal content is peculiar, for the general level is not established. If it is taken as *e,* the *d* which forms a flat seventh becomes a prominent part of the melody, and the play between the fourth below *e,* or *b,* and *d* is as pronounced as between *b* and *e.* If *d* is taken as the level with *e* as the major second above, then *c* becomes the flat seventh, and *b* the minor third below the level. The *f♯* above the level becomes the rare major third, in this tune very prominent, as is *c♯,* the seventh. If *c* is taken as the level, the presence of the third and the augmented fourth above it sets the chant apart from all the other hulas found. This may be a modern specimen, but it does not particularly resemble any tunes of European provenience. It may be an unusual case of native inventiveness overstepping the narrow limits of the hula and ranging free through a little piece that has no level, but which has a theme quite constantly adhered to. The change of melody beginning with the introduction of *f♯* is entirely foreign to the ancient type of Hawaiian chants, so far as the rest of the collection shows.

No. 136.—Hula called Kuhiau, chanted by Aiamanu Pauole, Hanalei, Kauai.

No. 137.—Hula composed by Kaehu, Wailua, Kauai, chanted by Wahineikeaouli Paa, Haena Wet Caves, Kauai.

Note: In the first measure of the sixth staff, the rest should be followed by a dot.

No. 138.—Hula ipu-wai, chanted by Hanohano Makea, Hanapepe, Kauai.

u-be_l   e a   H'e-a-i e ta i-no a_e ta ma-ka-ni̲

Nos. 136, 137, and 138 are the same mele adapted to various hulas by three chanters. They should be compared with No. 79—a still different tune.

The tonal content of these tunes is not different from that of the other hulas, except that in No. 137 the prominent major third appears above the level, which seldom has been observed. (See fig. 5, pp. 313-316, for a comparative table of tonal content.)

Hula kake.—One example, No. 139, with a second rendition, No. 140, was obtained of a rare hula known as a *kake*, a chant purporting to be a

No. 139.—Hula kake, or dialogue hula, chanted by Mrs. Kaimu Kihe, Puuanahulu, North Kona, Hawaii.

dialogue in code language between members of the royal family. It dates back to the time of Kamehameha III at the least. The informant thought it belonged to the period of Kamehameha I but this is declared wrong by several Hawaiian scholars. It probably was not intended to be used for dancing but appears to be more like the plain hulas. Kamehameha III asks Kalama, a beautiful woman, to go with him but she replies that she dares

No. 140.—Repetition of No. 139 by the same chanter.

Kamehameha: "Hea oe Kahaioa lama
Hele o mai o kaua iwaho nei"

Kalama: "Aole au e hiki aku o ana
Maka'u mai au ia Kaahuomanu"

Kamehameha: "No'u o luna a no'u a lalo
No'u o uka no'u o kai
No'u o na wahi a pau o loa"

---

a The italicized letters are for euphony only.

not, as she fears Kaahumanu, the queen. Kamehameha answers that she need have no fear as he is master of all he surveys and none can thwart his desires. The musical form of this chant is exceptionally good; the structural plan is rare, and it is worth noting that it was given by the same woman who sang the only chant containing a modulation. Whether this tune is her own invention or one that has been handed down is uncertain. I learned too late that often when speaking of chants the people were referring only to the words and not to the tune, which was usually a matter of comparative indifference.

I have marked the music with Roman numerals to indicate its tripartite division. Each part has three subdivisions, properly musical sections, of two measures each, except in two cases where there are three measures. In the first part the first section, composed of measures *a* and *b,* introduces the theme of the piece. The next two sections elaborate and extend it with the presentation of new material in *c,* its inversion in *d,* and the extension of *b* in *b'* and *e.* The *e* is properly an *a* measure, but as the single note followed by rests is used several times in contrast to the note repeated, I have given it a different letter. Because the second and third sections appear to elaborate and extend the first, I have combined them into a phrase, thus treating them as if they belonged together, which is further indicated by the single line of poetry which they accommodate.

Part II recapitulates the material of the first part, combining all the melodic content in the first measure, *cb,* of a three-measure section, which is finished with modifications of the first and final measures of Part I. The second and third sections of Part II are similar to the corresponding sections of Part I, although the first measure *cba,* is a new development of all the tonal material. Like the corresponding ones of Part I, these sections also cover but one long line of poetry and belong together. Part III, as would be fitting from an artistic standpoint, emphasizes the theme brought out in the second section of Part I, measure *c,* not only by repeating it once in slightly different rhythm, but by doubling the section, taking up for the first measure of the doubled part an exact repetition of the last measure of the first section and balancing it with another of the same melodic structure, but with sufficient rhythmic variation to avoid monotony. This quadruple statement of practically identical melodic ideas fits with great nicety the reiterations in the text, the rhythmic variations corresponding somewhat with the differences of direction stressed in the words *luna* (above), *lalo* (below), *uka* (landward), *kai* (seaward). With the beginning of the last line of poetry it is stated that not only in the four directions, but everywhere, lies the property of the king, so the beginning of the last half of Part III of the music again states the same measure, preparatory to summing up the thematic material of the chant and making the conclusion. This part is shorter by one measure than the corresponding divisions of Parts I and II, but the lengthened note at the beginning makes this less perceptible and adds emphasis. Not only in perfection of form, but in the adaptation of melody to words in a fashion which might be termed a miniature leitmotif, this little song is an extraordinary specimen, standing out among most of the pure Hawaiian tunes like a ray of light in the dark, indicating the kind of development that might have occurred had composers given fancy free reign instead of binding it for untold centuries to the narrow limits prescribed by custom, established probably as many other customs were, where a whole race was ridden by tapus.

Plain hulas.—These are mostly of late date, if the informant is correct who stated that in old times none but trained hula performers sang hula chants, and that plain hulas were the "pick up" productions of untrained imitators. I give here without comment a few of those which I collected merely for comparison with the dance tunes from which they do not vary noticeably.

No. 141.—Hula for Kalakaua, chanted by D. McKeague, Hookena, South Kona, Hawaii.

No. 142.—Hula, chanted by Kapeliela Malani, Kawaihaeuka, North Kona, Hawaii.

Au - he-a wa-lo - e ma-ka-ni Ko - na - i E la wě he-le ne-i ka'-

u a-lo- ha A- he-a la o-e ho'-i ho-i ma-i I ho-a-pi-li

RECORD CUt off HERE

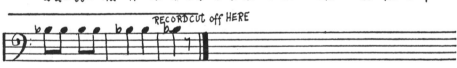

no ne-i a- i- na

Auhea wale oe e makani Kona	Ike ia Kuili mamua pono
E lawe hele nei i ka'u aloha	He pu'u kaulana no Keaukaha
A hea la oe ho'i ho'i mai	Ke pi'i ho'ola'i nei makou
I hoapili no nei aina	Mawaho pono iho o Keahole
Kaua i ka nani o Keawewai	Ike ia Hi'iaka au i ke kai
Ka iniki malie a ke kehau	Ka wahine noho anu o ke kuahiwi
Au aku ka mana'o no Mailekini	Ho'okomo i ke awa o Kailua
E ike i ke kai hāwanawana	Ke one hanau o ku'u pua
Ka ha'i a ka nalu pua ka ilima	Haina ia mai ana ka puana
Elima makou i ke ehukai	Eono pua loke lawa ku'u lei

No. 143.—Hula for Queen Emma, chanted by Kapeliela Malani, Kawaihaeuka, North Kona, Hawaii.

A Ki boi ha-na-a Ta-ba-nu la-kit Na-ha ma-i a Ha-na-be-i ba-kit A

te o-ne a o Ma-ha-mo-tu la-kit Meta wa-i a o Lu-maha-i la-kit A

na ba e ha-ba o Na-u-e ba-kit etc.

No. 144.—Hula for Queen Emma, chanted by Meloha Kenoi, Kapoho, Puna, Hawaii.

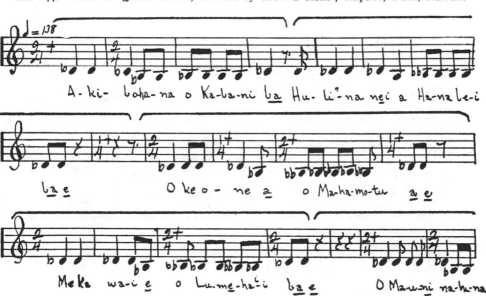

A-ki- boha-na o Ka-ba-ni ba Hu- li²-na nei a Ha-na-le-i

ba e   O ke o- ne a o Ma-ha-mo-tu a e

Me ba wa-i e o Lu-me-ha²-i ba e   O Ma-u-ni na-hu-na

A Kilohana o Kalani	Ke anu o Aipó
Naná ia Hanalei	O ka leo ka mea aloha
A ke one o Mahamoku	Ka heahea ana mai
Me ka wai o Lumaha'i	Mahea mai oukou
A na lae hala o Naue	Ma'anei ma ka mehana
Alai ia e ka noe	Kapi'ina nei ikiiki
Maunahina kai i luna	Kukala a ka manu
Ke ala kuhikuhi lima	Ho'omaha aku o Kalani
U'i a'e nei Emalani	I ka lehua makanoe
E huli ho'i kakou	Lehua lei a piki
I ke ala wai ohi'a	Pauku me ka painiu
Ala kiki Papaaola	E lalama i ka nui manu
Ke-awa-ko'o kai lalo	I ka ohi hua Mokihana
Naele o Alaka'i	I lei no ka wahine
Le'a kulou a Emalani	No Emalani he inoa

MODERN HULAS

A group of modern dance tunes is also given to show that the same old styles of composition are being produced even at the present time. These are about one-third of the modern hula tunes collected. For comparison with those that have been discussed, I have indicated the musical divisions as before, with the brackets above the notes. The tonal content will be found with that of all the hulas in figure 5 on pages 313-316.

No. 145.—Hula paiumauma, chanted by Waiwaiole Kala, Kapaa, Kauai. (Incomplete.)

Auhea wale oe makani kiu
Ka miki hau o ke aumoe
E moe oe a ho'olono mai
Kauwalo a ka leo o mi nei
Eia mai au waiolina
Pila honehone i ka pili o ke ao
E ao mai oe e ku'u aloha
O lohea wale ia mai kaua
Hamau ko leo kou pono ia

Hāwanawana li'ili'i ke kolohe
Eia e ka eu ua hiki mai
O makani kona o ke ano ahiahi
Nana i wawahi na pali pa'a
Naueue ka moana Iniana
Ua aná a'e nei ku'u makemake
I ke kono uilani i ka mana'o
Haina ia mai kahi puana
O ka liko iliahi o ka Uhiwai.

No. 146.—Hula kuhi no Wailuku, Maui, a gesture hula, chanted by Peter and Mrs. Kaawa, Kalaoa, North Kona, Hawaii.

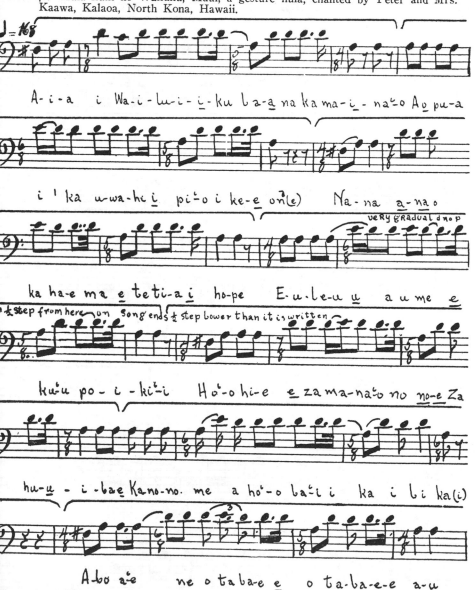

Note: In the fourth staff, fourth measure, the first *d* should be a quarter note. In the fifth staff, second measure, the *e* should be an eighth note.

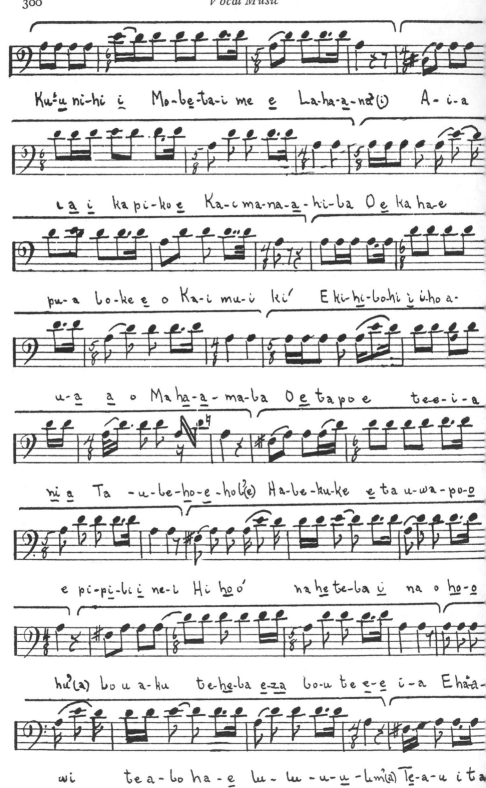

Ku-²u̱ ni-hi i̱ Mo-be̱-ta-i me e̱ La-ha-a̱-na̱ (i)   A-i-a

ta i̱ ka pi-ko e̱ Ka-o ma-na-a̱-hi-ta O e̱ ka ha-e

pu-a to-ke e̱ o Ka-i mu-i ki'   E ki-hi̱-bo-hi i̱ i-ho a-

u-a̱   a̱ o Ma-ha-a̱-ma-ta O e̱ ta po e   te e-i-a

ni̱ a̱ Ta -u-be-ho-e-hol(e) Ha-be-ku-ke e̱ ta u-wa-po-o̱

e pi-pi̱-ti i̱ ne-i Hi ho̱-o̱'   na he̱ te-ta i̱   na o ho̱-o̱

hu²(a) to u a-ku   te-he̱-ta e̱-za̱ to-u te e̱-e̱ i-a E ha̱a̱-

wi   te a-to ha-e̱ tu- tu -u-u̱ -tm(a) Te̱-a-u i ta

Notes: In the sixth staff, fourth measure, the two sixteenth notes on *d* should be one eighth note.

a-bo pe-be-na'lu-a a o-hu u be-i Ki-ka-a-ha Ka i-wa i

Ho'o -ba'-i-i-u'(a) A e-lu-a e a e-tolu u no ma

e-e to-u Makea-ba pii a-tu u a i Nu-u-au'(u)

I-ke i ta ba wa-i a o e Te-a-hu'-a-i-i-ba-na I a wa-

i li-po-li-po o ba'-i ka pa-a-la'(u) Ha-i-na

i na e o ma-i i a-na ka pu-a-na O e Ka na nu-i o

Ma-u-i i u-a ka-u-u ban(a)

i Wailuku lana ka manaʻo	Aia i ka piko o Kaimanahila	Kau i ka pela nolu ohuohulei
á ka uwahi piʻo i ke one	O ka hae pualoke o Kaimukí	Kikaha ka iwa i Hoʻolaʻilua
o ka hae ma ke kia hope	E kilohi iho au o Mamala	Elua a ekolu no makou
eu au me kuʻu pokiʻi	O ka poe keia o Kaulehole	Ma ke ala piʻi aku i Nuʻuanu
ie ka manaʻo no kahuila	Halekuke ka uwapo e pili nei	Ike i ka wai o Kahuaʻilana
onome hoʻolaʻi ia ka ili kai	Hi ó na kela na ohua	Ia wai lipolipo laʻi ka palai
ʻe o ka lae o Kalaau	Lou aku kela lou keia	Haina ia mai ana ka puana
ii Molokaʻi me Lanaʻi	E haʻawi ke aloha lululima	Ka nani o Maui ua kaulana.

No. 147.—Hula puili, chanted by H. W. Kahikina Kaoo, Hookena, South Kona, Hawaii.

Ma-i-no o-e a a ho ho-ni a-ha I ka wa-i u-a ba-na

ma-li-e Ma-i no o-e a a ho ho-ni a-ha I ka-wa-i

u-a ba-na-ma-be (Ko)o-pi-i a-e a u-a ne-i a-ha

(A)-ha-a-be i-ke ba-u o ka ha-u E a o pi-i a-e a-ha

u-a-ne-i a-ha A-ha-a-be i ke ba-u o ka ha-u

O ka-a-u ha-u-na no i-e a-ha U-a ko-mo i ka-a-u ki-pu-k

O-ka-a-u ha-u-na no i-e a-ha U-a ko-mo i ka-a-u

ka pi-i-ne U-a he-lu po-no i-a na pa̱e a̱-ha̱ Ma-i larbo

a-lu-na ka̱pi-i-ne I ke o-e ka-u-a-hi o-pi u-me a̱-ha̱

etc. record cut off.

I ka hu-e-hu-e. i ka pu-u-ko-le

Note: In the last line, first measure, *c* should read *c#*.

Mai no oe a ho'oni
I ka wai ua lana malie
O pi'i a'e auane'i
Ahaale i ka lau o ka hau
O ka'u hauna no ia
Ua komo i ka'u kipuka
Li'ili'i oi ala ma'anei
Ke mana'o a'e au e naue
Na'u i olali o Kahiki
Na aupuni kipi o ka hema
A he lohe olelo mai ko'u
I ke kani a ka ohe puili
Ua helu pono ia na pa
Mai lalo a luna ka pi'ina

Ike oe ka uahi opiuma
I ka hu'ehu'e i ka pu'ukole
Nawai e ole ke ko'i-i
I ka mea ono a ka paké
Ua hana mikioi ia mai
E na keiki o Kina
Ka'i huluhulu aku i ke ala
Ua ku i ka hewa kalaima
O ka mihi mua mai ka pakele
Pau ko'u mana'o ho'opi'i
Hoole pa'a loa mai oe
O kou holina no ia
A o Halemano ko Honolulu nei
Kahikina ko Ki'ilai nei

No. 148.—Hula puili, chanted by Mr. and Mrs. Keawe Nainoelua, Amaulu, Hilo, Hawaii.

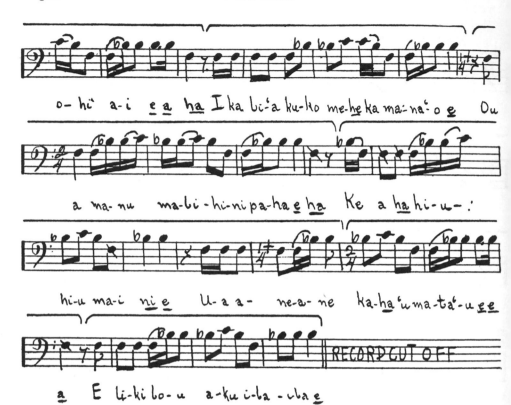

o-hï a-i   e a   ha   I ka li·'a ku-ko me-he ka ma-na'-o e   Ou

a ma-nu   ma-li-hi-ni pa-ha e ha   Ke a ha hi-u-:

hi-u ma-i   ni e   U-a a-   ne-a- ne   ka-ha'u ma-ta'-u e e

a   E li-ki lo- u   a-ku i-la -ula e

Malua, ki'i wai ke aloha
Ho'opulu i ka liko mamane
Uleuleu mai na manu
Inu wai lehua Panaewa
E walea ana keonaona
I ke one wali Ohele
Lele mai kou aloha
A lalawe i ko'u nui kino
E kuhi ana no paha oe
No Hopoe ne'i i lehua
Au i ka kaohi ai
I ka li'a kuko me ka mana'o
Ou a manu malihini paha
Ke a hiuhiu mai nei
Ua aneane ka'u maka'u
E liki lou aku ilaila
Kuhi au o oe ka makani
I ka ho'olale mai a ke anu
Anuanu Poliahu i ka { wai
                  { hau
He moa kani aumoe

O ko'u makemake no oe
Ke pa leo iki wale mai
A pili aku la ho'i au
Me oe no ku'u pu'uwai
I mea iho au e hihi'o
Hiki mai ana kou aloha
Huli a'e au ma ka paia
Ho'onaná ka mana'o
He mana'o no ko'u e pili
Me ka nalu ha'i mai o Huia
Hui pu'uwai ke aloha
Na mi nei no ia pua
O ka iwa oe o ka hikina
O paihi manu o Waiola
E ola oe Kapahukapu
No ke ahe pu'ulena ke aloha
O lili'i wai ohelo
O li'i hau anu o uka
Noenoe mai la i Ola'a
Haina ia mai ana ka puana
O Kaluluhi moku he inoa

No. 149.—Hula uliuli, chanted by Wahineikeaouli Paa, Haena Wet Caves, Kauai.

Note: In the last measure of the second staff, the fourth note should be followed by a dot.

a-u u-ho ne-i ma-a-ne'a i e e a Me za Ka-hi ki-hi-

e-i hu-lu-hu-lu Ha- i-na ka pu-an'o ku-u na-a ne e

a Ho-o-ke-le i ka i-hu o ka mok(u)

Note: The first note in the last measure of the second staff should be followed by a dot.

A kahi hoʻi au a ike
Na lio kakele i ke kula
Elua kahu nana i aʻe
Holo aku i ka pahu heihei
Eo i ka ahina pua kea
Ua hu Anemanu i ke kula
Aohe kahu e laka ai

Ua lilo i kamanu aukai
Aia i ka lae o Kekala
E kala kahiko i auwale
I niau iho nei maʻanei
Me kahi kihei huluhulu
Haina ka puana o kuʻu nane
Hoʻokele i ka ihu o ka moku

No. 150.—Hula uliuli, chanted by Wahineikeaouli Paa, Haena Wet Caves, Kauai. (Incomplete.)

A-u-he-a wa-a be o-e e ka i wa e a Ne-né a a-u

ka-i o Ta - ul'-(a) E - i-a i- ba i- ba ko-u h-hu he

a Ta- hi no-e a-u ma-i ai Te i a'-e

ne - i ta mai - na-a-o-e a A e hu-i ma-li - hi-m ta-a-

u'(a) O-i a-i ka pu - a-e ka-u ne' a-e he

a I za we-be-ta-u aza bi-hi - li?(hi) E i-te

o - e a a u-e ne'(i)a e he au I za ha-na a za

i-bi ba-ho-bi'(o)   Za-o-hi za-u-e-a u — mi-ki-e

a   I ka etc.

No. 151.—Hula uliuli, chanted by Wahineikeaouli Paa, Haena Wet Caves, Kauai. (Incomplete.)

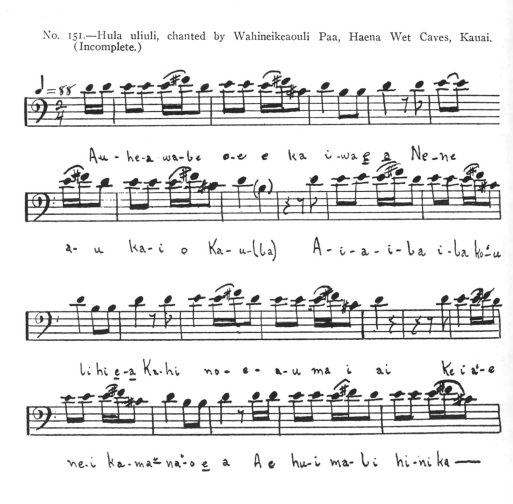

Au - he-a wa-be o-e e ka i -wa e a Ne-ne

a- u ka-i o Ka-u-(ba) A -i-a-i-ba i-ba ko-u

li hi e-a Ka-hi no- e- a-u ma i ai Ke i-a'-e

ne-i ka-ma= na'-o e a A e hu-i ma-bi hi-ni ka—

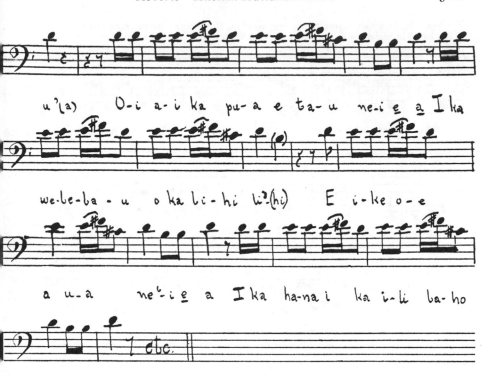

u'(a)   O-i a-i ka pu-a e ta-u ne-i e a̱ I ka

we-be-ba - u   o ka li-hi li²(hi)   E i-ke o - e

a u-a   ne²-i e̱ a I ka ha-na i ka i-li ba-ho

etc.

li-o e̱ a

Auhea wale oe e ka iwa	I ka hana a kaili laholio
Nené aukai o Kaula	Kaohi kauea umiki
Aia ilaila ko'u lihi	I ka pu'uwai Lokalia
Kahí no'eau mai ai	Pono ole na haku lehulehu
Ke i a'e nei ka mana'o	I ka uilani a ia ne'i
A e hui malihini kaua	E ola oe a mau aku
Oi ai ka pua e kau nei	A kau i ka pua aneane
I ka welelau o ka lihilihi	Haina ka pua a i ike ia
E ike oe a ua ne'i	O Kila opio he inoa

No. 152.—Hulá uliuli, name chant for Koolau, the famous leper, composed and chanted by Wahineikeaouli Paa, Haena Wet Caves, Kauai. (Incomplete.)

He mele he inoa no Koʻolau
No ke āiwaiwa noho kuahiwi
O oe ka mea i weli ia
I kaulana ai Hawaiʻi nei
Nau i olali hoʻokahi mai
Puʻuwai haokila me ka hopo ole
Pa lua, pa kolu i ke kekona
I ka haʻu o ka pu Kelemania
He loaʻa lihi paha i ka pana pua

I ka lula pololei a ka Hawaiʻi
Nau no ia i ka ike aku
Aloalo poká a ka pī ki
Ua puni na ailana i ka lohe
Na hana kaulana a kuʻu lei
O Wilikoki hoʻi ko Honolulu
Keiki Koʻolau ko Kauaʻi
Haina ka inoa oaʻu lei
Piʻilani Koʻolau a e o mai

FIGURE 5.—Tonal content of hulas. The numbers of the examples correspond with the numbers of the songs given in more complete form on pages. The slurs indicate that the examples connected are different versions of the same song. The names of the informants indicated by number are as follows:

(1) Peter and Mrs. Kaawa, Kalaoa, North Kona, Hawaii; (2) Mrs. Kaimu Kihe, Puuanahulu, North Kona, Hawaii; (5) Mrs. Kawaimakaonalii Hao, Kalaoa, North Kona, Hawaii; (7) Samuela Akoni Mika, Waiakea Homesteads, Hilo, Hawaii; (9) Mrs. Meloha Kenoi, Kapoho, Puna, Hawaii; (10) H. W. Kahikina Kaoo, Hookena, South Kona, Hawaii; (15) W. M. Kalaiwaa, Kamuela, South Kohala, Hawaii; (16) Mrs. Kaahaaina Naihe, Honolulu, Oahu; (18) J. P. Hale, Hilo, Hawaii; (19) Sam Kekoowai, Honolulu, Oahu; (20) J. S. Kiaha, Kohanaiki, North Kona, Hawaii; (22) Aiamanu Pauole, Hanalei, Kauai; (23) Waiwaiole Kala, Kapaa, Kauai; (24) Mrs. Koiahi, Hanalei Valley, Kauai; (25) Kapeliela Malani, Kawaihaeuka, South Kohala, Hawaii; (27) Paikulu, Haena, Kauai; (28) Solomono Huihui, Honolulu, Oahu; (29) Mrs. E. Lahilahi Webb, Honolulu, Oahu; (30) Samuela Waiki, Kawainui, Hilo, Hawaii; (31) Keawe Nainoelua, Kekaha, Kauai; (32) Mrs. Keawe Nainoelua, Kekaha, Kauai; (33) Moha, Kekaha, Kauai; (34) Antone Kaoo, Honolulu, Oahu; (35) Kamehaitu Helela, Hanapepe Valley, Kauai; (36) Hanohano Makea, Hanapepe, Kauai; (38) Louis Nakeu, Honolulu, Oahu; (39) Peter Pakele, Sr., Waiakea, Hilo, Hawaii; (40) Nahaleuli Nahialua, Kekaha, Kauai; (41) Wahineikeouli Paa, Haena, Kauai; (42) D. McKeague, Hookena, South Kona, Hawaii.

Figure 5.—Continued.

Hula Ka-laau

Hula olapa or ala'apapa

Hula manai

Hula kileleu

Hula ku'i Molokai-

Tunes serving more than one hula

FIGURE 5.—Continued.

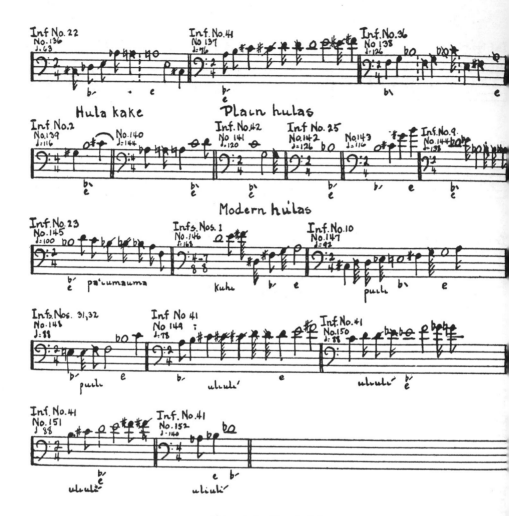

FIGURE 5.—Concluded.

PART SINGING

Ever since the days of Captain Cook the question has been raised as to whether the Hawaiians did or did not sing in parts. The following quotation, largely a footnote in King's Voyage to the Pacific Ocean (85, vol. 3, pp. 143, 144), is also given in part by Marques (104, p. 51):

Their music is also of a ruder kind, having neither flutes nor reeds, nor instruments of any other sort that we saw, except drums of various sizes. But their songs, which they sung in parts* and accompany, with a gentle motion of the arms in the same manner as the Friendly Islanders, had a very pleasing effect.

*As this circumstance, of their singing in parts, has been much doubted by persons eminently skilled in music, and would be exceedingly curious if it was clearly ascertained, it is to be lamented that it cannot be more positively authenticated.

Captain Burney and Captain Phillips of the Marines, who both have a tolerable knowledge of music, have given it as their opinion that they did sing in parts; that is to say, that they sung together in different notes which formed a pleasing harmony.

These gentlemen have fully testified that the Friendly Islanders undoubtedly studied their performances before they were exhibited. in public; that they had an idea of different notes being useful in harmony; and also that they rehearsed their compositions in private, and threw out the inferior voices before they ventured to appear before those who were supposed to be judges of their skill in music.

In their regular concerts each man had a bamboo which was of different length and gave a different tone: these they beat against the ground, and each performer, assisted by the note given by this instrument, repeated the same note, accompanying it by words, by which means it was rendered sometimes short and sometimes long. In this manner they sung in chorus, and not only produced octaves to each other, according to their different species of voice, but fell on concords such as were not disagreeable to the ear.

Now, to overturn this fact, by the reasoning of persons who did not hear these performances is rather an arduous task. And yet there is great improbability that any uncivilized people should. . . arrive at this degree of perfection in the art of music. . . .

The greater part of this quotation refers to the Friendly Islanders. Of Hawaiian part singing Marques says (104, p. 54):

Singing in unison was probably the most common; yet that the ancient Hawaiians did really sing in parts I do not now doubt, though their part singing may not have been anything near to what we call part singing. The part singing I have heard in hula was either *two parts*, the men singing the air and the women singing one octave and a fifth above, or else *three parts,* two as above and an intermediate one, chanting simultaneously on the mediant or major third. This did really produce harmony, but of what kind according to our modern notions will be explained by remarking that whilst the highest and lowest parts sung as I have said, in fifths, both following scrupulously the melodic design and producing what we call consecutive or forbidden fifths, the intermediate part kept on the mediant of the tonic even when the other parts passed to the dominant. Yet the effect of these combinations, often quite pleasant, was never as discordant as might be anticipated from the description, and any disagreeable sensation was avoided by the perfect time and "ensemble" of the performers. I have never heard four parts, nor anything approaching our fundamental bass parts, whose office in Hawaiian music seems to have been taken by the thumping of the calabashes on the ground, whilst the brisk snapping of the fingers on the same marked the pulsations and their subdivision.

With the *kaekeeke,* two to each performer, being played by a group of musicians, if there was any appreciable difference in the length or diameter of the tubes (and there seems to have been since exact measurements appear to have been regarded with indifference), there must have been many tones produced at the same time, as Captain Burney described of the Friendly Islanders, so that tonal combinations with these and with the *ukeke,* where two or three strings could be struck at once, must have been familiar. A certain incidental part singing must have existed if the accounts of Captain King and Dr. Marques are to be trusted, as they certainly are, or if an instance which I witnessed can also be taken as an indication, but there was probably no studied attempt to achieve a definite and constant performance, or it would seem that more traces of it would be left than is found in singing of the old style. The manner of harmonizing observable today in much of the native singing shows that the ideas of consonance and dissonance that we have never existed among the Hawaiians.

The one instance of part singing that I observed was when a man and his wife sang a hula. He pitched his voice a perfect fifth below hers and maintained this interval throughout.

SUMMARY

In summing up this study of hula tunes, it is advisable first to compare them broadly with the olis, both from the standpoint of the poetry and of the music, and secondly as accompaniments to different hulas, in the groupings followed here.

Hula meles are usually composed with lines of poetry nearly uniform in length, and in this respect they differ markedly from olis, where the lines may vary considerably in length at different points in the poem. Nearly all hula meles are capable of being scanned, with about the same number of accents to each line if not the same composition of feet, and the poetry is always composed in couplets. The music generally carries out this couplet plan with two short melodic themes, one for each line, the second being similar to the first, but likely to contain just sufficient change to complement it so that there is the effect of statement and answer. Occasionally only one theme appears which is repeated to complete the couplet, but whether the themes stand singly or in pairs they are given over and over with slight melodic or rhythmic variations, seldom with absolutely exact repetitions, until the song is finished.

Although many hulas are very limited in tonal content, there is more equal employment of tones, more *anuunuu,* that is, wavering, or interplay between pitches, than is found in the olis. Nevertheless, the general level is nearly always well established. On the other hand, many hula tunes have a fairly large number of melody tones, perhaps five or six, as well as others which, because of infrequent or inconsequential appearance, are to be considered merely as embellishments.

There is a very evident tendency to regularity of meter in all hulas, although in unaccompanied singing this is apt to break down as might be expected with any untrained singers. Unless the irregularities recur throughout the tune, in repetitions of the couplet phrases to the accompaniment of different texts, they may probably justifiably be considered as due to the absence of the steadying support of instrumental accompaniments or dancers, and to breathing exigencies which are likely to occur with old people and which would be bridged by other singers if the chanting were done in a chorus. In some tunes, however, No. 146 particularly, the irregularities are consistent and very attractive.

Almost without exception regular divisions of the music, either sections or phrases, accommodate the lines of the poetry, with not often a need for even those musical devices, extensions, contractions, or fillers commonly appearing in primitive music. Although two- or four-part meters characterize the great majority of hulas, three-part meters are not particularly rare, especially in what are generally thought to be the more archaic hulas, like those with animal names. A few are constructed on the principle of three, throughout, showing a nice conception of design or consistency. The modern tunes are mostly in two-four time.

As to the different types of hulas having characteristic music, such as certain meters or structural patterns, if these existed in earlier periods the lines of demarcation are practically obliterated. This is due to continual overlapping in one particular or another, so that as types, the tunes may no longer be identified except in a somewhat vague manner by examining a large number given by different chanters, and by discounting the constant exceptions in favor of certain features which they present as a mass. The *uliuli* tunes are the most clearly marked of any, perhaps, in being predominantly of two-four meter, and in having a large number which begin the phrases a beat and a half before the accent. Even with these tunes there are such exceptions as one in three-eight meter, and many which begin on the accent. The animal hulas tend to have six-part meters, or else three-part subdivided equally, but other meters were found. The *paiumauma* tunes have rhythms which tend to throw the weight of emphasis to the end of the melodic phrase, while the beats of the first three measures may be subdivided; the *puili* tunes, on the other hand, tend to distribute the weight of emphasis from measure to measure, and to begin on the unaccented part of a beat or on the second beat of the measure.

In melody tones and trend, the animal hulas and some of the other more classical types have very limited tonal material; some are confined to only two tones, and would be indistinguishable from olis except that the tones have more equal play instead of the upper being sounded almost continuously. *Uliuli* tunes, particularly, extend the tonal content to the first inversion of the major triad on the general level, to the major second above the level, and to the leading tone and subdominant below it, and many tunes for this hula begin low and work up to the level and above. Some of the other more modern hulas have tunes which also follow this plan.

Thus it appears that the meles, the kind of instrumental accompaniment, and the type of gestures, controlled to a large extent by the text of the mele, except in such hulas as the *paiumauma* and the *kui Molokai* of more or less well defined type, serve to distinguish the hulas rather than varieties of melody, meter, rhythms, or speed. This produces a situation the very opposite of that known to modern dance music. One informant thought that the *uliuli* tunes moved faster than the others, but figure 5, where the predominating meter and speed are indicated for each tune, will show that their rate is fairly uniform. As notes of smaller denomination than eighths are rare in all hula tunes, a misleading impression as to speed gained by the informant could not be accounted for in that manner.

Many tunes, presumably old, have become more or less stock melodies, used over and over again with various slight changes for different hulas. There is also a pronounced tendency on the part of any chanter to employ his own versions of these, or a tune of his own composition. (See those given by Antone Kaoo, Nos. 90, 106; Samuela Waiki, Nos. 80, 126; Solomono Huihui, Nos. 70, 75, 76, 82-85, 87-89, 107-111, 117, 131; Wahineikeouli Paa, Nos. 115, 116, 137, 149-152; and Samuela Akoni Mika, Nos. 121-123. Although opportunities for exercising individual preference and producing new effects thus exist, they are seldom seized, the tunes by Mrs. Kihe, Nos. 96, 139, 140, whatever their provenience, being rare instances of considerable range in variety and unusually good design.

The interchange of tunes from hula to hula is rendered exceedingly easy by the simple meters and rhythms and the paucity of melody. Dotted notes, contrasted with those of smaller value, even such simple combinations as were observed in the *ukeke* and nose flute tunes, are, oddly enough, very rare in hula chants or in their instrumental accompaniments, which are largely combinations of quarter and eighth notes and rests, while the olis are apt to be composed of notes of very small value with little contrast except in the trilled periods which give the impression of length. Olis consequently would appear to move much faster than hulas were it not for the long held notes and the time on one pitch. The hulas that are avowedly modern, are not particularly different from those that are quite old except in the few points already mentioned. No. 145, although probably an adaptation of a hymn, is constructed in the old style.

A large number of features which have become indispensable in the development of modern European music, like modulation, the regular use of extensions, contractions, inversions and reversals of motifs (all of which make possible thematic development), syncopation, dotted effects, and so on, are found in these little Hawaiian tunes, but so seldom that it is evident that although they were not unknown to Hawaiian ears, they had never come to be consciously recognized as possibilities in enlarging the melodic horizon. On the other hand grace notes, anticipations, slurs or portamentos, changing and passing tones, remarkable control in the volume of tone and trills, are what they relied on for variety. Runs, however, they seem never to have discovered.

In all of the old Hawaiian music there is one very noteworthy feature, aside from the stressing of the general level and one other tone in connection with it—the minor or major third or the fourth or fifth downward—and that is the corollary of this statement, that the music is conceived as lying downward from a level, and not as being built upward from it, as in European, much African and American Indian music. This point is important in tracing Hawaiian music to its source and will be discussed in that light in the next chapter. (See page 378.) The downward construction, together with the employment of a simple melodic idea over and over, embellishing and varying it to relieve the monotony, but never enlarging it, changing the structure, or playing with it for its own sake apart from accompanying texts, are the outstanding features of the art of music as it was known to the Hawaiians. The stamp of the old styles may still be noted in their manner of rendering modern music.

GEOGRAPHICAL DISTRIBUTION OF INSTRUMENTS AND MUSIC LIKE THE HAWAIIAN

Up to the present time few adequate studies of Polynesian, or for that matter, Micronesian or Melanesian music have been published with which the features of the ancient Hawaiian music may be compared. Various travelers have mentioned chanting or intoning of poetry as existing in different groups, but they have not been reduced to musical notation, so far as I am aware, and as yet few comparative studies of texts have been made. It is known that certain legends in groups like the Society and Hawaiian islands corroborate one another, but studies of styles in poetic composition, as of musical composition, are still wanting.

Therefore in looking beyond the Polynesian area for probable sources of the ancient phases of the art of music which the Hawaiians appear to have preserved more perfectly than most modern peoples have kept their ancestral heritages, it is necessary to depend largely on a comparison of instruments, inadequate though the descriptions of them by various travelers often prove to be. In making such comparisons the scope of this paper will permit only of tracing instruments like those of the Hawaiian complex, and even some of these perforce must be treated only casually. But in connection with some of them it will add greatly to the point I have to make, to take up allied forms which I will do as briefly as seems to me to be advisable. This chapter is admittedly but a preliminary survey upon which I hope to enlarge at a future time.

MUSICAL BOW

The geographical distribution of the musical bow has already been widely discussed and the study made by Balfour (9) very nearly covers the field. I am depending largely on his work for my information, and can add but little to what he has to give, in the matter of distribution. Only in so far as it is important for my argument will I quote him, but it will clarify much for the reader if at times I quote complete descriptions. The musical bow is a very widespread instrument which even in its simplest forms displays several distinct types. While these types are clearly in Balfour's mind, he has not differentiated them as sharply as necessary, perhaps, to a clear understanding on the part of the reader of their possible relationships.

It has been more or less tacitly assumed that the origin of the musical bow was the war or hunting bow, the musical possibilities of which were suggested when a powerful shot produced the agreeable humming of the vibrating string. That the bow may have had more than one independent origin seems unlikely, and it may be that the beginning of the musical bow is likewise to be referred to a very ancient period and to one locality, although the existence of several very different but all crude types suggest that its possibilities as a musical instrument were very early perceived and acted upon by the players in quite unrelated fashions.

There is first the simple long hunting bow, several feet long, with but a single string. Two methods of playing this seem to have been discovered, one of plucking the string, the other of hitting it with the arrow or with sticks. But in plucking the string a plectrum seems to have come into use in very ancient times. Both methods were known in Asia.

The desirability of a resonator to increase the faint sound of the string was also appreciated very early and one peculiar method of obtaining such a device was to place one end of the bow to the mouth as it was being held in the left hand extending horizontally to the left, while the string was manipulated with the right hand. Such a peculiarity, combined with the one way of holding the instrument, doubtless had but one origin at a very ancient time. The use of the mouth as a resonator has become one of the widest spread features. Whether the other methods were later or separate developments it is impossible to say. One was that of placing the bow, or even merely a string, over a hole in the ground or over an inverted pot, basket, gourd, or calabash. A more permanent form, probably an outgrowth of those just mentioned, was a bell-, bottle-, or bowl-shaped gourd or even a metal or wooden resonator, open on the side away from the bow, being fastened to it somewhere between the center and one end.

The Hawaiian bow had no permanent resonator, the mouth of the player serving as such, the bow being held in the left hand extending horizontally to the left, with one end of it placed between the lips, while a plectrum in the right hand manipulated the strings. (Pl. I, *D*.) But the Hawaiian bow was nevertheless not one of the simplest types since it had lost its hunting bow length, had substituted for the stick-like bow one which was definitely carved into a plano-convex form of great neatness narrowing toward the ends, and was fitted with a fish-tail spur at one end and a notched or perforated flange at the other for accommodating the strings which were increased from one to two or three. The strings were also raised from the flat surface of the wood by little bridges inserted one at each end. Therefore, in tracing the Hawaiian form it is necessary to keep these features in mind.

The musical bow appears in the Marquesas but it is not like the

Hawaiian. It is more than three feet long, instead of at most two feet. It is a round stick, with but one string tied about it at one end and carried through a notch at the other, or if there is an attempt at plano-convex form the flat side is away from the string. It is much more bowed, and yet in some instruments described by Linton (p. 24) stone bridges are used. The method of playing and the names are similar, Hawaiian *ukeke*, Marquesan *utete*. Both no doubt are to be traced to the same ancestor, but probably the Hawaiian which is far more developed and specialized has no direct relationship with the Marquesan. Far to the south in Raivavae in the Austral Islands the *titapu* was noted by Stokes. (See page 24.) It was not mentioned by Balfour, who wrote at an earlier date. According to description it more nearly resembled the Marquesan than the Hawaiian instrument, in fact, was even more crude, though fully as long and played in the same manner, and one bridge was used.

For the Society Islands, whence it is often assumed the Hawaiian Islands were peopled, Ellis and others make no reference to a musical bow. It would be very desirable to know if such an instrument existed there and what form it took. It appears also to be missing in Tonga, the Loyalty Islands, and Fiji. Probably, therefore, those who brought the bow to Hawaii came not from that direction. I have come across no reference to it in the Marshall, Caroline, Ellice, or Gilbert islands, although consider-ing the presence there of some of the other instruments of the Hawaiian complex, as in the south, its occurrence would be expected. The nearest point westward where it is found is in western Melanesia, that is, in New Britain, the Solomon, Santa Cruz, and New Hebrides islands. (See Bal-four, 9, pp. 75-78.) Here, instead of round sticks of wood or hollow tubes of bamboo being fitted with strings, which are the chief forms encountered elsewhere, from Malaysia to Africa, the bows are made generally of light, flat pieces of wood, bent only slightly by the tension of the strings. In size these instruments also correspond closely with the Hawaiian. Figure 6 illustrates specimens from the Solomon Islands given by Balfour. Two of the bows were collected rather late, in 1893-4 and the third before 1888, but there is no reason to suppose that they are particularly modern forms. Guppy (62, p. 142) says concerning the instruments of another island of this group:

> The women of Treasury Island produced a similar [to that of the jews-harp] though softer kind of music by playing, somewhat after the fashion of a jews-harp, on a lightly-made, fine-stringed bow about fifteen inches long. This is held to the lips and the string is gently struck with the fingers, the cavity of the mouth serving as a resonator.

Guppy informed Balfour that the string was held nearest to the lips in playing, which differs from the Hawaiian method, but Codrington (33, p. 336) says that the *kalove,* which is the name for the Florida Island instrument, is held with the curved back of the bow in the mouth. The Treasury Island specimen was made of a rough, flat strip of cane, not hollow, and

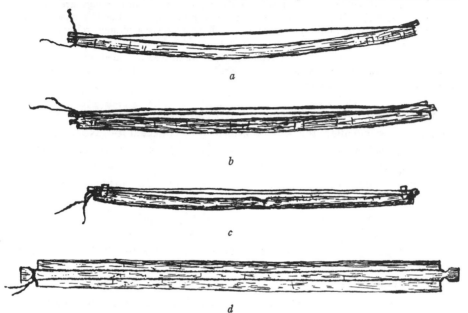

a

b

c

d

FIGURE 6.—Sketches of musical bows: *a, b,* from New Georgia Island, Solomon Islands, length about 18 inches; *c,* from Florida Island, Solomon Islands, length about 16 inches; *d,* bow used by a Pomo tribe of California. (Sketches of bows *a, b, c,* reproduced by courtesy of the Clarendon Press.)

Balfour pronounced it to be a "simpler and more primitive type than the other allied instruments found in this Melanesian group." Except that they are more crudely made than any specimens I have seen in Hawaii, the two New Georgia instruments might be mistaken for Hawaiian. Balfour says:

Of these, one is a short, slightly-curved bow of light wood, 18⅛ inches long and of uniform thickness throughout, with a small projecting spur at one end, and two at the other, round which the ends of the *single* string of twisted vegetable-fibre (? a creeper) are wound in a sailor's "half-hitch". The other, which is from the Mungeri district, has a bow of precisely similar form, and differs only in being furnished with *two* strings, or rather, as in the New Britain *pangolo,* one string fixed at the end having two spurs and passing round the single spur, to be fixed again at the two-spur end of the bow, thus making two strings for playing upon. Both instruments are, in fact, adapted for either one or two strings. In playing, one end of the bow is held in the mouth. A similar specimen from Rubiana Island is in the Rijks Ethnographical Museum at Leiden.

An almost identical instrument from Florida Island was sent to me for the Oxford Museum by Dr. R. H. Codrington in 1888. Its native name is *kalove.* The bow in this is made of hollow reed 15⅞ inches long and has a single little spur at each end round which are fastened the ends of two fine strings of twisted vegetable-fibre. A minute slip of reed pushed under the strings near each end, serves as a little bridge to raise the strings slightly from the bow, which is nearly straight. The bow is held in the teeth in playing. The strings are sounded by striking with a little plectrum of bamboo or reed held in the right hand. Both strings are tuned to one note; one string is permanently stopped with one finger of the left hand, raising the note by a certain interval; the other is alternately stopped and released higher up with another finger. The performer is thus master of three notes. . . .

A specimen identical with that from Florida Island was obtained by C. M. Woodford in Guadalcanar, and is now in the British Museum. There is also one in the University Museum at Cambridge.

In the Metropolitan Museum of Art, New York, is another Solomon Island specimen called the *kigulu* which was collected on Norfolk Island near New Zealand (110 vol. 2, pp. 30, 31). All the specimens described above have the short unbending bow, the spur feature, one or two strings, the same method of stringing. One specimen has bridges. All these features except the single-string and the reed forms distinguish the Hawaiian *ukeke*. No other musical bows I have read of except those of the Solomon Islands, Santa Cruz, or New Hebrides region have all of these characteristics. Evidently, too, the mouth was used as a resonator, the instrument being held to it by the left hand, while the strings were struck by a plectrum of grass or reed or a bit of stick held in the right hand.

There is a bow from Santa Cruz which Balfour thinks may have been carried from the New Hebrides, where it appears to be indigenous and of such "specialized form that it is unlikely to have been developed independently in the two groups." He says (9, p. 78):

The little bow is 19⅝ inches long, of wood, and curved. The shape is peculiar, being broad and more or less cymbiform, having a concavo-convex transverse section. One end is broad and rounded off, the other is shouldered and narrows suddenly into a long, straight spur. The single string is stout and seems to be made from a length of some creeping vine. At the rounded end of the bow it is passed through a small hole, being prevented from drawing right through by having a thickened, knot-like extremity. The other end of the string is wound round the spur, and is prevented by the shoulders from slipping.

The blunt end is held in the mouth, but the wood is directed in front of the player, like a horn, with the string uppermost, plucked by the thumb and first finger of the right hand.

In the New Hebrides the *vuhudendung* described by O. T. Mason (106, p. 379) is "a small, flat, thin bow of wood. The string passes from a hole near one end to a spur or stud formed on the other. It is held by the teeth and the string struck with a double stick." One answering the same description and having the same provenience is in the Metropolitan

Museum of Art. But it is said not to have been held in the mouth. Another, mentioned by Balfour, has a plano-convex transverse section. A good illustration of a flat bow from Ambrym is given by Speiser (141, table 102, fig. 5, spec. 3250).

Thus in these western Melanesian forms are encountered types closer to the Hawaiian than those nearer home which in their turn resemble others from far distant regions. Only in the reed bows occasionally seen in the Solomon Islands is there a significant departure from plano-convex or flat and short types. The presence of this second type in this region is noteworthy, yet to be expected, for this group of islands presents some of the most curious interminglings of culture of any islands in the Pacific. According to Guppy (62, introduction) some of the Solomon Islands are very ancient geologically, others very recent. In fauna and flora, in peoples and customs, are evidences of the many streams of life which have met there, as they have in Borneo and Java and the mainland of southeastern Asia. But elsewhere in the islands, at least, the reed bows and the solid bows appear to have traveled separately, although again in Africa both kinds are found.

In the vast region of Malaysia, where stringed instruments have been at home since time immemorial, the simple bow forms have long since been mostly displaced, apparently, by more elaborate types. Only here and there in isolated districts or in the marginal areas may they still be traced. Later developments of many Javanese, Siamese, Cambodian, Laosian, Burmese, and Indian stringed instruments reveal to the discerning eye the fact that simple wooden bows, even the plano-convex types, must have been ancestral to those instruments now in use. In the marginal region of Formosa, among the mountain tribes, ten Kate (153, p. 581) reports a musical bow of split bamboo with a wax-coated, twisted string of fiber. The bow is held in the left hand, the end resting against the shoulder. The lower part of the string is "struck with the fingers while the upper is put in vibration by the lips of the player." This must mean that the string is held to the mouth, rather than the back of the bow, but the principal vibrations must have been produced by the fingers. Those produced by the breath, if strong enough to have created audible tones, which is unlikely, were certainly secondary. It is more probable that the overtones of the string which was set in vibration by the fingers, being reinforced by the resonator formed by the mouth cavity, were faintly audible. Among the Tsoo of Central Formosa the name of the instrument is *porosu;* among the Vonum, northeast of the Tsoo, *radyok;* and on the southeast coast among the Puzuma, *ratok.*

Another bow from the Nicobar Islands in the Bay of Bengal, not unlike the Hawaiian, though very primitive, is described by Man (101, Pl. 25, fig. 5). It consists of a short section of a branch of a tree, in the round but with one side shaved away to flatten the surface beneath the string. A projection like a spur at either end is reinforced by pointed pieces of wood, one lashed to each spur and extending beyond the point of its conjunction with the main part of the bow well down on the flat surface. A single string of cane fiber, split at either end to form loops which are passed over the spurs, is raised from the surface by three little bridges placed close together in the central part of the instrument but nearer to one end. It was used on festive occasions and was called *danang* but the method of playing is not described. In extreme South Africa the Zulu have a short flat bow with a single string manipulated in the same way as the Melanesian and Hawaiian bows. The instrument is called *umqangala* (9, p. 13).

These are the only flattened forms of bow which appear to be closely related to the Hawaiian type that I have discovered west of Hawaii as far as Africa. In Melanesia, as I have intimated, mixtures of types appear. Thus in New Britain the *pangolo* (9, p. 73)

. . . . presents several features of well-known early types of musical bow. Though small, it is distinctly bow-shaped. The specimen . . . is 21 inches long, roughly finished and hardened with fire, and the ends are cut to form a spur and a shoulder. There are *two* strings made of a sort of bast. Actually the string is in one piece, which is fixed to one of the pegs, wound around the other peg, and carried back to the first peg, where the end is again fastened, two "bow-strings" being thus produced. One of these is braced to the bow with a piece of similar bast-string, a little below the center.

In this little bow are seen many features like those of Hawaiian bows for even the extreme bowing is not unknown in Hawaii in the "latest-style" *ukeke,* although apparently not a traditional form. But the tying of the string down to the bow to make it taut is a departure unknown in Hawaiian bows though it is to be noted from Malaysia to Africa, and even in the West Indies where this idea was carried by negro slaves. The *pangolo* is held like the *ukeke,* but a little more obliquely downward to the left. It is played with a plectrum.

In New Guinea the *pagola* (9, p. 72 and 106, p. 379) consists in a "bow, strung, held partly by the mouth, the string pressed by the thumb of the right hand and struck with a stick in the left." Balfour describes another specimen only five inches long and one inch wide, bi-convex in transverse section:

At each end is a spur, cut away from the solid, and to these are fixed the ends of a flat string made, apparently, from the rind of a reed. To keep the string away from the wood, a little bridge of stone is placed between them at each end.

It thus appears that the Hawaiian bow is a specialized type, highly perfected possibly since the time of its introduction to its present home. It resembles only in a remote way the musical bows of the Marquesas and Austral islands and its counterpart evidently does not exist in the Society Islands, Tonga, Fiji, or New Zealand. However, Best (167, p. 175) mentions a single, stringed, short musical bow, called *ku* by the Maori, which has become almost legendary. It was played with a plectrum. On the other hand, types which very closely resemble it, but which are more crude, are found in Melanesia, notably the New Hebrides and Solomon Islands, in the Bay of Bengal and in South Africa.

It has already been remarked that the region lying between the Malay Peninsula, the islands of Borneo, Sumatra, and Java, on the one hand, and Burma and India on the other, is preëminently the home of stringed instruments which show practically all stages from very simple bow types to the most ornate many-stringed members of the guitar and violin families. The stems of most of these instruments are plano-convex in cross section. The resonators of many of them are attached to one end, and range from half a coconut shell covered with the skin of some fish or animal to specially designed wooden forms. It therefore seems not unjustifiable to assume that the Nicobarese, Melanesian, and Hawaiian forms represent survivals of types ancestral to those now found in southern Asia and the East Indies. Whether the Hawaiian bow, more neatly finished and more highly developed than the Nicobarese or Melanesian forms, is a local development or a more perfect survival of a Malay Peninsula or Burmese type which had developed beyond the earliest forms, it is impossible to say unless exactly such a type might still be found in those regions. It is equally impossible to state whether the Melanesian and Nicobarese forms are degenerate types or crude copies of higher forms, or whether they belong as survivals to earlier stages than the Hawaiian, but it seems more probable that they are survivals of earlier forms. But at least the Hawaiian, the Nicobarese, and the Melanesian types which I have described are more nearly related to one another than the long stick bows or types where the string is tied down to the bow, with or without gourd or other resonators fastened not to the end of the bow but somewhere near its center, with the orifice turned away from the bow. They are also more closely related to one another than to the reed forms, where the reed itself acts to a certain extent as a resonator.

While still dealing with regions to the west of Hawaii, as far as the Atlantic Ocean, I propose to discuss briefly these other types. Taking first the simple stick bow, long and without a resonator, the Melanesian *pangolo* with the string tied down to the bow is the nearest in type to the forms found in the Marquesas and Austral islands, but the difference between the tied down string and the bridges prevents classing these two types together, especially as the *pangolo* is a comparatively short instrument and the others are long. In Timor, however, a simple stick bow has been noted with a wire string which was struck with a stick (9, p. 69). In Borneo a simple bow is laid with its back on a piece of wood which covers the orifice of an earthenware or metal jar (9, pp. 68, 69.) The string is struck with a plectrum. Since the resonator in this case is extemporaneous and not permanently fastened to the bow the instrument represents an intermediate form. Probably elsewhere in this region such simple contrivances are still to be found. In Malaysia, or at least in the Malay Peninsula, I have been unable to find reference to simple wooden bows, but Balfour (9. pp. 54, 55) and other writers on Indian music describe the *pinâka* and *darkun* of northern India which are simple long bows. It is not said by these writers whether the *pinâka* is held to the mouth as a resonator, but the *darkun,* which also is notched along one side of the bow near the end and which belongs, evidently, to the bow-rasp class of instruments, is held on a pot or basket in much the same way as the Bornean *busoi* and *aran.* To the *pinâka* the Hindus ascribe the derivation of all stringed instruments.

Simple bows are found in Africa among the Damara, in the southwest, who convert their hunting bows into musical bows by tying the string to the bow, and holding the bow at this point before the open mouth and striking the string with a small stick. (9, pp. 5-7.) The Mandingo near the Gold Coast also use simple bows, as do some tribes in the Cameroon district, and along the Niger and Benué (9, pp. 8, 10, 11). In fact, on the west side of Africa and in the center of the continent these simple forms seem to prevail, as they do also in the extreme south. But to the south, as among the Damara and Kaffirs, the expedient of tying the string to the bow has also become known. I have by no means named all the tribes among which the simple bows are found but am merely indicating that they appear to predominate largely on the western side of the continent though they are found in Central Africa and to the extreme south.

According to Balfour, extemporaneous resonators such as are used for the *busoi* and *aran* in Borneo and for the *darkun* in India are also used in Africa (9, p. 69) but he gives no instances. On the other hand, bows with bell-, bottle-, or bowl-shaped resonators, chiefly of gourds attached at some point along the bow, are very common. They are found all over the lower half of the continent, as well as in Madagascar, Réunion Island, and the Chagos Islands in the middle of the Indian Ocean (9, pp. 18-36.) Instruments of a more developed stage, like the *vina* of India, have evidently been derived from such forms and Balfour gives a picture of a figurine supposably representing one of the black Indian Hill-tribesmen carrying a bow with a resonator shaped exactly like many African forms (9, pp. 60, 61). Some Malay instruments also appear to have been derived from this type, but though simpler than the Indian *vina*, like it have tuning pegs for the strings (9, pp. 67, 68.) As far east as the Moluccas bows with centrally attached resonators having the orifice turned away from the bow are to be found (9, pp. 69-71), but instruments of this type do not seem to have spread into Melanesia.

To revert to the reed form of bow, it will probably be admitted by all thoughtful readers that a reed bow in its simplest form was secondary to a stick bow, and was first used where reeds were plentiful and sticks rare. The reed has not the resilience of the solid stick and usually cannot be bent very much without breaking. However, the long reed was sometimes used for simple bows, an example being furnished in Mashonaland in southern Rhodesia. Reed bows in Africa appear to be chiefly confined to the south and east. Being unsatisfactory they show some interesting approaches to reversion to solid wooden forms. For instance, among the Basuto (9, pp. 13, 14) is a type consisting of a central cylindrical part about 18 inches long, into either end of which are inserted slender and flexible sticks to which the bow-string is fastened. This instrument has the string drawn to the cylinder and tied down. The Zulu (9, p. 15) have a length of cane with the flexible stick inserted only in one end, the string being tied from the end of the flexible part to a spur on the far end of the cane.

In Madagascar short reed bows are used as well as the long form with attached gourd resonator (7, p. 31 and others) but the short types may have strings cut from the surface of the reed itself (110, vol. 2, p. 24). The *darkun* and *pināka* of India pictured by Balfour are of split reed but *pināka* of wood are also used. Many forms of stringed instruments in Malaysia and India would indicate that reed bows were their direct ancestors, and a few simple reed bows occur here and there, as among the Sakais near Perak River, who have a bamboo bow with three strings, and the Orang Berlanus in the Malay Federated States, who have a similar instrument (172, p. 296; 173, p. 295). Reed bows occur also in Formosa and the Philippines, as well as in the Solomon Islands.

To sum up, then, in the regions between Polynesia and Africa there are several types of primitive musical bow: (1) the simple stick form, long like the hunting bow with or without a flattened surface roughly planed down; (2) a variant and specialized type, usually short, flat or plano-convex (both of which types employ the mouth as temporary resonator); (3) bows laid on pots, gourds or baskets serving as resonators; (4) those having resonators attached at some point along the bow but not at the extreme end. (These attached resonators are bell-, bottle- or bowl-shaped and the orifice is turned away from the bow. I shall not consider forms with end-borne resonators, orifice uppermost, which are found from Borneo to eastern Africa and belong to a higher stage of development.) Then there are (5) reed bows, simple and round or concavo-convex, being split lengthwise, used with or without temporary resonators like types 1 and 3, and others with attached resonators like type 4, or those with strings cut from the surface of the reed which itself acts as a resonator with a hole cut in the side under the strings like the Philippine *agong* (110, vol. 2, p. 24). Solid wooden bows appear to antedate reed forms, their types having been carried over to the new material and a different type added in instruments like the *agong*.

The distribution of these types has lain through Polynesia, Melanesia, Malaysia, Burma, the Indian Ocean, the southern and western part of Africa including Madagascar. It is noteworthy that the simplest forms occur chiefly in the extreme east, west, south, and north, that is, in regions which are marginal to Malaysia and India, where there is a great wealth of development in the line of musical instruments and particularly of the strings or else among isolated or submerged tribes. North of this belt of distribution the bow of the chase was the legendary prototype of all stringed instruments in Greece and Rome, in China and Japan (9. pp. 3-4, and map). In the first two countries only legend remains, but in China and Japan instruments are still found which, if not musical bows, are of such simple structure that it is evident that they are closely related types.

In Japan legend has it that the old *koto,* one of the simple stringed instruments, was first fashioned from six long-bows tied side by side (121, p. 139). Concerning other simple stringed instruments there are similar tales. The evidence is not wanting, however, that these instruments were derived from China and that China, in turn, obtained much of its musical knowledge from India. (See pp. 340 and 121, p. 4, and pp. 143-144.)

There are a number of varieties of *koto.* It is supposed to have first been invented in China during the reign of the Emperor Fukki, about 2000 B. C. (121, p. 137) and was then over seven feet long and had five strings. There were smaller ones for travelers. The *Sagé-koto* was but two feet long, six inches wide at the upper end and about five inches at the lower. It had nine strings and was thought to have been invented in 3468 B. C. It is evident that these instruments by no means represented the earliest forms, legends notwithstanding, and the extreme age of these more elaborate types, even allowing considerable margin for error, shows at what an early time bows were first appreciated for their musical qualities.

It may be of interest to digress here and describe the *ichi-gen-kin,* another simple stringed instrument of Japan. In its simplest form it is a flat piece of wood four or five inches wide, about four feet long, fitted with one string which is raised from the surface by a bridge. There is no tuning peg and the string is played with a plectrum. This is either an instrument derived not from six long-bows, or else one that has degenerated. Other forms have pegs and varying numbers of strings. In some the body of the instrument is made of a longitudinal half-section of bamboo with a wooden surface glued on. Piggott (121) discusses the various types in full and several varieties may be seen in the Metropolitan Museum of Art in New York.

With simple musical bows in Formosa and very old instruments in Japan it might be expected that the Ainu would be found to possess a bow. Very little information is available concerning these people that is not in the Japanese language, but neither Batchelor (18) nor Bird (21), who give full and careful accounts, mention such an instrument although they refer to a guitar or fiddle, called the *tonkari* or *mukko*. This, however, is a quite highly developed instrument whose nearest relative appears to be the crocodile harp of Siam and Burma, called respectively the *ta'khay* and *meg-young*, names which in themselves suggest connection. A detailed study of the instruments reveals that the Ainu form is copied from the crocodile harp, but while the general shape of the body is the same, even to the peculiar nose form of the crocodile, the Ainu instrument has lost the carved features which positively identify the animal, although some of the markings not necessary to the functioning of the instrument and hardly explainable without comparison with more perfect southern forms, are shown by that comparison to be the same. All this is in keeping with Chamberlain's impression from his study of geographical terms (30) that the Ainu (or some of them, for they are a mixed people) once lived far to the southwest, and the pronounced "Hindu" features of some of them would strengthen this view.

The *kin* of the Chinese orchestra and some types of Japanese *koto* possess some of the features of the *tonkari* if descriptions are to be trusted, but it is not clear whether they are all manipulated in the same manner. A *kin* which is specimen No. 2850 in the Metropolitan Museum, is a rod of bamboo 24 inches long with a single narrow string of fiber attached.

It now becomes necessary to turn to the east of Polynesia, to the American continents, to examine the types of musical bow which occur there.

To the east of Hawaii the instrument showing the most striking resemblance to the *ukeke* is the *ha-hai-shin*, found in the possession of the Yokaia tribe of Pomo Indians, Kulanapan family, living in Ukiah Valley north of San Francisco near the coast of California. It is now specimen No. 3250, Metropolitan Museum, and is a flat strip of ash wood with a spur at each end. One side is painted red and decorated with arrowheads in black and white. It has two fiber strings and is 2 feet, 1¼ inches long and 1½ inches wide. (See fig. 6, *d*.) Morris says (110, vol. 2, p. 104):

In playing this instrument the performer places the unpainted side of the bow against his lips [which must mean the front side bearing the strings] and strikes the strings with a small piece of deer bone. The strings are usually of two tones and the size of the buccal cavity controls the pitch. Some of the tribes call this "silent music" as only the one playing the instrument can hear the sound produced. The bone striker is called *ga-di-so-liu*, which being translated means "bone music". Like the Winnebago courting flute, this instrument is popular with lovers. In this bow the strings lie close to the wood although originally they may have been raised from the surface by slips of wood as in the *ukeke* of Hawaii with which form of bow it is identical. It also resembles one in the Oxford Museum from the Mungeri district, New Georgia, Solomon Islands, illustrated and described by Balfour.

It is known that the Salinan Indians (176, p. 157) and some other California tribes like the Yokuts (178, fig. 33) and Diegneño (186, p. 349) had a musical bow with one string but little is known about it. The Salinan and Diegneño used the mouth as a resonator; the Yokuts' bow appears to have been made of reed.

A musical bow is also found among the Maidu (37, p. 221-2).

. . . . The Northeastern Maidu used the regular hunting bow for the purpose and played upon it merely as an amusement, there being nothing sacred or ceremonial about it. The Northwestern Maidu, however, at least in the foothills, seem to have considered the faint sounds produced as specially suitable for individual converse with the spirits, and in this region, therefore, the use of the musical bow is restricted to shamans. The bow here, moreover, appears to have been specially made for the purpose. . . The bow is a metre and a third long, thus exceeding the regular bow somewhat in its dimensions. . . . In playing the bow, it is held in the left hand, one end of the bow being placed in the mouth, the other end extending horizontally to the left. The string of the bow is then tapped gently with a small twig held in the left hand and the notes varied by opening and closing the mouth. . . . thus increasing or lessening the size of the resonance chamber.

Morris is therefore mistaken when, referring to Dixon's paper, she states that the Maidu, like the Mexican tribes, used the gourd resonator (110, vol. 2, p. 105). An even simpler form is reported by J. O. Dorsey (38, p. 350) among the Omaha of Nebraska, far east of the Maidu on the Great Plains. They used their hunting bows as musical instruments in one of their sacred dances, hitting the string of the bow at the same time that they shook the rattle.

These are the only instruments that I have found in North America that resemble the *ukeke* of Hawaii. It will be seen that of the instruments described only the Pomo type is closely allied and that the others are rather more like the Marquesan, Raivavae, or other long simple bows. But the Pomo method of holding the string side nearest the mouth is like that of the natives of Treasury Island, Solomon Islands, and that of one or two African tribes.

Two more examples of simple bows appear from regions so far remote that any connection with the North American bows is far less probable, considering the difficulties of coastwise or overland communications, than with the islands of the Pacific, through mishaps to early navigators. Quoting ten Kate (153, p. 93):

In August I had the opportunity to meet at the La Plata Museum a few Indians from Western Central Patagonia. One of them, a youth of mixed Tehuelche and Araucanian blood, had a . . . simple wooden bow, about 30 cm. long, with a single string made of a tuft of horsehair. When the Indian played upon the instrument one end of the bow was held between the teeth, the other was grasped with the left hand. The string was struck with one of the long bones of the condor, in a manner similar to the use of a fiddle-stick, and which was held in the right hand. . . . This instrument is called *koh'-lo* in Tehuelche, which name, it is curious to state, has a certain resemblance to the Maya name for the musical bow, *hool*, and the name *kolove*, given by the natives of Florida, in the Solomon Islands, to the same instrument. This *koh'-lo* was bought from the Indian for the La Plata Museum, where it is now kept in the Ethnographical section of that institution.

Mason (op. cit.) has criticised the suggestion that this Patagonian specimen could by any chance be pre-Columbian because it has a horse-hair string. I need only call attention to the "latest style" *ukeke* of Hawaii (p. 21) to show that the horse-hair string in that case was merely the substitution of handy, suggestive, and labor-saving material for the older twisted-fiber string on a more or less traditional form. The Patagonian form of bow lacks the resonator common to West Indian types or those of eastern South America, to which Mason and others would fain trace its origin, and is short, unlike most bows from those regions which lack resonators.

The second example in South America occurs in remote Central Brazil in the *umcunga* (106, p. 380) a "bow of rattan, string stretched from one end to about two-thirds its length and tied. Beaten with a small stick, the bow being held against the throat or vocal cords." On this Balfour comments (9, p. 48):

This method of holding the instrument against the throat is very peculiar, and reminds one of that curious Brahman instrument, the *nyastaranga*, or throat trumpet, although the effect would seem to differ in the two cases. I do not know of this method of playing in Africa, and probably it was not introduced from that continent, even supposing the Brazilian form of musical bow to be an offshoot from the immigrant African type, which, although probable, is by no means necessarily the case.

The Ashluslay, Choroti, Chané, and Mataco, living along the upper reaches of the Pilcomayo River just east of the Andes in the Paraguayan Chaco, are reported to have a musical bow (116, vol 1, pp. 168-9, p. 183; vol. 2, p. 116) but it is not described. These examples conclude the simplest types of plain musical bow found in the Western Hemisphere outside the

West Indies, Central America, and one or two spots on the east coast of South America, where they have evidently been carried by the negro slaves drawn from tribes in West Africa. It is necessary, however, to examine other types lying between these northern and southern extremes, namely in the southwestern United States, Mexico, Central, and South America. The first of these other types is hardly more than a simple bow, but one side of it is notched. It is described and figured by Bolinder (22, pp. 302-3) and belongs to the Busintana, a branch of the Arawak family in Colombia. It is a flat bow, like the Pomo, Hawaiian, Solomon Island, Nicobarese, and Zulu bows, and has but one string which is pictured as being held to the lips while being struck with a small stick. It is called the *marimba* and is properly a bow-rasp and will be discussed again.

Extemporaneous resonators consisting of a large gourd or pot on which the bow is laid string uppermost are described by Lumholtz (97, vol. 1, p. 475) as being used by the Tepehuanes and Aztecs of southwestern Mexico, in the neighborhood of Pueblo Viejo in the western and mountainous part of the state of Jalisco. The bow is one meter, 36.5 centimeters long and is called the *tawitól*. A flat stick is placed on the bow when in position on the gourd and is pressed by the foot of the shaman, who plays the instrument by beating the string with two sticks. To the south of these tribes the Huichol and Cora have the same instrument but the Cora, at least, have glued the bow to the gourd. They use two sticks to beat with, but the Huichol employ two arrows. This instrument is strikingly like that used in Borneo. Among some of the Mexican tribes a bow-rasp with notches on the side of the bow is substituted for the simple form. Both instruments are used in connection with very sacred ceremonies performed at the adolescence of both boys and girls at which the drinking of the juice of a certain cactus which is highly stimulating but not intoxicating, plays a prominent part. Personal adornment with flowers is also a ritualistic feature of the ceremonies, as is their performance in connection with the moon. Similar rites seem to have been performed by the ancient Aztecs. These recall ceremonies of a like nature in Northern India, including the floral decoration and altars on which the paraphernalia of the dancers is placed and the drinking of *soma* juice made from the moon-plant, as it is called (32, chapter on Dravidians). It will be recalled that the *darkun* of the Bhuiyârs of India is a bow-rasp, laid on a basket or pot as resonator. It is used at these ceremonies. Balfour (9, pp. 68-69) says that the extemporaneous resonator is used in like manner in Africa, but gives no explicit example.

Of the bows with attached gourd resonator placed somewhere along the bow with the orifice away from it, or for that matter, any bows with attached resonators, none are present in the western part of the two American continents. They are confined to the West Indies, Central America, and the eastern side of South America. They are described by Balfour (9, pp. 38-43), Morris (110, vol. 2), Stanley (144) and others. Most of them have the string tied down to the bow. Some are merely plain bows without resonators, such as are found on the west side of Africa. One, from San Salvador, is made of a long pliable reed (9, p. 41) but most of them are long, arc-shaped sticks of wood.

There are two examples which may or may not be of African derivation. One is an instrument from Yucatan, the *hool,* described by Saville (136, p. 272):

> . . . . made by stretching a piece of rope-like vine, called *ohil,* between the two ends of a pliable piece of wood, making a bow about two feet in length. One end of this bow is placed near the face, about one-third of the distance from the end, so that the mouth covers, but does not touch, the string, forming a resonator. Between the string and the bow a piece of wood is placed in such a manner that it may be pressed against the string or relaxed at will. The tones are produced by tapping on the string, thus producing a sound somewhat resembling that made in playing the jews-harp but more agreeable to the ear. The different notes are produced by the pressure or relaxation of the stick upon the string and by the opening and partial closing of the mouth over the same.

Balfour comments (9, p. 44) that this is a type commonly seen in Africa, and that the graduated pressure on the string is a method used by the Zulu of South Africa, so that it is not certain that this is really a Maya instrument. I would merely call attention to the fact that the Zulu are also the people who possess apparently the only African example of the short flat bow.

The other example is from Guatemala, "a light wooden bow about six feet long, strung with a thin creeper or with a string. A bracing loop draws the bow-string to the bow towards the middle. The bow is held to the mouth and the string is struck with a small stick. In this case there is no resonator." (9, pp. 41-2.) Probably this is of African derivation. Tied down strings are not found on the west side of the Americas.

In the *mawahellis* of the Tejon tribe of Tule River Indians of Central California (106, p. 377) occurs a type not hitherto discussed in this paper. It is a bow made of tule reed "with a longitudinal half-section of the upper joint removed and a hole made in the lower end for a tuning peg." The string, which is of gut, is strung between the peg and the spur formed by cutting away part of the reed longitudinally[9] an instrument almost identical with a Yokuts bow figured by Powers (178, fig. 33). Another[10] from a New Mexican pueblo is the *thlin-thli-no-me,* a "round stick, with a rude tuning peg

---

[9] This instrument is specimen No. 19,87, United States National Museum.
[10] Specimen No. 48,049, United States National Museum.

through one end. One string, supposed to be struck with a small stick."
(106, p. 380.)

Judging from the descriptions, these instruments and the *harpa* figured
by Balfour (9, p. 46) from the Rio Verde district, Mexico,[11] are identical
in construction and similar to another bow from Michoacan, Mexico (9, p.
46.) Both Mexican specimens are made of reed. The *harpa* is straighter
than the others and has a small sound hole cut in one side beneath the
strings, in which respect it is like the Philippine bow, the *agong*. Minus
the gourd resonator these instruments with tuning pegs are almost exactly
like certain Siamese, Cambodian, and Laosian instruments figured by Balfour (9, pp. 63-68) and others from Chota Nagpûr and Orissa in Northeastern India. That the American forms lack the resonator is an important
difference, to be sure, but the presence of the tuning peg device is a resemblance not so easily accounted for as would be the loss or lack of a resonator. There seems little doubt but that the Californian, New Mexican,
and Old Mexican forms are related to one another. So far as I have been
able to learn there are no tuning-peg devices on musical bows on the eastern
side of the continent, among the negroes.

Another still more developed type of musical bow is to be found among
the San Carlos and White Mountain Apache tribes of Southern Arizona.
It is a true fiddle, made of the cylindrical tube of the *agave* stalk, with a
tuning peg piercing it at one end and a spur, usually, at the other to which
a single string is fastened. The spur feature is exactly like the spur on the
Mexican instruments with tuning pegs (110, vol. 2, pp. 105-6). Apparently the Apache instruments have no bridges and some specimens lack the
spurs or tuning pegs. Sound holes are bored in the tube after the same
fashion as the *harpa* of Mexico, and the Philippine, Bornean, and Javanese
bowed stringed instruments. The Apache fiddles are played with a bow.
According to Morris (110, vol. 2, p. 106) they also resemble the Solomon
Island *kodili* and a specimen from New Guinea described by Balfour
(9, pp. 76 ff.) although these are not reported to be played with bows.
The Apache instruments are the only bowed stringed instruments in North
America, so far as is known. They do not in the least resemble any Spanish
instruments of the guitar variety. Spier (186, p. 349) reports that the
Dieguño Indians of California have a similar fiddle.

In South America Hawtrey (69, Pl. 41) has discovered one among the
Lengua Indians of the Paraguayan Chaco, who live now on the west bank
of the Paraguay River. He says that they do not belong to the Guarani
or Quichua families but are related to the Mataco, one of the tribes among
whom Nordenskiöld discovered a musical bow. (See page 335.) The

---

[11] Now in the Peabody Museum, Cambridge, Mass.

fiddle has a cylindrical body and a smaller cylindrical neck inserted in one end of it, with a tuning peg driven through it. It has one string which is raised from the cylindrical body by a bridge placed across the center. The instrument is played with a bow. In most respects it appears to closely resemble Apache fiddles. The Lenguas have some pottery and weave, using an upright loom. They practise tattooing, especially on the faces of the women. Their leather is tanned by a peculiar method characteristic of western Asia. They do not know about counting by the quipu, but use notched sticks. They are not musical and sing monotonous chants. They have a bamboo flute. One of their legends states that they came from the northwest and Hawtrey finds that there are evidences of this having been the case.

In Patagonia among the same tribes which have the musical bow in a simple form, with a horse-hair string (see p. 335), namely the Tehuelche and Araucanians, Musters (113, p. 200) says that he saw "a wind instrument, formed of the thigh bone of a guanaco, with holes bored in it, which is applied to the mouth, and played on with a small wooden bow, having a horse-hair string." Balfour thinks that Lieutenant Musters' remarks must have referred to a simple musical bow placed to the lips and struck with a bone, hardly a flute, since it is so difficult to conceive of a flute being blown and played at the same time with a bow. The account that Balfour read, however, was in another work of Musters' and not so clearly explicit as this. I prefer to leave Musters' statement unchallenged, particularly in view of the presence of a bow-played instrument among the Lengua Indians and the other evidence I have to present. (See also 110, vol. 2, p. 265, for several other similar descriptions by various authors.)

Since primitive bow-played musical bows are apparently lacking on the eastern side of the Americas and in the West Indies and the invention of playing with a bow is sufficiently peculiar in itself to warrant a suspicion that it originated but once, it is necessary to look to the west for other examples of this technique. It has already been remarked that bow-played instruments are found in the Philippines, Borneo, and Java, while ten Kate (135, p. 581) reports them among the primitive tribes of Formosa. It is well known that in Malaysia and India they have had a very long history. Concerning the *ravanastron*, the oldest stringed instrument of the Hindus to be played with a bow and generally accepted by historians of music to be the ancestral form of all bow-played instruments, Engel says (46, p. 56):

The Hindus claim to have invented the violin bow. They maintain that the *ravanastron*, one of their old instruments played with the bow, was invented about 5,000 years ago by Ravanon, a mighty king of Ceylon. [Day, 36, p. 102, calls him Râbana and credits him only with the invention of the art of bowing.] However this may be, there is great probability that the fiddle bow originated in Hindustan, because Sanskrit scholars inform us that there are names for it in works which cannot be less than from 1,500 to 2,000 years old. The non-occurrence of any instrument played with a bow on the monuments of the nations of antiquity is by no means so sure a proof as has been generally supposed, that the bow was unknown. . . . If the *ravanastron* was an importation of the Mohammedans it would most likely bear some resemblance to the Arabian and Persian instruments, and it would be found rather in the hands of the higher classes, in the towns; whereas it is principally met with among the lower order of people, in isolated and mountainous districts. It is further remarkable that the most simple kind of *ravanastron* is almost identical with the Chinese fiddle called *ur-heen*. . . . The *ur-heen* has not been mentioned among the most ancient instruments of the Chinese, since there is no evidence of its having been known in China before the introduction of the Buddhist religion in that country. From indications which to point out would lead too far here, it would appear that several instruments found in China originated in Hindustan. They seem to have been gradually diffused from Hindustan and Thibet, more or less altered in the course of time, through the East as far as Japan.

Concerning the *rebec* of Arabia, conceded to be the ancestral form of the more western bow-played instruments which reached Europe and northeast Africa, Engel (46, p. 56) says that the Arabians themselves assert that it came from Persia. The *rebec* was introduced into Europe during the 11th or 12th centuries. Engel says that it is certain that at that date it was not bowed in Arabia although it was so played about that time in Europe. Ancient Egypt and Assyria appear not to have known such instruments and those which are found in Africa therefore have another and comparatively late origin. They are rather widely spread in this continent (7, pp. 11-16) one being even found among the Bushmen in South Africa (9, p. 29) which is merely a bow with attached gourd resonator like the primitive types, played with another plain bow. This instrument is not considered original with them, however, but in all probability the idea of bowing was copied from European instruments (9, p. 30). The other African instruments pictured by Ankermann (7) even to their names show traces of relationship to Arabian forms while the harps are singularly like those of Malaysia.

Summing up the situation of the musical bow in the Western Hemisphere it appears that here also are all types of bow from the simple war bow of the Omaha and Maidu to crudely developed fiddle forms (which however, are cylinders instead of having end-borne resonance chambers) and that they include the solid long wooden bows, the flattened short wooden forms, and those made of reed. Their distribution calls for discussion. The long simple bows are found in three regions—in the Sacramento drainage in California among the Maidu; on the Great Plains among the Omaha; and in the West Indies, Central America and the eastern side of South America, where they appear to be connected with the negro slave importations. It is difficult to conceive how the Maidu have had any connection with the negroes. There is nothing in their culture to warrant such an assumption, in fact, their material culture, their other musical instruments, their elaborate work in feathers and shells, would seem to link them with Mexican tribes through southern California routes. The feather headdresses of the Maidu (37, pp. 149 f.), the Tulare Indians[12] and the natives of Easter Island (157, Pl. 5, 54, 55; 132, p. 218) are so alike that they might almost be mistaken, one for the other.

It is almost as difficult to connect the Omaha with the southeast, especially as their legends point to an early home in the southwest and their agricultural ceremonies, together with those of the Pawnee and other allied tribes, are in their general aspects, according to a personal communication of Dr. Clark Wissler who has made an exhaustive study of the Pawnee creation ritual, very much like those of the southwest. Their manner of cutting the hair into curious patterns is paralleled in many parts of the South Seas.

Therefore it seems that the long musical bows of the Maidu and Omaha must be distinguished from those in the West Indies from the standpoint of provenience, although in appearance they are practically the same.

As to the short forms of simple bow, the Pomo instrument with its flat shape comes first to mind. The only other flat form which is short is that of the Busintana of Colombia, but this has deep notches on the side and is a rasp as well. The Pomo instrument, on the other hand, is so like Hawaiian and Solomon Island forms, even being played with the string rather than the bow toward the mouth, after the fashion of Solomon Islands bow, that it could hardly be associated with the one in Colombia except indirectly.

The Patagonian bow is the third short type. Apparently it is not flat or plano-convex. Its name, however, links it with the Pacific also. (Compare Patagonian *kohlo* with Solomon Island *kolove* or *kalove*.) The bows of the tribes along the Pilcomayo River have not been described so that they could be classified. As to the *umcunga* of Central Brazil, no description is given of the form of the bow, but the peculiar practice of holding it to the throat it will be recalled was not known by Balfour to have occurred in Africa but was known in India.

The types with extemporaneous resonators occur in western Mexico. Although such forms are known in Africa they are apparently not known in the West Indies or on the eastern coasts of Central and South America. The Mexican forms, together with the ceremonies in which they are used, show striking resemblances to those of northern India while an identical form occurs in Borneo, although nothing is said concerning ceremonies there.

On the other hand the bows with attached bell-, bottle- or bowl-shaped resonators, fixed to the bow somewhere near the middle with the orifice

---

[12] Personal observation.

turned away from it, are common forms among the negroes of the West Indies and the eastern coasts of Central America and South America. They do not occur on the west coasts nor in the Pacific east of Melanesia. Their presence in the Western Hemisphere is undoubtedly due to the negro slaves.

The types with tuning pegs and the fiddle forms, which are either of reed or else cylindrical in form occur in California, Arizona, New Mexico, Old Mexico, Patagonia and Paraguay, are not common in West Africa, and apparently have not come to the Americas with the negroes. On the other hand they are like forms found from the Solomon Islands, the Philippines, Borneo and Java as far west as Siam, Burma, and India.

In Java, Siam, Burma, and India the great wealth of development of stringed instruments of all types, descended from both reed and solid bow forms, with and without resonators, would indicate that these regions have been centers of influence from remote times. The legend concerning the *ravanastron* and the very early date (about 3000 B. C.) assigned to the invention of playing a string with a bow, together with the evidence from China and Japan pointing to India or that general region for the derivation of many of their musical instruments, lends weight to this assumption. Greece, too, according to Strabo, ascribed most of her knowledge of music to Asia, the country from which Orpheus came (p. 376).

The solid wooden bow, the ancestor of all the stringed instruments, probably, lacking a more powerful resonator than the mouth, never developed beyond the stage reached by the Hawaiians who utilized in addition the natural resonance of certain woods. But very early in the Asiatic regions temporary resonators in the shape of gourds, baskets or pots, or even holes in the ground were utilized and from these developed the resonator fastened to the bow, either at one end or somewhere nearer the center. All these stages are represented in southern Asia.

Reed bows, too, appear to have found a place in the early history of music in these lands and to have suggested themselves as more resonant than solid bows at a time when resonators were still not generally adopted. The practice of boring a hole in the side of the tube to increase the resonance, besides occurring in these regions, reached west to Madagascar and east to Borneo and the Philippines and I would venture to say even to the west side of North America, although at present evidence of the occurrence of reed resonators in the intermediate regions is lacking, except in Melanesia. The use of the reed in this form was a significant step in the development of the psaltery family of stringed instruments through the exchange of large reeds for elongated box resonators like those of the Burmese crocodile harps, the Japanese *ichi-gen-kin* and others. In the reed form having a flexible stick inserted in one end of the reed and the string forming a triangle with the body of the instrument, probably lies the beginning of the harp family.

The practice of attaching resonators, at least on the arc of the bow, extends from Africa, on the west of the central region just defined, across the Atlantic by means of negro carriers to eastern America, but on the east of southern Asia evidently no farther than Melanesia. On the other hand, the practice of placing the bow on temporary resonators seems not to have gone across the Atlantic with the slaves, yet it is found in western Mexico with ceremonies which are strikingly like those of India which are associated with similar instruments.

Bowing probably did originate in Ceylon or India. It has gone both east and west of the center. The similarity of Apache fiddles and the Lengua Indian form in western Patagonia to Malaysian types of reed musical bows is extraordinary, while the African forms of bowed instruments are quite different and appear to have been influenced by Arabian instruments of comparatively high development. To my mind there are but two interpretations to be made of the evidence presented, either that of independent development or that of diffusion. With the region between Malaysia and India forming a center of very high development and of very ancient history, Africa on the one hand and Melanesia, Polynesia, and the Western Hemisphere on the other become marginal areas. (See fig. 7, p. 382.) The Americas by means of later negro carriers become the extreme margin by way of Africa. Although the African types of bows coming by way of the Atlantic, and the Asiatic by way of the Pacific have met in the Americas, they have not intermingled to any extent, but have come near to so doing. The Maya and Guatemala specimens may be African, along with some central American bows, but considering the name and description of the Mayan *hool* and the connections between the Aztec and Mayan civilizations, the provenience from Africa seems doubtful, at best. Some writers would consider the Brazilian bows African, but the *umcunga* resembles the Hindu throat trumpet and no known African type, while the notched Busintana bow from Colombia has no exact parallel in Africa, and a less close one only reported once.

It seems to me far more likely that the types of bows found in California, the Great Plains, Arizona, New and Old Mexico, Paraguay, Central Brazil, and Patagonia are pre-Columbian, and reached the Western Hemisphere through the agency of as many carriers as there are types, and at different periods, than that they should be due to negro influence of which few similar and no very close results are found on the east side of the continents. The Pacific was a far more active region in pre-Columbian times than has yet been freely admitted. The ease with which canoes could be blown over thousands of miles of ocean in a comparatively short time, having once been driven off their course, has been demonstrated again and again. Although the prevailing winds blow west, not east, in storms they vary as do also currents.[13]   References occur in Hawaiian legends to long voyages and *Kahiki-Ku,* meaning, as some Hawaiians insist, the foreign land to the east as distinguished from *Kahiki-Moe,* that to the west. Mendaña, whose ability as a sailor was considerable for his time, was driven far north on his return from the Solomon Islands to Peru, and must have come near the Hawaiian Islands on his way to Lower California, where he eventually arrived and made his way down the coast to his destination.

It is a commonplace that the Easter Islanders are to be connected with Polynesia.   It is another that the Maori of New Zealand were in part of Hawaiian stock.   There are legends of trips made between Hawaii and Tahiti more than once, and also of some Marquesans reaching Hawaii. Not only the Polynesians but the Micronesians and Malays, and the Melanesians to a lesser extent, have always been great sailors and think nothing

---

[13] It is frequently stated even today, despite the numerous citations of contrary evidence, that, owing to adverse winds and currents voyages eastward across the Pacific could not have been undertaken, especially as far east as America. It is even argued that the Polynesians came to their present homes from the east, that is, America, although it is admitted that the Melanesians farther west must have spread east into the Pacific. I have therefore thought it might be useful to cite the following writers on winds and currents in the Pacific. W. L. Ranken, writing on the South Sea Islanders, says (123a, p. 238) :

Then in regard to the winds, the prevailing winds are mostly from the east, but every navigator can corroborate Cook's experience of the Society Group, that he had frequently a fresh gale from the S. W. for two or three days, and sometimes, though very seldom, from the N. W. It is also well known that in October, November, and December the trade winds disappear, and as a rule S. W. winds prevail. One instance of a migration against the course of prevailing winds is as good as many. Captain Beechey picked up a canoe which had sailed from Chain Island for Tahiti, a voyage of about 100 miles west, down the trades. Two westerly gales had blown them to Banoir Island, 600 miles out of their course. On board were 26 men, 15 women, and 10 children, quite enough to form a colony, and this against prevailing winds. By such gales alone all the Tuamotus and Marquesas might have been colonized from the Society Isles.

Whitmee says (165, p. 269) :

A difficulty is felt by many as to the possibility of such an eastward movement, directly against the prevailing trade winds and the usual currents. But it is well known to voyagers in the tropical regions of the Pacific that sometimes there are strong westerly winds blowing there; and also that occasionally there are strong currents setting from the west to the east. These are exceptional. But the probability is that, if the voyage were involuntary, the people would be more likely to be taken off their guard by exceptional winds and currents than by those which usually prevail. If, on the other hand, the people went of their own will—a vanquished tribe determining to seek a new home in the east—I imagine their canoes would lie close enough to the north-east to fetch the Samoan or Tongan Islands.

On reviewing the studies of Captain Powell on Ocean Currents, the reviewer says in vol. 3 of the same Journal, p. 339:

Now Captain Powell has shown that there is a drift-current following eastwards [in the Pacific] caused by winds which at certain seasons blow in a direction contrary to the trades, and that this current after sweeping round Easter Island is deflected northwards.

This reviewer argued that such a current might carry canoes from the west to Easter Island, and that a boat starting from this island might be carried in a north-easterly direction and landed on the coast of Peru, in the neighborhood of Truxillo. This migration, he said, would well accord with certain South American traditions.

of undertaking long voyages. It is unnecessary to multiply examples to prove that there were in all probability many pre-Columbian and pre-Magellanic journeys on this great ocean.

Notwithstanding the fact that no positive evidence has come to light for the landing of the Oceanic voyagers on America's shores, in far Patagonia occurs a musical bow of a type used in the Solomon Islands, with a name almost the same, and among the Pomo Indians north of San Francisco in California is another so like one of the New Georgia, Solomon Islands, types, that it might be called identical.

The carriers of the *ukeke* to Hawaii would seem to have been different people from those who brought the bow to the Marquesas and Austral Islands, to the Maidu of California and others having the long simple forms, but more closely related to those who carried the *kalove* to the Solomon Islands, the related forms to Santa Cruz and the New Hebrides, and the Patagonian and Pomo types just mentioned. The Nicobar Islands bow appears to occupy a position ancestral to all of these, while the Zulu *umqangala* may be due to carriers voyaging in that direction from the center.

The fingering of the strings, of which a hint was found in Hawaii (p. 25) may have first been suggested in an earlier home, since it occurs in the Solomon Islands, Malaysia, and the Asiatic mainland, or it may be merely the result of holding so narrow an instrument in the palm of the hand where the fingers necessarily touched the strings. The method of tuning being different from that in the Solomon Islands, with the almost invariable interval of a perfect fourth established, suggests more direct connection with the ancient Asiatic world, where that interval influenced the entire musical systems of India and, in Europe, of ancient Greece.

As to the remainder of the complex of musical instruments found in Hawaii, and even of some which do not occur there, their distribution and

---

There are numerous references to Japanese junks having been encountered off California, and to early trade between that country and America, as well as to Japanese junks landing on various islands in the Pacific. One case cited by Whitmee (op. cit., p. 273), of a Japanese junk having landed in December, 1832, on one of the Hawaiian islands, only four living of an original crew of nine, who had been ten or eleven months at sea in a junk originally bound from one of the southern Japanese islands to Yeddo, laden with fish, when they encountered a typhoon. Such Japanese junks ran north of Micronesia, usually.

A final example is the most striking of all, and is cited by Ranken (123a, p. 238).

There is no difficulty in making a voyage from the Society Group to Rarotonga, down the trades; and to show how, at some seasons, voyages eastward can also be made, we will instance one made by John Williams, exactly from Samoa to Rarotonga, other isles and Tahiti. Sailing from Samoa, he was at first 15 days in making Niue, 300 miles south. Here he got a westerly breeze, and ran to Rarotonga, 800 miles east by south, in 7 days. This in a small schooner of his own building in the islands. Carrying on the same breeze, he visited Mangaia, south of Rarotonga, called at Rurutu, and thence made Tahiti, 350 miles, in 48 hours. "After the fair wind sprang up, 200 miles west of Savage Island," he says, "we sailed, in the short space of 15 days, a distance of about 1,700 or 1,800 miles to the eastward."

relationships are fully as interesting as those of the bow and are equally important in furnishing evidence concerning the migrations of peoples. With such instruments as the drums, the jew's harps, and the bull-roarer, which are either too undifferentiated or of too many types to have made possible a thorough survey, I shall deal very lightly. In the time available it has not been possible to cover the literature completely and perhaps for this present study it would not be necessary to do so.

THE NOSE FLUTE

Perhaps it is only fair to myself, as well as to Foy, to state that his paper on the distribution of the nose flute (57) was not read until I had covered the main part of the work on this section. He has gone over much of the same ground in working out distributions, but often with different authorities, so that I shall refer to him only for data new to me. The other authorities I have followed are Andree, Meyer, Ihering, Morris and Stanley, together with many of their sources. (See Bibliography.)

The peculiar custom of playing a flute with the nose is in itself sufficiently unnatural to afford a feature by which to trace connections. It is said by Tylor (161, p. 403), Engel (45, p. 166), and Day (36, p. 103) to have originated with the Brahmans who, because others of lower caste played flutes with the mouth, could not allow themselves to be defiled by doing the same. Two varieties of nose flute were known in India, the single, and the double form which was played with both nostrils. The single flute, *murali* (36, p. 104), was very sacred in southern India and was thought to have been the companion of the god Krishna in his wanderings. The double flutes were called *kural* at least in one locality (36, p. 104). Stanley (144, p. 78) gives a description of one from Jeypore. Double nose flutes are also used by the wild Malay tribes (182, p. 132). The *poongi,* the familiar snake charmer's instrument, consisting of a series of pipes placed in a gourd, was given the name *nâsajantra* when sometimes also blown with the nose (36, p. 104). Another instrument made of a small gourd with a blow hole in the top and one or two holes for stops in the side (resembling an *okarina*) has, in some parts of the world, including parts of Africa and some of the Pacific islands, been blown with the nose, but I have no reference to such an instrument in India, although it is not improbable that it was known there.

West of India, Foy (57, p. 245) quotes Frobenius as mentioning the presence of the nose flute in the Cameroon district and in the Lulua district in the Congo, and Torday and Joyce as reporting it among the Ba-Huana. That it should be found in West Africa and apparently be lacking in East

Africa is not so surprising as might be thought, if its original home was India, for it seems that many old culture traits once presumably covering a greater part of that continent now survive chiefly on the western side, or to the south, having been pressed back by later cultural waves from the north and east. I have not yet found a reference to its presence in Madagascar or in Réunion or the Chagos Islands.

East of India, Foy (57, p. 240) reports it among the Chingpaw in Upper Burma. It is mentioned by various writers, but not Foy, again and again in the Malay Peninsula (for instance 23, vol. 1, p. 147; 87, p. 3145. In Sumatra, among the Nias tribe it is called *sigu-nihu* (144, p. 81). (Compare the Hawaiian *ohe-hano-ihu, ihu* meaning nose.) It is found among the Nias Islanders who name it *seroene* (144, p. 78); in Java, where it has six holes and is called *souling* (144, p. 83; 110, vol. 2, p. 7 and elsewhere); in Bali (109, pp. 195-6); in Borneo, where it is called *silinguit* in Sarawak (110, vol. 2, p. 18 and elsewhere); in various parts of the Philippines, in Palawan and especially in northern Luzon (57, p. 240 and 110, vol. 2, Pl. opp. p. 26); in Formosa (153, and 32, p. 138), particularly among the Tosarri tribe; in different parts of Celebes (109, pp. 195-6; 57, pp. 239-40); in the Moluccas (57, pp. 239-40); in Sangi (109, pp. 195-6); in Tinian (57, pp. 239-40); among the coast peoples in the southern and central parts of New Guinea as well as along the north coast (57, p. 240); in Yap (57, pp. 240-1); in Pelew and various parts of the Caroline Islands (57, pp. 240-1), where Christian (32, p. 138) thought it missing, but Andree reports it from Ponapé (4, p. 150), Meyer from Ruk (109, pp. 195-6), Foy from Mortlock and Truk (57, pp. 240-1). Foy remarks that its occurrence in the New Hebrides, New Britain (or New Pommerania), and New Caledonia is very doubtful. In fact he says that it does not occur in New Britain at all, and thinks that on that account it is probably not to be found in the Solomon Islands either. On the other hand, the Crosby Brown collection in the Metropolitan Museum contains a nose flute from New Caledonia (110, vol. 2, p. 40); another is cited by Mahillon (99, vol. 1, p. 409, specimen 364); a third by Edge-Partington and Heape (39) and a fourth by Stanley (144, p. 80). Other writers cite the New Hebrides, New Britain and the Solomon Islands, possibly, as Foy states, through error or confusion of the nose flute with an instrument like the okarina. Foy cites Uea in the Loyalty group as a new locality hitherto not mentioned by writers on the distribution of the nose flute (57, pp. 240-1), while various writers have reported it from Fiji, where it is said to have been played only by women and called *mbi-ta-ni-tanga* (110, vol. 2, p. 40). Rougier (131, p. 468) gives a fine description of it. In Tonga it varied in size, and had from three to five holes (144, p. 83, and others). Mariner says that it was called *fangofango* (102, vol. 2, pp. 331-2). St. Johnston (134, pp. 133-4) gives a description of a Tongan virtuoso playing on it. In Samoa it was evidently given the same name as in Tonga (32, p. 138). It is reported as the *vivo* from the Society Islands, especially Tahiti, where Ellis (40, vol. 1, p. 285) saw it, and Edge-Partington and Heape illustrate it (39); from Niue (57, pp. 240-1); from the Marquesas as *puhckuheku* (88, p. 406); from Hawaii (*ohe hano ihu*); and from New Zealand (122, p. 184, and others). Best (167, p. 146) gives *nguru* as the Maori name. Foy says that its presence in North Australia is recent (57, p. 240). Ihering, whom Foy overlooked, refers to its presence among the Coroados or Caingang of Central Brazil (76, p. 375), while Teschauer (155, p. 21) says of the same tribe:

> Ihre Musikinstrumente bestehen aus Rohrstücken, die sie mit der Nase blasen, und aus Ochsenhörnern die zu einander gestimmt sind und eine "pathetische, traurige Musik" vernehmen lassen. Ferner haben sie für Signale in weiteren Entfernungen eine Art Trompete, die sie aus den grossen festen Blütenscheiden einer Palmenart (*coqueiro*) herstellen.

Lastly, A. H. Keane (84, p. 206) discussing the Botocudos of Brazil says:

> An instrument of a more peaceful character is a small bamboo flute, which is played on through the nose. This strange habit was probably occasioned by the *tembeitera*, which prevented the lips from being conveniently used for the purpose. Similar nose flutes are common in India and other parts of the East where the custom has been explained by the caste system. But however this may be, we have here another instance of apparently eccentric customs originating in independent centres.

All the authorities I have quoted who have written on the distribution of the nose flute have overlooked this reference, as I nearly did. It may be, as Keane is inclined to think, a case of independent development, but considering that this region of central South America furnishes so many instruments of types like those which are being discussed, and so many other phases of culture which recall Polynesia and beyond there, Malaysia and India, it is at least possible that this peculiar trait may be traced to the west, the lip plug notwithstanding.

GOURD WHISTLE

It will be recalled that in Hawaii the *kamani* nut and small gourds were used as whistles and are said to have been played with the nose or with the mouth. Edge-Partington and Heape (39) picture two such whistles from Tahiti, one with four holes, made from a small nut, another of gourd with two holes, and one from Fiji made from a coconut shell. Gourds as mouth whistles are used by the Taranaki tribe in New Zealand (159, p. 65) and Edge-Partington and Heape (39) illustrate one from there. An *okarina*-like flute occurs in the New Hebrides, the Solomon Islands and New Britain (57, p. 240). Among the Tugeri of British New Guinea there is a whistle made of a small coconut shell. (See Annual Report of the District for 1890.) Whistles of the same types are reported by various writers from among the Malay tribes. The Chinese call them *foön* (110, vol. 1) and not only blow them with the mouth, but fasten them to pigeons' tails to protect the birds when they are flying from birds of prey. I have encountered no reference to them in India, although the *poongi*, being a type of gourd whistle with reeds inserted vertically in a bunch, through which the air escapes that is blown into the gourd through another tube, is a combination type of gourd whistle and flute. Such an instrument is also known in China and Japan (144), and in Borneo (130, p. 62), Sumatra (110, vol. 2, Pl. opp. p. 20), Laos, Siam, and Burma (144, pp. 102-30).

Although gourd rattles were popular enough in the Americas, as they were indeed in other parts of the world, I have only two references to them as whistles, and none to nuts. A gourd whistle has been found in a Peruvian grave (107, p. 335). Gourd whistles are used by the Bororo of Central Brazil (170, p. 388). Other whistles, shaped like a gourd but made of pottery, are found in the district of Manizales in Northwestern South America (187, p. 240). Gourds were used as trumpets in some parts of the South American continent (116, vol. 2, p. 119)[14], and also in New Zealand (167, p. 158).

TI LEAF WHISTLE

I had abandoned hope of finding a reference to any instrument like the ti leaf whistle elsewhere, until this paper was ready for the printer. There was then brought to my attention a note in the Internationales Archiv für

---

[14] Gourd whistles were supplanted by those of clay, bone or wood in the Americas. Round clay whistles, with faces in relief on one side are common archaeological finds in Peru, for instance. (Bowls so ornamented are made in the Solomon Islands [39]). In this connection it is worth noting that clay whistles called *pulik* are made by Malay tribes (8, p. 9) and the Chinese (144, p. 125; 110, vol. 1), fashioned like birds, the air being driven through the tail. In Mexico bird whistles are blown through the beak (144, p. 73). These bird whistles recall the bird rattles of the northwest coast of America, but there they are carved of wood. All American whistles were mouth-blown, apparently.

The distribution of bone whistles and flutes is by no means practically confined to America as Morris has stated (110, vol. 2, p. 109, note 3). In addition to Thibet where trumpets have been manufactured from the thigh bones of human beings, an exception which she gives, as well as the bone pipes of Arabia and Egypt known as *meijiwiz*, they were known in India at Bhutan, also made of human thigh bones (108, Pl. VI); among the Maori of New Zealand in two sizes, a larger called *koauau* and a smaller, a fife, made from the wing bone of an albatross (159, pp. 65-6). Miss Morris herself reports them from Borneo (op. cit., p. 19) and the Bismarck Archipelago (p. 43). Stanley also mentions one from the same region and both he (144, p. 14) and Ankerman (7, p. 927) mention specimens from Africa. A neolithic bone flute with three holes has been exhumed from the pile village of Concise, Department of Vaud, Switzerland (98, vol. 2, p. 140). A specimen very like it, but not positively identified as a flute, has been found in a Magdalenian site at La Placard Cave, Charente, France (98, vol. 1, p. 286), while other positively identified specimens were exhumed by the American School of Archaeology in France during the summer of 1925 which are said to be Magdalenian.

Ethnographie for 1911-12, which referred to a short paper by Balfour (11), on a primitive musical instrument which survived until about seventy years ago in Oxfordshire, England, in the villages of Hailey, Crawley, and Whitney. According to a very old charter these three villages were allowed a hunt once a year in the forest preserves and the men of each village were permitted to kill one stag for the village. The hunt took place on Whit-Monday and in order to rouse the villagers from their slumbers for the early start a horn of bark was used. It was made of long strips of willow bark, two to three inches wide, twisted spirally and the ends pinned with hawthorn or buckthorn spines. From a twig of willow about half an inch in diameter a cylinder of bark was removed, thinned at one edge, and inserted in the small end of this rustic horn as a mouthpiece, the thinned edge being pressed flat or pinched together to form a reed like that in an oboe. The instrument in its entirety was about eighteen inches long. It was brought to Balfour's notice and two samples were made by an old man who said at the time (1896) that it had not been used for forty years. Balfour's article elicited the note referred to, by J. D. E. Schmeltz, on pages 89-90 of the journal above mentioned, who adds after commenting on Balfour's article:

A similar instrument named May-flute is mentioned by E. Neumann (Musikge-schichte I, pg. 244) as the most primitive form of the "Schalmei," in use among the peasants of the lower Rhine, which Mr. Balfour believes, although he has not seen the instrument itself, to be possibly identical with that described by him.

In connection with this communication of Mr. Balfour we observe that at the wedding feast of the "Huzules" in Galicia an instrument is played which is also made of strips of willow-bark and which form answers very well to that of the "Whit-horn" (Viz "Zur Guten Stunde, 10ter Jahrgang (1897) p. 29, with illustration, representing a wedding procession).

Specimens of instruments allied to the Clarinette type with a sound-funnel, made of strips of palm leaf from Central Sumatra (Inv. No. 268/278), Flores (Inv. No. 842/182) and Southern Celebes (Inv. No. 697/38) are preserved in the National Museum of Ethnography at Leiden, of which we give the figures here; one of them shows no sound-holes.

It is unfortunate that the photographs of the three Malaysian types accompanying this note may not be given here. The whistles are clearly more highly developed than the English Whit-horn or the Hawaiian ti leaf whistle. The Hawaiian diminutive specimens, measuring but three inches long, lacked any mouthpiece and had only the end of the ribbon bent so that it would cut across the tube formed by the spiral twisting, to serve as a reed, when the breath blew on its edge. The English form had a separate cylinder of bark inserted in the tube and pressed flat, making two edges, but achieving somewhat the same result. The Malay spiral tubes are less extended, making a more squat form of whistle, more like a bell in outline, and into this at the apex is thrust a cane or reed, several inches long, to judge from the photographs, with or without finger-holes bored in the side, after the fashion of a flute. Some types have a reed mouthpiece of still smaller diameter than the cane inserted within it. The Flores Island one has both the cane and the reed mouthpiece but no finger-holes. The Sumatran form has the cane and holes but no mouthpiece. That from Southern Celebes has all three.

This note of Schmeltz' elicited another from H. Ling Roth in the same periodical (p. 162), who adds to these localities that of the Niger coast country in West Africa, where similar horns or whistles occur made also of strips of palm leaf, wound in a spiral. One of the specimens he cites had a strip of bast tied about the horn at the end of the spiral. (Compare the Hawaiian method of fastening, p. 45.) The other end had two old iron screws inserted at the end of the last spiral to hold it together. These African horns are made of several strips, the ends of which overlap. There is no mouthpiece. The horn is finished, however, in a manner different from the other specimens described, in that near the end it suddenly flares into a flange lying in a plane almost at right angles to the length of the horn. The English specimen illustrated was exactly like the Hawaiian in shape.

Since receiving proof of this paper, I have received page proofs of Elsdon Best's Games and Pastimes of the Maori, from which I quote:

A kind of temporary trumpet was occasionally made of the leaves of the flax (Phormium) plant. These leaves were split down the middle, and the pieces wound in a spiral manner to form the instrument. They were useable merely so long as the material remained green. These frail instruments were termed *tetere*.

In describing the methods of the hostile natives during the fighting in the Wai-koto district, General Alexander says: "To imitate the Pakeha (Europeans), they used to fire off a gun at tattoo, and call 'All's well,' and made a horn of native flax to imitate the bugle calls."

A traveller in the interior in 1854 wrote: "Under the artistic hands of our [native] comrades, a horn emerged from a flax bush, and a merry blast poured across the water."

THE CONCH

The antiquity and wide distribution of the conch shell trumpet, not a musical instrument, strictly speaking, but of the greatest sacred import in religious ceremonies from the earliest times, are facts almost too well known to mention. As it gradually lost its sacred significance which it probably first acquired through its awe-inspiring sound of great power, it was still retained in some localities as a very practical means of summoning people from far and near, or for herding animals; although its sacredness has not diminished even now in some lands with a high culture having a long history, as well as among more primitive folk. It is worth noting, too, that the distribution of the conch shell as a trumpet does not correspond to its natural geographical distribution, although it is found more frequently in regions where large shells grow.

As was the case with the nose flute, I had covered considerable ground before discovering Jackson's very valuable paper on the distribution of shells (78). I have been able to add to this report many localities as well as important points to be considered, through his researches and may, on my side, contribute some which he did not have. In instances where the sources are different I will quote mine, then simply Jackson. Far from being universal, the conch shell trumpet has a most peculiar, if wide-flung, distribution which it is important to consider in connection with that of the other instruments forming this significant complex.

In India (36, p. 103 and others) the conch has been in daily use in the temples from the very earliest times of which Indian legends treat. The custom has been maintained up to the present time. The conch, like the flute, is supposed to have been first used by the god Krishna. In the Ramayana it is called by the name *devadata,* while this term as well as *goshringa* is found in the Mahabharata. The later common term for it was *sankha,* and is still used but spelled differently by different writers. This is the chank of Jackson. A Bengalese name is *barataka,* referring to the species of shell (144, p. 114). The *sankha* was usually provided with a metal mouthpiece, but shells which seem to lack them are mentioned by different writers. So far as I have been able to gather from Day, Engel, Fox Strangways, Jackson, and others, all Indian *sankha* have the blow hole at the apex of the shell. In fact, the trumpet is made by simply grinding or knocking off the apex. Two types of trumpet must be kept in mind, that with the apical hole and that with the lateral.

To begin with the localities from which it has been reported west of India, the point farthest west is Great Britain. Here it is found in North Wales and Staffordshire in pastoral use (78, p. 32). Farther north Jackson reports it from Lithuania and Muscovy but in none of these references has the type been given, that is, whether the blow hole is apical or lateral. As Jackson makes a point of differentiating where possible, it is assumed that his authorities are silent on this. Shell trumpets have also survived in southern France. In Nice the type is definitely given as apical and presumably all Mediterranean types are (op. cit., p. 34). They are still used. A reference to the occurrence of one in Portugal is taken from Pliny (78, p. 30). They occur on the islands of Elba and Corsica (op. cit., p. 33), all over Italy, including Genoa, where they are not only used by herdsmen but are blown in the churches during Holy Week, on the island of Ischia near Naples, and in Sicily and Crete. In Crete conch shells have been unearthed which belong to the Minoan period (66, p. 155) where they have since been common, even to the present day (78, pp. 33-35). They were used in ancient Greece (78, p. 30). Sir William Ridgeway, to whom I wrote concerning their occurrence in Greece, replied that he had no evidence of their having been used there from the classical period on, although that did not preclude their use in prehistoric times. The cow's horn trumpet was probably used in Greece very early, as it went on into the classical period and the name Βμκανη, derived from that of a cow's horn, was the ordinary military term for a trumpet in the latter part of this period.[15]

The conch has not been reported by any of my authorities from Africa, including Egypt, nor from Assyria, Babylon, or any of the ancient countries between Asia Minor and Persia and Afghanistan, where it again occurs (144, p. 114). The name in Afghanistan is *mir-sang*. Sir Ernest Budge, formerly keeper of Egyptian and Assyrian antiquities in the British Museum, Dr. Ludlow S. Bull of the Metropolitan Museum, New York, Professor Jean Capart of the University of Liege, and Professor Albert T. Clay of Yale University, all have responded to my inquiries with negative evidence for the appearance of the conch in Egypt or Babylonia. The Hebrews, Assyrians, and Africans, as well as the peoples of India to some extent, used the horns of animals and later created instruments of metal in their semblance, as indeed the Greeks did at a period later than the prehistoric. Apparently none of the negro tribes of Africa have the conch, although if it should be found there one would look for it on the west coast, but Engel (45) classes the animal horn trumpets which they use as of comparatively recent date. Ankermann (7) omits all mention of the conch in Africa and I am assured by my friend, Mrs. A. C. L. Donohugh, who has devoted years to covering the literature on Africa, that she has never encountered a reference to the conch trumpet in that continent. The conch has been found in Madagascar, however, for the Metropolitan Museum of Art contains a much broken specimen, a trumpet called *antsiva*. (See 110, but old edition of 1907, vol. 3, p. 37, and plate.)

---

[15] This distribution around the north shore of the Mediterranean and along the Atlantic coast corresponds in a curious manner very nearly to that of the variety of Alpine race discussed by Fleure and James (54, pp. 137 ff), which is encountered here and there in nests which "stretch at least from southern Italy to Ireland by way of the Straits of Gibraltar and across France by the dolmen line." These authors question their being true Alpine men, on account of their huge stature, their black hair and their coastal distribution as against the typical mountain distribution of the brachycephalic type generally called Alpine. Such dark broad heads are highly characteristic of Dalmatia, the Aegean, and Crete, as well as Asia Minor. From this, if there is any connection between the conch and this race, we should expect to find the conch in Ireland, especially as a Greek colony is rumored to have been made there about 1100 B.C. On the other hand the authors have not reported the dark broad heads from Lithuania and Muscovy.

In both the southern and the northeastern parts of India the conch with the apical hole was used. It occurred in Ceylon and the Laccadive Islands (78, p. 38) but the type is not given. Presumably it is apical. Types described as chanks are reported from Siam (op. cit., p. 37). Various authorities including Lavignac (87, p. 3094) report them from Thibet, where they are also called chanks by their describers. In Mongolia, Van Oost says (117, p. 394) that they are used for religious purposes and are called *dung* or *labai*. No doubt they are the same form as the Thibetan. In China they were called *hai-lo* or *lozeu* (144, p. 113; 110, vol. 1), in Japan, where they were carried in netted cord bags, *rappakai* (144, p. 113; 110, vol. 1). The Japanese type is apical with a brass mouthpiece (78, p. 39). One is a *Triton variegatus* (144, p. 113). The Malay type is apical as is that from Borneo (78, p. 39). Conches in the Philippines are mentioned by a number of writers (78, p. 40; 110, vol. 2, p. 25); they occur also in Gilolo and Ceram (78, p. 40).

In Celebes shell trumpets belong to the second type with a lateral hole and are possibly a southern importation (78, p. 40). In Papuan New Guinea (op. cit., p. 40) and the Admiralty Islands (op. cit., p. 40), in Torres Straits, where it is called *bu* and is either a Fusus or Triton (64, vol. 4, p. 283), and in the Solomon Islands, the shell trumpet has a lateral hole (62, p. 143; 127, vol. 2, p. 459; 110, vol. 2, p. 34). But at Humboldt Bay, New Guinea, where the Strombus shell is used, the type is again apical (78, p. 40) and the two types appear to have met throughout Melanesia (127, vol. 2, p. 459; 78, p. 41). Jenness (80, p. 120) reports shell trumpets in the Northern D'Entrecasteaux and writes me that the hole is lateral. Conch shells are found in the Banks Islands (127, vol. 1, pp. 64, 98, 186). At Efate in the New Hebrides Triton trumpets are apical in type (127, vol. 2, p. 459; 78, p. 42; 110, vol. 2, p. 39), but at Tanna presumably lateral. They are found in New Britain, Mallikolo, and the Ellice Islands, where the Cassis is used (78, p. 43), but Cassis horns (found only in Aoba) are apical (141, p. 422). Bamboo mouthpieces are used at Vao (141, p. 422). In New Ireland, at St. Matthias and the neighboring islands, Triton trumpets of the lateral type occur called *kaué* (118, p. 328). In New Caledonia the *Fusus proboscidiferus* is used but the type is not specified (144, p. 114). In Fiji shell trumpets (*davui*) are apical (110, vol. 2, Pl. opp. p. 40) with a heavy carrying rope of braided fiber fastened near the lip of the shell or with a woven band about it.[16] Edge-Partington and Heape (39) picture a Triton from there with a small finger hole as well. In the Loyalty Islands trumpets were made from the Triton or Stramonita (65, pp. 134-5). Tregear (159, pp. 65-6) and Edge-Partington and Heape (39) report an apical Triton trumpet with a wooden mouthpiece among the Maori, who call it *pu moana* or *potipoti*. In Samoa *o-le-pu* was the name (142, p. 135) and the type was apical (24, p. 423).[15a] The conch was used in Tonga (102, vol. 2, p. 197) and Manahiki (78, p. 45). In Tahiti and the Society Islands generally, the *Triton tritonis* was the shell employed. The blow hole was near the apex and in some specimens a mouthpiece was inserted (39; 40, vol. 1, chap. 8). Jackson (78, p. 46) reports the conch from Tubuai. In the Marquesas both types occurred (88, p. 405); the Cassis, without a mouthpiece, belonged to the apical type; the Triton, with a mouthpiece of reed, to the lateral. The Marquesans called their trumpets *pu* and carried them about by a band of sennit cord woven about them to which was fastened a string.

So far, the distribution of the conch has been carried through the islands south and east of New Guinea. To return to the north and east, namely, through the Micro-Polynesian area, several of my authorities and Jackson as well, report it from the Caroline and Ascension islands (Ponapé). In Ponapé the conch is called *chaui* (32, p. 138). Shell trumpets occur in Pelew and the Marshall islands but the type is not given (78, p. 46). In the Hawaiian islands both the Triton and Cassis are used. The native name for the trumpets is *pu* and I have never seen or heard of any that were not of the apical type, nor of any that had mouthpieces attached.

According to old Spanish accounts cited by Morris (110, vol. 2, p. 189) and by other authorities, the conch was part of the ceremonial equipment of the Aztecs of Mexico. Its native name was *tecciztli* or *quiquiztli* according to the Spanish manuscripts. The first name is undoubtedly connected with that of the moon god *Tecciztecatl*. He wears the conch shell on his brow or on the back of his neck in illustrations shown in the Codex Vaticanus, No. 3, 773, or the Codex Telleriano Remensis (78, pp. 50-59). This same god with the same equipment was a prominent Maya deity, and Jackson has shown the similarity of this cult to that followed by the Hindus. He says (78, p. 53): "The remarkable identity in the Hindu and Mexican use of shell trumpets in temple worship and harvest rites, and the association of the conch shell with the god of the moon, has been pointed out in a previous article" (78, *a*).

Aztec shell trumpets were apical if the specimen illustrated in the Codex Magliabecchiano xiii, 3, f. 35 is typical. Bandelier (15, pp. 149, 152, 220 and 231) reports exhuming conches several times at the great Toltec sites, the pyramid of Cholula and at Acozac, Mexico. He does not say that they

---

[15a] Best (167, p. 160, figs. 100 and 101 A, B) gives excellent illustrations of these instruments, and a number of names, viz:—*pu tara, pu pakapaka, pu taratara, pu toto, pu tatara, kakara, pu moana, puhaureroa, potipoti,* and *kaeaea.*

[16] Linton tells me that they are also lateral.

were apical but merely that they had a number of holes in their lower volute (p. 152). The Fasciolaria and Turbinella were both used in Mexico (78, p. 50).

To the present time the Huichol Indians employ a shell trumpet in their ceremonies, which they call *kúra* (95, p. 185). The location of the hole is not given by Lumholtz and a Murex shell which he obtained with difficulty as being quite as sacred as those used in the ceremonies, like the trumpet shells but smaller, has no hole. Fewkes excavated apical shell trumpets at Casa Grande, in Arizona (51, pp. 144-5), and G. H. Pepper unearthed several of the same type at Pueblo Bonito in New Mexico, one of which was made from the Strombus (120, figures 46, 77). The Arizona specimens are all from the Pacific Ocean or the Gulf of California. Jackson draws attention to the existence of a very sacred shell possessed by the Omaha tribe which was wrapped in one of their sacred bundles and carried with them on all of their tribal hunts (78, p. 64). It was supposed to guide tribal actions by speaking. Fletcher (53, pp. 454-8) has described and pictured this shell which was not a trumpet, however, but a bi-valve, *Unio alatus,* which occurs in the valleys of the Mississippi River and tributaries and around the Great Lakes. However, the central Siouan tribes wore as gorgets cross-sections of conch shells, which were thought to be related to the moon.

The Maidu, who, it will be remembered, have the musical bow in its simplest forms, though slightly more developed in one type than the Omaha bow, have no sacred shells. I have no data at present for the pueblo at Jemez, New Mexico, for the Zuni or the Hopi, where the bow or the bow rasp with gourd resonator occurs, but it would not be surprising if the conch were to be found there.

South of Mexico a Strombus shell trumpet occurs in the Usumatsintla Valley in Central America (78, p. 47). In Panama the Guaymis Tribe, which seems to have had some ancient connection with the Chiriquian civilization, also employs a marine conch (op. cit., p. 47). The types of these two trumpets is unfortunately not given. It is quite commonly known that the conch was an ancient Peruvian instrument. It had two names, the *putatu* (op. cit., p. 48), undoubtedly the original native name with which should be compared the Polynesian terms for various kinds of trumpets and wind instruments, and *bosina* (op. cit., p. 46) which is probably of Spanish derivation. Jackson says (op. cit., p. 46) that the name *bosina* was given on account of the sound resembling that of the roar of a bull, referring back to Hutchinson's "Two Years in Peru" for the explanation. Hutchinson described a finely plaited leather carrying band on a trumpet found at

Canete. It is a singular coincidence that this name should so closely resemble that given by the old Romans to the same instrument, *buccina* or *buccinum* (op. cit., p. 30), unless the conch has also been known to the Spaniards. Jackson has not discussed this resemblance in terms or given any reference to a conch in Spain, but the probability of its presence there in prehistoric times, at least, is likely, considering the surrounding distributions on the north coast of the Mediterranean, in Portugal, and up the Atlantic coast and here and there inland in France.

Cow horn trumpets are reported from the island of Titicaca, Bolivia (14, p. 93), called by the natives *pu-tu-to,* almost exactly the same name as the native Peruvian one. Morris, quoting Bandelier (110, vol. 2, p. 245) says that these cow horn trumpets replaced the conches of earlier times but Bandelier does not say so, and Morris gives no other authority for this statement. Nordenskiöld (116, vol. 2, p. 122), who reports horn trumpets, end blown, with mouthpieces of reed, among the Ashluslay, Choroti, and Chané living at the head waters of the Pilcomayo River, who also have a musical bow, is inclined to think that they are derived from western horns, originally of other material, such as sea shells. The Lengua Indians have an apical cow's horn trumpet with reed mouthpiece (69, pp. 280-299). Strombus trumpets were reported by early writers to be in use in Brazil in the latter part of the sixteenth century (78, p. 48). In most of the South American countries and Mexico these trumpets were used, as they were in Polynesia and India, in connection with religious ceremonies. This was apparently the case in Minoan Crete and the early Mediterranean cultures, where shell trumpets are depicted on early coins and gems in the hands of deities or votaries near altars (op. cit., pp. 30, 33).

Although the conch appears not to have travelled to Africa, and therefore could not have been brought to the West Indies or South America by negro slaves, as has been claimed by Bolinder and others for the musical bow and Hawley for the notched rattle, with probable justification in some instances, Hawtayne (68, p. 198) relates that conch shells have been exhumed from Carib graves on the island of St. Vincent in the West Indies, but he makes no mention of them as trumpets. In the Stearns collection of musical instruments at the University of Michigan is an apical shell trumpet, a *Turbinella pyrum,* from Nassau in the Bahama Islands (144, p. 113) which is described as unplayable, but from what cause has not been stated.

Perforated conch shells have been found at Marco, in the southwestern part of the state of Florida, but it is thought they might have been used as axe heads. The perforations are lateral.[17]

Curiously enough, also, up to the present time I have been unable to find a reference to the presence of the conch trumpet in Australia.

JEW'S HARPS AND BAMBOO TUBES

Before leaving the breath blown instruments to consider the bull-roarer, I will mention the problematical winds, the jew's harps and the bamboo tubes. The jew's harp may be passed with a word that there is probably scarcely a locality around the world where its presence has not been noted, at least for the belt mentioned. It takes different forms but in most the vibrating tongue is cut in one piece with the frame, with a slit underlying it. To work out the distributions of the different forms would perhaps prove valuable but I have not been able to do so. Evidently the Hawaiian jew's harp mentioned by Emerson and already discussed (pp. 46-48) was one of the commoner types. Only one other of the type in the Bishop Museum called *niau kani,* with the coconut leaf stem fastened to the board (p. 47) has been encountered by me in my search. It has been described by Parkinson (118, p. 137) as belonging to the coastal peoples of the Gazelle Peninsula, New Britain, and is called the *ngap.* It is, to translate Parkinson, a piece of bamboo, lancet-shaped, 15 to 20 cm. long and about 2 or 3 cm. broad running to a point at one end. In the midst of this a long narrow leaf is loosely fastened with its base at the broad end of the instrument. The leaf tapers to a point corresponding to the shape of the instrument. This sounding leaf vibrates freely. When in use the jew's harp is held in the left hand and the pointed end with the sounding leaf is laid against the front teeth. With the right hand the player gives a gentle tug on a thin cord fastened to the base of the instrument, setting the leaf in vibration so that it produces a light droning sound. Somewhat similar instruments are used by the wild Malay tribes.

Bamboo tubes, especially of the type notched in the rim at the end held to the lip while the flute remained in a vertical position, the notch coming against the lower lip, were not found by me in Hawaii, but were referred to by one of my older informants. It is therefore worth noting that such flutes occur in Malaysia (the reference to which I have mislaid); the Torres Straits (64, vol. 4, pp. 282-3); New Britain (Edge-Partington and Heape [39], and Parkinson [118, p. 136] who says that they are called *kaur* in the Gazelle Peninsula); from Ambrym and Gaua in the New Hebrides (141, table 108, figs. 24-27, Spec. 3498, 3500, 3314, 3316); and

---

[17] See the American Naturalist for November, 1895, an article by Colonel Dunford on his excavations at that site.

also in northwest Brazil (110, vol. 2, p. 245). Probably their distribution is much wider. Bamboo tubes open at one end or both are found in New Caledonia and elsewhere in that general region, while open flutes are characteristic of California.

BULL ROARER

The only Hawaiian bull roarer that I came across is of specialized form, the small gourd or coconut shell with a small hole in the top, a string being tied through minute holes on either side of the orifice so that the shell could be whirled about. No other information concerning it was obtained. Edge-Partington and Heape (39) illustrate a *kamani* nut from Hawaii used in the same way. One other reference to such a bull roarer that I have come across is given by Parkinson (118, p. 137) who describes one from the Gazelle Peninsula, northern New Britain. He says that it is called the *bai-bai* and is made of the nut of a kind of *cycas*. It is pierced by two pairs of holes on two sides of the nut, 8 to 10 cm. apart. Through each of these pairs a cord is threaded and the player takes the ends of each cord, one in either hand, and swings the nut in a circle, so that the doubled cord on each side of the nut winds itself up. When the winding is sufficiently tight, the player pulls the cords lightly from both sides, or increases the tension, which causes the cord to untwist and sets the nut whirling, producing a light humming or whistling noise. Then the rotating nut rolls itself up again in the other direction far enough to continue the whistling noise before the force is spent making it necessary for the player to repeat his operation. Speiser (141, table 98, fig. 4, Spec. 3538) pictures what appears to be a gourd bull roarer from eastern Malekula. It has a pronounced neck, about which is tied a string and a hole is made in the side of the gourd just below the neck. Speiser has questioned this instrument as being musical but describes the manner of its use thus (p. 422): *"Schwingt man den Kürbis wie ein Schwirrholz, so entsteht ein schwacher Ton."* He mentions a similar instrument from Santo. Best (167, p. 158) evidently refers to similar instruments in New Zealand.

I have not followed the distribution of the ordinary bull-roarer. It is of very wide-spread occurrence, according to Meerwarth (108, pp. 2 and 3) being found in some form in all the five continents and apparently belonging to a very ancient period of human culture. But it is interesting to observe that the flat rhombus form, besides occurring in the Pacific and in the Old World (notably, perhaps, in ancient Greece) is also used by the Apache tribes in the southwestern United States and has been found among the remains of the Cliff Dwellers of the Mesa Verde, the peoples of the Rio Grande pueblos, the Zuni, Navaho, Hopi and Ute Indians (110, vol. 2, pp. 176-8).

DRUMS

The numerous specialized varieties of drums and the practically world-wide distribution of one form or another preclude the possibility of tracing the distribution of various types at this time. However, there are a few forms concerning which it is necessary to treat, however briefly and inadequately, merely to indicate that in this class of instruments it is to be expected that much will come of an examination and classification of types and a study of their geographical distribution.

It is well known that the *pahu,* or large wooden kettle drum of Hawaii, with one skin head, was brought there by Laa, presumably (or so the legend states) from Tahiti during a comparatively late migration. The distribution of this type of drum in some respects approaches that of the musical bow but the form seems to be primarily Melanesian. Wooden drums are reported from the Solomon Islands by some writers, but according to Codrington (33, p. 336) wooden drums are missing in Florida of that group, and in Santa Cruz. This is exactly the region where musical bow forms most like the Hawaiian have been found, and the significant fact of the absence of wooden drums here would appear to have some bearing on their early absence in Hawaii if people from the Santa Cruz region or neighboring Solomon Islands influenced Hawaiian culture at an early time. Probably it will not be disputed that instruments of percussion like the resonant sticks called *kalaau,* which the Hawaiians used for one of their ancient hulas, and small drums made from stretching a skin over a coconut or a gourd shell, are in all likelihood older than those hollowed from logs by means of long slits, or, as with the *pahu,* from either end toward a central septum, which required considerable labor in either case when accomplished with crude implements. The *pahu* had some vogue in Hawaii, owing perhaps to the popularity of Laa and his followers, but has dropped out of use, while the original calabash drums still survive, along with the sticks and the small coconut drums.

In this connection it may be worth noting that small hand drums, less than a foot high and in diameter, are especially common in India, with the body made from a pot or calabash, but old pictures show what appear to be coconuts as well. No large drums are listed with the specimens in the Indian Museum at Calcutta (108) although there are small ones made from hollowed wood. Meerwarth says (op. cit., p. 17): "Drums in India are beaten with the full hands and fingers. To play with sticks is considered inartistic and occurs only during processions and ceremonies where the aim is to produce a maximum of noise."

Although possibly the *pahu* introduced by Laa was beaten with sticks in later times, Ellis saw it played with the hands (40, vol. 1, p. 74). In the Marquesas the huge drums which far excel the Hawaiian in size were so manipulated (88, pp. 403-5) as were the drums of the ancient Aztecs of Mexico, called *tlapan huehuetl* (15, p. 151). The nearest approach to stick playing among the Hawaiians was the beating of the little *puniu* or coconut drum with a bit of braided fiber, and the tapping of the resonant stick, the *kalaau,* with the small one, which produced a clear, musical tone. Like the Hindu, the Hawaiian instinct seems to reject blatant noises. In addition to India, Hawaii, and ancient Mexico, hand drumming is characteristic of some parts of primitive Africa, although there, as in Melanesia, there are huge drums beaten with clubs which carry messages over miles of country. The conveying of messages by drum beats is common to North India (59, pp. 85-86), Africa, Melanesia, and Hawaii, and is practised also by the Jibaros Indians in South America (175, p. 260; 181, p. 387). Bandelier (15, p. 152) says a small drum is reported by some authors to have been used in battle by ancient Mexican war captains for the purpose of signalling. In the New Hebrides signalling is also achieved by blowing the conchs, varying the tone by placing the hand in the opening (141, p. 422).

Those individuals who peopled Hawaii could not have passed through Melanesia after the huge wooden drums, so important a feature of the culture there, had been developed, and remained for any length of time without acquiring a knowledge of them. In all likelihood they had gone east before this development had occurred or else passed by a route where such drums were unknown. Parts of the Solomon Islands and the Santa Cruz group offered such a route. Ray (179, p. 32) finds that the Oceanic and Polynesian migrations flowed north of New Guinea and not by way of Torres Straits.

It is remarkable that despite a search for mention of calabashes or large gourds used for drums I have discovered no reference to them outside of India and Hawaii except those with a skin top from the Soudan, Uganda, and Uschachi in Africa (144, pp. 46, 47). Oddly enough Day (36, p. 100) speaking of India says, "These gourds are used for many purposes and the best are trained in their growth to the shape for which they are required." (See also p. 52 of this report, and compare the fact that the Hawaiians also treated calabashes in this fashion, and that they used them as receptables for food and clothing as well as for drums.) Again (op. cit., p. 106) the calabash drums in India are beaten with the hands and thrown into the air at intervals, which is the same procedure followed by the Hawaiians in executing the *hula pa-ipu.* Calabashes are also specially grown in New Zealand (152, p. 27). Lumholtz (97, vol. 1, p. 520) refers to gourds as playing an important part in the material culture of the Indians of western Mexico, although as drums they are not mentioned. In central South

America are gourds made into trumpets by the tribes along the upper Pilcomayo (116, vol. 2, p. 119), by the Shavajé Indians in Brazil (144, p. 114) who call them *loku,* by some West African tribes and the Maori of New Zealand (167, p. 158). In Africa, India, the Pacific, and the Americas they are common in smaller sizes as rattles, resonators, cups, water bottles and food containers, but no very large specimens appear to have been used elsewhere than in India and Hawaii to any extent. The Edge-Partington and Heape album (39) pictures one calabash from New Zealand.[18]

Aside from the occurrence of hand played drums in India, the Malay Peninsula, parts of Africa, Hawaii, the Marquesas, and ancient Mexico (and probably elsewhere), they are found in the West Indies (128) where they are undoubtedly a West African slave importation, and among the present-day Huichol of western Mexico who have a hollow log open to the ground, which stands on three legs, the top covered with skin (97, vol. 2, p. 32). Although missing in Hawaii, a log drum which has incisions like a capital "H" running lengthwise of its walls forming two tongues which are beaten, is found in Africa in several localities, one being the French Congo (99, vol. 2, pp. 137-140; 144, p. 43); another the Upper Congo region (144, p. 43); and Mexico (15, p. 151-2), where it is called *teponaztle* and beaten with two sticks, each tongue giving a different tone. Since log drums with slots are common all over Melanesia and in New Zealand and are found in the Marquesas, perhaps this peculiar form of tongue occurs in the Pacific, but so far I have encountered no references to it. This type of drum is mentioned as an instrument belonging to the aboriginees of Haiti or Hispaniola (180, p. 278).

Large bamboo pipes struck on the ground (the *kaekeeke* of the Hawaiians) have been reported from the Malay Peninsula among the Semang and Sakai (110, vol. 2, p. 231); from Korea (op. cit.); from New Guinea (169, p. 111); from Fiji (34, p. 60); from Tonga (102, vol. 1, p. 129) where the septum is cut away but the end of the tube is plugged with a piece of soft wood and where bamboos producing different tones are selected according to the tune to be rendered. They occur in Samoa (160, p. 125). Their use in Hawaii is well known but Linton seems to have overlooked it. In British Guiana they were used with one end covered with snake skin (110, vol. 2, p. 230) for which the author quotes Im Thurn[19] and by the Arawaks of Wakapoa Lake, for which she quotes Brett.[20]

---

[18] Ellis (41, p. 349) gives a very interesting account of the old Hawaiian method of staining and decorating calabashes with dots and lines in crude patterns. Only a few of the decorated specimens are to be found in the Bishop Museum. The type of decoration suggests that used by the inhabitants of Java and Borneo on their flutes. A further investigation of this subject might lead to more definite clues as to connection between these regions, particularly an investigation as to the treatment of calabashes in India.

[19] Im Thurn, Among the Indians of Guiana, p. 323.

[20] Brett, The Indian Tribes of Guiana, p. 157.

Lastly the San Gabriel Indians of Brazil had a bamboo instrument, the *ambnuba,* of which one end was closed by a joint. The instrument was held vertically and the closed end thumped on the ground (op. cit., vol. 2, p. 231). Doubtless there is a much wider distribution than I have given, although possibly the absence of this instrument in some regions may be accounted for by the absence of bamboo. I have no reference to its use in Africa.

RESONANT STICKS

Resonant sticks were comparatively rare instruments in Hawaii, and at the time of my visit they had almost completely disappeared. Some informants thought they had been confined to the island of Kauai, but Ellis (41, pp. 48, 49) mentions having seen them in use at a dance on Maui. The Cyclopedia of Fiji (34, p. 60) says, speaking of some natives of Fiji: "Several of them elicited clear notes from the long stick by hitting it with a shorter one." At dances the Marquesan men sometimes beat time with two short sticks (88, p. 408), one being held in the palm of the left hand and tapped with the other held in the right. Tregear (159, pp. 66, 67) says that the Maori had two varieties, the *pakuru* and the *pakakau.*

The principal stick (*pakuru*) was about fifteen inches long by one and a half inches wide, with one flat and one convex side. Sometimes it was carved and at others only notched with "parrot nibbles" (*whakakaka*) along its side. One end of the stick was held between the teeth, flat side down, and the other held in the left hand, while the right hand struck the wood with the other stick in time to an accompanying song.

Can it be that Tregear is referring to a degenerate form of musical bow, which in some way has been combined with the rasp feature and the resonant stick? (See p. 367 ff. for discussion of rasp.)

Tregear continues: "The other form of the pakuru was a bar of wood about eighteen inches long, held in one hand and struck lightly with a small mallet; both mallet and bar being highly decorated with carving."

This is practically the same as the Hawaiian *kalaau.* Such instruments are very primitive types of xylophones. In addition to Hawaii, the Marquesas, Fiji, and New Zealand, they are reported (110, vol. 2, p. 46) from Australia where they are named *mirambura* in one locality; on Jaluit Island in the Marshall group far to the north, where the name is *dimuggemuck;* in New Britain, where they are known as *atidir.* Haddon (171, p. 374) reports them from Torres Straits. The Edge-Partington and Heape album (39) pictures specimens from Tahiti. Linton mentions the presence of a true xylophone in the Marquesas (88, p. 409) almost like the African *marimba,* and speaks of a cruder but related form in New Zealand which may be that already mentioned here.　Parkinson (118, p. 132) describes simple forms in the Gazelle Peninsula, laid across the knees or on two banana stalks and struck with two sticks.　The Nias Islanders use three pieces of wood over a hole in the ground to increase the resonance (144).　Malaysia appears to be the region in which this type of instrument reaches the highest stages.　All through Siam, Cambodia, and Burma elaborate forms are found and in Java perhaps they are even more developed.　The wild tribes of the Malay Peninsula, the Semang, Sakai, and Jakun, still use the two sticks (182, p. 132).　The African xylophone, the *marimba,* already mentioned, has become well known.　It is interesting to note that xylophones are found in South America (72) and the western coast of Central America near the Gulf of Nicoya (110, vol. 2, p. 210).　No doubt they are far more widely scattered over the Pacific than I have indicated here.

FOOTBOARDS

It will be recalled that aside from the fact that slightly curved, resonant footboards were used by the Hawaiians in connection with the *hula kalaau,* no further information could be obtained concerning them, not even the name, up to the present time of writing.　Meerwarth (108, Pl. VIII) pictures a specimen which comes closer to the Hawaiian than any other contrivance I have been able to find.　It is used in the Andaman Islands.　Concerning it he says:

> The shield which covered the warrior serves always as the prototype of a war-drum; beaten with the club or spear it is calculated to create awe in the hearts of the enemy and to increase the courage of the warrior.　Such a shield-like contrivance, though only used to accompany the peaceful art of dancing, is the Andamanese sound-board (Nos. 157, 158); its indigenous name is *Pukuta-yemnga.* It represents more or less the only musical equipment of this primitive people.　The shield is laid on the ground and the dancer strikes it from time to time with his feet.

The specimen illustrated is about three feet long and one foot wide so that it is as large again as the Hawaiian specimens, but in general contour it is identical with them.　It has been apparent all along that the Hawaiian instruments of music belong to a very archaic stage in the development of the types which they represent.　To my mind they are survivals of a very early period, and if one needed the proof it would seem to be forthcoming in the presence here of this rare and very crude and primitive instrument. Man (101) also describes it.

It is even more remarkable that among that very Yokaia tribe of the Pomo of California, who have a musical bow so like the Hawaiian, Powers (178, p. 166) reports that at the death dance where a mournful chant on two tones was sung, the instrumental accompaniment was that of split sticks and stamping on a hollow slab of wood. The Kabinapek tribe have the same two instruments (op. cit., p. 211).

A somewhat related device not found in Hawaii so far as I know, is a slab of wood planted in the ground over a pit which serves as a resonator, and the wood is stamped upon by the bare feet of the dancers. Guppy (62, p. 144) describes one used at Treasury Island in the Solomon group:

A board, which was fixed in the pit about half way down, covered it in with the exception of a notch at its border. On this board stood two women, and as they danced they stamped their feet, producing a dull hollow sound, to which the women of the circle timed their dancing. . . .

Considering that the Maidu of California have a musical bow of very primitive type, it is worth noting what Dixon has to say concerning a similar dancing pit among them (37, p. 221):

Drums were simple, and consisted either of a pit dug in the ground and covered with a sheet of bark, or of a section of a log hollowed out by fire. Both sorts were beaten with the bare feet of the performers, who stood on the drum and stamped.

Barrett (166, p. 400) mentions this type also among the Pomo. On the other hand, Powers (178, p. 286) found the simple slab without the pit resonator, apparently, among the Maidu.

In the New Hebrides, at Ureparapara, a board is placed over a hole in the ground and struck with sticks but not danced on (141, p. 421). A similar device has been reported from Easter Island (132, p. 239). A hole was dug in the middle of a house at the bottom of which was placed a gourd covered with a stone to act as a drum. On the top of this a man danced, being hidden in the hole. The occurrence of this type of drum is by no means common, and it seems to be a survival of a very ancient custom. No doubt a more prolonged search would bring to light other regions where it occurs. In itself it might not mean much, but in connection with other instruments of the complex and traits of material culture it cannot be entirely ignored.

CASTANETS

Hawaiian castanets are the simplest and most primitive that could be imagined, merely two pebbles held in the palm of the hand. To the west, castanets of the shells of nuts or seeds occur in the Solomon Islands (33, p. 336). Castanets are reported from Gaua in the New Hebrides (141, table 108, fig. 7 and p. 422) and possibly elsewhere in Melanesia, but I have found no record of them. They occur in Burma, Siam, Anam (87, p. 3094), China and Japan (110, vol. 1) of wood and of metal. In India small instruments described as hand or finger cymbals (148, p. 78) are called *jallali*—a name not unlike the Hawaiian *iliili*. But there are also castanets (108, Pl. IX, no. 189) called *kartali,* consisting of two small bars of iron held in the palm. They are peculiar to Bengal (op. cit., p. 16). In Burma they are called *wale kau* (87, p. 3094). Small cymbals were known in Persia, Arabia, Syria and Egypt while according to Burney (27, vol. 1, p. 66) the ancient Greeks used oyster shells. Iron castanets are found in the Soudan (144, p. 23). From Arabia the castanets were carried to Spain, and being there made of chestnut wood, *castaña,* they took the name now associated with them in Europe, the mere mention of which has come almost to mean Spain (143, p. 16).

East of Hawaii, in South America, Stanley (144, p. 23) reports them from Patagonia, made of copper. Fewkes (52, p. 265) mentions that the Hopi of Arizona have shell rattles which, if not castanets, have a name, *mo-si-'li-li,* recalling the Hawaiian. Shell castanets were used in Haiti among the aboriginees (180, p. 278).

GOURD RATTLES

Gourd rattles are known practically wherever the gourd grows. Since Nature thus provides the suggestion for the rattle in so marked a fashion, the fact that its musical possibilities have been discovered, probably independently, in many localities, makes its discussion unnecessary here. The *ulili,* the Hawaiian gourd rattle and top combined, was not at all common, the Bishop Museum specimens having both come from one locality on the west side of the island of Hawaii. While I have encountered no mention of precisely this form elsewhere, the Maori had top-rattles made of wood, hollow and pierced with a stick which served as the spinning agent. These were also known in Java and on Nias Island (110, vol. 2, p. 8). In the Solomon Islands they are made of coconuts or cane, one to a stick (39). In Central America, Porto Rico, Venezuela and British Guiana globular gourds are pierced with straight wooden handles (110, vol. 2, pp. 211-235), but it is possible they are not spun. North American rattles are not.

The string attached to the center stick, so prominent a feature of the Hawaiian top-rattles, by which they were twisted first one way and then another, is not mentioned for these other areas. Humming tops are playthings in several central South American tribes but Nordenskiöld does not consider them as musical instruments (116, vol. 2, p. 114).

ANKLET RATTLES

In different forms anklet rattles are no doubt found in many more regions that I have discovered in this survey. Used in the dance, in the same ways as the Hawaiians used them, they are reported by Codrington

(33, p. 336) from the Solomon Islands, the Bismarck Archipelago and New Hebrides. (For the New Hebrides see also 141, table 106, figs. 1, 7, 9; table 109, fig. 14, and p. 422.) Haddon reports them from Torres Straits (64, vol. 4, pp. 282 f.). Edge-Partington and Heape (39) picture them from New Guinea and the Marquesas. Day (36, p. 105) speaks of their use in India where the process of tying them on was attended with much ceremony. Meerwarth (108, p. 16) remarks that once a female dancer had been decorated with the ankle bell she could not abandon her profession, but unfortunately he does not illustrate the instrument. Whatever may be its form, the ceremonial donning of it recalls the Hawaiian ceremonial donning of the regalia before Laka's altar. Flower wreaths, also so important a part of Hawaiian culture, were used in connection with the dance in India.

The anklets of cocoons filled with pebbles, or else empty palm pods, strung, have been reported by Lumholtz (97, vol. 1, p. 475) as used by the same tribes in Mexico as have the musical bow. According to this authority the Huichols, both men and women, wore flowers in the dance and had an altar decked with green on which was hung the paraphernalia of the dancers. The same kind of anklets, according to Morris (110, vol. 2, p. 203) were also used by the Papago of southern Arizona and the Yaqui and Tarahumare of northwestern Mexico. Cocoon rattles were used among the Maidu (37, p. 221) and in Africa (144, p. 19) while those of nuts occurred in Africa and Peru (op. cit., p. 19).

This concludes the survey of the distribution of instruments of types similar to those found in Hawaii, but it is interesting to note three or four instruments which, if not found in Hawaii, have otherwise about the same peculiar distribution as those just discussed.

THE NOTCHED STICK RATTLE

The notched stick rattle is clearly an early offshoot of the musical bow, in its crudest form, but in Malaysia it had an elaborate development which apparently later affected many other regions. The simple bow form belongs to a far more ancient layer of culture and is very wide-spread, although now the traces of it are scattered and higher forms occupy the intervening areas. To take the simple bow form first, Balfour (9, p. 16) mentions in West Africa among the Mussorongo or Muschikongo who are south of the mouth of the Congo River, a specimen called the *massunda* with a notch at one extremity for holding the knotted end of the string which is wound about the other end of the bow, while on both sides near one end are cut a series of notches over which the stick is rubbed, throwing the string into vibration. Balfour says that he has not observed these notches in any other African bows which, as a class, are well represented. A more elaborate specimen, possibly an indigenous invention or later importation among the Usambara, consists of a solid piece of wood from which is lightly bent a notched stick over which another is stroked (67, p. 344). It is called the *charra* or *kwatscha*. These are the only examples of bow rasp which I have encountered from Africa, although the use of jawbones of animals seems to have been widespread there.

Apparently only one example is known in Europe, a "primitive bow consisting of a long stick with serrated edge. This form is still used in country dances in France for the rustic *Bumbass*." (110, vol. 3, p. 244.)

Among the Bhuiyârs of Mirzapur, North West Province, India, and the Korwas Balfour (9, pp. 56, 57) reports the presence of a simple notched bow which the Bhuiyârs call the *darkun,* one end of which is placed on a temporary resonator consisting of an inverted basket containing a brass pot. The rasp is rubbed with another stick.

Some Hawaiian *ukeke* have very shallow notches on either edge of the wood, hardly deep enough to be used for rasping, and, were it not for these other examples, I should be inclined to consider them rather the natural result of rubbing down the wood when finishing it with a tool which jumped under strong pressure. Form, however, is occasionally retained when meaning is lost, and in the light of the distribution of this instrument in connection with the musical bow and that it may be that the practice of rasping was once known to the ancestors of the Hawaiians, the presence of these notches on some of their bows should be recorded.

Bolinder (22, p. 302) pictures a bow found among the Busintana, a tribe with Arawak affiliations living in the mountains of Colombia in South America. It is very like the Hawaiian *ukeke,* being flat and comparatively short, except that it has but one string and the notches along one side of the bow are very deep. He would derive it from Africa through the agency of negro slaves. This may be the correct deduction, although Balfour remarked that the musical bow forms in some parts of South America (the *umcunga* of Brazil, for instance) closely resembled some of the types in India and need not necessarily be related to Africa, while as to notched bows, although Balfour had considerable African data, only one specimen, from the Muschikongo, was familiar to him, while Hawley has added only that of the Usambara. Neither of these writers cited cases of bow rasps with resonators from Africa.

These are the instances of the occurrence of the bow rasp with which I am familiar. Closely connected with this instrument is the simple stick rasp, without any string. It may be an earlier type, or a degenerate form. And of the same class with the simple stick rasp is that made of a notched bone. I will treat of these as one type of instrument.

The *pakuru* of the Maori has already been described as a form of instrument combining the rasp with the resonant stick, having the same methods of manipulation common for that instrument and the musical bow. According to old Spanish accounts quoted by Morris (110, vol. 2, p. 189) the ancient Aztecs had a notched stick called the *omichichauoztli*. Lumholtz says (97, vol. 1, p. 362) that a similar instrument occurs in Mexico today among some of the isolated western tribes. Among the Tarahumare and possibly among the Tepehuane and Aztecs, from whose burial caves he secured a specimen, it is associated with a ceremony which involves the drinking of the juice of a plant and is performed at the adolescence of the youths and maidens of the tribe. In fact, the distinction between the use of this rasp, which is laid on a resonator, and of the musical bow, is not very clear. It will be recalled that the bow-rasp, laid on a resonator, has a similar association among the Bhuiyârs of northern India (9, pp. 56, 57; and 35, chapter on the Dravidians). In this connection it is well to remember that one of the oldest ceremonies in India at which the Samaveda chant is recited, which is a Brahman religious rite of great sacredness, the juice of a plant known as the moon-plant, *soma,* was imbibed as one of the central steps in the ritual, while the Samaveda is especially connected with the worship of ancestors whose abode was supposed to be the moon (148, p. 249). These notched rattles of the Huichol, consisting of a stick of Brazil wood or else the shoulder blade and metatarsal bone of a deer, are called *kalatsiki* (95, pp. 205-6), while the Cora have a form made from deer bones with a gourd resonator (97, vol. 2, p. 155). Some of the ceremonies are performed in connection with the moon. Lumholtz, too, feels that these instruments in western Mexico could hardly have reached those tribes through negroes, and in this opinion ten Kate concurs (153).

Mason (176, p. 158) reports a very similar instrument used by the Salinan Indian in California and gives an excellent illustration of it.

Notched stick rasps with resonators somewhat resembling the instruments of the Bhuiyârs and Korwas of India are used by the Hopi Indians of Oraibi, Arizona (67, p. 344; 110, vol. 2, p. 180 and Pl. opp. p. 184). The stick is more than a foot long with grooves cut in the face held uppermost, which is rubbed with a bone scraper as it rests on a gourd at one end. It is given various names—*patcikyopi, zhegunpi-hopi,* or *truh-kun-pi.* Simple sticks, one notched, the other serving as a scraper, are employed in a certain dance by the Pueblo Indians of Jemez, New Mexico (158, p. 351). A resonator is used. The Tonkaway Indians of western Texas had a similar instrument (67, p. 344). Practically the same type is found among the Ute used during a bear dance in which the bear is represented as the ancestor, but the scraper may be merely another stick. The name reported

by Hawley is *pam-pu-ni-wap* (op. cit., p. 344). This dance and the instruments have also been described by other writers. Lowie (92, p. 827,) observed Ute ceremonies at Navaho Springs, Colorado and says:

> In the pit I found a considerable number of notched instruments [*wüñürügüñap,
> wüñorōÈnop*] as well as several rasps. . . Max Joy, my interpreter, explained that
> during the performance the tub was placed in the pit, the case over the tub and a
> sheet of tin on the case [which was a wooden packing case, open to the ground].
> When the notched stick is rasped on this series of resonators, the noise produced is
> said to be tremendous. In former times a large basket took the place of the tub.

> At Whiterocks . . . the place of the pit was taken by a trench. . . This was
> covered by a wooden box and on this were tin sheets. The ground was strewn
> with several notched wooden sticks and rasps of cattle bone. . . At Whiterocks
> my interpreter said that one end [of the instruments] ought to be carved into the
> head of a mule, horse, bear or rattlesnake and that the stick should be daubed all
> over with red or yellow paint. At Navaho Springs I was told that the origin of
> the notched instrument is ascribed to an old woman.

Again, speaking of the Northern Shoshone (94, p. 219) he says:

> Somewhat fuller information is available as to the wöhö-nökakin of which
> [ceremony] the name is derived from a musical instrument called wöhönög (fig. 20).
> This consists of a notched wooden board held up in a slanting direction and resting
> on a parfleche or piece of tin, and a second stick or bundle of twigs, which was
> rapidly drawn down the scale of notches. A somewhat similar instrument was found
> by Alexander Henry among the Assiniboine and is used by the Hoof-Rattle society of
> the Cheyenne. . . . Within recent times an open box was substituted for the
> rasping stick. Mr. Sherman's authority regards the dance as old, but as having
> been originally introduced by the Ute. . . . The bear dances of the Ute however,
> are described as purely social entertainments by Clark while the homologue of the
> wöhönökakin was an annual religious ceremony performed in February or March.

Concerning the Assiniboine we read (89, p. 26):

> Another instrument was one that was no more than a piece of wood, of three
> feet, with notches cut on its edge. The performer drew a stick backward and for-
> ward, along the notches, keeping time.

> A similar instrument was found by Long's expedition among the Oto and Iowa.

Lowie is here quoting Edwin James and Alexander Henry. It appears
that the Hidatsa also had the notched stick rasp. This is the most interesting instrument of all for it is roughly carved in the form of an animal with
a well defined head and the ridges of the spine are used for rasping (93, p.
238). Lowie pictures it in his fig. 1, p. 238. The instrument was used by
the Notched Stick Society called *miraraxúxi,* which was also the name of the
rasp.

> An ordinary stick was rubbed up and down the notches. The unnotched side of
> the miraraxúxi seems to have been encased in rawhide. . . . The notches on the
> lower stick represented a snake's backbone. . . . The notched stick was always
> rubbed downward.

Another specimen is described as being shaped like a snake with two
horns in front, with two front legs, two hind legs, and a tail. The Crow and

Hidatsa were once more closely related than they are now and the Crow have borrowed much from the Shoshone. Both Crow and Hidatsa apparently had some contact with the far west before their separation (91, p. 199). The Ute language is connected with the Uto-Aztekan family of languages. Thus it would seem that the Ute are near the apex of a rough triangle of distribution of that linguistic stock which has its base in Mexico. It would thus seem that the rasp in various forms has been disseminated generally among the Shoshonean or Uto-Aztekan speaking peoples. The animal forms of rasps show distinct affiliation with such types used by the Aztecs. That the animal forms have been lost in the intervening area to the south may be interpreted in the light of greater intermingling of cultures, while the marginal tribes have to some extent retained the original forms. Other forms have been described among the Ute. It is said that a piece of wood is carved like a jawbone, the teeth of which are rubbed (110, vol. 2, p. 183). This is called *morache*. I have not examined Morris' authority, but although rasps shaped like jawbones are not western forms, but actual jawbones serve this purpose in the West Indies, this need not be taken as a sign that all the Ute rasps have been due to negro influence. The West Indian negroes do not carve rasps in the form of animals, nor do any negroes, so far as I am aware. The ancient Mexicans did. I should want to see the jawbone-shaped rasps of the Ute before linking them with eastern forms, and would be inclined to consider them merely sporadic developments, independent of the negroes, rather than due to their influence.

Mr. Francis La Flesche tells me that the Omaha also used a notched stick or elk bone for a rasp, but he did not mention a resonator, nor with what ceremonies it was employed. Probably this occurrence is due to contact with these other plains tribes or to a survival from an earlier residence in the Southwest. According to Morris (op. cit., vol. 2, p. 184) the Seneca Indians of New York had a flat stick with the narrow edge serrated, which they called the *ga-no-ska*. She does not mention a resonator nor with what the stick was rubbed. Some of the Iroquois tribes, notably the Tuscarora, originally lived much farther south, and seem to possess a number of cultural traits savoring of the Pacific.

From Nassau, in the Bahama Islands, a notched stick rattle called locally the "hog fiddle" was collected (144, p. 18), presumably a negro instrument. West Indian rasps generally appear to have been the jaw-bones of cattle, the teeth of which were rubbed with a stick or another bone, or notched gourds acting at the same time as rasp and resonator. A Cuban form called the *maruga* is a notched cylinder of tin and is allied to a modern Spanish instrument.

It would be desirable to pursue further the investigation into the question of bow, stick and bone rasps, together with the ceremonies with which they are associated. Although one writer states that the Ute ceremonies are purely of a social nature, another says they are performed with rites connected with ancestor worship, as they are in Asia and in Mexico, apparently. The scope of this paper will not permit of enlarging on this subject at present.

I have not discussed the more elaborate types of rasps carved in the form of animals, the ridges of the spines of which furnish the notches. Again, it is necessary to look to Malaysia and India for types which appear to have reached this perfection, if the term may be allowed. The *slentem* of Java takes any number of animal forms richly carved. The *yu* of China, also animal in form, appears to have been used in connection with Confucian ceremonies (110, vol. 1 ; 127), which would imply ancestor worship. The *gyo* of Japan are also elaborately carved animal forms (op. cit., vol. 1 ; 127), probably derived from China. In ancient Mexico these animal forms followed the peculiar art of the country and have been well illustrated and discussed in an article by Seler (138). Strangely the Hidatsa forms are more like the Javanese in their attitudes and less involved symbolism than the Aztecan.

Rasps made of pieces of wood of various shapes, but crude, occur in the Banks Islands, Torres Straits, New Hebrides, and Tonga (39). In the last two named localities the wood is covered with shark skin. In the Solomon Islands a type which appears to be a rasp Edge-Parkington and Heape doubtfully class as a breadfruit grater. A New Britain type is a notched bamboo tube (39) and a similar instrument called *clara carshi* (67, p. 345) occurs among some of the tribes along the Amazon River in South America. The name should be compared with that given by the Usambara of Africa to their rasp, the *charra* or *kwatscha,* but the African instrument is a solid piece of wood from one end of which is lightly bent a notched stick over which another is stroked.

THE CLAPPER

Various writers on the ethnography of Melanesia, particularly New Guinea, have mentioned clappers made of a tube of bamboo cut in half, longitudinally, nearly the entire length, leaving only a piece long enough to serve as a handle. The "flail" ends were shaken or struck on the palm of the hand to produce a rhythmic knocking. The Edge-Partington and Heape album (39) pictures from New Guinea one having several tongues which is beaten at sea on long journeys. Haddon mentions the presence of clappers in the Torres Straits (64, vol. 4, p. 271) and Jenness (80, p. 165) says that they were used in the Northern D'Entrecasteaux. Morris (110, vol. 2, p. 22) reports them from Borneo.

Balfour (8, p. 15) discusses those belonging to the Sakai or Semang of the Malay Peninsula, which he says are made by the Malay. They are called *genggong Sakai*. There is a hole on either side of the handle and the instrument is struck on the thigh, the sound being modified by closing one or both holes. He remarks that an identical instrument occurs in the Philippines where it is called *buncacan*. Several years ago Mr. Charles W. Mead of the American Museum of Natural History, New York, called my attention to specimen No. 70. 1/4493 from the Philippines, a tube of bamboo 19 inches long, 1½ inches in diameter, closed at one end by a septum. This end, used for the handle, was entire for a distance of several inches. The remainder was slit into two parts. The septum was pierced by a small jagged hole, possibly accidental, but on one side of the "handle" not far from the end was a round hole burned in about a half inch in diameter. The "flail" ends did not clap as loudly as in some similar clappers, for they were stiff and had been whittled away on either edge so that the tongues did not meet. They produced a buzzing sound more like the Hawaiian *puili*. When the ball of the thumb was placed over the hole and the two ends of the clapper were struck on the arm, quite a clear musical tone was emitted which became a minor third higher if the thumb were removed from the hole. One more such specimen, evidently identical except for the hole in the septum, has been described by Morris (110, vol. 2, pp. 29-30) from New Guinea. She also mentions bamboo clappers, without the holes, evidently from Burma, where they are known as *wahle khoht* (op. cit., vol. 1) and from Japan.

I have discovered no form exactly like the Hawaiian *puili* with its finely fringed ends, elsewhere, but that of New Guinea having several tongues, which was beaten at sea on long journeys, comes the closest to the Hawaiian specialized form. Nor does the true clapper occur in Hawaii. The Hawaiian instrument when shaken affords only a "murmurous breezy rustle," instead of the sharp clap of the clapper, another evidence of the Hawaiian preference for soft sounds.

While I was working in 1922 with some old Indians belonging to tribes who once lived near Lake Tulare and as far east as Visalia, California, an old man, seventy-five years of age, the last of his tribe, used a clapper made of elder wood as an accompaniment for his songs. The pith of the wood had been carefully removed. The instrument, about 20 inches long, and less than an inch in diameter, had been slit into two sections nearly the entire length, with four or five inches left entire to serve as a handle. It was named *tra-wat-tr'wil*. When shaken it emitted a sharp clap. The old man handled it so deftly that he was able to create a number of complicated rhythms, wholly at variance with those of his songs or his dance steps, and reproduced them exactly, time after time. He was much amused at my clumsy efforts to imitate him or to execute the rhythms I had written in my note book.

Dixon (37, pp. 221-2) reports that the Northern Maidu have such a clapper made of willow, from 30 to 50 centimeters long, which is used only in ceremonial dances in the winter season in Sacramento Valley and the foot-hill area. Mr. John P. Harrington of the Smithsonian Institution in Washington discovered by personal investigation that the clapper was used by the Indians of Santa Barbara and the channel islands, as well as on Santa Catalina and San Clemente. It occurred generally in the state as well as in Lower California. It is used by the Yokaia Pomo, while the Hupa (178, fig. 33) have a many-pronged type shaped like the sticks of a fan.

Mr. Harrington does not know of its use among any other tribes of North America, and Miss Frances Densmore, whose studies in North American Indian music in other areas have been so extensive, told Mr. Harrington that she had never encountered it. Mr. La Flesche tells me that the Omaha did not have it, although they had the deer hoof rattles, which were tied in bunches and placed at the tip of a stick and shaken, like the cocoon rattles sometimes were among other tribes and in the Pacific when they were not used as anklets.

As with some of the other instruments already discussed, such as the musical bow, the shell trumpet and the nose flute, it is interesting to note that the clapper idea has been carried over into other material where the bamboo was lacking. The original musical bow of solid wood was made of reed where wood was lacking; the shell trumpet was made of any variety of shell which could be utilized and was carried beyond the natural distribution of such shells; the peculiarity of blowing an instrument with the nose was carried over from the flute, which was the first, to other instruments, like the gourd whistle; and where the bamboo for the clapper was missing, as on the west coast of America, the instrument was made of elder or willow.

FLUTES AND PANPIPES

Flutes with cup-shaped appendages at the lower end, usually of gourds, although missing in Hawaii, have formed part of the musical equipment of ancient India, Greece, and Mexico (144) and are found among the Papago and Hopi of Arizona, the Zuni of New Mexico, and the Sioux of the Plains (110, vol. 2). Edge-Partington and Heape (39) picture Maori war trumpets of the same shape. See also Best (167, pp. 156 *b*, 157).

An aeolian flute made of a number of bamboos bound together and hung in a tree that the wind might play its melodies is reported by Codrington from the island of Aurora in Melanesia (33, pp. 336 ff.). Tylor somewhere compares the forms found in the Malay Peninsula and Sumatra to those in the province of Picara, Colombia, in South America, but I have only found one incorrect reference to it while Morris (110, vol. 2, p. 233) mentions them as occurring in ancient Peru.

Lastly there is the distribution of panpipes worked out by von Hornbostel (72) for Java, Oceania and Central Brazil which I have not gone into here, not only because von Hornbostel covered the ground, but because panpipes are entirely lacking in Hawaii.

VOCAL MUSIC

As has been intimated, little may be said concerning the singing of the inhabitants of most of the regions mentioned in connection with the distribution of instruments. Comparison with ancient Hawaiian methods is prevented for the most part because specimens of the songs have not been available and the music has not been thoroughly discussed. India and Greece are the notable exceptions as countries whose music has been written upon by numerous authorities. In India singing had reached a high degree of development by the beginning of the Christian Era if not long before and treatises were being written upon music in Sanskrit revealing its long past. On the other hand, from Greece, as one writer has said (86, pp. 398-402) have survived only a few fragments of musical theory and songs. Of other ancient nations even less is known. The same author continues, summing up the situation in Greece:

> The character of Greek music has consequently been the subject of much fruitless speculation and the most varied theories and opinions have found currency in the learned world, all being the product of fancy rather than research. On one point, however, there has been a general consensus of opinion, to wit, that in the field of music the Greeks had accomplished very little. This view has been supported by a grim fact, the absence of musical compositions.

This, however, is a prelude to his discussion of the then recently discovered and now celebrated Hymn to Appollo which, nevertheless, adds but one more to the dozen or so fragments extant, and while it shows a Wagnerian treatment of melody, can not be taken as an indication that the art of music in general had reached a high level of melodic development. The Greeks appear not to have been a partcularly musical people, even though their physicists worked out mathematically the laws which are today the foundation of European music.

Tod, whose discussion of Hindu music is included in Rajah Tagore's anthology, remarks (151, p. 278):

An account of the state of musical science amongst the Hindus of early ages and a comparison between it and that of Europe is yet a desideratum in Oriental literature. From what we already know of the science it appears to have attained a theoretical precision yet unknown to Europe, and that at a period when even Greece was little removed from barbarism.

As has been said, according to Strabo who is quoted by Tod, the Greeks considered music as originating from Thrace and Asia, "of which countries were Orpheus and Musaeus; others who regard all Asia as far as India as a country sacred to Dionysius attribute to that country the invention of nearly all the science of music."

Greek notation was not invented prior to the 27th Olympiad, or about 670 B. C., when Terpander discovered its adaptation to the science and introduced its use (111, p. 32). It has evidently not been possible to fix more than an approximate date for the first introduction of notation in India for none of the writers on Indian music that I have examined give a date, but instead remarks such as the following are encountered. Emil Naumann's History of Music (114, vol. 1, p. 20) states that hymns intended for music occur in the Rigveda at about 1500 B. C. An article by J. D. Paterson (151, p. 177) says that music must have been cultivated in very early ages by the Hindus as the abridged names of the seven notes are said to occur in the Samaveda; while French (op. cit.) says, "Sanskrit notation goes back to a period before authentic history," and the oldest Sanskrit characters are those used to designate the notes. According to Fox Strangways (148, p. 114) the highly elaborate system of 'srutis may be dated before Aristoxenus, to the fifth century B. C. and like his system, points to a long antecedent period of development. (See also Weber, 164, vol. 8, pp. 662 and 271.)

Of the Sāman chants, of which specimens are preserved in modern as well as ancient notation, but which are rendered differently today by various Brahman priests, Fox Strangways says (148, p. 249): "Great care was taken not to deviate from the original melody-types and rhythms, and the religious efficacy of the hymns was held to depend largely on the right application of directions contained in the Brahmanic explanations of the Vedic text."

Brāmaṇa is to be dated not later than sixth century B. C., according to this authority. Day (36, p. 3) says that the earlier music of the Sanskrit period, that is, the Vedic chant composed in the simple Sanskrit spoken 3,000 years ago, "bears a close resemblance, so far as we can judge, to that of the ancient Greeks, going far to prove that music has been derived from the same Aryan source, which seems probable and has been discussed freely by different writers."

Fox Strangways remarks (op. cit., p. 263), after a long comparison of Indian and Greek systems:

We have other hints which point to a correspondence between the Greek and Indian scale. The Aryans came into India from the north. Gāndhāra is the same word as Kandahar, which as late as Alexander's time (the fourth century B. C.), included Afghanistan and the Panjab, with a capital near Peshawar. The Gāndhāra grāma is the oldest of the three grāmas and may preserve an early Aryan tradition. . . . Evidence of the correspondence of the Greek and Indian systems has been accumulating in these pages and that the fundamental scale of Greece, the Doric tetrachord, should be identical in form with the oldest form of Indian tetrachord would be more striking evidence than any. But it is unfortunately not more than circumstantial.

These remarks, though indefinite and merely circumstantial, as Fox Strangways says, nevertheless at least seem to indicate that a highly developed music in India is as old as any in Greece. Although in theory, Hindu music has not gone beyond the principles of Greek music, it has "enormously refined the detail," while remaining true to its type as outlined in early times. It is therefore possible to compare its stylistic features with the Hawaiian, isolated survival as it is of a most archaic stage of musical development, for traces of common principles.

It will be recalled that the chief features of Hawaiian singing were first, a form of chanting practically on one tone with very slight variations above or below it; second, the somewhat freer but also very limited melodic range and content of the hula songs which had only one main pitch level, but about it a small and near group of tones contrasting with a group of other tones clustered about a lower level, generally establishing a perfect fourth, or more rarely a perfect fifth or even a third below. Hula songs were composed either of one or two short melodic phrases repeated *ad infinitum* with slight variations.

Until near the end of my survey, the similarity of this music to what little was known of that of ancient Greece, especially in the prominence of the perfect fourth interval and the custom the Greeks had of composing long epics and odes adulatory of heroes, together with many other similarities of culture, inclined me to the feeling that there might be a connection between the Hawaiians and those early dark peoples of Greece and possibly Crete, who had been overwhelmed by northern invaders more than a thousand years before Christ. Therefore the discovery of numerous and intimate correspondences between not only the instruments and the singing, but many other cultural traits of the Hawaiians and early peoples of India or Indonesia was all the more surprising.

Concerning the Brahminical instructions for singing, Day says (36, pp. 6-11) that they refer constantly to mythological traditions even more ancient, and that the musical learning of the sages is couched in language so figurative and purposely so worded that none but Brahmans skilled in sacred lore could decipher and interpret the real meaning. While no musical treatises exist, or even very clear ideas on musical questions are to be obtained from the old generation of Hawaiians still living, Day's remarks on Hindu music could not have been better adapted to fit the situation in regard to the information contained in the meles or poetry which go to make up Hawaiian history, individual and national.

Features that specially characterize ancient and even modern Hindu music are lack of pronounced accent, the frequent use of grace notes or appogiaturas, small intervals, the prominence of one tone in chanting, the scale being conceived of as lying in a downward progression from a level, the absence of harmony, necessitating a purely melodic structure, all of which are likewise noticeable to a marked degree in Hawaiian music of the old style. It was customary in Hindu chanting, as in Hawaiian, to depend upon the development of great lung capacity to sustain the chanter over long periods without taking a new breath. Meter, in India, as well as in Hawaii, was only in its infancy in chanting. A few quantities were fixed, the others were optional and, although the actual rhythms depended somewhat on the words rather than on arbitrary divisions as in European music (where, as Fox Strangways remarks [148, p. 217] the development has been from the dance or march rather than from song), the poetical meter and rhythm were often completely ignored by the chanter due to the fondness for inserting syllables between those of the text, and to the modification, prolonging and vocalizing of the vowels. What could more perfectly describe the rendition of an Hawaiian oli?

But at the time these methods of Hindu chanting were first being recorded, the interminable theorizers, as Fox Strangways calls them, had rules and terms well defined and exactly followed, with names for the long and short syllables. Thus at so early an age the Hindus were far in advance of the Hawaiians unlesss it be conceded that the Hawaiians have lost all this by the way, if they were in contact once with this culture, or that they were not in direct contact with it, being possibly among those earlier hordes that were dispersed to the east.

Fox Strangways (op. cit., p. 203) remarks on the comparative rarity of genuine Hindu songs in three-time: "Although what we should call 3/8 and 6/8 are not unknown, they are not favorite meters and are common in Mohammedan music." Nor are they common in ancient Hawaiian tunes. However, all time or meter, in this distant period when the early treatises were written in India, had been reduced to modes in the same manner as tunes. In Hawaii apparently neither time nor tunes have submitted to any formal analysis and regulation, although the tendency to two-part meters and certain divisions of the single beat are noticeable in the hula tunes as is that to split the single beat into quarters in chanting an oli. On the other hand, according to Fox Strangways, the trill or quavering, which is prominent in oli chanting in Hawaii, was apparently not known in India until the Mohammedan invasions about the ninth century.

Fyzee (59, p. 48) observes: "Among the list of undesirable traits . . is to sing with the words all jumbled up together and rolling in the throat so as to be incomprehensible." This indicates that such a mode of singing had crept into Hindu performances. This "undesirable trait" the Hawaiians have cherished to the present day although with the introduction of *kepakepa* chanting which has as its object the clear enunciation of syllables, was recognized here also the necessity for better rendition, particularly within earshot of royalty in whose praise chants were composed and recited.

Fox Strangways says (148, p. 100) that it makes no difference whether progressive step intervals or leaps are used in Hindu songs, the melody pivots on two notes which are a fourth apart, much more rarely a fifth. "A chromatic melody tends to center in the cluster of semitones and to treat the leap as an occasional excursion" (p. 122). This is characteristic of the oli. "A transilient melody moves more freely and the leap is the most important material of the song." In the hula particularly, the leap of the fourth or fifth is especially prominent. But the majority of Hindu songs, judging from hundreds given by this author and other writers, differ from the Hawaiian in beginning low and transferring to higher levels, and most of them do not stress the leap or the difference between the two levels as much as one is led to suppose. They more frequently contain minor thirds and even sixths, and embody more melodic material than hula tunes. Hindu melodies descend gradually. Hawaiian melodies as often drop a fourth as they ascend by that interval. The older Hindu chants extant resemble the Hawaiian the most. Thus Felber's collection (49, examples 458-460) more nearly approach Hawaiian olis than any others which I have seen, but even so the Hindu chants contain a wider range of tones. Some of the Sāman chants are not unlike the Hawaiian but they are much slower moving, the grouped sixteenth notes being altogether lacking. "The essence of the Sāman chant is that it circles about one note and only leaves that to form a downward cadence" (148, p. 253). There are "characteristic prolongations of notes by vocalizing syllables which add so much to the solemnity of the chant." The specimens which I have examined do not show this so clearly and have much more evidence of form than Hawaiian olis, in which, however, it will be remembered this vocalizing was a prominent feature.

As to the transilient melodies, as Fox Strangways calls them, which stress the leap as a principal feature, he remarks (148, p. 122), "We found a hint in the Gurkha and Garhwālī songs that these transilient scales had their home in the east of India" and of all the numerous examples he presents the songs of these tribes are almost exactly like many hula tunes. In later Hindu songs the development of chromatics and the habit of gliding gradually from tone to tone appears more marked and the difference between them and the Hawaiian becomes very wide indeed. On the whole, however, it may be said that there is more than a casual connection between very early styles of Hindu singing and the Hawaiian although some of the features they both have in common with much primitive singing all over the world. It would seem at every turn that in Hawaiian music one is encountering an ancestral type in which may be discerned the germs of the music which later developed more broadly in India, and so far as may be judged, in Greece.

Unfortunately there is very little published that is helpful on the early stages of music in Burma, Siam, Laos, and Cambodia. If, as seems likely, the music of northeastern India, while it was still in early stages of development, influenced that which later became isolated in Hawaii, it would seem that in these regions east and south of India should be found traces of relationship, although not necessarily. However, the instruments pictured by various writers, Sir James Scott, W. Joest, Sir John Bowring, and the contributors to Lavignac's Encyclopédie de la Musique et Dictionnaire du Conservatoire, are for the most part highly developed and consist chiefly of elaborate stringed instruments, gongs and drums, xylophones, and rasps. The melodies that I have been able to find in various books dealing with these regions are entirely different from the Hawaiian and the more ancient Hindu chants. For the most part they are modern and have developed far away from the chants.

Information concerning Ceylon, Java, and Sumatra is almost as disappointing. The music reported upon has been largely influenced by Europeans. After a discussion of physical and cultural traits which do not ill describe the Hawaiians Gomes gives the following concerning the music of the Sea Dyaks of Borneo (60, p. 225):

> The music [of the love song] is to our ideas monotonous, and it is not always easy to understand the meaning of what is sung, as many archaic expressions are used and the singer sometimes calls his love by one name, sometimes by another; at one time she is spoken of as a bird, and then, in the next line, perhaps, the name of some animal is applied to her. A similar song is sung by the women.

This is somewhat akin to the Hawaiian custom of clothing direct speech in metaphor and describing human beings by other than human attributes, in which those of natural scenery, however, seem to predominate. Gomes continues that the use of metaphor is common in all Dyak songs and that some of them are of great length. The songs or incantations are not set to any particular melody but are sung to a "kind of chant" and "long sentences are often repeated on one note."

But they have several distinct settings for the different songs and incantations and these seem to suit the subject. The song of mourning, for instance, sounds very sad and pathetic even to one who does not understand the language.

However, wailing songs all over the world would be apt to sound the same. Nevertheless the description and the fact that there are songs which imitate wailing would fit the situation generally as it exists in ancient Hawaiian styles of singing.

Of Tongan music Mariner says (102, vol. 1, pp. 306-7):

The following song is very often sung by them, or, to speak perhaps more correctly, is given in a sort of recitative by either sex; and in the Tongan language has neither rhymes nor regular measure, although some of their songs have both. It is perhaps a curious circumstance that love and war seldom form the subject of their songs, but mostly scenery and moral reflections.

This apparently comes not so close to Hawaiian styles, although if metaphor is used, especially that of a scenic character, which is very typical of Hawaiian poetry, there are points of resemblance. Many localities in the Pacific are characterized by different writers as having chants which lack melody and which are long odes dealing with ancestral prowess. Of Fijian poetry Rougier (131, p. 467) says there are no rhymes but assonance, a feature which, it will be recalled, also characterizes Hawaiian poetry. Probably for many groups of islands in the Pacific the underlying conceptions and styles are the same, but until more material is available for comparison, it is impossible to say which groups are most closely related. However, in no respect, unless it be texts, is the comparative study of chant-songs to be relied upon to the same degree as that of instruments. The very lack of melodic development, although on the one hand valuable as contributory evidence, in contrast with groups where the tendency to melodic development is more marked (as with many of the negro peoples, for instance) on the other hand is less valuable in tracing inter-relations between the groups within a region so characterized, simply because of the lack of distinguishing features.

With the dance it is more easy to trace connections through some island groups from Hawaii to the Asiatic mainland. The dances of the Samoans and Tongans are in many respects like those of the Hawaiians, although special types of dances appear to be purely local. Mariner describes certain Tongan dances which had been taken over bodily from Samoa. In Fiji the dramatic talent is very strongly marked. Very beautiful symbolic dances are described by St. Johnston, which are entirely of native conception. Humorous animal dances, evincing clever mimicry, are products of this group and recall the Hawaiian animal dances. In Furness' account of Yap (58, p. 86) we read:

> . . . the first number on the program was a sitting-down dance or *tsuru*. (Compare *hura, hula*.) This posture belongs to the same class as those to be seen in Japan, Anam, Siam, the Malay States, and Java.

The *hula olapa* or *alaapapa* is one of the few Hawaiian dances in which the dancers move about freely, and for this reason is usually a solo dance. In Day's treatise (36, p. 40) I note the Hindu word *alâpa*, which is nearly the same, used in connection with music. Its application in India to melody is practically the same as to dancing in Hawaii. Day says:

> To convey in writing an idea of in what an alâpa consists is somewhat difficult; it is not exactly a song, the music not being set to any particular words; neither is it an air, for it is not confined in its rhythm. An alâpa may be said to be rather a kind of rhapsody, which abounds with grace and embellishments of all kinds and is formed by an extension, according to the murchana (style), of the notes of the raga *in such a way that all the characteristics of that raga are prominently shown—and scope is given to the performer's power of improvising.*

The italics are mine. In the *hula olapa* the dancer is given just this sort of license to improvise, to enlarge upon the theme of the mele and to show prominently the characteristics of the person about whom the mele is composed—in other words, he "takes off" the person who is the subject of the mele, with the utmost freedom.

It is characteristic of dancing in India, Burma, Java, Siam, Cambodia, and Laos, and in a measure of dances in Japan, for the hands and arms, or the trunk, to take far more active parts in the dance than the feet and legs. The hands and arms in southern Asiatic dancing are used to the utmost nicety in delicate pantomime, interpreting the words of the song which accompanies the dance. Dexterity and liveliness are not attempted.

The subject of dancing, like that of poetry, is however, a field in itself, into which it is impossible for me to go at the present time. I can merely indicate that there lies an almost untouched field for investigation, especially in a comparative way, which might lead to important results furnishing evidence for the relationship of peoples. That in this hasty survey so much should come to light indicating the fundamental similarity through these regions should stimulate inquiries into differences.

In making comparison of these features of the arts of Malaysia and further India with the features of Hawaiian musical instruments, music, and dancing, it seems most surely that the points of resemblance between these complicated arts, in which the range of possibilities of development is unlimited, are far too many to be due to chance. Just how close the connection between the original peoples may have been it is not yet possible to state, for there is a vast region between them in which closer relationships might more properly be thought to exist and may still be traced. However, either most of the intervening localities have yet to be investigated even more searchingly than has so far been done or else the musical evidences of relationship have largely disappeared. Only in the north of Melanesia, in the neighborhood of the Solomon, Santa Cruz, and New Hebrides islands, or in the south in New Zealand, where it is known that the Maori arrived at a comparatively late date, probably from Hawaii, and in Tahiti, with which there was also some intercourse in the Middle Ages, are specially intimate connections discernible.

Glancing back over the evidence presented by the musical instruments it appears that the region between Malaysia and India has for thousands of years been a center of extraordinarily high development, not only in stringed instruments but in instruments of percussion of all sorts and in wind instruments. The other nations of antiquity show nothing comparable to it. In India, at least, the forms now in use have not altered in two thousand years for they are the same as those described in the early treatises (36, p. 99).

The poverty of music and instruments in Egypt, Babylonia, and Greece is painful by comparison. Although concrete records in the shape of documents and archæological finds which may be dated, may be wanting in the regions of southern Asia for periods as far back as such criteria carry the civilizations of countries farther west, on the other hand the fact must not be overlooked that definite attempts to unearth them here have as yet been few and that the enormous number of millions of people covering every bit of these lands render such search the more difficult and unlikely to prove fruitful. On the other hand the very presence here of more people crowded into one fairly limited section of the earth's surface than are found together perhaps anywhere else would suggest it as a center from which streams of population must have been thrown off from time to time in all directions, but particularly southeast and southwest, away from the great mountain barriers to the north. If southern Asia is the original home of mankind, as seems now to be generally accepted, then it would be but natural that here culture had its earliest beginnings.

If, then, it be conceded that this region was the center in which music as well as other phases of culture flourished from time immemorial, which will be allowed for the sake of argument, what does the distribution of

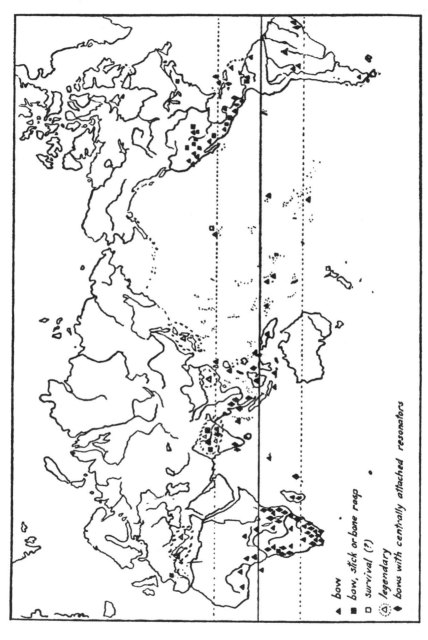

FIGURE 7.—Map showing distribution of simple musical bow and bow rasps.

musical instruments show from the data already available and such as is presented here? Taking the musical bow, and for the moment ignoring the diffusion of the simple bow and other types to America by way of Africa in post-Columbian times, the simplest form is marginally distributed, as regards southern Asia, the circle narrowing progressively with the more developed types, especially north and south. (See fig. 7.) The conch has not the same distribution as the stringed instruments (fig. 8), since it is apparently absolutely lacking in Africa, including Egypt (as well as in Assyria). It extends along the north shore of the Mediterranean and up the Atlantic, while the bow can be traced in this region only legendarily in Greece and Rome and in the bow-rasp still surviving in the country districts in France. The fact of the absence of the conch in Egypt would go far to disprove the theory that the Egyptians were the dispensers of all the early culture that swept the world in a belt eastward, along with sun worship and megalithic monuments, since the conch appears to have been associated with megaliths not alone along the north shore of the Mediterranean, roughly, but through the Pacific and in the early cultures of middle America, intimately bound up with religious rites of great sacredness having to do with sun and moon. Possibly both the conch and the bow belonged originally to a proto-Mediterranean race, between the extremely far-flung distributions of which east and west, communication was subsequently interrupted from Persia to Crete. The bow apparently (or the bow-rasp and allied forms) had not as much sacred significance as the conch, perhaps because its tone was not as awe-inspiring. This may account for its failure to survive in regions where higher cultures developed. The apical type of conch is undoubtedly the oldest. It may be certainly dated as far back as the Minoan period in Crete, possibly much earlier farther east. It appears to be characteristic alike of the northern shore of the Mediterranean, Asia, parts of Melanesia and Polynesia, as well as the middle American cultures. A later lateral type appears east from Torres Straits and mingles with the apical from New Guinea as far east as the Marquesas. This second distribution is wedge-shaped with its apex to the east, and in this general region is also found the still more developed type with the attached mouthpiece.

Although very old, the nose flute appears not so ancient as the conch or musical bow. It is not reported in regions north of the Mediterranean, although it is found pressed back into West Africa, having evidently been lost or overlaid in the eastern part of the continent when later cultural waves came from the northeast. (See fig. 9.) Although present practically everywhere in the Pacific, it appears to be missing in the Americas, except in Brazil. It is even missing in the West Indies and on the eastern

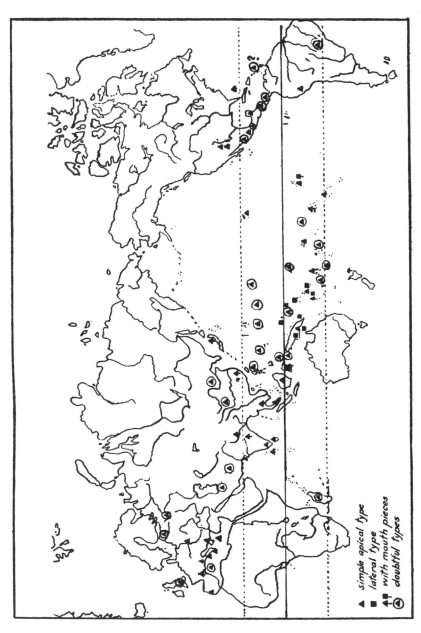

Figure 8.—Map showing distribution of shell trumpets.

simple apical type
lateral type
with mouth pieces
doubtful types

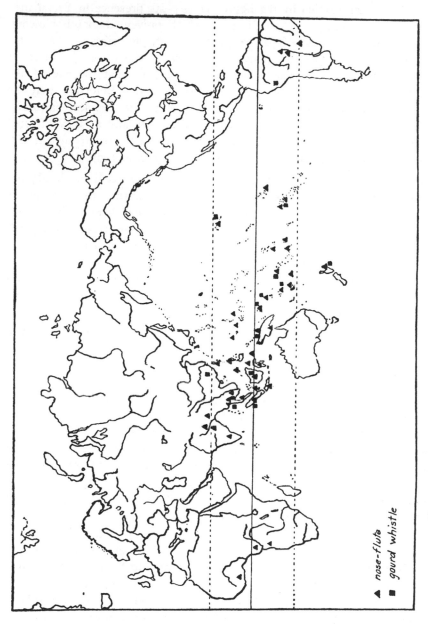

FIGURE 9.—Map showing distribution of the nose flute and gourd trumpets.

coasts of South America where bows and other features of west African cultures have been carried by the negro slaves. Its presence in Brazil may be due, as Tylor suggests, to a lip-plug which prevented mouth blowing, and thus it may be a case of parallel development, but tribes in the center of South America possess so many cultural traits which are like those of the South Seas that it seems to me equally possible that the use of the nose flute among such people as the Coroados and Botocudo may be merely a survival among some of the less fortunate peoples, culturally speaking, who reached America from the west, especially as they affected enormous ear-plugs, like the people of the west coast, certain ancient elements in the Pacific, and the Indo-Chinese and Malayan peoples.

The distribution of gourd and spiral whistles (fig. 10), bamboo pipes and the clapper, the castanets, anklets and other instruments corresponds roughly, if not always so widely, to those outlined here. The entire complex may not, of course, be taken as a unit, nor is it possible to say, without much further study, which are most nearly related in point of age, or have been carried to certain localities by the same group of carriers. Since it is evident that the Pacific has been from remote times a region of great activity, introductions at most points have probably been made more than once.

This is particularly evident in Hawaii, far north though it lies off a main line of travel by way of Melanesia and the Marquesas. The Hawaiian islands were originally peopled by a race known to the present people as menehune, to whose efforts are ascribed the stone-walled fish ponds which border the islands at every turn and which have withstood centuries of action from the waves, though they are but a few feet wide and hardly above high water level and are built without mortar. The original race has had accessions from the northwest, probably; from Melanesia and from Tahiti and the Marquesas, perhaps, as well as from Samoa, in very early times, and the Hawaiians have in turn sent expeditions far and wide. Legends tell of stranded or wrecked ships leaving survivors in the Hawaiian islands in later days.

As a whole, however, the Hawaiian complex of instruments represents, as I have already said, a very archaic stage of development, as indeed much of the native culture did. It is not, perhaps, to be ascribed so much to degeneration through isolation as to survivals of a very ancient period, since here are found existing early types of instruments known in southern Asia and from there to the British Isles, mostly as prehistoric survivals. In the bow, the conch of the apical type and the ti leaf whistle are three of the oldest of these. The Hawaiian ti leaf whistle is the most archaic of all such spiral horns in type, though the English is next. Some of the

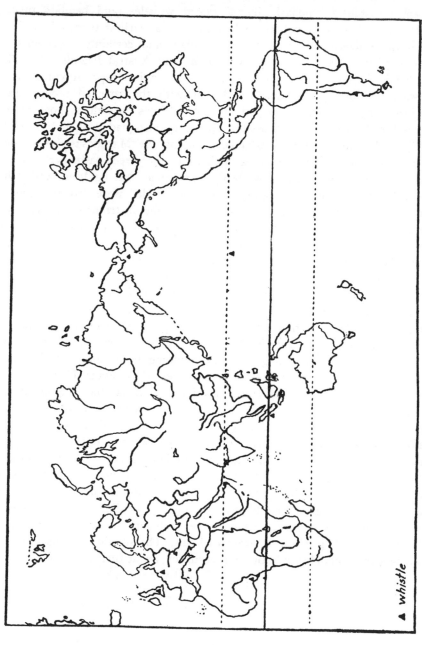

▲ *whistle*

FIGURE 10.—Map showing distribution of the spiral twisted horn or whistle.

other older instruments are probably the resonant sticks, the footboard, the pebble castanets, calabash drums, gourd whistles, and bamboo tubes. The Hawaiian bow, although related to one of the earliest types of musical bow, is more developed in a specialized way, and certainly represents a higher stage than the bow of the Marquesas and Austral Islands. On the other hand, the Marquesans have not only the apical type of conch, but the two later forms, the lateral, and that with the attached mouthpiece, as well as large wooden drums, mouth blown flutes as well as nose flutes and developed xylophones. Possibly once they also had a shell lyre (88, p. 408). The more southerly islands, including the Marquesas, lay in the road of much of the later travel as well as in the direct path, perhaps, of one of the earliest migrations, while the Hawaiians, having been settled in very early times, and by slightly different people, were isolated thereafter for long periods. Thus the carriers of the instruments to Hawaii were not quite so closely related to the early peoples of the Society and Marquesas islands as has been supposed. There was a large element in the population of the more northern islands which powerfully influenced what few people may have come there from the south. Ellis (40, vol. 1, chap. 8) who describes the musical instruments of Tahiti with great care, does not mention the musical bow and I believe it has not been reported from there. The Tahitians (and the Marquesans) had huge wooden drums which the early Hawaiians lacked. Nor has the rasp been mentioned for the two southern groups, or anything been said of calabashes as drums. The singing of the Tahitians and Marquesans is also much more developed than that of the Hawaiians, that is, the singing uninfluenced by Europeans. In fact, the musical evidence seems to somewhat support Ellis' view, derived from quite other evidence, that the Hawaiian islands were peopled first. At any rate they were peopled before the later waves whose culture dominated the southern groups. If the earliest Hawaiian settlers came by way of the southern islands, then it was a migration which took away with it traces which would ordinarily be left along the way as well. The highly developed Hawaiian bow, as against the cruder Marquesan form, presents one difficulty in settling the point of the earlier peopling of the Hawaiian islands. The solution of this problem as well as many others brought out in this survey, await further study.

BIBLIOGRAPHY

1. ALEXANDER, W. D., compiler, Hawaiian antiquities, from Kamakau of Kaawaloa, in manuscript, B. P. Bishop Mus., Honolulu.
2. ALEXANDER, W. D., History of the Hawaiian islands, in manuscript, B. P. Bishop Mus., Honolulu.
3. ANNANDALE, NELSON, see Balfour.
4. ANDREE, RICHARD, Die Nasenflöte und ihre Verbreitung: Globus, Band, 75, p. 150, Bawnschweig, 1899.
5. ANDREWS, LORRIN, Remarks on Hawaiian poetry: The Islander, vol. 1, pp. 26, 27, 30, 31, 35, Honolulu, 1875.
6. ANKERMANN, BERNHARD, L'ethnographie actuelle de l'Afrique méridionale: Anthropos, vol. 1, 1906, pp. 926-928.
7. ANKERMANN, BERNHARD, Die Afrikanischen Musikinstrumente: Ethnologisches Notizblatt Kgl. Mus. f. Völkerkunde, vol. 3, pt. 1, Berlin, 1901.
8. BALFOUR, HENRY, Report on the collection of musical instruments from the Siamese Malay Straits and Perak: Fasciculi Malayensis (Nelson Annandale and Herbert C. Robinson, Editors), London, 1903.
9. BALFOUR, HENRY, The natural history of the musical bow, Oxford, 1899.
10. BALFOUR, HENRY, The goura, a stringed-wind musical instrument of the Bushmen and Hottentots: Roy. Anth. Inst. Jour., vol. 32, N. S. 5, 1902, pp. 156-177.
11. BALFOUR, HENRY, A primitive musical instrument: Reliquary and Illustrated Archaeologist, Oct., 1896, pp. 221-224.
12. BALLANTYNE, A., See Jenness.
13. BALTZELL, J., History of music, Philadelphia, 1905.
14. BANDELIER, ADOLPH F., The islands of Titicaca and Koati, Hispanic Society of America, New York, 1910.
15. BANDELIER, ADOLPH F., Report of an archaeological reconnaissance into Mexico in 1881: Am. Arch. Inst. of America, Papers, Am. Ser., vol. 2, 1884.
16. BARROT, ADOLPHE, Visit of the French sloop of war, Bonite, to the Sandwich Islands in 1836: translated for The Friend, vol. 8, no. 5, pp. 33-35, Honolulu, May, 1850.
17. BARRY, PHILLIPS, Greek music: Musical Quarterly, vol. 5, no. 4, New York, 1919, pp. 578-613.
18. BATCHELOR, JOHN, The Ainu of Japan, Religious Tract Society, London, 1892.
19. BECKWITH, MARTHA W., The Hawaiian hula dance: Jour. of Am. Folklore, vol. 29, no. 8, 1916, pp. 409-412.
20. BECKWITH, MARTHA W., The Hawaiian romance of Laieikawai: reprinted from the 33rd Ann. Rept. of the Bur. of Am. Ethnology, Washington, 1918.
21. BIRD, ISABELLA L., Unbeaten tracks in Japan, New York, 1880 (?).
22. BOLINDER, GUSTAF, Busintana-indianernas musikbåge: Ymer, Årg. 37, Stockholm, 1917, pp. 300-307.
23. BOWRING, JOHN, Siam, London, 1857.
24. BROWN, GEORGE, Melanesians and Polynesians, London, 1910.
25. BROWN, J. MACMILLAN, The languages of the Pacific: B. P. Bishop Mus., Occ. Papers, vol. 7, no. 2, 1920.
26. BURGER, FRIEDRICH, Die Küsten und Bergvölker der Gazelle-halbinsel, Stuttgart, 1913.
27. BURNEY, CHARLES, A general history of music, 4 vols., London, 1789.
28. CADWELL, HELEN, Hawaiian music: Hawaiian Ann., Honolulu, 1916, pp. 71-79.
29. CAMPBELL, ARCHIBALD, Voyage around the world, New York, 1819.

30. CHAMBERLAIN, BASIL HALL, The language, mythology and geographical nomenclature of Japan, viewed in the light of Aino studies: Mem. Literature College, Imperial University, No. 1, Tokyo, 1887.
31. CHAMISSO, ALBERT VON, A voyage of discovery into the South Seas and Behring's Straits, by Otto von Kotzebue, 3 vols., London, 1821: excerpt in The Friend, N. S., vol. 2, no. 2, p. 15, Honolulu, February, 1862.
32. CHRISTIAN, F. W., The Caroline Islands, London, 1899.
33. CODRINGTON, R. H., The Melanesians, Oxford, 1891.
34. Cyclopedia of Fiji, Sydney, New South Wales, 1907.
35. DALTON, EDWARD T., Descriptive ethnology of Bengal, Calcutta, 1872.
36. DAY, CHARLES R., The music and musical instruments of Southern India and the Deccan, London, 1891.
37. DIXON, ROLAND B., The northern Maidu: Am. Mus. Nat. Hist., Bull., vol. 17, part 3, 1905, pp. 119-346.
38. DORSEY, JAMES O., Omaha Sociology: Bur. of Am. Ethnology, Ann. Rept. for 1881-2, Washington, 1884.
39. EDGE-PARTINGTON, JAMES, AND HEAPE, CHARLES, Ethnographical album of the Pacific islands, drawn from examples in public and private collections in England, Manchester, 1890.
40. ELLIS, WILLIAM, Polynesian researches, 4 vols., London, 1831.
41. ELLIS, WILLIAM, Narrative of a tour through Hawaii, London, 1826.
42. EMERSON, NATHANIEL B., Pele and Hiiaka, a myth from Hawaii, Honolulu, 1915.
43. EMERSON, NATHANIEL B., The unwritten literature of Hawaii: Bur. of Am. Ethnol., Bull. 38, Washington, 1909.
44. EMERSON, J. S., Catalogue of Hawaiian ethnological specimens formerly constituting the J. S. Emerson collection, manuscript on loan in the Bishop Museum.
45. ENGEL, CARL, A descriptive catalogue of musical instruments in the South Kensington Museum, London, 1874.
46. ENGEL, CARL, Musical instruments, New York, 1876.
47. EVANS, IVOR HUGH NORMAN, Among primitive peoples in Borneo, London, 1922.
48. Fasciculi Malayensis, see Balfour.
49. FELBER, EDWIN, Die indische Musik der vedischen und der classischen Zeit: Sitzungsberichte der Kais. Acad. der Wissenschaften in Wien, Band. 170, Abhand., 7, Wien, 1912.
50. FERNANDO, C. M., The music of Ceylon: Royal Asiatic Society, Ceylon Branch Jour., vol. 13, Colombo, 1895, pp. 183-189.
51. FEWKES, J. WALTER, Casa Grande, Arizona: Bur. Am. Ethnol., 28th Ann. Rept. for 1906-7, Washington, 1912, pp. 25-181.
52. FEWKES, J. WALTER, Flute observances at Walpi: Jour. of Am. Folklore, vol. 7, 1894, pp. 265-287.
53. FLETCHER, ALICE C., and LAFLESCHE, FRANCIS, The Omaha tribe, Bur. of Am. Ethnol., 27th Ann. Rept., Washington, 1905.
54. FLEURE, H. J. AND JAMES, T. C., Anthropological types in Wales, Roy. Anth. Inst. Jour., vol. 46, pp. 35-154.
55. FORNANDER, ABRAHAM, An account of the Polynesian race, its origin and migrations, 3 vols., London, 1878.
56. FORNANDER, ABRAHAM, Fornander collection of Hawaiian antiquities and folklore: B. P. Bishop Mus. Mem., vols. 4-6, 1916-1919.
57. FOY, W., Zur Verbreitung der Nasenflöte: Ethnologica, vol. 1, Leipsig, 1909, pp. 239-245.
58. FURNESS, WILLIAM H., The island of stone money, Uap (Yap) of the Carolines, London, 1910.
59. FYZEE, RAHAMIN, Indian music, London, 1919.

60. GOMES, EDWIN H., Seventeen years among the Sea Dyaks of Borneo, Philadelphia, 1911.
61. GRAEBNER, F., Die melanesische Bogenkultur und ihre Verwandten: Anthropos, vol. 3, 1908, vol. 4, 1909.
62. GUPPY, H. B., The Solomon Islands and their natives, London, 1887.
63. HADDON, ARTHUR CORT, Races of Man and their distribution, London, 1910.
64. HADDON, ARTHUR CORT, Reports of the Cambridge anthropological expedition to Torres Straits, 4 vols., Cambridge, 1912.
65. HADFIELD, E., Among the natives of the Loyalty Group, London, 1920.
66. HALL, H. R., Aegean archaeology, London, New York, 1915.
67. HAWLEY, E. H., The distribution of the notched rattle: Am. Anthropologist, vol. 11, 1898, pp. 344 ff.
68. HAWTAYNE, G. H., Remarks on the Caribs: Roy. Anth. Inst., Jour. vol. 16, 1886-7, pp. 196-9.
69. HAWTREY, SEYMOUR, H. C., The Lengua Indians of the Paraguayan Chaco: Roy. Anth. Inst., Jour. vol. 31, N. S. 4, 1901, pp. 280-299.
70. HEAPE, CHARLES, see Edge-Partington.
71. HITCHCOCK, ROMYN, The Ainos of Yezo, Japan: U. S. Nat. Mus. Report for 1890, Washington, 1892, pp. 429-502.
72. HORNBOSTEL, ERICH M. VON, Über ein akustisches Kriterium für Kulturzusammenhänge: Zeit. f. Ethn., vol. 43, Berlin, 1911, pp. 601-615.
73. HOWORTH, HENRY H., Buddhism in the Pacific: Roy. Anth. Inst. Jour., vol. 51, 1921, pp. 279-287.
74. HUTCHINSON, T. J., Explorations amongst ancient burial grounds of Peru, Roy. Anth. Inst. Jour. vol. 4, 1874-5, pp. 2-13.
75. HUGUENIN, PAUL, Raiatea la sacrée, Neuchatel, 1902.
76. IHERING, H. VON, Nasenflöte: Globus, Band. 75, Bawnschweig, 1899, p. 375.
77. IYENGAR, P. T. SRINIVAS, Did the Dravidians of India obtain their culture from the Aryan immigrant: Anthropos, vol. 9, 1914, pp. 1-15.
78. JACKSON, J. WILFRID, Shells as evidence of the migrations of early culture, Manchester, 1917.
78a. JACKSON, J. WILFRID, The Aztec moon cult and its relation to the chank cult of India: Lit. and Phil. Soc. Mem. vol. 60, pt. 2, 1916.
79. JAMES, T. C., see Fleure.
80. JENNESS, D., and BALLANTYNE, A., The Northern D'Entrecasteaux, Oxford, 1920.
81. JOEST, W., Malayische Lieder und Taenze aus Ambon und den Uliase (Moluken), Leiden, 1892.
82. KAMAKAU, S. M., Ka moolelo o na Kamehameha: Honolulu Nupepa Kuokoa, Dec. 21, 1867; translated for the Hawaiian Historical Commission by John H. Wise.
83. KEANE, A. H., Man, past and present, London, 1921.
84. KEANE, A. H., On the Botocudos: Roy. Anth. Inst. Jour. vol. 13, 1883-4, pp. 199-213.
85. KING, JAMES A., A voyage to the Pacific Ocean, vol. 3, London, 1785.
86. KUBA, LUDOVIK, A Greek musical composition of the third century, B. C.: Music, vol. 11, pp. 398-402.
87. LAVIGNAC, ALBERT, Encyclopedie de la musique et dictionnaire du Conservatoire, Paris, 1913-4.
88. LINTON, RALPH, The material culture of the Marquesas Islands: B. P. Bishop Mus. Mem., vol. 8, no. 5, Honolulu, 1923.
89. LOWIE, R. H., The Assiniboine: Am. Mus. Nat. Hist., Anth. Papers, vol. 4, pt. 1, 1911, pp. 1-270.
90. LOWIE, R. H., Crow military societies: Am. Mus. Nat. Hist., Anth. Papers, vol. 11, pt. 2, 1913.

91. Lowie, R. H., The Crow tobacco society: Am. Mus. Nat. Hist., Anth. Papers, vol. 21, pt. 2, 1920.
92. Lowie, R. H., Dances and societies of the Plains Shoshone: Am. Mus. Nat. Hist., Anth. Papers, vol. 11, pt. 10, 1915, pp. 801-835.
93. Lowie, R. H., Hidatsa and Mandan societies: Am. Mus. Nat. Hist., Anth. Papers, vol. 11, pt. 3, 1913, pp. 219-358.
94. Lowie, R. H., The Northern Shoshone: Am. Mus. Nat. Hist., Anth. Papers, vol. 2 pt. 2, 1909, pp. 165-306.
95. Lumholtz, Carl, Symbolism of the Huichol Indians: Am. Mus. Nat. Hist. Mem., vol. 3, Anth. 2, 1900.
96. Lumholtz, Carl, The Huichol Indians of Mexico: Am. Mus. Nat. Hist., Bull. vol. 10, 1898.
97. Lumholtz, Carl, Unknown Mexico, 2 vols., New York, 1902.
98. MacCurdy, George Grant, Human origins, 2 vols., New York, 1924.
99. Mahillon, Victor Charles, Catalogue descriptif et technique du Conservatoire Royale de Musique de Bruxelles, 1893-1912.
100. Malo David, Hawaiian antiquities, edited and translated by N. B. Emerson [B. P. Bishop Mus. Sp. Pub. No. 2], Honolulu, 1903.
101. Man, E. H., On the Andamanese and Nicobarese objects: Roy. Anth. Inst., Jour. vol. II, 1881-2, pp. 268-290.
102. Mariner, William, An account of the natives of the Tonga Islands, compiled and arranged by John Martin from the letters of William Mariner, London, 1817.
103. Marques, A., Ancient Hawaiian music: Hawaiian Annual, Honolulu, 1914, pp. 97-107.
104. Marques, A., Music in Hawaii Nei: Hawaiian Annual, Honolulu, 1886, pp. 51-60.
105. Marx, B. L., The Hawaiian mele from a musical standpoint: Hawaiian Annual, Honolulu, 1904, pp. 154-162.
106. Mason, Otis T., The geographical distribution of the musical bow: Am. Anthropologist, vol. 10, 1897, p. 377.
107. Mead, Charles W., Musical instruments of the Inca: Am. Mus. Nat. Hist., Anth. Papers, vol. 15, pt. 3, 1924.
108. Meerwarth, A. M., A guide to the collection of musical instruments of the Indian Museum, Calcutta, 1917.
109. Meyer, A. B., Die Nasenflöte im Ostindischen Archipel: Globus, Band. 75, 1899, pp. 195-6.
110. Morris, Frances, Metropolitan Museum of Art catalogue of the Crosby Brown collection of musical instruments, 4 vols., New York, 1914.
111. Moseley, W., The quantity and music of the Greek chorus discovered, Oxford, 1847.
112. Moss, F. J., Through atolls and islands in the great South Seas, London, 1889.
113. Musters, G. C., On the races of Patagonia: Roy. Anth. Inst. Jour., vol. 1, 1871, pp. 193-207.
114. Naumann, Emil, History of music, translated by Ferd. Praeger, London, 1886 (?).
115. Nell, Louis, An introductory paper on the investigation of Singhalese music: Roy. Asiatic Soc. Jour., Ceylon Branch, 1856-8, pp. 200-206.
116. Nordenskiöld, Erland, Comparative ethnographical studies in South America, Goteborg, 1919-1924.
117. Oost, P. Joseph van, La musique chez les Mongols des Urdus: Anthropos. vols. 10 and 11, 1915-6, pp. 358-396.
118. Parkinson, R., Dreissig Jahre in der Südsee, Stuttgart, 1907.

119. PASTOR, WILLY, The music of primitive peoples and the beginnings of European music: Smithsonian Institution Ann. Rept., Washington, 1912, pp. 679-700.
120. PEPPER, G. H., Pueblo Bonito: Am. Mus. Nat. Hist., Anth. Papers, vol. 27, 1920.
121. PIGGOT, F. T., The music and musical instruments of Japan, London, 1893.
122. POLAK, J. S., New Zealand, a narrative of travel, London, 1838.
123. POPLEY, HERBERT A., The music of India, Madras, 1921.
123a. RANKEN, W. L., Roy. Anth. Inst., Jour., vol. 6, pp. 223 ff, 1876.
124. REEVES, EDWARD, Brown men and women, London, 1898.
125. RIDGEWAY, WILLIAM, Dramas and dramatic dances of non-European races, 1915.
126. RIDGEWAY, WILLIAM, The origin of tragedy, Cambridge, 1910.
127. RIVERS, W. H. R., The history of Melanesian society, 2 vols., Cambridge, 1914.
128. ROBERTS, HELEN H., Some drums and drum rhythms of Jamaica: Natural History, vol. 24, no. 2, 1924, pp. 241-251.
129. ROBINSON, HERBERT C., see Balfour.
130. ROTH, H. LING, Low's Natives of Borneo: Roy. Anth. Inst., Jour., vol. 22, 1892-3, pp. 22-64.
131. ROUGIER, P. EMMANUEL, Danses et jeux aux Fijis: Anthropos, vol. 6, 1911, pp. 466-484.
132. ROUTLEDGE, K., The mystery of Easter Island, London, 1919.
133. SACHS, CURT, Die Musikinstrumente Birmas und Assam im K. Ethnog. Mus. zu München, K. Bayerische Acad. der Wissens., Sitzungsb. philosophische-philologische und historische Klasse, Jahrg. 1917, Abh. 2, 1917.
134. ST. JOHNSTON, ALFRED, Camping among cannibals, London, 1883.
135. ST. JOHNSTON, T. R., The Lau Islands (Fiji), London, 1918.
136. SAVILLE, MARSHALL H., A primitive Maya instrument: Am. Anthropologist, vol. 10, 1897, p. 272.
137. SCOTT, JAMES G., Burma, a handbook of practical information, London, 1921.
138. SELER, E. G., Altmexikanische Knockenrasseln: Globus, vol. 74, 1898, pp. 85-93.
139. SELIGMANN, C. G., The Melanesians of British New Guinea, Cambridge, 1910.
140. SELIGMANN, C. G., and B. Z., The Veddahs, Cambridge, 1911.
141. SPEISER, FELIX, Ethnographische Materialien aus den neuen Hebriden und den Banks-Inseln, Berlin, 1923.
142. STAIR, J. B., Old Samoa, London, 1897.
143. STANFORD-FORSYTH, A history of music, New York, 1916.
144. STANLEY, ALBERT A., Catalog of the Stearns collection of musical instruments, Ann Arbor, 1918.
145. STEWART, GEORGE W., Poetry of the Polynesians; reprinted from the Overland Monthly by permission, revised by the author: Hawaiian Annual, Honolulu, 1919, pp. 97-117.
146. STOBART, J. C., The glory that was Greece, London, 1911.
148. STRANGWAYS, A. H. Fox, Music of Hindustan, Oxford, 1914.
149. SULLIVAN, LOUIS R., Marquesan somatology, with comparative notes on Samoa and Tonga: B. P. Bishop Mus. Mem., vol. 9, no. 2, Honolulu, 1923.
150. SULLIVAN, LOUIS R., New light on the races of Polynesia: Asia Magazine, January, 1923, pp. 17 ff.
151. TAGORE, SOURINDRO MOHUN, Hindu music from various authors, Calcutta, 1882.
152. TAYLOR, RICHARD, Te ika a Maui, or, New Zealand and its inhabitants, London, 1870.
153. TEN KATE, H., The geographical distribution of the musical bow: Am. Anthropologist, vol. 11, March, 1898, p. 93.
154. TEN KATE, H., The musical bow in Formosa: Am. Anthropologist, new ser., vol. 5, 1903, p. 581.
155. TESCHAUER, P. C., Die Caingang oder Coroados-Indianer im brasilianischen Staate Rio Grande do Sul: Anthropos, vol. 9, 1914, pp. 16-35.

156. THOMSON, BASIL, The Fijians—a study of the decay of custom, London, 1908.
157. THOMSON, W. J., Te pito te henua, or, Easter Island: U. S. Nat. Mus., Ann. Rept., Washington, 1899, pp. 447-552.
158. THOMPSON, GILBERT, An Indian dance at Jemez: Am. Anthropologist, vol. 2, 1889, p. 351.
159. TREGEAR, EDWARD, The Maori race, Wanganui, New Zealand, 1904.
160. TURNER, GEORGE, Samoa a hundred years ago and long before, London, 1884.
161. TYLOR, E. B., Notes on the Asiatic relations of Polynesian culture: Roy. Anth. Inst., Jour. vol. 11, 1881-2, pp. 401-405.
162. TYLOR, E. B., Researches into the early history of mankind and the development of civilization, London, 1865.
164. WEBER, ALBRECHT, Indische Studien: Beiträge für die Kunde des indischen Altertums, Band. 8, Berlin, 1863.
165. WHITMEE, S. J., The ethnology of Polynesia: Roy. Anth. Inst. Jour. vol. 8, pp. 261 ff.

———

166. BARRETT, S. A., Ceremonies of the Pomo Indians: Univ. of California, Am. Arch. and Ethn., vol. 12, 1917, pp. 397-441.
167. BEST, ELSDON, Games and pastimes of the Maori: Dominion Mus., Bull. 8, Wellington, 1925.
168. CHRISTIAN, F. W., On Micronesian weapons, dress, implements, etc.: Roy. Anth. Inst., Jour., vol. 28, 1898, pp. 288-306.
169. COMRIE, —, Anthropological notes on New Guinea: Roy. Anth. Inst., Jour., vol. 6, 1876-77, pp. 102 ff.
170. FRIC, VOJTECH, AND RADIN, PAUL, Contributions to the study of the Bororo Indians: Roy. Anth. Inst., Jour., vol. 36, 1906, pp. 382-406.
171. HADDON, A. C., The ethnography of the western tribe of Torres Straits: Roy. Anth. Inst., Jour., vol. 19, 1889-90, pp. 297-440.
172. HALE, ABRAHAM, On the Sakais: Roy. Anth. Inst., Jour., vol. 15, 1885-6, pp. 285-301.
173. KNOCKER, F. W., The aboriginees of Sungei Ujong: Roy. Anth. Inst., Jour., vol. 37, 1907, pp. 290-305.
174. KROEBER, A. L., A Mission record of the California Indians: Univ. of California Am. Arch. and Ethn., vol. 8, 1908, pp. 1-27.
175. MARKHAM, C. R., A list of tribes in the valley of the Amazon: Roy. Anth. Inst., Jour., vol. 24, 1894, pp.236-285.
176. MASON, J. A., The ethnology of the Salinan Indians: Univ. of California Am. Arch. and Ethn., vol. 10, 1912, pp. 97-240.
177. NELSON, N. C., The Ellis Landing shellmound: Univ. of California Publ. Am. Arch. and Ethn., vol. 7, 1910 ,pp. 357-426.
178. POWERS, STEPHEN, Contributions of North American ethnology, vol. 3, The tribes of California, Washington, 1877.
179. RAY, S. H., The languages of British New Guinea: Roy. Anth. Inst., Jour., vol. 24, 1894, pp. 15-39.
180. ROTH, H. LING, The aboriginees of Hispaniola: Roy. Anth. Inst., Jour., vol. 16, 1886-7, pp. 247-286.
181. SIMSON, A., Notes on the Jivaros and Canelos Indians: Roy. Anth. Inst., Jour., vol. 9, 1879-80, pp. 385-394.
182. SKEAT, W. W., The wild tribes of the Malay Peninsula: Roy. Anth. Inst., Jour., vol. 32, 1902, pp. 124-141.
183. SKEAT, W. W., AND BLAGDEN, C. O., The pagan races of the Malay Peninsula, London, 1906.

184. SOMERVILLE, B. T. Ethnographical notes in New Georgia, Solomon Islands: Roy. Anth. Inst., Jour., vol. 26, 1896, pp. 357-413.
185. SOMERVILLE, B. T., Ethnological notes on New Hebrides: Roy. Anth. Inst., Jour., vol. 23, 1893, pp. 363-393.
186. SPIER, LESLIE, Southern Diegueño customs: Univ. of California Publ. Am. Arch. and Ethn., vol. 20, 1923, pp. 297-358.
187. WHITE, R. B., Notes on the aboriginal races of the northwestern provinces of South America: Roy. Anth. Inst., Jour., vol. 13, 1883-4, pp. 240 ff.

PLATE I

HAWAIIAN MUSICAL INSTRUMENTS: *A*, JEW'S HARP, NIAUKANI; *B*, THREE-STRINGED UKEKE; *C*, TWO-STRINGED UKEKE; *D*, HAWAIIAN PLAYING UKEKE.

PLATE II

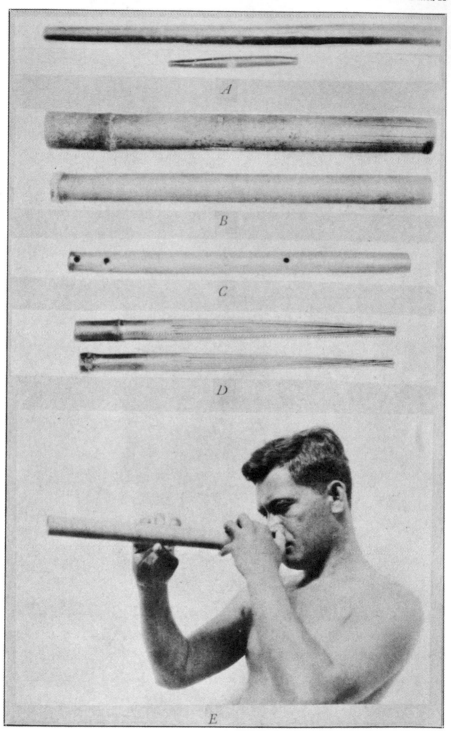

HAWAIIAN MUSICAL INSTRUMENTS: *A*, KALAAU STICKS; *B*, KAEKEEKE; NOSE FLUTE (OHE); *D*, PUILI; *E*, HAWAIIAN PLAYING NOSE FLUTE.

PLATE III

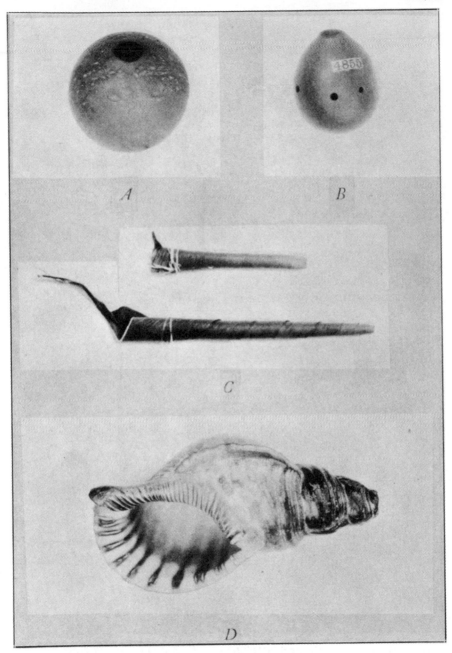

HAWAIIAN MUSICAL INSTRUMENTS: *A*, BULL-ROARER; *B*, GOURD WHISTLE (HOOKIO); *C*, TI LEAF WHISTLES (PULAI); *D*, THE CONCH (PU).

PLATE IV

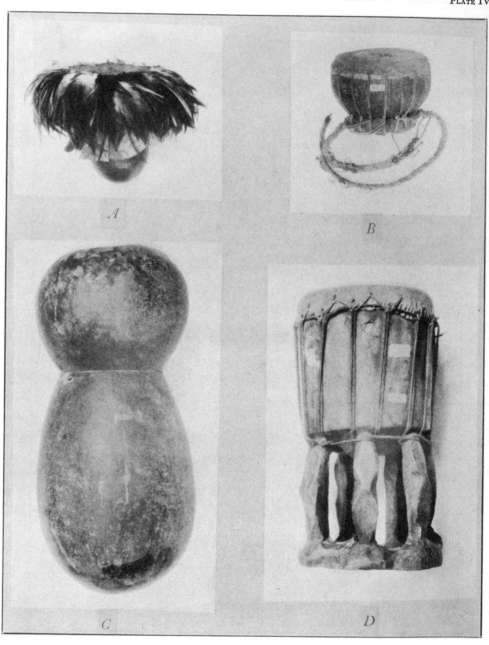

HAWAIIAN MUSICAL INSTRUMENTS: *A*, RATTLE OF COCONUT SHELL (ULIULI); *B*, COCONUT SHELL DRUM (PUNIU); *C*, CALABASH DRUM (IPU); *D*, WOODEN KETTLE DRUM (PAHU).

PLATE V

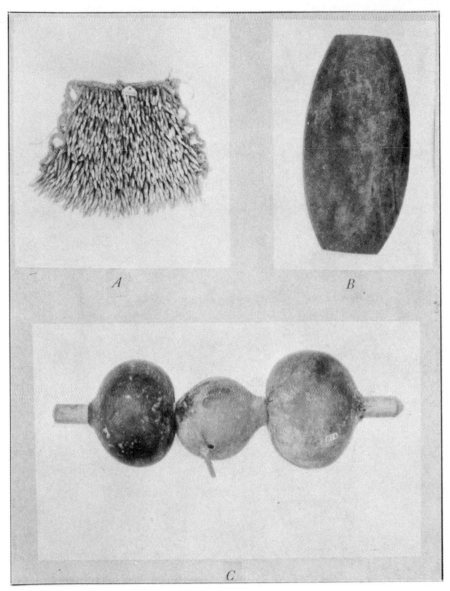

HAWAIIAN MUSICAL INSTRUMENTS: *A*, DOG'S TEETH ANKLE (KUPEE NIHO ILIO); *B*, FOOTBOARD USED IN THE HULA KALAAU; *C*, GOURD TOP RATTLE (ULILI).

INDEX OF MUSICAL EXAMPLES